DEBATING REFORM

Third Edition

CQ Press, an imprint of SAGE, is the leading publisher of books, periodicals, and electronic products on American government and international affairs. CQ Press consistently ranks among the top commercial publishers in terms of quality, as evidenced by the numerous awards its products have won over the years. CQ Press owes its existence to Nelson Poynter, former publisher of the *St. Petersburg Times*, and his wife Henrietta, with whom he founded *Congressional Quarterly* in 1945. Poynter established CQ with the mission of promoting democracy through education and in 1975 founded the Modern Media Institute, renamed The Poynter Institute for Media Studies after his death. The Poynter Institute (*www.poynter.org*) is a nonprofit organization dedicated to training journalists and media leaders.

In 2008, CQ Press was acquired by SAGE, a leading international publisher of journals, books, and electronic media for academic, educational, and professional markets. Since 1965, SAGE has helped inform and educate a global community of scholars, practitioners, researchers, and students spanning a wide range of subject areas, including business, humanities, social sciences, and science, technology, and medicine. A privately owned corporation, SAGE has offices in Los Angeles, London, New Delhi, Singapore, and Melbourne, in addition to the Washington DC office of CQ Press.

DEBATING REFORM

Conflicting Perspectives on How to Fix the American Political System

Third Edition

Richard J. Ellis
Willamette University

Michael Nelson
Rhodes College

Editors

FOR INFORMATION:

SAGE Publications, Inc.

2455 Teller Road

Thousand Oaks, California 91320

E-mail: order@sagepub.com

SAGE Publications Ltd.

1 Oliver's Yard

55 City Road

London EC1Y 1SP

United Kingdom

SAGE Publications India Pvt. Ltd.

B 1/I 1 Mohan Cooperative Industrial Area

Mathura Road, New Delhi 110 044

India

SAGE Publications Asia-Pacific Pte. Ltd.

3 Church Street

#10-04 Samsung Hub

Singapore 049483

Printed in the United States of America

Library of Congress Cataloging-in-Publication Data

Names: Ellis, Richard (Richard J.) | Nelson, Michael, 1949-

Title: Debating reform : conflicting perspectives on how to fix the American political system / Richard J. Ellis and Michael Nelson, Willamette University Rhodes College

Description: Third edition. | Los Angeles : SAGE/CQ Press, 2016. | Includes bibliographical references.

Identifiers: LCCN 2016010223 | ISBN 978-1-5063-3364-9 (pbk. : alk. paper)

Subjects: LCSH: United States—Politics and government. | Political participation—United States. | United States—Social conditions. | United States—Economic conditions.

Classification: LCC JK274.D398 2016 | DDC 320.60973—dc23 LC record available at https://lccn.loc.gov/2016010223

This book is printed on acid-free paper.

Acquisitions Editor: Michael Kerns

Editorial Assistant: Zachary Hoskins

Production Editor: Laura Barrett

Copy Editor: Michelle Ponce

Typesetter: C&M Digitals (P) Ltd.

Proofreader: Dennis W. Webb

Cover Designer: Glenn Vogel

Marketing Manager: Amy Whitaker

Certified Sourcing
www.sfiprogram.org
SFI-00453

16 17 18 19 20 10 9 8 7 6 5 4 3 2 1

CONTENTS

Senate

Presidency

Bureaucracy

Judiciary

Domestic Policy

National Security and Foreign Policy

PREFACE

The best American government textbooks do a superb job of conveying how the American political system works: who votes and who doesn't, how the electoral college operates, how members of Congress make decisions, how judges are appointed, how presidents manage the executive branch, and so on. The best textbooks also document how American politics has changed over time: the development of mass media, trends in voting behavior, the changing relationship between the president and the parties, the expansion of the federal government, the evolution of civil liberties and civil rights, and so on. These books provide, in short, the political knowledge that is an essential part of good citizenship.

Imparting this knowledge is a necessary but not, we believe, a sufficient condition for a successful American government and politics class. The most successful classes are not those in which instructors treat students as passive receptacles to be filled with the knowledge that political scientists possess. Instead, the most successful—and certainly the most memorable—classes are those that invite active student engagement through discussion and debate. We want to foster the development of citizens who are not only well-informed but also politically involved. We also want our students both to know the answers to test questions and to believe that the questions are worth thinking and arguing about, even after the class bell has rung.

There are, of course, many ways to promote student engagement in the classroom. We do not pretend to have discovered the one true way. But we do believe, based on many years of undergraduate teaching, that inviting students to debate concrete proposals to reform the political system they are studying is an excellent vehicle for promoting active learning.

Why a debate format? And why debates on reform? A standard textbook, no matter how well it is put together, can be very intimidating. This has less to do with the complexity or quantity of material that students are asked to absorb than with the authoritative tone of most texts. Scrupulous evenhandedness is a virtue in a textbook, but it can leave students feeling that there is almost nothing for them to contribute, no room for them to argue back. In a standard American government text, the loose ends seem neatly tied up. The accent is on what political scientists agree upon, not the many things they disagree about.

Our book reverses that pattern. By inviting accomplished scholars to debate resolutions, we highlight argument and disagreement. Summarizing existing knowledge through evidence can make for a good lecture, but vigorous classroom discussions and engaged student writing, we believe, are best spurred by contests between competing perspectives. Students listening to a lecture or reading a textbook chapter expect the author to sift through the evidence and lead them to a more balanced understanding. The debate format, in contrast, places the onus on students to sift through competing claims and evidence and then take sides.

Why make institutional reform the focus of these debates? First, reform proposals are explicitly normative: they are about what *should* be done. Many debates in political science are empirical; that is, they are mainly descriptive, explanatory, or predictive. Scholars debate the best way to measure voter turnout, the best model for predicting the winner in a presidential election, and whether the political parties have become more ideological. Each of these empirical debates is important and should be taught to undergraduates. Yet, when the question is solely empirical, classroom debates are understandably circumscribed. Discussion is generally oriented around the teacher trying to help students understand an argument rather than the students staking out and defending positions. Normative arguments invite students to offer their own judgments and thus help to build students' confidence that they can contribute productively to the intellectual conversation. They can make and defend claims of their own rather than just ask questions of the teacher.

A second reason we have chosen to focus on debating institutional reforms is that we want to minimize ideological arguments about liberal or conservative public policies. Although it is not difficult to have passionate classroom debates about abortion, same-sex marriage, or affirmative action, these arguments tend to run in well-worn grooves, and students tend to line up on the same sides in debate after debate. These debates may be vociferous, but they are unlikely to lead students to reexamine their views. Because institutional reforms generally do not strike familiar ideological chords, students are more willing to change their minds based on evidence and arguments and are less prone to array themselves in predictable patterns of support or opposition.

Policy debates are also unsatisfying in the introductory course because often they seem divorced from the institutional core of the course—more like an entertaining sideshow than an integral part of learning to think more deeply about American politics and government. Debating reforms, in contrast, connects the classroom conversation directly to the core of the course: American political institutions and processes.

The third reason we focus on debating institutional reform is that we want students not only to understand how American government functions but also to think about how it can be made to work better. Too often we take our institutions for granted, assuming that what has been must always be, and that it is for the best. Many of the reforms debated in this book—such as limiting the terms of Supreme Court justices, abolishing the electoral college, establishing a national initiative and referendum process, and making it easier to amend the Constitution—would require constitutional amendments. Others—such as removing the caps on the amount that individuals can contribute to candidates for federal office, bringing back earmarks, and doing away with the filibuster—could be achieved through statutory changes. At least a few of the proposed reforms debated in this book stand no chance of being adopted, most notably, changing the two-senators-per-state rule. Yet, even reforms that are unlikely to be enacted make for valuable debates because they require us to think carefully about the principles that underlie our constitutional system and to evaluate how well our political institutions help us to realize our deepest values and beliefs.

The introduction to American government course is not and should not be the gateway to graduate school. Only a minority of students in the course will even become political science majors. For many students, this will be their only politics course. As political scientists, we naturally want to teach students how to think like political scientists, but even more important in the introductory course is that we help students to think like democratic citizens—citizens who understand how and how well their political institutions are functioning. Inviting students to debate fundamental political reforms helps to model active and engaged citizenship.

Our focus on reform does not necessarily mean that we think our political system requires fundamental change. This book is not an argument for a particular political agenda; instead, we want to start an argument. Some readers may come away from these debates with a renewed appreciation for American political institutions; others may find that these debates open their eyes to problems of which they had been blissfully unaware. We want students to enter the debate about American politics, not to come out on a particular side.

Debating Reform is designed not to replace a standard textbook but to supplement it. That is why we have organized the debates around the chapter topics that generally structure American government texts: The Constitution, federalism, civil liberties, civil rights, political participation, the media, political parties, interest groups, Congress, the presidency, bureaucracy, the judiciary, foreign policy, and so on.

Thirteen debate resolutions have been retained from the second edition and revised to reflect recent scholarship and events. This new edition also has eight new debate resolutions that we hope will ignite spirited classroom discussion on a diverse range of new topics, including voter identification laws, the 22nd

Amendment, campaign finance reform, the role of secrecy in American democracy, and whether higher public education should be free for all Americans. For this new edition we welcome seventeen new authors: Gary D. Bass, Keith Gunnar Bentele, Danielle Brian, Richard Briffault, Bruce E. Cain, Mark Cheathem, Michael Colaresi, David A. Crockett, Brad DeWees, John Dilulio, Norman Eisen, Stephen F. Knott, Michael J. Korzi, Neal McCluskey, Erin O'Brien, Robert Samuels, and Brian A. Weiner.

One final word of explanation is owed the reader. Unlike other debate-style readers, our book includes only original essays that we commissioned specifically for this volume—no reprinted selections here. We chose to solicit original essays because we wanted each author to address a specific, concrete debate resolution directly. Nothing is more frustrating than a debate in which the participants do not actually address the same question, as often happens in books that try to fit a debate topic around a set of existing essays. We invited each of our contributors to take a side and defend it as vigorously as he or she could; the author's charge was not to weigh the evidence on all sides judiciously but rather to present the most persuasive case he or she could for the position taken. We hope that teachers and students will have as much fun reading these debates as our contributors had writing them.

In deciding which debate resolutions to retain and which to add, we were greatly assisted by sage advice we received from many teachers who adopted the previous edition of this book. We would particularly like to thank the reviewers commissioned by CQ Press: Scott Meinke, Bucknell University; Anthony Rodin, Whitworth University; Kate Scheurer, University of North Dakota; and Chris Shortell, Portland State University, as well as two who chose to remain anonymous. We also remain grateful to help we received from reviewers of the first edition: Molly Andolina, DePaul University; Larry Berman, University of California, Davis; Jeremy Busacca, California Polytechnic University, Pomona; Whitney Court, Saint John's University/College of Saint Benedict; William Cunion, Cuyahoga Community College; Christopher Ellis, Bucknell University; Michael Farlow, Salisbury University; Gerard J. Fitzpatrick, Ursinus College; Brian Frederick, Bridgewater State University; James Hill, Central Michigan University; Mack Mariani, Xavier University; and Amy Moreland, Sul Ross State University.

Our task as editors was made much easier and more enjoyable not only by our talented and conscientious contributors but also by the skilled and experienced crew at CQ Press. Our special thanks go to editorial assistant Zachary Hoskins, copy editor Michelle Ponce, and production editor Laura Barrett. There is no debating the debt we owe to each of them for helping us bring the third edition of this work to fruition.

CONTRIBUTORS

Douglas J. Amy is professor of politics at Mount Holyoke College. He has published a number of books, including *Real Choices/New Voices: How Proportional Representation Elections Could Revitalize American Democracy* (2002), which won the George H. Hallett Award from the American Political Science Association. His most recent book is *Government Is Good: An Unapologetic Defense of a Vital Institution* (2011).

Gary D. Bass is the executive director of the Bauman Foundation and affiliated professor at Georgetown University's McCourt School of Public Policy. He founded and for three decades ran OMB Watch, an organization that promoted greater government accountability and increased civic engagement. He is a recognized national expert on government transparency issues: co-founded OpenTheGovernment.org in the aftermath of the 9/11 terrorist attacks; played a key role in creating USAspending.gov and advocating for federal spending transparency; spearheaded a coalitional effort that resulted in open government recommendations to the incoming Obama administration; and received awards for his leadership on government transparency, including induction into the Freedom of Information Hall of Fame.

Keith Gunnar Bentele is an Associate Professor of Sociology at the University of Massachusetts Boston. He received his bachelor's degree from New College of Florida and his doctorate from the University of Arizona. His research has examined the passage of state level voter restrictions and multiple types of state legislation sought by the conservative Evangelical movement (e.g., faith-based initiatives and abortion restrictions). In addition, he has examined the consequences of welfare reform, rising earnings inequality, and trends in poverty in the US.

Jason Brennan is Robert J. and Elizabeth Flanagan Family Chair of ethics, economics, and public policy at Georgetown University. He has written extensively on voting ethics, political liberty, and civic virtue. His current work examines whether citizens have a right to competent government. His books include *Against Democracy* (2016), *Markets without Limits*, with Peter Jaworski (2015), *Why Not Capitalism?* (2014), *Compulsory Voting: For and Against*, with Lisa Hill (2014), *Libertarianism: What Everyone Needs to Know* (2012), *The Ethics of Voting* (2011), and, with David Schmidtz, *A Brief History of Liberty* (2010).

Danielle Brian has been the Executive Director of the Project on Government Oversight since 1993. POGO is a nonpartisan independent watchdog that champions good government reforms. At her direction POGO works to expose and remedy corruption, misconduct, and the undue influence of money on public policy. She works on issues across the federal government, frequently testifying before Congress and provoking agency officials towards reforms. Ms. Brian serves on the board of Taxpayers for Common Sense, is chair of the Steering Committee for Openthegovernment.org, and in 2012 was appointed to serve on the U.S. Extractive Industries Transparency Initiative Federal Advisory Committee.

Richard Briffault is the Joseph P. Chamberlain Professor of Legislation at Columbia Law School. His research, writing, and teaching focus on state and local government law, the law of the political process, government ethics, and property. The author of numerous legal texts and more than seventy-five law review articles, he is also the Chair of the New York City Conflicts of Interest Board; was a member of New York's Moreland Commission to Investigate Public Corruption; and is the Reporter for the American Law Institute's project on Principles of Government Ethics. He is a graduate of Columbia University and Harvard Law School.

Justin Buchler is associate professor of political science at Case Western Reserve University. He received his doctorate from the University of California, Berkeley, in 2004. He is the author of *Hiring and Firing Public Officials: Rethinking the Purpose of Elections* (2011) and numerous articles on electoral competition, including "The Social Sub-Optimality of Competitive Elections," in *Public Choice,* which received the Gordon Tullock Award for 2007.

Bruce E. Cain is a Professor of Political Science at Stanford University and the Spence and Cleone Eccles Family Director of the Bill Lane Center for the American West. He received a BA from Bowdoin College (1970), a B.Phil. from Oxford University (1972) as a Rhodes Scholar, and a PhD from Harvard University (1976). He taught at Caltech (1976-89) and UC Berkeley (1989-2012) before coming to Stanford. Professor Cain was Director of the Institute of Governmental Studies at UC Berkeley from 1990-2007 and Executive Director of the UC Washington Center from 2005-2012. He was elected to the American Academy of Arts and Sciences in 2000 and has won awards for his research (Richard F. Fenno Prize, 1988), teaching (Caltech 1988 and UC Berkeley 2003), and public service (Zale Award for Outstanding Achievement in Policy Research and Public Service, 2000). His areas of expertise include political regulation, applied democratic theory, representation, and state politics.

Mark Cheathem is professor of history at Cumberland University, his under-graduate alma mater, having completed his Ph.D. at Mississippi State University. He is the author or editor of five books, including the award-winning *Andrew Jackson, Southerner* and *Andrew Jackson and the Rise of the Democrats*. He is currently completing book projects on the 1840 and 1844 presidential elections. Cheathem also serves as project director for the new Papers of Martin Van Buren.

Roger Clegg is president and general counsel of the Center for Equal Opportunity. He writes, speaks, and conducts research on legal issues raised by civil rights laws. He is also a contributing editor at *National Review Online*. From 1982 to 1993, he held a number of positions at the U.S. Department of Justice, including assistant to the solicitor general and the number-two official in the Civil Rights Division and Environment Division. From 1993 to 1997, he served as vice president and general counsel of the National Legal Center for the Public Interest, where he wrote and edited a variety of publications on legal issues of interest to business. He is a graduate of Rice University and Yale Law School.

Michael Colaresi is Professor of Political Science and Director of the Social Science Data Analytics initiative at Michigan State University. He is also co-editor of the journal *International Interactions* and has published articles and books on topics related to national security secrecy, international rivalries, the role of militias in conflict, the domestic politics of international war, the use of text as data, and time series analysis. His most recent book is *Democracy Declassified*: The Secrecy *Dilemma in National Security* (2014, Oxford University Press). He was co-awarded the Gosnell Prize for Excellence in Political Methodology in 2006.

David A. Crockett is a professor and chair of the Department of Political Science at Trinity University. Often asked if he is related to the famous Davy Crockett, he says that he is not a direct descendant, but a first cousin five times removed. He is the author of *The Opposition Presidency: Leadership and the Constraints of History* (2002) and *Running against the Grain: How Opposition Presidents Win the White House* (2008), as well as numerous articles on presidential politics. He received his doctorate from the University of Texas at Austin in 1999.

Captain Brad DeWees is an instructor of political science in the United States Air Force Academy's Department of Political Science. He teaches courses on American government and a senior seminar titled "Innovation in Government." Captain DeWees was the top overall graduate from the

Air Force Academy's class of 2009. He is a Tactical Air Control Party (TACP) and Air Liaison Officer (ALO) by career, and has deployed to Afghanistan.

John Dilulio is Frederic Fox Leadership Professor at the University of Pennsylvania, a Brookings Institution Nonresident Senior Fellow, and a National Academy of Public Administration member. His academic awards include the Association of Public Policy Analysis and Management's David N. Kershaw Award and the American Political Science Association's Leonard D. White Award in Public Administration. He served as first Director of the White House Office of Faith-Based Initiatives. His books include *Bring Back the Bureaucrats* (Templeton Press, 2014), *American Government* (with James Q. Wilson and Meena Bose, Cengage, 2014), and *Godly Republic* (University of California Press, 2007).

Brendan J. Doherty is associate professor of political science at the United States Naval Academy. He earned his PhD from the University of California, Berkeley and his BA from Dartmouth College. He is the author of *The Rise of the President's Permanent Campaign* (2012), an empirical examination of the evolving ways that U.S. presidents handle electoral concerns throughout their terms in office. His other published work has examined presidential travel and fund-raising, the electoral college, U.S. Senate leadership, speech restrictions in judicial campaigns, the Marshall Court and federalism, the political participation of dual citizens, and the targeting of Spanish-speaking voters in presidential elections.

Todd Donovan is professor of political science at Western Washington University in Bellingham, Washington. He has published scores of articles in scholarly journals and has coauthored or coedited several books. His most recent coauthored books are *State and Local Politics: Institutions and Reform* (third edition, 2013) and *The Limits of Electoral Reform* (2013).

George C. Edwards III is University Distinguished Professor of Political Science and Jordan chair in presidential studies at Texas A&M University. He has written or edited twenty-five books on American politics and is also editor of *Presidential Studies Quarterly* and general editor of the *Oxford Handbook of American Politics* series. His most recent book, *Overreach*, analyzes the politics of leadership in the Obama presidency. He has served as president of the President and Executive Politics Section of the American Political Science Association, which has named its annual dissertation prize in his honor and presented him with its Career Service Award.

Ambassador (ret.) **Norman Eisen** is a Visiting Fellow in Governance Studies at the Brookings Institution, where his research focuses on good political and corporate governance. He served as the U.S. Ambassador to the Czech Republic from 2011 to 2014, developing an innovative anticorruption strategy that was adopted as a State Department model and training all new U.S. ambassadors in economic statecraft in 2013–14. Before that, Eisen served from 2009-11 in the White House as Special Assistant and Special Counsel to the President, where he was dubbed by the press as "Mr. No" and "the Ethics Czar" for his tough compliance and anti-corruption program. His portfolio also included open government, financial regulatory reform, campaign finance, and other political law issues. Before entering government, Ambassador Eisen was a litigator whose cases included *Enron*, the ADM antitrust case, the subprime financial collapse, and the 2000 and 2004 Presidential recounts, and he was named as one of Washington's top lawyers by *Washingtonian Magazine*. He co-founded Citizens for Responsibility and Ethics in Washington (CREW), a government watchdog group. Ambassador Eisen received his JD from Harvard Law School in 1991 and his BA from Brown University in 1985, both with honors.

Richard J. Ellis is Mark O. Hatfield Professor of Politics at Willamette University. His books include *The Development of the American Presidency* (2015, second edition), *Debating the Presidency: Conflicting Perspectives on the American Executive* (with Michael Nelson; third edition, 2014), and *Judging the Boy Scouts of America: Gay Rights, Freedom of Association, and the Dale Case.* In 2008, he was named Carnegie Foundation for Advancement of Teaching Oregon Professor of the Year.

Ward Farnsworth is dean and holder of the John Jeffers Research Chair at the University of Texas School of Law. He has written many articles on the Supreme Court and related subjects; he is also the author of *The Legal Analyst: A Toolkit for Thinking about the Law* (a guide to analytical methods for lawyers and law students) and *Farnsworth's Classical English Rhetoric.*

James C. Fell is a Principal Research Scientist with the National Opinion Research Center (NORC) at the University of Chicago in the Bethesda, Maryland, office. From 2001 to 2015 he was a Senior Research Scientist at the Pacific Institute for Research & Evaluation (PIRE) in Calverton, Maryland. Since 2001, he has completed over 50 research projects in the areas of impaired driving, underage drinking, alcohol policies, and traffic safety. Mr. Fell formerly worked at the National Highway Traffic Safety Administration from 1969 to 1999 and has 49 years of traffic safety and alcohol research experience. He has authored over 150 publications.

Scott A. Frisch is professor and chair of political science at California State University Channel Islands. His recent coauthored books include *Cheese Factories on the Moon: Why Earmarks Are Good for American Democracy* (2010), *Jimmy Carter and the Water Wars: Presidential Influence and the Politics of Pork* (2008), and *Committee Assignment Politics in the U.S. House of Representatives* (2006). His research interests include Congress, public budgeting, and the use of archival methods in political science. He is currently working (with Sean Q Kelly) on a book about congressional appropriations politics.

Gary L. Gregg II holds the Mitch McConnell Chair in Leadership at the University of Louisville, where he is also the director of the McConnell Center. He has written widely on the American founding, the electoral college, and presidential leadership and has authored two novels. He is author or editor of ten books, including *Thinking about the Presidency: Documents and Essays from the Founding to the Present* (2005), *The Presidential Republic: Executive Representation and Deliberative Democracy* (1997), *Securing Democracy: Why We Have an Electoral College* (2008), and *America's Forgotten Founders* (2012).

Elaine C. Kamarck is a senior fellow in the Governance Studies program and the director of the Center for Effective Public Management at the Brookings Institution. She is also a lecturer in public policy at the Harvard Kennedy School of Government. Kamarck is an expert on government innovation and reform in the United States, OECD countries and developing countries. In addition, she also focuses her research on the presidential nomination system and American politics and has worked in many American presidential campaigns. Kamarck is the author of *Primary Politics: Everything You Need to Know about How America Nominates Its Presidential Candidates*.

David Karol is associate professor of government and politics at the University of Maryland, College Park. He studies parties, interest groups, political institutions, and American political development. He is the author of *Party Position Change in American Politics: Coalition Management* (2009), coauthor of *The Party Decides: Presidential Nominations Before and After Reform* (2008), and coeditor of *Nominating the President: Evolution and Revolution in 2008 and Beyond*. His research has also appeared in several journals and edited volumes.

Sean Q Kelly is professor of political science at California State University Channel Islands. He is a former American Political Science Association Congressional Fellow (1993–1994). He has coauthored three books with Scott A. Frisch: *Cheese Factories on the Moon: Why Earmarks Are Good for American Democracy* (2010), *Jimmy Carter and the Water Wars: Presidential Influence and* *the Politics of Pork* (2008), and *Committee Assignment Politics in the U.S. House of Representatives* (2006). He is also coeditor of two books, including *Doing Archival Research in Political Science* (2012). Utilizing archival data, he is currently working with Scott Frisch on a book about the politics of congressional appropriations earmarks.

Stephen F. Knott is a professor of national security affairs at the United States Naval War College. Prior to accepting his position at the War College, Knott co-chaired the Presidential Oral History Program at the Miller Center of Public Affairs at the University of Virginia. His books include: *The Reagan Years; Alexander Hamilton and the Persistence of Myth; Secret and Sanctioned: Covert Operations and the American Presidency; At Reagan's Side: Insiders' Recollections from Sacramento to the White House; Rush to Judgment: George W. Bush, the War on Terror, and His Critics;* and *Washington and Hamilton: The Alliance That Forged America.*

Michael J. Korzi is Professor of Political Science at Towson University. He teaches and researches the presidency, Congress, American political development, and political philosophy. He has published on a range of topics, including the presidency and public opinion, presidential signing statements, and William Howard Taft's theory of presidential leadership. His most recent book, *Presidential Term Limits in American History: Power, Principles, & Politics* (2011), a theoretical and historical survey of the subject, received the American Political Science Association's Richard E. Neustadt Award for the "Best Book on Executive Politics" in 2012.

David E. Kyvig held the rank of Distinguished Research Professor Emeritus in the department of history at Northern Illinois University. He was the recipient of fellowships from the American Council of Learned Societies, the National Endowment for the Humanities, and the Woodrow Wilson International Center for Scholars. His book *Explicit and Authentic Acts: Amending the U.S. Constitution, 1776–1995* (1996), which won the 1997 Bancroft and Henry Adams Prizes, recently appeared in an updated edition (2016). His book *The Age of Impeachment: American Constitutional Culture since 1960* was a *Choice* Outstanding Academic Title for 2008.

Jeffrey Lazarus is associate professor of political science at Georgia State University. His research focuses on American elections and congressional organization. Much of his research explores how members of Congress use the policies and procedures of the legislative branch to help themselves win reelection. Toward this end, he has written extensively on earmarks but has also explored other types of pork-barrel spending as well as conference committees, the motion to recommit, and bill introduction. His research has appeared in several journals, including the *American Journal of Political Science, Journal of Politics,* and *Legislative Studies Quarterly.*

Sanford Levinson holds a chair at the University of Texas Law School and is also professor in the government department of the University of Texas, Austin. He is the author of many books and articles on the Constitution, including, most recently, *Framed: America's 51 Constitutions and the Crisis of Governance* (2012). He was elected to the American Academy of Arts and Sciences in 2001.

John McCardell is vice chancellor and president of Sewanee: The University of the South. He previously served as professor of history at Middlebury College, where he was also president from 1991 to 2004. He received his bachelor's degree from Washington and Lee University and his doctorate from Harvard University. In 2006, he founded Choose Responsibility, an organization whose mission is to engage the public in informed and dispassionate discussion about the place of alcohol in the lives of young adults. A scholar of nineteenth-century America, he has written and spoken extensively on the effects of alcohol policies, especially the National Minimum Drinking Age Act of 1984.

Neal McCluskey is the director of the Cato Institute's Center for Educational Freedom. Prior to arriving at Cato, McCluskey served in the U.S. Army, taught high-school English, and was a freelance reporter covering municipal government and education in suburban New Jersey. McCluskey is the author of the book *Feds in the Classroom: How Big Government Corrupts, Cripples, and Compromises American Education.* He holds an undergraduate degree from Georgetown University, where he double-majored in government and English, a master's degree in political science from Rutgers University, and a PhD in public policy from George Mason University.

Michael Nelson is Fulmer Professor of Political Science at Rhodes College. He is also a senior fellow of the Miller Center at the University of Virginia, senior contributing editor and book editor of the Cook Political Report, and a former editor of the *Washington Monthly.* In 2015, the American Political Science Association gave Nelson the Richard E. Neustadt Award for the Outstanding book on the Presidency and Executive Politics published during the previous year for *Resilient America: Electing Nixon in 1968, Channeling Dissent, and Dividing Government.* He and coauthor John Mason won the Southern Political Science Association's 2009 V.O. Key Award for Outstanding Book on Southern

Politics for *How the South Joined the Gambling Nation: The Politics of State Policy Innovation*. More than fifty of Nelson's articles have been reprinted in anthologies of political science, history, music, sports, and English composition.

Erin O'Brien is Chair of the Political Science Department at the University of Massachusetts Boston and co-director of the Scholars Strategy Network Boston chapter. Her research focuses on voter access, the politics of poverty, and gender in political representation. Dr. O'Brien's scholarship has been covered by *The New York Times, Boston Globe, Dallas Morning News, Houston Chronicle, Miami Times*, MSNBC, NPR, and *The Washington Post*. She is author of two books and articles appearing in *American Journal of Political Science, Perspectives on Politics, Political Research Quarterly, Newsweek*, and *Women & Politics*. Professor O'Brien is also a frequent media expert on issues of American politics.

Bruce I. Oppenheimer is professor of political science at Vanderbilt University. He earned his bachelor's degree from Tufts University and his master's degree and doctorate from the University of Wisconsin. He specializes in research on Congress, congressional elections, and American political institutions. With Frances Lee, he is coauthor of *Sizing Up the Senate: The Unequal Consequences of Equal Representation* (1999). In addition, he is coeditor of *Congress Reconsidered*, the eleventh edition of which will be published by CQ Press in 2017. He is currently working on a book examining Congress' role in the development of energy policy over the past fifty years.

John J. Pitney Jr. is Roy P. Crocker Professor of American Politics at Claremont McKenna College. He received his bachelor's degree from Union College and his doctorate from Yale University. He has been a New York State Senate Legislative Fellow and a Congressional Fellow of the American Political Science Association. He has written articles for *The Washington Post, The Wall Street Journal*, and *Politico*, among others. His most recent books are *After Hope and Change: The 2012 Elections and American Politics* (with James W. Ceaser and Andrew E. Busch; rev. ed., 2015) and *The Politics of Autism: Navigating the Contest Spectrum* (2015).

David P. Redlawsk is James R. Soles Professor and Chair of the Department of Political Science and International Relations at the University of Delaware. He received his bachelor's degree from Duke University, MBA from Vanderbilt University, and doctorate from Rutgers University. His most recent book, *The Positive Case for Negative Campaigning* (with Kyle Mattes; 2014) examines the role negativity plays in political campaigns. Other books include *Why Iowa?*

How Caucuses and Sequential Elections Improve the Presidential Nomination Process (with Caroline J. Tolbert and Todd Donovan; 2011), *How Voters Decide: Information Processing during Election Campaigns* (with Richard R. Lau; 2006), and *Feeling Politics: Emotion in Political Information Processing* (2006).

John Samples directs the Center for Representative Government at the Cato Institute. He is the author of *The Struggle to Limit Government: A Modern Political History* (2010) and *The Fallacy of Campaign Finance Reform* (2006). He is coeditor of *The Marketplace of Democracy* (2006) as well as other volumes on public financing of elections and on the legacy of James Madison. He blogs at http://www.cato-at-liberty.org.

Robert Samuels is the author of seven books, including *Why Public Higher Education Should Be Free* (2013). He teaches writing at the University of California, Santa Barbara, and is president of the faculty union, UC-AFT, which represents 5,000 lecturers and librarians at the University of California system. He writes the blog *Changing Universities*. His main interests are public discourse, political rhetoric, higher education research, and political economy.

Wendy J. Schiller is professor of political science, international & public affairs at Brown University. She served as a legislative staff aide to Senator Daniel P. Moynihan and as a federal lobbyist in the office of Governor Mario M. Cuomo, and she has held fellowships at Princeton University and the Brookings Institution. She is the author of *Electing the Senate: Indirect Elections before the Seventeenth Amendment* (with Charles Stewart III; 2015), *Partners and Rivals: Representation in U.S. Senate Delegations* (2000), *The Contemporary Congress* 4th-7th editions (with Burdett Loomis; 2003, 2005, 2015, 2017), and *Gateways to Democracy* 1st-4th editions (with John G. Geer, Jeffrey A. Segal, Richard Herrera; 2011, 2013, 2015, 2017). She is a frequent political commentator for local and national news outlets.

Steven S. Smith is Kate M. Gregg Distinguished Professor of Social Sciences, professor of political science, and director of the Murray Weidenbaum Center on the Economy, Government, and Public Policy at Washington University. He has taught at George Washington University, Northwestern University, and the University of Minnesota, where he was Distinguished McKnight University Professor of Political Science and Law. He has authored or coauthored several books on congressional politics, including *The Senate Syndrome* (2014). He has worked on Capitol Hill in several capacities, served as a Congressional Fellow of the American Political Science Association, and was a senior fellow at the

Brookings Institution. He has served as an editor of *Legislative Studies Quarterly* and on the editorial boards of the *American Journal of Political Science, Journal of Politics,* and *Congress and the Presidency.*

Robert J. Spitzer is Distinguished Service Professor and Chair of the Political Science Department at the State University of New York, College at Cortland. He is the author of over six hundred articles and papers appearing in many books, journals, and newspapers on a variety of American politics subjects, and he has published fifteen books: *The Presidency and Public Policy, The Right to Life Movement and Third Party Politics, The Presidential Veto, The Bicentennial of the U.S. Constitution, President and Congress, Media and Public Policy, Politics and Constitutionalism, The Right to Bear Arms, The Presidency and the Constitution, Saving the Constitution from Lawyers, Gun Control, The Encyclopedia of Gun Control and Gun Rights, We the People: Essentials Edition, The Politics of Gun Control* (6th edition), and *Guns Across America.* He is also series editor for the book series American Constitutionalism for SUNY Press. In 2003, he received the SUNY Chancellor's Award for Excellence in Scholarship.

Caroline J. Tolbert is professor of political science at the University of Iowa and the author of more than a dozen books and dozens of scholarly journal articles. Her latest book is *Digital Cities: The Internet and the Geography of Opportunity* (2012). She is also coauthor of *Digital Citizenship: The Internet Society and Participation* (2008) and *Virtual Inequality: Beyond the Digital Divide* (2003). *Digital Citizenship* was ranked as one of twenty best-selling titles in the social sciences by the American Library Association for 2008. Another of her recent books, *Why Iowa? How Caucuses and Sequential Elections Improve the Presidential Nomination Process* (2011), examines how presidents are nominated in the United States and ways to reform the process. She is editor of a *PS: Political Science and Politics* symposium titled "Reforming the Presidential Nomination Process" and coeditor of *Democracy in the States: Experiments in Election Reform* (2008), and *Citizens as Legislators: Direct Democracy in the United States* (1998).

Martin P. Wattenberg is professor of political science at the University of California, Irvine. His first regular-paying job was with the Washington Redskins, from which he moved on to receive a PhD at the University of Michigan. He is the author of two books on voter turnout in the United States: *Is Voting for Young People?* and *Where Have All the Voters Gone?*

Brian A. Weiner is Associate Professor of Politics at the University of San Francisco. His research focuses on American political thought, democratic theory, and the intersections between political theory and contemporary political and legal issues. He is the author of *Sins of the Parents: The Politics of National Apologies* (Temple University Press) and is currently working on a book tentatively titled *Visual Cacophony: Contemporary Visual Public Culture, Democratic Theory and Practice* that examines debates over the visual materials (art, graffiti, billboards) that appear in public spaces.

Erika L. Wood is professor of law at New York Law School, where she directs the Voting Rights and Civic Participation project. Professor Wood specializes in voting rights, criminal justice reform, and racial justice issues. Her work has been featured in numerous media outlets across the country, including the *New York Times, Newsweek,* the *Wall Street Journal, USA Today,* and National Public Radio. Previously, Professor Wood was deputy director of the Democracy Program at the Brennan Center for Justice, where she designed and launched major reform campaigns around the country and provided legal counsel and strategic guidance to advocates, legislators, and policy makers nationwide. Her most recent article, *One Significant Step: How Recent Reforms to Prison Districts Begin to Address Political Inequality,* was published in the fall 2015 volume of the University of Michigan Journal of Law Reform.

RESOLVED, Article V should be revised to make it easier to amend the Constitution and to call a constitutional convention

PRO: Sanford Levinson

CON: David E. Kyvig

The final article in the Articles of Confederation declared that no "alteration at any time hereafter [shall] be made" to any of the articles unless "agreed to in a Congress of the United States, and be afterwards confirmed by the legislatures of every State." Unanimous consent meant, in practice, that institutional deficiencies could not be corrected. Unable to amend the Articles of Confederation, those who were dissatisfied were forced to overthrow them instead. And that is precisely what happened in Philadelphia in 1787, when those whom we now call the "framers" or the "Founding Fathers" ripped up the existing constitution and wrote a new one.

The starting point for the constitutional convention's business was not the Articles of Confederation but the "Virginia Plan," authored principally by James Madison and presented to the delegates at the outset of the convention by Virginia Governor Edmund Randolph. The Virginia Plan's thirteenth resolution stated "that provision ought to be made for the amendment of the Articles of Union whensoever it shall seem necessary, and that the assent of the National Legislature ought not to be required thereto." Madison and his Virginia colleagues were determined to avoid a situation in which a single recalcitrant state could prevent the rest of the nation from amending the federal constitutional charter.

When the convention took up the Virginia Plan's thirteenth resolution on June 5, only two delegates spoke, one against and one in favor. South Carolina's Charles Pinckney "doubted the propriety" of excluding the national legislature from the amendment process. Massachusetts Governor Elbridge Gerry offered his support, arguing that the "novelty and difficulty of the experiment" on which his colleagues were embarking suggested the wisdom of allowing for "periodical revision." Gerry argued that they were unlikely to get everything right and so would need an amendment process to fix their missteps and miscalculations. The delegates were in no mood, however, to contemplate how to change a constitution they had not yet created, and so they voted to put off consideration of the resolution.

Nearly two months later, the delegates were no closer to resolving the question, and so the task of devising an amendment procedure fell to the five-man Committee of Detail, which worked for ten days from the end of July to the beginning of August to compose a rough draft of the Constitution. On August 6, the committee presented its handiwork to the convention, including Article XIX, which read: "On the application of the Legislatures of two thirds of the States in the Union, for an amendment of this Constitution, the Legislature of the United States shall call a Convention for that purpose." On August 30, the delegates unanimously approved Article XIX.

The question of how the new constitution should be amended was reopened on September 10, only a week before the delegates affixed their signatures to the final document. New York's Alexander Hamilton asked the delegates to make it easier to remedy "the defects which will probably appear in the new System." In Hamilton's view, those defects were most likely to be spotted by the national legislature, so he proposed that the article be modified to allow Congress, contingent on a two-thirds vote in each house, to call a constitutional convention. Madison also urged the delegates to take a second look at the article. He was particularly bothered by the "vagueness of the terms." How would the convention be formed, he asked, and what rules would govern its decisions?

Doubts about the article were sufficiently widespread that nine of the eleven state delegations voted to reconsider. Connecticut's Roger Sherman seized the opportunity to amend the article in order to allow the national legislature to propose amendments but to require that any such change be "consented to by the several States." Pennsylvania's James Wilson was quick to modify the proposal so that a constitutional amendment would require the approval of only two-thirds of the states. The proposal narrowly lost, but a compromise proposal of three-fourths of the states was agreed to without a dissenting vote. Madison then proposed wording that incorporated both Hamilton's earlier proposal and the three-fourths approval mechanism.

The delegates overwhelmingly approved it, although only after adding a provision that forbade any amendment relating to the slave trade for the next two decades.

The Committee of Style was charged with polishing the final draft of the Constitution, and on September 15, the committee presented to the delegates the wording of what had now become Article V. Several delegates remained dissatisfied, however. Sherman wanted a guarantee that no change could be made to the Constitution that deprived states of "equality in the Senate." Initially, the convention rejected the change, prompting an angry Sherman to propose that Article V be struck altogether. "Circulating murmurs" of discontent moved Gouverneur Morris to play peacemaker; he proposed that Article V be amended so that "no State, without its consent shall be deprived of its equal suffrage in the Senate." Eager to bring their proceedings to a close and to avoid jeopardizing the carefully crafted compromises between large and small states, the delegates agreed to Morris's proposal.

One further change was made to the work of the Committee of Style. The committee's Article V included no method for calling a constitutional convention, and Morris and Gerry proposed to remedy this by requiring a constitutional convention on application of two-thirds of the states. Their proposal was endorsed unanimously, and the opening sentence of Article V was revised into its final form: "The Congress, whenever two thirds of both Houses shall deem it necessary, shall propose Amendments to this Constitution, or, on the Application of the Legislatures of two thirds of the several States, shall call a Convention for proposing Amendments, which, in either Case, shall be valid to all Intents and Purposes, as Part of this Constitution, when ratified by the Legislatures of three fourths of the several States or by Conventions in three fourths thereof, as the one or the other Mode of Ratification may be proposed by the Congress." Two days later, the delegates—although not Gerry, Mason, or Randolph—signed the Constitution. Their work was done, but the debate over the wisdom of Article V had just begun.

Sanford Levinson and David E. Kyvig renew this centuries-old argument. Levinson seconds the complaint that was first voiced by Patrick Henry at the Virginia ratifying convention in 1788: "The way to amendment," Henry thundered, had been "shut." Levinson agrees that Article V is "an iron cage" and fundamentally undemocratic. Kyvig, in contrast, thinks that Article V gets it just about right, endorsing Madison's judgment in *Federalist* No. 43: "It guards equally against the extreme facility which would render the Constitution too mutable; and that extreme difficulty which might perpetuate its discovered faults." Twenty-seven amendments later, we are still debating the question of whether the framers got it just right or made constitutional reform too difficult.

PRO: Sanford Levinson

The United States has the hardest-to-amend national constitution in the world, at least among democratic nations.[1] Indeed, even illiberal constitutions, such as that of Saudi Arabia, may be easier to amend because rulers often have the unilateral power to change them. It is not merely that the U.S. Constitution stands out among world constitutions; with some exceptions, the fifty state constitutions within the United States also have much easier amendment procedures than does the federal constitution. Most states require that an amendment be passed by a simple majority of both houses of the legislature followed by a majority vote of the people. Some states, especially in the American West, permit an initiative process that enables a majority of voters to change the states' constitutions while bypassing the legislature entirely. There is, then, no "American consensus" that foundational documents should be extremely difficult to change. In fact, judging by what John Dinan has aptly called America's "state constitutional tradition," there is arguably an American consensus in favor of easy constitutional change.[2]

Be that as it may, we are stuck with Article V and all of its difficulties. It sets out two paths toward amendment, one going through Congress (and requiring the assent of two-thirds of both the House and the Senate), the other going through a convention that must be called by Congress upon a petition of two-thirds of the states. The text also establishes two paths for ratification: approval by three-fourths of the state legislatures or by three-fourths of specially convened state conventions. Which "mode of ratification" shall be used is left up to Congress to decide, and with one exception (the 21st Amendment), Congress has always opted for approval by state legislatures. Since all state legislatures, save for Nebraska's, are bicameral, any amendment needs to be approved by a minimum of seventy-five legislative houses in thirty-eight states, whereas any proposed amendment can be defeated by the negative vote of only thirteen legislative houses in separate states.

Congress is far too busy to spend its time reflecting on the inadequacy of our eighteenth-century Constitution to our twenty-first-century reality. Even if one sets aside the obscene amount of time that legislators must spend raising money for the next election, Congress has too much on its plate as it seeks to address pressing issues such as national security, the environment, and the economy, both domestic and global. Congress's inability to devote adequate time to thinking about possible changes in our basic political structures, even were its members predisposed to do so, is why I strongly support a new constitutional convention. I also hope that any such convention will modify Article V and make its own handiwork easier to amend.

The United States is stuck with Article V not because of a nonexistent national commitment to the idea that constitutions should be close to unchangeable but instead because of decisions made in the waning days of the Philadelphia convention of 1787 when delegates were eager to wrap things up and return to their respective homes. The convention was a ringing repudiation of Article XIII of the Articles of Confederation, which required the unanimous assent of the state legislatures in order to amend the Articles. No one at the convention defended this change-prohibiting system. So a key question is, Did those who wrote the Constitution decide, after significant debate, that two-thirds of each house plus ratification by three-quarters of the states was the right decision rule, the Goldilocks-style "just right" between a method of change that would be "too hot" (by being too flexible) and one that would be "too cold" (by emulating the Articles)? The answer is no. Almost all of the debate in Philadelphia and thereafter about Article V concerned the roles of states and Congress in the amendment process. Wariness about entrusting the process exclusively to Congress is what accounts for the ability of the states to trigger a new constitutional convention should two-thirds of them petition Congress to do so. Most of the framers of the Constitution would likely be surprised that this part of Article V has seemingly become moribund and that constitutional change now, realistically, must go through Congress. To be sure, there are currently attempts, sponsored largely by conservative political groups but with some left-wing support, to trigger a so-called "Article Five Convention" by going through state legislatures, but it is unlikely that the constitutionally required 34 states will accept the need for a new constitutional convention; Congress will therefore remain the only practical source of constitutional amendment. In any event, no one at the constitutional convention actually addressed why the formula of two-thirds for either proposing new amendments or triggering a new convention and then three-quarters for ratification was just right for the new United States.

The first discussion in the Philadelphia convention of the numbers required for amendment took place on September 10, a mere week before the delegates signed the final document. Elbridge Gerry of Massachusetts was among those who pointed out that one of the major defects of the Articles of Confederation was the unanimity requirement of Article XIII. "It was," said Gerry, "desirable now that an easy mode should be established for [correcting] defects which will probably appear in the new System." Article V reflected the delegates' view that the new constitution would in fact be more flexible than the one it was replacing. This is truly faint praise.

At least one leading critic of the Constitution condemned it for making change still too difficult. At the Virginia ratifying convention, Patrick Henry warned his fellow citizens that only one-tenth of the American people might be able to block necessary changes. "It will be easily contrived," he suggested, "to procure the opposition of one tenth of the people to any alteration, however judicious." Interestingly, James Madison, who was the Constitution's primary defender at the Virginia ratifying convention, chose not to confront Henry directly on this point. One searches in vain for any ringing endorsement of Article V. All that its defenders were willing to say in its behalf was that it was better than the disastrous Article XIII.

It is worth elaborating on Henry's reference to the "one-tenth" who could block needed change. His calculation was based on the fact that the total population (including slaves) of the four smallest states at the time (Delaware, New Hampshire, Rhode Island, and Georgia, with approximately 325,000 people) could block an amendment supported by the nation's other 3.6 million people. Consider the contemporary reality. The population of the United States as of the 2010 census was 308,143,815; the thirteen smallest states had a combined population of approximately 13,750,000. So the decision of a single legislative house in states constituting less than 5 percent of the nation's population would be sufficient to veto an amendment desired by states with 95 percent of the American population. Anyone who defends the present Article V should note that there is no correlation whatsoever between the percentage of states required to ratify an amendment and the percentage of the nation's population. No system that pretends to be based on the principle of one person, one vote, should take any pride in Article V, which in almost every respect resembles the justly despised Article XIII of the Articles of Confederation.

Perhaps one should place Article V alongside other unfortunate compromises made in Philadelphia, such as reinforcing the power of slave states and acquiescing to Delaware's demand for equal representation in the Senate, which were the price of gaining the Constitution in the first place. This may explain the decision reached in 1787, but it would be as crazy to embrace Article V because that is what the framers decided as it would be to embrace the sanctity of recognizing property rights in other human beings, as was done by the notorious Three-Fifths Compromise and the Fugitive Slave Clause.

For those who think it is important to remain faithful to the specific decisions made by the founders, consider the closing lines of James Madison's *Federalist* No. 14:

> Is it not the glory of the people of America, that, whilst they have paid a decent regard to the opinions of former times and other nations, they have not suffered a blind veneration for antiquity, for custom, or for names, to overrule the suggestions of their own good sense, the knowledge of their

own situation, and the lessons of their own experience? . . . They formed the design of a great Confederacy, which it is incumbent on their successors to improve and perpetuate.

We should, then, turn to the lessons of our own experience—including the history of American state constitutions and, for that matter, the history of every other country that is committed to the principles of liberal democracy—in deciding whether or not "improvement" of the "great Confederacy" designed in 1787 requires radical surgery on what is, in significant respects, its most important article, Article V.

Any discussion of the present adequacy of Article V requires that we answer two quite different questions: First, how does one evaluate the possible gains attached to risking changes in the status quo against the fear that such changes will generate negative costs? It is obvious that Article V has a tremendous bias toward the status quo and places an extremely high burden on anyone who believes that change is desirable. Second, can we develop some way of measuring, over our 220-year history, whether we have procured enough gains from this bias that any costs attached to the near impossibility of amending the Constitution are worth it?

I will return to those questions. A third question, however, needs to be considered first: How important are constitutional amendments? A number of distinguished law professors, including Bruce Ackerman, Stephen Griffin, and David Strauss, have argued that most important changes in the American constitutional order have taken place outside Article V.[3] If they are right, then this debate is much ado about relatively little. Although I believe that much important constitutional change has occurred outside Article V, I also believe that many needed changes have not. Much of the Constitution is "hardwired" against interpretive cleverness.

Perhaps the easiest, and least controversial, example has to do with when we inaugurate new presidents. A recurrent feature of the American political system is the election of a new president who has run on a platform repudiating key policies of the incumbent. A hiatus of about eleven weeks ensues between the repudiation of the sitting president and the inauguration of the successor on January 20. The United States pays a real cost in having simultaneously a legal president who has been repudiated by the electorate and a politically legitimate president without any legal authority to act. This is surely not the most serious defect in our Constitution, but it is perhaps the clearest example of a "hardwired" feature that cannot be "worked around," at least in the absence of an unusually public-spirited incumbent president and vice president both of whom must be willing to resign their offices immediately after the election in order to pave the way for their perhaps despised successors. This example should prove chastening to those who proclaim the irrelevance of formal amendment.

So let me return to the first two questions, which are more central to the debate. In his defense of Article V, David Kyvig remarks that the rigors of Article V have "contributed to a stable but not cripplingly inflexible government for more than two centuries." The appropriate response to this is, Says who? What, precisely, are the proper tests of flexibility and, for that matter, of stability? Indeed, whatever the test, could any reasonable person believe that we really have had "two centuries" of stability? What about the Civil War, a conflagration that was to a significant degree generated by the Constitution of 1787? William Lloyd Garrison described that Constitution as a "covenant with Death and agreement with Hell" because of the hardwired support it gave to slavery. It is difficult to argue that he was wrong. The Three-Fifths Compromise, for example, gave slave states enhanced representation in the House of Representatives and directly contributed, through the electoral college, to the election of American presidents who either owned slaves or were part of national political coalitions dedicated to protecting the interests of slave owners. This also helps to explain why the Supreme Court, consisting of presidential appointees, was so consistently pro-slavery prior to the Civil War.

As for the Fourteenth Amendment, which became part of the Constitution after the war, Bruce Ackerman has demonstrated that it is almost impossible to shoehorn it into a plausible Article V framework.[4] Proposal of the amendment by Congress was made possible by the refusal of the Republican Congress in December 1865 to seat most southern representatives and senators whose elections were viewed as valid by President Andrew Johnson. Had they been seated, it would have been impossible to procure the needed two-thirds majorities in each house. As for ratification, military reconstruction was established in order to engage in the kind of "regime change" that would generate approval by the South. Moreover, the defeated states were told that their representatives and senators would not be seated unless they had ratified the amendment.

No historian should pretend that the Fourteenth Amendment is evidence of the flexible operation of Article V. Constitutional reform literally grew out of the barrel of a gun. One must, therefore, reject Kyvig's notion that the Fourteenth Amendment reflects in any unproblematic sense "the high threshold of consensus required for amendment." Indeed, precisely because it reflected no such "consensus" and because the so-called Compromise of 1877 signaled *de facto* capitulation to the return of White rule in the ostensibly defeated Confederate states, the Reconstruction Amendments (Thirteenth,

Fourteenth, and Fifteenth) went into hibernation, so far as racial justice was concerned, for at least three-quarters of a century.

At this point, invariably, defenders of Article V will play the "risk aversion" card, suggesting that the wonderful thing about a functionally unamendable Constitution is that it prevents bad amendments. That it certainly does. An anti–flag burning amendment, for example, would have been a terrible addition to the Constitution, as would, I believe, the addition of a "balanced budget" amendment that is behind the current efforts to achieve an "Article V Convention" by petition of thirty-four states. The possibility of such amendments being enacted would certainly count as a cost of a more flexible system of amendment. What those who endorse such arguments never do, however, is ask about the potential risks (and costs) of our *not* being able to make desirable changes. Are we better off, for example, not having the Equal Rights Amendment in the Constitution, even though it received the support of both House and Senate and two-thirds of the states with well over a majority of the national population? Nor do proponents of Article V address the cost of having a political system in which there is no serious discussion of our "hardwired" structures because of an altogether rational belief that it is impossible to change them in our era. Kyvig proffers the Seventeenth (direct election of senators), Twentieth (moving up the inauguration date), and Twenty-second (two-term limit for the president) Amendments as examples of change, and they are. But they were added between sixty and one hundred years ago.

Although we were close to third party–induced electoral train wrecks in 1948 and 1968, and many people believe that such a train wreck occurred in 2000, there has been no serious attempt to amend the electoral college because at least one-fourth plus one of the states would view any change as negatively affecting their parochial interests. It is even more utopian to suggest changing the indefensible allocation of power in the Senate, by which Wyoming gets the same voting power as California, which has seventy times the population, because Article V at that point becomes like the Articles of Confederation, requiring unanimity for amendment.

One of the worst features of Article V is that it infantilizes our entire political dialogue. We are totally unlike the founders in our systematic refusal to discuss the adequacy of our institutions and to think of needed improvements, in part because the founders imprisoned us in an iron cage that makes change nearly impossible. And the success of Article V is in part our refusal to perceive ourselves as trapped in such a cage! Proponents of Article V basically argue that "Article V isn't broken and therefore doesn't need fixing." I am far more pessimistic. I think it *is* one of the most important parts of a broken Constitution. And, what is worse, precisely because most of us believe, perhaps rationally, that Article V works to stave off any realistic possibility of fixing what is wrong, we adopt the classic mechanism of denial: "If it can't be fixed, then it really isn't broken to begin with." We are, as a citizenry, much like a battered spouse who perceives no real possibility of exit and therefore is inclined to put the best spin on what might well be described, by an objective outsider, as a situation that merits escape.

Thus, I enthusiastically support a new constitutional convention that would, as one of its most important actions, significantly modify Article V. It is possible that most Americans, even in a world that made constitutional change easier, would disagree with me and come to the conclusion that things are basically fine as they are. That would disappoint me, but at least one might say, "Well, at least We the People have really thought about our polity, and one can respect the process by which the conclusion was reached even if one disagrees with the ultimate decision." In our present reality, however, there is only a deafening silence with regard to the adequacy of our political institutions, even as we are engaged in vigorous national debates about fundamental reform of our economy and our health care system. Those debates are taking place because of a perception that change is possible, and so it is worthwhile to organize and participate as democratic citizens in political struggles. Because Article V generates, in the minds of most rational people, the perception of impossibility of change, there is no serious debate about the article at all. Some people may be cheered by this. I obviously am not. I see it as cause for alarm, and perhaps even despair, if the policy changes we need (and desire) are thwarted by an outdated and undemocratic Constitution that is kept that way by the barriers to institutional change created by Article V.

CON: David E. Kyvig

When the men who would frame the U.S. Constitution first met in Philadelphia in May 1787, a fundamental question faced them: How should they design a government to strike an effective balance among competing desires for popular sovereignty, functional effectiveness, stability, and adaptability to changing circumstances? The framers were committed to establishing a government that would ultimately reflect the will of the people while at the same time not be so sensitive to momentary public enthusiasms that it would constantly change its character or direction and thus be considered unsteady. The solution that they devised for balancing the competing pressures of democratic responsiveness and government stability, the mechanism of constitutional amendment embodied in Article V of the Constitution, was a vast improvement over previous constitutional arrangements and has since proven its worth over the course of more than two centuries.

The question at hand is whether Article V still serves America's best interests or whether its rules for constitutional reform should be relaxed. No doubt, Article V is a daunting obstacle to those eager for change. Taken as a whole, however, the history of efforts to use Article V suggests that its high standards have not been an insurmountable barrier to needed reform. At the same time, Article V has saved the United States from adopting some momentarily popular but fundamentally imprudent measures. Dramatic declines in approval of the conduct of a president, such as confronted Richard Nixon between his overwhelming reelection in 1972 and his resignation to avoid impeachment twenty-one months later or as George W. Bush experienced between his high point after the terrorist attacks of September 11, 2001, and the lows of his last months in office, should remind us that temporary enthusiasm for or unhappiness with those leading government should not be confused with endorsement of or dissatisfaction with the design of government itself. The functional utility and simplicity of a structure have more lasting importance than does the conduct, for good or ill, of its temporary occupants.

The idea of constitutions—legal instruments defining the responsibilities, powers, and limitations of governments—originated in 1215 with the English Magna Carta, a negotiated agreement between King John and the principal peers of the realm regarding the limits of royal authority. In a series of further agreements over the next 500 years, British monarchs and Parliaments refined their definition of governmental structures and powers in a series of acts collectively, if not entirely accurately, referred to as an unwritten constitution. The distinguishing feature of Great Britain's master plan of government was less its haphazard manner of construction in several parts and more the fact that it could be and several times was radically altered by a simple parliamentary majority. Allowing a bare majority to define the law and thus the rules of government proved to be a prescription for sudden, dramatic shifts in government.

Britain's North American colonies developed on the basis of less flexible, more precisely defined instruments; for the most part, corporate or royal charters set forth the terms by which the colonies operated. The colonies grew more comfortable with such specific written instruments of government as they observed the erratic evolution of British government through the English Civil War, the Restoration of the monarchy, and the Glorious Revolution of 1689. By the time of the 1776 Declaration of Independence, the newly independent American states had all opted for written constitutions, either modeled on earlier instruments or created anew. The idea of a charter delegating the authority of the sovereign people to a government functioning under agreed-upon rules was widely embraced not only at the state level but also in the creation of a confederation of the states. A written constitution that could be read and comprehended by all seemed necessary and valuable for maintaining a well-defined and limited government under democratic control. Yet written constitutions carried with them the question of how they should be altered if experience proved they needed reform.

Any change to the Articles of Confederation required the unanimous agreement of all thirteen states. This system of amendment quickly proved unworkable, since it allowed a single state to thwart any constitutional reform, something that happened repeatedly and quickly rendered the Articles unpopular. Dissatisfaction with a rigid and unsatisfactory government of too few powers led to the call for states to send delegations to a constitutional convention in Philadelphia in the summer of 1787. Once the delegates gathered, every aspect of the Articles of Confederation was regarded as eligible for reform.

High on the agenda of the Philadelphia convention—along with the creation of a more effective national government with a balance of structures to carry out necessary legislative, executive, and judicial tasks without any one of them being able to exercise unlimited power—was the objective of devising a workable amending mechanism. The founders repeatedly demonstrated a concern for protecting minority interests while still respecting majority preferences. The Constitution won approval from every sector of the new nation by reassuring each of them that its interests would not be abused. Important decisions, those with long-lasting consequences, would require the greatest degree of consensus to take effect. To ratify an international treaty, one with the highest legal status, or to remove from office a properly chosen but subsequently impeached president or judge required a two-thirds vote by the Senate. Adoption of laws that Congress had passed but the president had vetoed required a two-thirds vote in each house of Congress. The most significant change, an alteration of the powers or procedures of government, should require the highest degree of consensus, the founders believed. Thus, they agreed that an amendment should be approved by two-thirds of Congress or by a constitutional convention called by two-thirds of the states. But to make such a basic change in the rules of government, the amendment would also have to be ratified or approved by legislatures or democratically elected conventions of three-fourths of the states. The founders did not insist on unanimity for constitutional change, but they clearly feared that if the fundamental rules of government were too easily altered, this could lead to changes being made without sufficient thought or agreement. Were they too cautious? More than 200 years of experience offer evidence that they were not.

Article V, the amending provision, proved one of the Constitution's great selling points. As the original states considered whether to ratify the Philadelphia convention's proposal, many had doubts about one aspect or another. A common complaint was the absence of a bill of rights providing specific protections for individuals against overweening governmental power. The ratifying convention in Massachusetts was the first to call for the immediate addition of a bill of rights, and it showed its confidence in the functionality of the new amending process by proceeding to approve the Constitution on the assumption that it would be promptly amended. Several other states did likewise, affirming their faith that the amending system would work by accompanying their ratifications with calls for a bill of rights. The two late ratifications critical to putting the Constitution into effect, those of Virginia and New York, were both obtained on the basis of pairing ratification with calls for amendment. Without the presence of a method of amendment that the founding generation regarded as workable, it is unlikely that the Constitution would have won approval.

James Madison, one of the Constitution's principal architects elected to the first Congress, perceived that the new framework of government would not be fully accepted until its amending system could assuage the concerns of various ratifying conventions. He devoted himself to drafting a set of amendments that would constitute a bill of rights on the basis of the host of proposals emanating from state ratifying conventions. Madison's amendments were approved by the House, modified by the Senate, and emerged from the first session of the first Congress. Ten of Madison's package of twelve amendments gained ratification within two and a half years. The incorporation of the Bill of Rights into the Constitution brought about the full acceptance of the new charter of government, an affirmation made possible only by the successful functioning of Article V.

The early discovery of oversights and flaws in the original Constitution led to two more amendments in short order, a further indication that the amending process could function when needed. Otherwise, the Constitution remained unaltered until the end of the Civil War. It is hardly surprising that this would be the case, since the matter most likely to provoke amendment—slavery—was what most deeply and evenly divided the country. A consensus on fundamental changes in the nature of government was hardly possible until one side or the other in the slavery debate gained a firm upper hand, as occurred only with the South's surrender in 1865. The amendments that ended slavery (the Thirteenth), guaranteed equal treatment and due process of law regardless of race (the Fourteenth), and secured black suffrage (the Fifteenth) reversed the terms of the racial settlement in the original Constitution and demonstrated the power of Article V to transform the entire government and society. Such authority, as the framers had foreseen, was not to be used lightly. The high threshold of consensus required for amendment anchored the fundamental reorientation of the United States from a confederation of powerful states to a centralized national government—not a transformation to be taken lightly.

Following the Civil War amendments, no more constitutional reform occurred until the early twentieth century, and the belief grew that the requirements for amendment might be insurmountable. But then the image of amendment as difficult under the terms of Article V was repeatedly refuted. Progressive reformers, unhappy with a Supreme Court ruling that a federal income tax was unconstitutional and disenchanted with the process for selecting U.S. senators, found constitutional amendments effective and achievable remedies. Indeed, as a growing number of states demanded a constitutional convention to draft a direct senatorial election amendment, and as Congress began to contemplate that such a convention would be as unrestrained as its 1787 predecessor in proposing changes to the basic terms of government, the House and Senate moved quickly to adopt a direct election amendment and send it to the states for ratification. As soon as the income tax and direct election of senators amendments were ratified early in 1913, advocates of women's suffrage and national prohibition of alcoholic beverages launched amendment campaigns. By the end of the decade, organized political crusades for each of these reforms achieved success. Once the belief that amendment was impossible was overcome, these fundamental changes in income distribution, democratic participation, and social practice were rapidly achieved. Two more amendments followed in little more than a decade—one an important speeding up of the presidential and congressional transition after a national election and the other a reversal of the national ban on alcohol.

The prohibition amendment delivered several lessons about the nature of constitutional amendment. First, it demonstrated that the threshold for adoption of even a radical constitutional reform was not beyond reach. The required two-thirds of each house of Congress and majorities in three-fourths of state legislatures were not merely assembled but exceeded. Events of the next decade demonstrated that the adoption of an amendment did not guarantee that it would be universally embraced; widespread violation of the liquor ban suggested that there were limits to public respect for the Constitution. The most important lesson may have been provided by the repeal of the Eighteenth Amendment only fourteen years after its adoption. Passage of the Twenty-first Amendment showed that the high standards of Article V were not an insurmountable obstacle to the construction of a public consensus overwhelming enough to reverse a previous constitutional agreement, even one of fairly recent standing. The Twenty-first Amendment, the one constitutional reform that directly reversed another, was a measure whose ratification Congress removed from the hands of state legislatures and gave to popularly elected state conventions. The use of bodies of delegates chosen solely on the basis of their position on this one issue underscored the democratic intentions of the Constitution. Prohibition and its repeal also made clear the liabilities of dramatic shifts in fundamental government practice, a cost that would increase if standards for achieving amendment were relaxed. At the same time, the episode demonstrated the capacity of a democratic polity operating under the terms of Article V to repair a constitutional error.

The prohibition episode is not the only evidence of the possibility that questionable amendments may be adopted, despite the elevated standards of Article V. The Twenty-second Amendment, limiting a president to two terms in office, was speedily approved by a conservative coalition of Republicans and southern Democrats following the death of Franklin Roosevelt, who had been elected four times to the presidency. The anti-Roosevelt sentiment that spawned the amendment produced a situation that thereafter politically hobbled every second-term president, ironically many of them conservatives, by barring them from running again. As a result, Presidents Dwight Eisenhower, Richard Nixon, Ronald Reagan, Bill Clinton, and George W. Bush all found themselves politically weaker in their second terms. The Twenty-second Amendment stands as a reminder that constitutional change can restrict democratic choice. Such reform ought to be approached cautiously and adopted only if a substantial national consensus is supportive.

Four amendments adopted during the 1960s demonstrated once again that the Article V process could work effectively. As public attention became focused on various issues, the necessary degree of consensus was attained for measures broadly perceived as worthwhile: racially progressive steps to prohibit poll taxes and grant electoral votes to the District of Columbia, a complex measure to replace departed or disabled presidents, and a grant of voting rights for eighteen- to twenty-year-old citizens. At the same time, certain measures that divided the society were unable to attain the political support necessary to move forward. Reaction against various Supreme Court decisions also led in the 1960s to proposals for amendments that would strengthen the authority of states while restricting that of the federal government, overturn the requirement of equal representation of citizens in state legislatures, and authorize state-sponsored school prayer composed by a local majority. Adoption of these amendments, each of which enjoyed support—in the last two cases substantial support—would have had significant, arguably antidemocratic and liberty-restricting, consequences. Advocates of anti–equal representation and prayer amendments once again proposed a constitutional convention and stirred concern that such a convention could produce radical change. As a result, interest in such measures rapidly declined. A lower threshold for amendment approval could have conceivably facilitated the adoption of such measures.

The battle for women's rights showed both sides of the Article V question. The Equal Rights Amendment (ERA), first proposed to Congress in 1923, did not achieve two-thirds support in both houses until 1972. It was ratified by thirty-five states, 70 percent of the necessary total but not the required three-quarters. The failure of the ratification effort did not prevent the Supreme Court from repeatedly during the 1970s and 1980s deciding to extend women's rights to due process and equal protection under the law. At the same time, widespread opposition to the Court's *Roe v. Wade* decision acknowledging a woman's right to choose to have an abortion spurred calls for an amendment to invalidate the ruling. In this case, the same high Article V standard that frustrated ERA supporters prevented abortion foes from achieving an anti-abortion amendment even though they had the support of President Reagan. The framers' notion that a high degree of consensus should be required for constitutional empowerment kept either side in an ongoing social debate from imposing its will on a still fundamentally divided society.

A lower threshold for adoption of constitutional amendment combined with the momentary enthusiasm displayed in the 1980s for proposed amendments to ban flag burning and require balanced annual federal budgets might well have facilitated adoption of imprudent amendments. The anti–flag burning amendment would have overturned a Supreme Court ruling that such acts represent symbolic free speech and would have constituted the first significant constriction of the free speech guarantees of the First Amendment. Such an outcome might have encouraged attempts to restrict through amendment other provisions of the Bill of Rights, ranging from gun possession to criminal justice protections. The so-called Balanced Budget Amendment would have posed difficulties for the federal government in responding to an economic or military emergency with large-scale economic stimulus or defense spending. While the anti–flag burning and balanced budget amendments enjoyed wide support at the moments they were first introduced, enthusiasm gradually faded as their consequences became evident. Had the Article V threshold for adoption of such amendments been lower, they might well have been installed in the Constitution, to the detriment of effective government.

The original constitutional principle that the fundamental rules governing the conduct of government should be based on a widespread public consensus is a concept that has served the United States well for more than two centuries. Each adoption of a constitutional amendment, the most recent in 1992, has represented a reaffirmation of the consensus that in other respects the terms of the existing Constitution remain acceptable. The repeated unwillingness to embrace a new constitutional convention offers additional evidence that easier amendment is not widely sought. Even the high standards of Article V have allowed such amendments as national prohibition and presidential term limits to win approval. Easier requirements for constitutional change might well allow other ill-considered measures to be installed in the basic framework of government, measures that would then be difficult to remove. While it is certainly possible to think of possible attractive changes to the Constitution— from electoral college reform to broader protection of individual human rights to clearer articulation of federal government responsibilities—it is hard to imagine continued confidence in the Constitution and the steady functioning of the federal government in the absence of a high degree of consensus on the terms of constitutional design. Article V, with its requirements of two-thirds congressional agreement and three-quarters state approval for constitutional change, has contributed to a stable but not cripplingly inflexible government for more than two centuries. Article V has served the nation well and deserves to be retained.

NOTES

PRO

1. Donald S. Lutz, "Toward a Theory of Constitutional Amendment," in *Responding to Imperfection: The Theory and Practice of Constitutional Amendment,* ed. Sanford Levinson (Princeton, NJ: Princeton University Press, 1995), 237–74. It is true that several constitutions, the most important being Germany's, include certain sections that are "unamendable." Save for this caveat, it remains true that the U.S. Constitution is the most difficult constitution to amend in the democratic world; in fact, it is easier to amend the "non-unamendable provisions" of the German constitution than it is to amend any provision of the U.S. Constitution.

2. John J. Dinan, *The American State Constitutional Tradition* (Lawrence: University Press of Kansas, 2006). It should be noted, however, that several American state constitutions, by requiring that two successive legislatures propose an amendment before sending it out for popular ratification, make it harder to engage in rapid amendment than is the case with the United States Constitution. The difficulty with the latter is surmounting the two-thirds requirements in both the House and Senate and then gaining the approval of three-quarter of the states. But, as the history of several amendments has demonstrated, the time from proposal to ratification can be relatively quick, which is impossible in, say, Massachusetts or Iowa, which have the "double-legislature" requirement.

3.   See Bruce A. Ackerman, "Higher Lawmaking," in Levinson, *Responding to Imperfection,* 63–88; Stephen M. Griffin, *American Constitutionalism: From Theory to Politics* (Princeton, NJ: Princeton University Press, 1996); and David Strauss, "The Irrelevance of Constitutional Amendments," *Harvard Law Review* 114 (2001): 1457–1505. See also Sanford Levinson, "How Many Times Has the United States Constitution Been Amended? (A) < 26; (B) 26; (C) 27; (D) > 27: Accounting for Constitutional Change," in Levinson, *Responding to Imperfection,* 13–36.

4.   Bruce A. Ackerman, *We the People: Transformations* (Cambridge, MA: Harvard University Press, 1998), 99–252.

RESOLVED, American democracy needs less sunshine and more closed-door negotiations

PRO: Bruce E. Cain

CON: Gary D. Bass, Danielle Brian, and Norman Eisen

"Selfishness, injustice, cruelty, tricks, and jobs of all sorts shun the light; to expose them is to defeat them." So wrote James Bryce in his classic 1888 treatise, *The American Commonwealth*. Bryce's suggestion that the "sunlight" of publicity invariably "kills . . . those noxious germs which are hatched where politicians congregate" caught the imagination of a brilliant lawyer and intellectual leader of the Progressive reform movement, Louis Brandeis. Writing in 1913 on "What Publicity Can Do," Brandeis gave to Bryce's idea the turn of phrase that is still quoted to this day: "Publicity is justly commended as a remedy for social and industrial diseases. Sunlight is said to be the best of disinfectants; electric light the most efficient policeman."[1]

The notion that publicity is essential to cleaning up the corruption of politicians, party bosses, and industrialists was central to the Progressive movement in the United States. It was the reason that Progressives pushed to replace smoke-filled party conventions with primary elections, provided (through passage of the Seventeenth Amendment in 1913) for direct popular election of U.S. senators rather than selection by state legislators, enacted the Federal Corrupt Practices Act (a.k.a. the Publicity Act) of 1910 requiring the disclosure of election contributions by political parties, and celebrated "muck-raking" journalists like Ida Tarbell and Lincoln Steffens, whose investigative reporting brought to light the shameful working conditions, widespread poverty, and corruption of urban America. A century later, the Progressives' equation of democracy with publicity continues to frame the ways Americans think about politics.

But don't we need to recognize that closed-door negotiations and back room deals also have their place in a democracy? After all, the nation's most revered document, the Constitution of the United States, was created behind closed doors and drawn curtains. The delegates' first act was to adopt a rule of absolute secrecy "that nothing spoken in the House be printed, or otherwise published or communicated without" the convention's permission. James Madison, often called the father of the Constitution, defended the rule on the grounds that it was necessary "to secure unbiased discussion within doors." Delegates would be much freer to speak their minds if they knew what they said would not end up on the front page the next day. Most historians would agree, moreover, that the secrecy that enveloped the convention's closed-door negotiations enabled the delegates to reach the compromises between large and small states as well as northern states and southern slaveholder states that were pivotal to the success of the Constitution.

If closing the doors to the public can be important in a functioning democracy, then the question is not whether publicity is better than secrecy or vice versa but rather whether in today's politics our commitment to these values has become out of balance. The resolution defended by Bruce E. Cain suggests that indeed we have swung too far in the direction of publicity, and that, as a result, we too often lack the political spaces that can enable politicians to hammer out agreements that require painful concessions by both sides. According to Cain, we need to recognize that excessive sunlight can be harmful because it leads politicians to become overly responsive to short-term interests and partisan pressures at the expense of the hard choices and uncomfortable compromises that are necessary to make effective public policy that is in the long range interests of the country. Gary D. Bass, Danielle Brian, and Norman Eisen aren't buying this argument, however. They believe that the politics of the past century have only confirmed that Brandeis and the Progressives had it right. What the United States needs to make government more responsive to the people is not less sunshine but more.

PRO: Bruce E. Cain

The idea that American democracy needs "less sunshine and more closed door negotiations" might seem counter intuitive. How could less sunshine improve American government? Isn't it obvious that politicians, untethered from public scrutiny, would just line their pockets with taxpayer money and sell the public interest short? Surely, Americans are best served by keeping their public officials on the shortest possible leash at all times.

Actually, determining the right amount of democratic transparency is surprisingly complicated, because public officials must also govern effectively, not simply in the most democratically pure way. When we make naïve assumptions about citizen capacity, democratic opportunities to observe and participate can be captured by highly motivated and well-resourced interest groups and individuals. And because the political world constantly evolves, the rules we adopt in one era do not always work as effectively in another. Political reform is a process of continuous adaptation. Reform advocates who fail to recognize the changing political context and blindly defend the status quo may be protecting their own turf at the expense of the public interest.

WHY DO WE WANT TRANSPARENCY?

Because democratic values are so deeply embedded in American culture, we rarely question the purposes they serve. Democracy is a form of government that is designed to make public officials responsive to the citizen majority. The key institution in any democracy is the election, which enables eligible voters to hold public officials accountable by the threat of removing them from office. In order to be informed adequately, voters need to know what opposing candidates are promising and what incumbents have done in office. That provides a baseline level of government transparency. But how much is enough?

The answer is a balance of competing citizen expectations. A political system based on majority consent and voter equality resonates with us because it respects our individual dignity to a greater degree than other forms of government. But the personal affirmation we derive from democratic values is not enough. Americans also expect their government to solve problems and be effective. The public's attachment to the political system is highly instrumental. Americans like their government when things are going well and dislike it when conditions sour.

What does this imply for transparency? It means that transparency should not be simply maximized for its own sake. It should also be compatible with effective government. Consider an obvious example. The government must have the ability to keep secrets about national security and law enforcement in order to protect its citizens adequately. A country cannot tip off its enemies or criminals about the specific ways it defends itself. That is why freedom of information laws protect the nation's need for state secrecy by blocking a citizen's right to obtain sensitive public safety data until it is no longer threatening to release it.

Currently, many states have open meeting laws that require government bodies to conduct their deliberations in public. The federal government has similar laws governing its advisory committees (i.e., the Federal Advisory Committee Act, 1972) and government agencies (i.e., The Government in the Sunshine Act, 1976). Federal laws, however, exempt the Congress and the Supreme Court from these rules. Open meeting laws vary in their strictness, but in general, they set out rules for when meetings must be open to the public, what topics can be discussed at any given meeting, when discussions can be closed to public observation, and what penalties can be assessed when there are violations of these rules.

Given the possible tension between effectiveness and transparency, the question is whether laws that force public decision making into the open strike the right balance between accountability and effective government. In too many instances, they do not. When rigidly enforced, for example, open meeting laws encourage rigid posturing rather than negotiation and compromise. Any final vote, decision, or action should of course be announced and explained publicly. But government officials should have enough deliberative space to permit frank exchanges, persuasion, and the airing of preliminary conclusions. Too much sunshine can have the opposite effect.

Retrospective accountability does not require that citizens know all preliminary thoughts and discussions that led up to particular decisions or actions. Moreover, if public officials were held accountable for every suggestion they made in conversation, e-mail, and memo before they acted, it would deter the kind of devil's advocate questioning that prevents groupthink (the dangerous tendency in government circles to go along in order to get along).

Excessive public scrutiny can also hamper compromise and deal making. If a public official announces a position in public, and then later changes his or her position in the interest of compromise, that official can be accused of inconsistency, hypocrisy, or opportunism. But the American political system with its many divisions of power across branches and levels of government cannot act without negotiation and bargaining. The consequence of purity and rigidity is often stalemate.

Open meeting laws constrain the ability to find compromise by broadly defining the meaning of a "public meeting." Under some sunshine laws, members of a government body are prohibited from having separate individual conversations or informal discussions at a social gathering about matters they are considering. In 1986, I was hired by the LA City Council to come up with a remedy to a voting rights violation in their city council districts. There were several ways that we could have altered the city council lines to meet the Justice Department's objections, but as the city's consultant, I was prohibited from meeting with the city council members individually and serially to assess their willingness to accept certain proposals. This was a problem because if a member first publicly announced that he or she was willing to trade away a given area of his or her district but ended up with that area in the final plan, his or her loyalty to those constituents could be questioned by an opponent.

Sometimes showing a united front is in the public interest. This, for instance, applies to the Federal Reserve Bank because its decisions can affect market reaction and confidence adversely. In the fall of 2015, the Federal Reserve Board was divided as to whether to raise interest rates. The chair, Janet Yellen, held a series of back-to-back calls and one-on-one meetings to pull together a consensus of the seventeen members that they should postpone a decision until the economic signals were clearer.[1] Prohibiting this kind of pre-meeting discussion and forcing it into the open as some strong open meeting laws do would have undermined her efforts.

Moreover, the general public rarely has the time, interest, or resources to take advantage of sunshine laws. Normally, only interested parties or occasionally the press corps show up to witness agency, commission, or local government deliberations. The press would like to tell the inside story, especially if there is conflict or drama, but when public officials are present, they are pretty guarded about what they say and do. Being watched drives the real political conversation underground. The inside story usually comes in deep background leaks by inside sources, not from press conferences, hearings, or debates on the floor.

Interested parties monitor meetings and hearings in order to influence outcomes. This is particularly true at the implementation stage. State and federal environmental laws, for instance, mandate public input and official responses before agencies can issue permits or make rulings on specific projects. But the "public" at these meetings is rarely the general population or even a representative sample of the electorate. More often, the "public" consists of private and nonprofit stakeholders. With enough resources, they can use transparency opportunities to hold up major projects for many years.

An example I have discussed elsewhere is the failure for two decades to obtain the necessary permits to build floodwalls along the San Francisquito Creek to protect the economically disadvantaged minority community of East Palo Alto, because various well-resourced NIMBY and environmental groups have used their opportunity to observe and comment to hold up the floodwall construction in order to gain leverage for such issues as wildlife protection and wetlands preservation.[2]

The problem is transparency capture: If transparency practices assume that the general public will take advantage of them when that is not the case, then the opportunity to monitor and influence will fall to those with the greatest resource advantages and self-interested motives.

THE MODERN CONTEXT AND TRANSPARENCY

All of this was troubling enough when the modern wave of transparency laws were enacted in the 1970s, but these problems have worsened over time. Today's more contentious political environment has fundamentally altered the way American government now operates. Consider the demise of regular order in the House of Representatives. Congressional leaders routinely bypass the textbook steps of committee consideration of bills, public hearings, opportunities to amend, and the like. Speaker Paul Ryan vowed in the fall of 2015 to restore regular order to the House but immediately had to abandon his promise in order to get a bill on the floor that revised the rules for the U.S. refugee program in the wake of the Paris shootings.[3]

The reality is that in order to be effective in the current political environment, Congressional processes have had to adapt to the increased prospects of political obstruction. Procedural purity inevitably gave way to instrumental need. Tolerance for process for its own sake at the expense of being effective is limited. In the end, democratically elected governments are judged in large measure by what they do for their constituents, not by the processes they follow.

Partisan polarization has risen to levels reminiscent of the late nineteenth century.[4] This means that there are fewer instances of bipartisan support for legislation and willingness to compromise. When obstruction is the goal, every step in the legislative process is a potential opportunity for delay and obstruction. Hearings become showcases for partisan viewpoints, not opportunities for fair-minded investigation. Amendments are opportunities to weaken bills or embarrass the opposition, not to improve the legislation. And votes on complicated bills become fodder for thirty-second campaign ads.

Increasing political professionalization has also shaped contemporary politics. Political consultants, lobbyists, and interest groups are much more sophisticated and experienced today than in earlier periods of history. They have learned how to use the system to their advantage. Opposition researchers, a modern political consulting subspecialty, routinely use Freedom of Information

Act (FOIA) requests to gather information about opposing candidates. Over the two years before the 2016 presidential election, the Republican National Committee's opposition researchers made more than 330 FOIA requests for over 11,000 pages of public records concerning the Clintons at taxpayer expense.[5] The efforts of such extensive searches have been trivial to date from a policy point of view. Similarly, when Hillary Clinton handed over her 55,000 e-mails, we learned very little about the pressing issues of the day and a great deal about her desire to get in touch with Lady Gaga and Ben Affleck and her many communications with Sidney Blumenthal.[6]

Transparency laws enable the press to play a role in maintaining government accountability, but the press corps has changed dramatically since the seventies. Reporting standards have declined, and many more media outlets function as outlets of partisan and ideological viewpoints. Media that resist the partisan sirens tend to place a higher priority on entertainment and sensationalism over the boring details of policy and government performance. Good for business but not what we had in mind when the transparency laws were put in place.

Achieving policy closure is more difficult than before. Policies are contested through the stages of implementation and judicial review. As with regular order, opportunities for the public to observe and participate in these later stages have become potential veto points—that is, procedural openings for more policy obstruction. As a consequence, it gets harder to achieve policy closure and regulatory certainty.

THE CASE FOR REVISING TRANSPARENCY

Despite significant changes in the American political system, there are few innovative ideas coming from the reform community. The solution as most reformers see it is more of the same. Tighten disclosure laws to put more information online. Restore regular order in Congress. Make sure that open meeting laws are followed to the letter of the law and that no deliberations among officials are hidden from the public, and so forth.

Does this mean that open meeting laws should be scrapped entirely—of course not. But it does mean adapting them to fit the demands of the contemporary period. Here are my suggestions.

1. *Resist the temptation to extend sunshine laws to Congress or the Supreme Court.* Many people are unhappy with Congress. They dislike its high level of polarization and suspect that interest groups have too much influence over it. When the government disappoints, the populist temptation is to tighten the level of public monitoring. But strict open meeting rules would hamper

negotiation and strengthen the hands of interest groups and ideologues to keep party leaders from cutting deals that their base voters and financial supporters disapprove of. Many former members of Congress believe that the current polarization is rooted to some degree in the fact that current members do not live in DC and socialize with one another anymore. If we cut off the capacity for one-on-one and social meeting conversations, we will further inhibit the capacity for consensus building in the Congress.

2. *Focus on retrospective rather than in-process transparency in order to create more deliberative space.* Voters need to know which actions were taken and what their consequences have been in order to vote in an informed way. Most voters do not know or care about the arguments and discussions that led up to a given decision. The value added by forcing discussions to be held in public or demanding the publication of e-mails, memos, and other materials relevant to a given action is usually far less than the negative effect it has on the capacity for deliberation and willingness to negotiate. Polarization and professionalization make it harder for public officials to compromise without angering their core supporters and interest groups. And yet, the American political system, fractured as it is, cannot operate unless there is a willingness of negotiate and bargain to some resolution. Public officials need to be accountable for what they do in office (*retrospective accountability*) not monitored closely while they are considering what to do (*in-process transparency*). They need to be able to change their minds and make bargains without the constant scrutiny of outside interests guarding their narrow agendas.

3. *Streamline decision-making processes to reduce public opportunities for obstruction.* There is a rampant sore loser problem in the United States. As a consequence, it is hard to achieve closure on policy matters. Democratic opportunities to observe or participate in the policy-making process that were originally intended for the public are instead used by strong partisans and interest groups to continue policy battles they lost in the Congress. The Affordable Care Act ("Obamacare") passed in 2010 but is still contested five years later. The ability to do something about the excessive number of veto points in the U.S. political system is limited given the Constitution's separation of powers and federalism features. But we can improve matters on the margin by accepting the demise of regular order in Congress and by providing stricter guidelines about public input at the implementation stage of many laws.

CONCLUSION

While Americans are quite vocal about their government dissatisfactions, they are often unwilling to examine the basic premises that undergird their political system. More transparency and openness is not always the answer to our governance problems. We need more deliberation, compromise, and consensus. We need less partisan posturing, ideological rigidity, and obstruction. In our everyday lives, we practice ways to tamp down emotional disagreements and quietly settle our differences, but we hesitate to give our elected officials the same options. A democracy that works for the people needs to be able to make effective decisions without undue special interest pressures and incentives to grandstand. That sometimes means providing shade from the glare of excessive transparency.

CON: Gary D. Bass, Danielle Brian, and Norman Eisen

If you follow the news, it only takes a second to realize how important transparency is to a robust democracy, and that, if anything, we need more of it.

Public institutions thwart us in trying to get information about police beatings in our cities and sexual assaults on our campuses. Trade agreements are negotiated in near secrecy—with the big businesses affected by the deals enjoying privileged access to the negotiations. Behind closed doors, Wall Street deploys powerful lobbyists to Capitol Hill to undo disclosure and accountability requirements.

Openness is the means by which we, as the owners of our democracy, make judgments about necessary political corrections and policy reforms that can improve the quality of life in America. Sunshine is the first step to bringing accountability to our political system and to ensuring that the powerful in our society follow the rule of law.

So why is there a need to debate this resolution? Incredibly, some now claim that transparency is a cause of government dysfunction and polarization. They assert that although transparency is a good thing, we have too much of it today—and it is undermining deliberation in government and therefore government's effectiveness.

To understand why this claim is false, let's start with some background. Today's transparency requirements are built upon a series of laws passed in the aftermath of the Watergate scandal of the 1970s. The intent of these laws—the Federal Advisory Committee Act (FACA), the Government in Sunshine Act (Sunshine Act), and a revised Freedom of Information Action (FOIA)—was to address growing corruption in the executive branch and to rebalance power between the legislative and executive branches. FACA required various steps, including transparency, when the executive branch sought advice from people outside the government on policy matters. The Sunshine Act required various agencies to meet openly when making deliberations. FOIA required the executive branch to disclose records when requested by the public. Congress hoped these laws would bring accountability to government, although good government advocates would be the first to say these laws have fallen short of their goals.

Over the years, open government efforts moved beyond these Watergate-era laws by addressing transparency in specific areas. For example, in 1986 Congress passed a law requiring chemical companies to disclose information to the public about toxic chemicals being released to the air, water, and land. This affirmative release obligation under the Toxics Release Inventory (TRI) went beyond FOIA in that it no longer required the public to request the information and also established the notion that government agencies should be providing searchable databases on the Internet.[1]

In 2006, building on the advances of the TRI, Congress passed a law that required information about government grant and contract spending to be made available through USAspending.gov. The website allows anyone to see who is getting how much money from which government agency and program—an important tool to make sure taxpayer money is used wisely and to spot corruption. In 2009, in another step forward, Congress required a searchable website of all emergency funding appropriated under the Recovery Act to address the "Great Recession" economic collapse.

Today, there are literally hundreds of other examples of cutting-edge efforts to strengthen transparency. For example, state regulators and researchers are advocating for a searchable website of charity registrations and federal tax information in order to stop fraudulent charitable solicitations and other misuses of funds by charities. Others are seeking greater disclosure about beneficial corporate ownership so that the public and regulators can find out who is really behind shell corporations and combat fraudulent activities such as tax evasion. Numerous whistleblower protection provisions have been passed in order to shed light on wrongdoing inside government agencies, government contractors, and regulated entities in the financial sector. Transparency helps those inside government enforce the laws on the books, and it helps the public build confidence that our government is doing the right thing.

Yet, instead of celebrating this new era of openness and accountability, the transparency critics bemoan it. For example, Francis Fukuyama, echoing sentiments from his recent book *Political Order and Political Decay*, writes that transparency has actually harmed government operations. He says FACA and the Sunshine Act "put a serious damper" on deliberation, with FACA imposing "onerous requirements" on federal agencies seeking advice from those outside of government. Fukuyama adds that FOIA can be "weaponised" by political opponents (e.g., using FOIA to obtain Benghazi documents to blame Hillary Clinton for the 2012 attack on the U.S. compound in Benghazi, Libya), and that television coverage of Congress is linked "to the decline of deliberation in that body." Fukuyama characterizes openness laws as "a straitjacket of rules specifying how [legislators and government officials] must talk to each other, and to citizens."[2]

Or take Jason Grumet of the Bipartisan Policy Center. He argues that "it's time to revisit . . . the reforms inspired by the mistrust of government that Watergate helped engender [that were] aimed at transparency, openness and the monitoring of decision-making."[3] His solution is to replace transparency with more secrecy, or what Grumet euphemistically calls "privacy." Others make a similar case, although they often maintain that they are not opposed to transparency in theory, just that the current balance of transparency to secrecy is off.[4]

In broad strokes, their theory is that politics needs to be left to politicians, and that incessant interference by forces such as the media, open meetings laws, public records requests, campaign contribution disclosures, and even smartphone videos of town halls recorded by citizens, has resulted in gridlock. The necessary backstage wheeling and dealing of politics has ground to a halt, these critics claim, and we need to give political professionals their privacy back so they can get to work. As Fukuyama says, solutions do not "lie in the proliferation of formal accountability mechanisms or in absolute government transparency. . . . Citizens must trust the government to make good decisions."[5] We firmly disagree with that premise. While Fukuyama does add that government should earn our confidence, we argue it should not expect our blind trust.[6]

SECRECY AND DEAL MAKING

On December 13, 2014, there was a collective national sigh of relief when, less than one hour before a looming government shutdown, Congress passed the "cromnibus" bill, so-called because it combined a shorter term continuing resolution and a longer term omnibus spending bill containing eleven appropriations bills funding government operations. However, it turned out that the bill, negotiated behind closed doors, was riddled with tacked-on provisions, or "riders," many of which were put there by powerful special interests. Prior to voting on the bill, Sen. Elizabeth Warren (D-MA) called attention to one such provision, reportedly pushed by Citibank, that let big banks gamble on derivatives inside their taxpayer-insured depository institutions, unwinding legislation (the Dodd–Frank Wall Street Reform and Consumer Protection Act of 2010) that had been enacted to limit this risky behavior that was one of the causes of the 2008 economic meltdown. Others spotted changes to campaign finance law that raised the limit contributors can give to political parties to over $1.5 million each election cycle.

While those two riders gained national attention, there were dozens of others added. But because of the secrecy surrounding the spending bill, we will likely never know who inserted each specific rider. Big trucking companies got a temporary rollback of safety rules aimed at ensuring truck drivers get enough rest. The potato industry won a reversal on the ban against buying white potatoes through the Women, Infants, and Children nutrition program, despite Institute of Medicine research that shows low-income families already get plenty of white potatoes. Another part of the bill blocks EPA from regulating certain water sources for the farming industry, risking dangerous chemicals entering our food supply. The list goes on.

Was secrecy really needed for deal making? There is plenty of evidence that real deals can still be made in public. For example, the massive and controversial Dodd-Frank Act happened under the glare of television cameras, including the conference committee negotiations where important compromises were struck. Given that lobbyists representing opponents of derivative reform reportedly outnumbered reformers by an 11-1 margin,[7] the decision to televise the proceedings may have been a key ingredient in holding the special interests at bay and turning the bill into a law.

There are many other examples. As we write this piece, it appears that a deal has been struck on reauthorizing the No Child Left Behind law. That bipartisan deal was accomplished in openness after several years of gridlock. Similarly, a highway bill to fund transportation infrastructure projects was passed in the open without unnecessary secrecy. These bills were initially locked up because key actors would not compromise, not because of undue transparency. All of these instances show that failure or success in passing bills has little to do with transparency and more to do with the political courage to compromise.

To take another example, some maintain that the private, bipartisan negotiations that generated the Senate's initial immigration bill demonstrate the importance of limiting transparency. True, it resulted in a bill, but has that bill or *any* bill on immigration reform become law? No. The reasons have almost nothing to do with transparency but instead result from dramatically different attitudes toward the underlying issue and a refusal to compromise.

Furthermore, secrecy creates potential dangers. Under the cromnibus, numerous special interests got special deals. Under Dodd-Frank, written in full public view, a number of deals for Wall Street were stopped. Given the influence wealthy individuals and powerful corporations have today, secrecy in the legislative process allows for sweetheart deals and policies that do not reflect the needs of most people or the country. It is not surprising that 74 percent of voters believe our elected leaders put their own interests ahead of the country's interest.[8]

That is precisely why transparency is so important: It can restore confidence in government decision making. Disgraced former lobbyist Jack Abramoff said that simply mentioning to a legislator or regulator that a lucrative lobbying job might be available to him or her upon leaving government was an extremely effective way to get the bill or rule changes he wanted.[9] And few doubt that large campaign checks help deliver enormous payback. Letting the sun shine on issues like the so-called revolving door (jobs top government policy makers get when leaving government) and campaign contributions may not on its own end corruption, but it helps identify it and, with other enforcement tools, can stop it.

The bottom line is that secrecy isn't necessary for deal making; it's necessary for *bad* deal making.

TRANSPARENCY IS NOT THE REAL PROBLEM

Jonathan Rauch, a senior fellow at the Brookings Institution, doesn't see it that way. The title of his recent article expresses his view succinctly: "Political Realism: How Hacks, Machines, Big Money, and Back-Room Deals Can Strengthen American Democracy." Despite examples like Dodd-Frank, Rauch maintains that a twenty-first-century version of Tammany Hall is necessary to get government working again. "In order for government to govern, political machines or something like them need to exist, and they need to work." Rauch sums up his argument as follows:

> Professionalizing the civil service, formalizing welfare programs, prosecuting bribery and extortion, opening more political deliberations to public view—those and other reforms of a century ago were justified and mostly wholesome. But what began as a necessary rebalancing acquired its own momentum and ideology and created an imbalance of its own, pushing relentlessly to extirpate corruption and defining corruption ever more broadly . . . what began as a useful correction of Tammany-style excess has become a neurotic obsession.[10]

We disagree with Rauch. As we have pointed out here and elsewhere, anti-corruption transparency measures are not significant factors contributing to government gridlock.[11] Instead, hyperpartisanship has become a political tool that has turned gridlock into an end in itself.[12] This shift began in the past decade or so, with the congressional leadership of both parties instructing their members to stop cosponsoring bipartisan legislation with moderate colleagues in swing districts because leadership wanted to target those moderates. The disincentive to work across the aisle became more acute as Tea Party Republicans, whose disdain for government operations is a core feature of their agenda, were elected to office. This vocal minority in the House of Representatives has forced a government shutdown, inched the country to the brink of default, forced a Speaker of the House to resign, initiated repeated votes on repealing Obamacare, and launched other efforts that promote gridlock. Given that this bloc in Congress and their supporters believe government is part of today's problems, they have no incentive to compromise.

Furthermore, the arguments positing that transparency threatens our democracy are often grounded in exaggeration and hyperbole. Consider Fukuyama's argument that FOIA can be "weaponised" by those with an axe to grind. That is precisely what makes our democracy so precious. We don't limit access to records just to those whom the government decides need to know—and we certainly would never support a plan to allow the government to ask how requesters plan on using the information.[13] Instead, we premise our democracy on the public's right to know what the government is doing in the people's name, making that information available to everyone. That is how we enable meaningful accountability, by allowing open access. If anything about FOIA needs fixing, it is that there should be more proactive disclosure by government (more like the TRI), instead of the burden being on the public affirmatively to request access to records.

Moreover, FOIA already provides appropriate restrictions from disclosure, such as for confidential business information and national security. The problem is that too often the government uses the more discretionary exemptions in FOIA to withhold information. One such exemption protects recommendations and advice that are part of the "deliberative process" involved in governmental decision making. The rationale is to protect the integrity of agency decision making by encouraging both full and frank discussions of policy proposals while at the same time preventing premature disclosure of policies under review. Citing research by the Associated Press, conservative journalist Mark Tapscott points out "there were at least 81,752 'deliberative moments' in the federal government" in 2013 when records were withheld from public disclosure for that reason, "the most ever [of] such denials."[14] In other words, there is already lot of opportunity for government to operate out of the spotlight.

There is no doubt that FACA and the Sunshine Act need improvement. But their main problem is the exact opposite of the ones the critics claim. There are actually *too many* loopholes to disclosure and open meeting requirements. When Fukuyama and others criticize the Sunshine Act, they may not realize that it only applies to a small number of executive agencies and that approximately 40 percent of those agencies responding to a survey report using loopholes in the law more than 75 percent of the time, circumventing disclosure.[15]

Remember the supposedly onerous requirements of FACA that Fukuyama claims? A closer look shows that these "onerous" requirements are that committee membership be "fairly balanced in terms of the points of view represented," and that the advice provided by committees be objective, independent, and accessible to the public.[16] Strikingly, few of FACA's critics seem to know that the law allows committees to hold closed meetings.[17] In fact, the Congressional Research Service reports that in fiscal year 2014, more than seven in ten of all FACA meetings were closed![18]

The Washington Post's Christopher Ingraham drew attention to the dangers regarding secrecy, imbalance, and potential abuse by the FACA committees that advise the government on trade policy and trade negotiations. Ingraham noted that the committees "are heavily dominated by corporate interests and their related trade associations."[19] In all, those companies and groups "represent 85% of the voices on the trade committees" and "get access to documents that the public cannot see."

It is essential to know who the government is getting input from, and not just after the fact, as Professor Bruce Cain would have it.[20] If government is contemplating a new energy policy, it is important that government not only get advice from coal-burning companies, for example. Imagine if bank policies were shaped in secret with Wall Street bankers and no one else. Sunshine is a means for the news media, nongovernmental organizations (NGOs), activists, and others acting to benefit the public to bring accountability to, and build confidence in, our government.

Some critics, such as Cain, criticize the role of these intermediary organizations. "Relying on intermediaries to monitor public officials is . . . fraught with its own uncertainties and incentive misalignments."[21] In a later article, Cain notes that "democratic opportunities can be hijacked for individual gain and special interest."[22] He fails, however, to acknowledge that the role of intermediary organizations and institutions that have no financial stake in the game is a powerful countervailing force to government capture by special interests. These intermediary organizations enable a fairer, more participatory form of democracy by helping the general public become aware of issues and assist them in taking on civic responsibilities, such as speaking out, petitioning government officials, and voting.

Critics also argue that cameras in Congress have had an impact on deliberation. To be sure, they have some effect; we do not deny that there are trade-offs for transparency. Critics note that members of Congress are far more careful about what they say at a hearing or on the floor of Congress. And we say, thank goodness; they should be. But the data show that cameras did not change Senate productivity; other factors did.[23] Moreover, there are no restrictions on members of Congress informally talking to one another, discussing ideas, or even sharing drafts of bills—and all of this can be done outside the reach of cameras and other open government laws.[24]

Those who really win when the cameras are removed are the powerful special interests. Should we return to the pretransparency days when, as a practical matter, lobbyists and their wealthy clients had preferential access to congressional hearings and to what was happening in Congress generally? We say a resounding no. It strengthens democracy when anyone sitting at his or her desk or at home is able to see what Congress is doing.

The goal of a healthy democracy is for public policy to benefit the common good, not just the economically powerful. The latter already have excessive influence over the political system. Increased secrecy only allows this imbalance to worsen, and further tips the scales of political inequality.

SUMMARIZING SECRECY'S DANGERS

Out of the many reasons why secrecy is a danger to our democracy, three stand out:

1. ***Corruption.*** The core of our argument is the proposition that corruption will flourish when there are gaps in transparency and openness. Corruption often involves special deals for political elites with pecuniary interests at stake. Special provisions like those riders slipped into the "cromnibus" bill are examples. That is why it is essential to shine a light on things like the exchange of money with our elected and appointed leaders (e.g., campaign contributions), the contracting process, the revolving door in and out of government, and the regulatory system.

2. ***Effectiveness of Government.*** The public perceives government as ineffective and does not trust it.[25] Secrecy just exacerbates the problem. When the public does not know what government is doing, it creates uncertainty about the role of government. Openness reinvigorates the Constitutional concept of "We the People" by not only assuring transparent government actions but also by inviting public engagement in that decision making.

3. ***Inequality.*** When it comes to political power, new research confirms that the power elite largely pull the levers of government. A 2014 analysis found that the "preferences of the average American appear to have only a miniscule, near-zero, statistically non-significant impact upon public policy."[26] The authors concluded "that economic elites and organized groups

representing business interests have substantial independent impacts on U.S. government policy, while mass-based interest groups and average citizens have little or no independent influence."[27] Not surprisingly, this political inequality is mirrored by increasing economic inequality, which has grown to the levels not seen since the 1920s.[28]

Most voters get that the system is rigged or even stacked against them. Today, trust in government is close to the lowest level since monitoring of the topic started. Can anyone doubt that lingering government secrecy has helped perpetuate official decision making against the public interest that has helped produce this state of affairs? Shining a bright light on government provides a powerful vehicle to rectify special interest influence and redress inequality.

It makes little sense to devise and allow backroom deals, as Cain, Fukuyama, Grumet, and others advocate, if those deals open opportunities for corruption, create perceptions of government ineffectiveness, and perpetuate inequality. Our standard for success should not be how many bills get passed by legislatures but the quality of those bills in tackling the major social, economic, and political issues of the day. Participatory democracy, premised on plenty of sunshine, may not always be pretty, but it is what makes our nation vibrant and keeps us moving toward, as the Constitution puts it, "a more perfect Union."

NOTES

INTRO

1.   James Bryce, *The American Commonwealth*, 505 (Chapter LVII). Louis Brandeis, *Other People's Money* (New York, NY: Stokes, 1914), 92 (Chapter V).

PRO

1.   Yian Q Mui, "Fed Chair Janet Yellen Is Learning the Importance of Politics in Economics," *Washington Post*, December 4, 2015.

2.   Bruce E. Cain, "The Democracy Paradox," *The American Interest* 11 (October, 2015):2.

3.   Dana Milbank, "Paul Ryan Restores the House's Regular Disorder," *Washington Post*, November 18, 2015.

4.   Christopher Hare and Keith T. Poole, "The Polarization of Contemporary American Politics," *Polity* 46, no. 3 (2014): 411-429.

5.   Elizabeth Williamson, "Inside the Republicans' Opposition Research Machine," *New York Times*, November 27, 2015.

6.   Nick Gass, "The 13 must-read Clinton emails," *Politico*, October 30, 2015, http://www.politico.com/story/2015/10/hillary-clinton-must-read-emails-215407.

CON

1. The TRI is available at http://www2.epa.gov/toxics-release-inventory-tri-program.

2. Francis Fukuyama, "Why Transparency Can Be a Dirty Word," *Financial Times* (Aug 9, 2015), http://www.ft.com/cms/s/0/1d78c194-2c8d-11e5-acfb-cbd2e1c81cca.html; and Francis Fukuyama, *Political Order and Political Decay: From the Industrial Revolution to the Globalization of Democracy*, (New York, NY: Farrar, Straus and Giroux, 2014), 504.

3. Jason Grumet, "When Sunshine Doesn't Always Disinfect the Government," *Washington Post* (Oct. 2, 2014), http://www.washingtonpost.com/opinions/laws-aimed-at-transparency-have-hindered-serious-debate/2014/10/02/7c5eb022-48dd-11e4-b72e-d60a9229cc10_story.html?wprss=rss_opinions.

4. See David Frum, "The Transparency Trap," *The Atlantic* (August 13, 2014), http://www.theatlantic.com/magazine/archive/2014/09/the-transparency-trap/375074. See also Bruce E. Cain, *Democracy More or Less: America's Political Reform Quandary* (New York, NY: Cambridge University Press, 2014); and Bruce E. Cain, "The Transparency Paradox," *The American Interest*, Vol. 11, No. 2 (October 10, 2015), http://www.the-american-interest.com/2015/10/10/the-transparency-paradox.

5. Fukuyama, *Political Order and Political Decay*, 522.

6. We are not transparency absolutists. We understand the need for government secrets and for private discussions when negotiating policy development. But we believe there must be openness at key decision points in policy development so that our officials are held accountable for their actions. Our views are elaborated in Gary D. Bass, Danielle Brian, and Norman Eisen, "Why Critics of Transparency Are Wrong," *Brookings Institution* (Nov 2014), http://www.brookings.edu/~/media/research/files/papers/2014/11/24-why-critics-transparency-wrong-bass-brian-eisen/critics.pdf.

7. Alexander Cohen and Lincoln Taylor, "Eleven to One: Pro-Reform Derivatives Lobbyists Vastly Outnumbered by Opposition," *Public Citizen* (May 18, 2010), http://www.citizen.org/documents/DerivativesLobbyistsReport.pdf.

8. Carroll Doherty, Jocelyn Kiley, Alec Tyson, and Bridget Jameson, "Beyond Distrust: How Americans View Their Government," *Pew Research Center* (Nov. 23,2015),http://www.people-press.org/2015/11/23/beyond-distrust-how-americans-view-their-government/?wpmm=1&wpisrc=nl_daily202.

9. Jack Abramoff, "'Willing Vassals' in Congress Do Lobbyist Bidding," *Bloomberg View*(November 18,2011),http://www.bloomberg.com/news/articles/2011-11-18/-willing-vassals-in-congress-do-lobbyist-bidding-jack-abramoff; and Jack Abramoff, *Capitol Punishment: The Hard Truth About Washington Corruption from America's Most Notorious Lobbyist* (New York, NY: WND Books, 2011).

10. Jonathan Rauch, "Political Realism: How Hacks, Machines, Big Money, and Back-Room Deals Can Strengthen American Democracy," *Brookings Institution* (May 2015),

8, 14, and 16, at http://www.brookings.edu/~/media/Research/Files/Reports/2015/04/political-realism-rauch/political-realism-rauch.pdf?la=en.

11. Bass, Brian, and Eisen, "Why Critics of Transparency Are Wrong."

12. See Thomas E. Mann & Norman J. Ornstein, *It's Even Worse Than It Looks: How the American Constitutional System Collided with the New Politics of Extremism* (New York, NY: Basic Books, 2013).

13. Cain, "The Transparency Paradox." Cain calls for prioritizing certain FOIA requests "by making the requester designate a reason for a particular FOIA request." This inappropriately politicizes the FOIA process by allowing government to determine what is worthy.

14. Mark Tapscott, "Transparency Critics Are Peddling Public Ignorance to 'Fix' Government," *Washington Examiner* (Oct 4, 2014), http://washington examiner.com/transparency-critics-are-peddling-public-ignorance-to-fix-government/article/2554376.

15. See Administrative Conference of the United States, "Recommendation 2014-2: Government in the Sunshine Act" (Adopted June 5, 2014), 2, at https://www.acus.gov/sites/default/files/documents/Recommendation%202014-2%20%28Sunshine%20Act%29.pdf.

16. 5 U.S.C. (FACA) Appendix, §5(b) (2); P.L. 92-463; 86 Stat. 771, October 6, 1972.

17. According to 41 C.F.R. §102-3.155, a committee can hold a closed meeting with prior approval from either the agency head or GSA's Committee Management Secretariat. For more information, see 41 C.F.R. §102-3.120.

18. Wendy Ginsberg, "The Federal Advisory Committee Act: Analysis of Operations and Costs," *Congressional Research Service*, (7-5700, R44248, Oct 27, 2015), https://www.fas.org/sgp/crs/secrecy/R44248.pdf.

19. Christopher Ingraham, "Interactive: How Companies Wield Off-the-Record Influence on Obama's Trade Policy," *Washington Post* (Feb 28, 2014), https://www.washingtonpost.com/news/wonk/wp/2014/02/28/how-companies-wield-off-the-record-influence-on-obamas-trade-policy. To be precise, these committees generally operate under FACA but with some exemptions including a discretionary one from open meetings and transparency rules.

20. Cain, "Transparency Paradox."

21. Cain, *Democracy More or Less*, 42.

22. Cain, "Transparency Paradox."

23. Bass, Brian, and Eisen, "Why Critics of Transparency Are Wrong," 3-5.

24. Many of the openness laws that are being criticized, such as FOIA and FACA, do not even apply to the legislative branch.

25. Doherty, Kiley, Tyson, and Jameson, "Beyond Distrust: How Americans View Their Government."

26. Martin Gilens and Benjamin I. Page "Testing Theories of American Politics: Elites, Interest Groups, and Average Citizens," *Perspectives on Politics*, Vol. 12, No. 3, 564-581 (Sept 2014): 575, https://scholar.princeton.edu/sites/default/files/mgilens/files/gilens_and_page_2014_-testing_theories_of_american_politics.doc.pdf.

27. Gilens and Page, "Testing Theories of American Politics: Elites, Interest Groups, and Average Citizens," 565.

28. Emmanuel Saez and Gabriel Zucman, "Wealth Inequality in the United States Since 1913: Evidence from Capitalized Income Tax Data," *National Bureau of Economic Research*, Working Paper #20625 (Oct. 2014), http://www.nber.org/papers/w20625; and Emmanual Saez, "Striking it Richer: The Evolution of Top Incomes in the United States," University of California, Berkeley (September 3, 2013), http://eml.berkeley.edu//~saez/saez-UStopincomes-2012.pdf.

3

RESOLVED, Andrew Jackson should be removed from the $20 bill

PRO: Brian A. Weiner

CON: Mark Cheathem

The subtitle of Harold D. Lasswell's 1936 book *Politics: Who Gets What, When, How* has become political science's most famous definition of politics. At the time Lasswell wrote and for several decades afterward, the "what" in this phrase was thought to mostly involve economic benefits and costs. What would be the federal income tax rate for the rich, the middle class, and the poor? What benefits would the government confer on business owners, widows, the unemployed, and other groups? What share of the federal budget would go to national defense and what share to domestic programs? What projects would be built in which states and cities?

Of course, politics has always been about more than economics. Recent years have been marked by a rising number of political controversies over cultural issues, many of them involving the symbols with which the nation chooses to remember its past in view of contemporary concerns about racial, ethnic, and gender equality. In 2015 alone, outrage over the slaying of nine prayer group members at Emanuel African Methodist Episcopal Church in Charleston by an avowed White supremacist prompted the state legislature to remove the Confederate flag from display outside the South Carolina State House; students at Yale persuaded the university's president to stop using "master" as the title assigned to the heads of its residential colleges because of the title's historical association with slave owning; the University of Texas, Austin, took down a statue of Jefferson Davis, the president of the Confederacy during the Civil War; students at Princeton University pressured its administration to consider renaming the Woodrow Wilson School of Public and International Affairs on the grounds that Wilson, a former president of the university before becoming president of the United States, was a racist; and the New Orleans city council voted to remove a prominent statue of Robert E. Lee and other Confederate memorials from public display.

Similar controversies have broken out in multiple states, cities, and campuses across the country. For example, at the College of William and Mary, which Thomas Jefferson attended, and the University of Virginia, which he founded, critics have objected that President Jefferson, no less than General Lee, was a slave owner. So, for that matter, was George Washington, after whom the nation's capital, a western state, thirty counties, and several universities (George Washington University, Washington and Lee University, Washington and Jefferson College, among others) are named.

Some groups representing women and Native Americans have aimed much of their fire at a different cultural target: the nation's currency. Feminists object to the monopoly that men have on every bill that Americans carry in their wallets: Washington on the one-dollar bill, Lincoln on the five, Alexander Hamilton on the ten, Andrew Jackson on the twenty, Ulysses S. Grant on the fifty, Benjamin Franklin on the hundred. Even bills that never circulate, such as the thousand (Grover Cleveland) and ten thousand (Salmon P. Chase) dollar bills feature men. In 2015, Secretary of the Treasury Jacob Lew spoke to these groups' concern by pledging to place a woman on the redesigned ten-dollar bill. He later reconsidered in response to the runaway popularity of the Broadway musical Hamilton. In 2016, he reversed course and announced that Hamilton would stay on the ten but Jackson would be moved to the back of the twenty and replaced on the front by Harriet Tubman.

Jackson was long a hero of American liberals for fostering the spread of democracy in the United States in the form of wider voter eligibility, more elected offices, and greater turnover in government positions. In 1948, for example, liberal historian Arthur M. Schlesinger Jr.'s celebratory *The Age of Jackson* won the Pulitzer Prize in history. More than a half century later, however, many Native Americans, with considerable liberal support, based their demand that Jackson be removed from the currency on his harsh policies toward Indians. One such critic, Brian A. Weiner, suggests that Jackson should be replaced by "Wilma Mankiller, a descendant of the survivors of the Trail of Tears, the first elected principal chief of the Cherokee Nation." In defense of Jackson, Mark Cheathem highlights his role as "champion of democracy," battler against "concentrated economic power," and staunch supporter of the Union.

PRO: Brian A. Weiner

Secretary of the Treasury Jack Lew's announcement in 2015 that the redesign of the $10 bill would feature a portrait of a woman sparked great excitement and no little controversy. The announcement came two months after New Hampshire Senator Jeanne Shaheen had introduced the Women on the Twenty Act, legislation that was inspired by a grassroots effort to put a woman in place of Andrew Jackson on the $20 bill. Shaheen and some supporters of the "Women on 20s" movement were pleased by Lew's announcement but devotees of Alexander Hamilton were less supportive, arguing that the nation's first secretary of the Treasury was a founding father who fully deserved his place on the nation's currency. If a dead White male should make way for a woman, surely the treasury department should remove Jackson, the racist slaveholder who was an architect and instrument of Indian removal.

Secretary Lew attempted to answer his critics by explaining that the $10 bill was the next in line to be redesigned to foil counterfeiting threats, and with the rollout set for 2020, it was fitting to mark the 100th anniversary of women's suffrage by putting a woman on the $10 bill. Lew then attempted to mollify Hamilton's defenders by suggesting that Hamilton would still appear somewhere on the bill, an announcement that provoked a new round of criticism on the grounds that a woman should not have to share her place on the bill. As Lew ruefully admitted, his initial announcement "expanded the scope of conversation in this country in more areas than we might have anticipated."[1] In 2016, Lew came up with a new compromise: Hamilton would stay on the front of the $10 bill and Jackson would be moved to the back of the $20 bill, replaced on the front by Harriet Tubman.

It is fitting that Lew's announcement has inspired a broad conversation about who should appear on the nation's money—and who should decide. Each redesign of a bill (since 2003, the $5, $10, $20, $50, and $100 have all been redesigned) has been guided by a theme, and the theme of the current redesign of the $10 bill is democracy. Democracy means "rule by the people" and places political power in the hands of ordinary people. Under democracy, governmental officials have the authority to initiate policy discussions, but they cannot control where ordinary citizens take those conversations.

The question of who should be placed on the nation's currency raises fundamental questions about how the present generation should relate to the past and whether the choices made by previous generations about whom to honor should be accepted today. These questions have been argued recently in debates over whether the Confederate flag should continue to fly over Southern statehouses, whether statues memorializing Confederate war "heroes" should be removed from public parks and state universities, and most recently, whether private universities should continue to name colleges, buildings, or schools after former slaveholders, defenders of slavery, or those who espoused racist views.

This essay argues that democracy requires each generation to reinterpret its political history and reassess the figures and symbols it honors. A belief in democracy therefore required that Andrew Jackson be replaced by a more fitting symbol of our diverse nation on the front of the $20 bill.

CURRENCY'S ROLE IN REPRESENTING THE IDENTITY AND VALUES OF THE NATION

At first glance, the question of whose portrait should appear on our money may appear inconsequential, but currency performs more than a strictly financial function. Along with other symbolic representations such as flags and stamps, and material ones such as statues, a nation's currency conveys the government's presentation of its identity and values and serves as a means to create the "imagined community" that is the nation.[2] A nation's currency is one of its most visible symbols—just consider how often everyday citizens come into contact with paper money. Our choice about who we put on our currency is a public declaration about who we deem worthy of emulation and the deeds we wish to honor.

The seven figures whose portraits adorn our most widely circulated currency are Washington ($1), Jefferson ($2), Lincoln ($5), Hamilton ($10), Jackson ($20), Grant ($50), and Franklin ($100). All are from the eighteenth and nineteenth centuries. Five were presidents, and the two nonpresidents (Hamilton and Franklin) were instrumental in the founding of the nation. All are White. All are men.

Compared to other countries, the United States has been unusually conservative in its willingness to change who is represented on the currency. The last change to the pantheon of the Greats who appear on the most widely circulated paper bills occurred in 1928.

If currency serves as a means by which a nation represents its identity and values, then the absence of women, African Americans, and other racial minorities implicitly conveys their status as outsiders who are not full members of our political community.[3] We are not the same nation we were in 1928, when women had only recently been granted the right to vote but were still denied the right to serve on juries, and African Americans were systematically discriminated against and disenfranchised through Jim Crow legislation. Our currency should reflect our still imperfect, yet more inclusive political community.

WHO SHOULD DECIDE WHOSE PORTRAITS APPEAR?

Congress has given the Treasury Secretary the authority to "engrave and print United States currency . . . from intaglio plates on plate printing presses [he] selects."[4] In 1928, the last time the government replaced the portraits of those who appear on our paper bills, a special panel of citizens was appointed by the Treasury Secretary, but we do not know whether the panel was simply advisory or whether the Secretary accepted all of the panel's recommendations.[5]

Secretary Lew did not chose to convene a citizens' panel, but he did seem conscious of the incongruity of having made "democracy" the theme of the new $10 bill, and yet the sole authority to make decisions regarding its design to rest in the hands of an unelected official. Lew embraced the tools of new media to solicit public opinion on the matter, a nod in the direction of democratic input. A website, "The New 10" was created, complete with a Twitter feed, along with a link to "share your ideas," which registered over 1 million such ideas.

Lew never made clear, though, precisely *how* the decision was made as to who will appear on the $10 bill and the $20 bill. The lack of transparency about how the decision was made, along with the attenuated sense of accountability for the decision, undermines Lew's promise that the theme of the redesign of the bill is "democracy." However, the willingness to reconsider which historical figures deserve to appear on our paper bills and hence to provide the present generation an opportunity to reinterpret its political history recognizes a fundamental democratic right.

HOW OFTEN SHOULD WE REDESIGN OUR CURRENCY?

If currency communicates a nation's understanding of its identity, then critical questions related to whether to replace some historical figures on our currency focus our attention both on who we understand ourselves to be as a political body and how our political identity is related to our past. The question, then, of whether to replace Andrew Jackson on the $20 bill is bound up with the broader question of the relationship between our political past, present, and future.

One defense of Jackson remaining on the $20 bill depends less on Jackson's virtues and more on the argument that we should not lightly change the enduring symbols of the polity, including its financial and banking system. As the Declaration of Independence warns about revolution more broadly, "prudence . . . dictate(s) that Governments long established should not be changed for light and transient causes." Echoes of this argument, emphasizing the importance of stability, may be heard as well in battles over constitutional interpretation, voiced by advocates of "original intent," who contend that courts should interpret the Constitution as it was understood at the time it was drafted and ratified. But ours is a revolutionary history. Our nation was founded by those who chose to dissolve their former political connection and who feared that maintaining the status quo for the sake of stability ossifies political energy and imagination and infantilizes the current generation.

Jefferson was especially attuned to the dangers of past political generations ruling from the grave. In a 1789 letter to James Madison penned while he was in Paris, Jefferson asked "whether one generation of men has a right to bind another." His short answer was that they did not because "the earth belongs to the living and not to the dead." Jefferson even sought to define the parameters of each political generation. He imagined "a whole generation of men to be born on the same day, to attain mature age on the same day, and to die on the same day, leaving a succeeding generation in the moment of attaining their mature age, all together." Employing this fiction allowed Jefferson to suppose that "each successive generation would . . . come and go off the stage at a fixed moment, as individuals do now." Consulting mortality tables, and discovering that at the time an average lifespan was fifty-five years, and asserting that individuals reach political maturity at twenty-one years, Jefferson determined that each generation should be accorded thirty-four years of sovereignty. To ensure that the present generation's sovereignty is not encroached upon by past generations, Jefferson concluded, "Every constitution . . . and every law naturally expires at the end of 34 years."[6]

Underlying Jefferson's thought experiment was the claim that if we are to take democracy seriously, then we must guard against the present generation becoming enthralled by the past and failing to assume responsibility for the constitution, laws, and mores under which the present generation lives. Those untroubled by the thrall of the past will not be concerned that the portraiture on our paper currency has not changed for close to 90 years. But those who take Jeffersonian principles seriously will recognize that each generation has the right and the duty to decide for itself who deserves the honor of appearing on the nation's currency. Granted Americans live longer than in Jefferson's day but not so long that we should be bound by the judgment made by our political ancestors in 1928. Jackson may have been our ancestors' hero; he is not ours.

DOES ANDREW JACKSON CONTINUE TO DESERVE HIS PLACE ON THE $20 BILL?

We do not know precisely why in 1928 Andrew Jackson was selected to replace Grover Cleveland on the $20 bill. We do know that Jackson had appeared on

$10 Federal Reserve Notes first issued in 1914, but when the decision was made in 1928 to standardize the national currency, Alexander Hamilton was assigned to the $10 bill, Jackson the $20 bill, and Grover Cleveland relegated to the more valuable but much rarer $1,000 bill.

Since the historical record is silent as to why Jackson was placed on Federal Reserve notes in 1914 and the $20 bill in 1928, we can only speculate as to why government decision makers placed his portrait on our currency. What we do know is that Jackson was no stranger to controversy in his lifetime. His military and political career were marked by violent and highly publicized disputes with major figures of the day, including his Vice President John C. Calhoun, Bank of the United States President Nicholas Biddle, Senator Henry Clay, arguably the leading statesman of the time, and Cherokee Indian chief John Ross. Jackson's national reputation was built upon his military conquests; he served as a major general in the War of 1812, and his victory over the Creek Indians in 1814 marked the American army's first dramatic military success, transforming Jackson into a national hero.[7] Jackson's triumph over the British at The Battle of New Orleans in 1815 cemented his reputation as America's greatest military hero since Washington. He continued his military efforts to expand the nation, and dispossess Native Americans, in 1818 by invading Florida in pursuit of Seminole Indians. After Spain ceded Florida, Jackson became its territorial governor. He then served as a United States senator, representing Tennessee, unsuccessfully ran for president in 1824 (in a contested election that was ultimately decided by the House of Representatives), and handily won the presidency in 1828 and again in 1832.[8]

Jackson's presidency featured a number of high-profile battles in which he painted himself as the People's Tribune and pitted himself against those he deemed a danger to the nation. In the "Nullification Crisis," South Carolina, incensed by protective tariffs on imports that it believed advantaged Northern economic interests, declared the tariff to be unconstitutional and blocked its enforcement within the state. Although not a fan of a high protective tariff, Jackson saw South Carolina's actions as treasonous and acted to uphold federal supremacy. Jackson gave a rousing speech on the occasion, declaring the Union to be indissoluble, an inspiration to Lincoln years later. In his second term, Jackson wrangled with the Second Bank of the United States, a corporation chartered by Congress and analogous to the Federal Reserve today. Jackson portrayed the Bank as a tool of the Eastern moneyed interests and in vetoing a bill to extend the Bank's charter, Jackson argued that he did so to protect "the humble members of society—the farmers, mechanics, and laborers" from "the rich and powerful (who) too often bend the acts of government to their selfish purposes."[9] Unfortunately for the nation, Jackson's policies to destroy the bank, by moving federal deposits to state-chartered banks, led the country into a severe depression, and his unilateral action prompted the Senate to censure him.

As a number of Jackson's critics have pointed out, there is an irony to the effort to maintain his place on the $20 bill given his ardent opposition to central banking and a national paper currency. But, as Jackson's rhetoric in his famous Bank Veto Message suggests, he was skillful in portraying himself as the defender of "the humble members of society," many of whom had recently gained the franchise and had helped to sweep him into office in 1828 and again in 1832.[10] It is the image of Jackson as the champion of western farmers and ordinary laborers against the predations of the rich and powerful, one that progressive historians like Charles Beard presented at the time that Jackson was placed on our currency, that most explains his spot on the $20 bill. Contemporary defenders of Jackson's place tend to rely on this image of Jackson, arguing that he was "key to birthing the expansive American democracy we know today."[11]

However, the expansion of the United States came at a tragic cost to Native American land rights, sovereignty, and lives, and it is that central legacy of Jackson that most forcefully demands his replacement on the $20 bill. Indian removal and destruction of the primary southeastern Native American tribes was not a marginal aspect of his career; rather, as political scientist Michael Paul Rogin has written, Jackson was "the single figure most responsible for Indian destruction in pre-Civil War America."[12] His political career was built upon his military conquests of Native American tribes, and throughout his later political career he used all means at his disposal to forcefully remove tribes and gain control over much of Alabama, Florida, Georgia, Tennessee, Mississippi, Kentucky, and North Carolina. Jackson's principal if not sole legislative achievement was to push through the Indian Removal Act of 1830, an attempt to induce tribes to move west of the Mississippi.

Tribes who resisted removal from their lands suffered aggressive action from states and land-hungry Whites, and the federal government under Jackson refused to protect Native American rights or enforce court rulings. When the Cherokees turned to the federal courts to protect their rights and won a court ruling that recognized their sovereignty, Georgia, encouraged by Jackson, ignored the Court's ruling.[13] Jackson next turned to trickery and negotiated a removal treaty with a small faction of unrecognized leaders of the Cherokees. The Supreme Court recognized the treaty, even though a petition signed by the great majority of the tribe was submitted to them by Chief John Ross asking them not to. The Cherokees were given two years to leave their land; only a very small number did so, and in 1838 the federal government (under Jackson's hand-picked successor, Martin Van Buren) sent in 7,000 troops who brutally evicted the Cherokees from their lands, beginning the march known as "The Trail of Tears," in which 4,000 Cherokee people died of hunger, cold, and disease. By the end of his second term, the Jackson administration had removed close to 50,000 Native American people from their lands east of the Mississippi and often under the threat of coercion had secured treaties with a similar number leading to their removal. Jackson's brutal treatment of Native American peoples, the related expansion of slavery into formerly Native American lands, his defense of slavery, and contempt for the law are argument enough that he does not deserve to be one of the select figures who grace our paper currency.

One final argument offered in Jackson's defense is that it is unfair of the present generation to judge him by current standards, and that criticism of Jackson reflects a self-righteous "Monday morning quarterbacking." But Jackson was no mere bystander following the mores of the day; he made use of his near monopoly of military and political authority to single-mindedly force Native American peoples off their land, contrary to law, treaties, and in the face of contemporary opposition by many leading statesmen, including Senators Henry Clay and Daniel Webster and Chief Justice John Marshall.

It must also be remembered that Jackson's placement on the $20 bill was itself a case of a later generation judging him by the standards of their time. United States law forbids the government from placing the portrait of a living individual on our coins and bills (a sign of our antimonarchical roots), so the question of whose portrait is to appear unavoidably is a matter of historical interpretation.[14] Jackson's selection in 1914 and then again in 1928 is best explained by the judgment probably made at the time that he symbolized a populist figure, "a champion of the working class against the business community."[15] And although it is the case that scholarship at the time did not highlight the central role that the mistreatment of Native American peoples played in Jackson's career, it was not completely unacknowledged. The grave misgivings regarding honoring a figure so closely linked to the brutal treatment of Native Americans is not ours alone. Even at the time, D.H. Lawrence, in his *Studies in Classic American Literature*, attempted to bring to our attention "the under-consciousness" of the Jacksonian destruction: "The deliberate consciousness of Americans so fair and smooth-spoken, and the under-consciousness so devilish. Destroy! Destroy! Destroy! Hums the under-consciousness."[16]

As we have become more conscious of "the under-consciousness" of Jackson, his central, indispensable role in the dispossession and brutal treatment of Native American peoples, it is now our responsibility to wrestle with how to acknowledge that legacy. It is no longer unproblematic to venerate Jackson with a prominent place in our nation's currency pantheon. As Jefferson reminds us, it is every political generation's right to rethink its history and to decide which actors and deeds deserve honor. Just as the nation in the wake of the 2015 shootings in South Carolina decided that it was high time to take down the Confederate Flag from the statehouse and other public places, we should do the same with Andrew Jackson's place on the $20 bill. I believe the most powerful acknowledgment of Jackson's stained legacy would have been for us to replace his portrait with that of Wilma Mankiller, a descendant of the survivors of the Trail of Tears, the first elected principal chief of the Cherokee Nation, and a striking reminder of the ultimate failure of Jackson's efforts to eliminate tribal sovereignty, if not Native Americans.[17] But just as important as who should be honored is the process by which that decision should be made.

In order to live up to the theme of "democracy" chosen for the redesign of the $10 bill, the selection of whom to place on the $20 bill should not be in the hands of a single unelected official but rather placed before an inclusive citizen panel, one that reflects who we are today—a land of, as Cornel West has written, "hybridity, heterogeneity, and ambiguity."[18] Ours is an "ambiguous" history, but we are not alone in having inherited a legacy of both deeds and misdeeds. We are fortunate that our history is so much richer than the one currently portrayed upon our currency. An inclusive, democratic process engaged in by members of our present political generation surely should be able to select a figure whose deeds better reflect who we are and aspire to be than do those of Andrew Jackson's blood-stained legacy.

CON: Mark Cheathem

Arguments for Jackson's removal from the $20 bill center on two major facets of his life: his treatment of Native Americans and his ownership of the enslaved people who worked on his plantations. But Jackson is not the only slaveholder whose face can be found on the nation's currency. Both Washington (on the $1 bill and the quarter) and Jefferson (the $2 bill and the nickel) owned slaves. Nor do Washington or Jefferson have clean hands when it comes to Native Americans: General Washington ordered his officers to "lay waste" to Indian settlements, while President Jefferson plotted the forced removal of Native Americans from their land. Were Jackson's sins worse than those of Jefferson, who likely had several children by his slave concubine

Sally Hemings? To single Jackson out for removal from the nation's currency not only overlooks the sins of our other presidents but ignores Jackson's many historic contributions to the development of democracy in the United States. Jackson democratized the presidency and the polity, opposed the corrupting influence of big money in politics, and courageously defended the Union against slaveholding secessionists. For all these reasons, Jackson deserves his place on our nation's money.[1]

JACKSON WAS A CHAMPION OF DEMOCRACY

Political culture in the early American republic generally focused on voters electing elite White men, whose education and intellect were deemed sufficient to make decisions for the good of the nation. Elected officials expected the people to defer to their wisdom. Some U.S. politicians, particularly those affiliated with the Federalist cause, also argued for a strong central government that would be insulated from public pressures.

Jackson disagreed with this philosophy. He insisted on the democratic ideal that politicians should be responsive to the people's will. During the early part of his political career, while a member of the House of Representatives, Jackson criticized the monarchical trappings of George Washington's presidency. He also vowed never to vote for a candidate unless he reflected and carried out "the will of his constituents." Jackson's commitment to equality and distrust of aristocracy ran deep. During his short tenure as Florida territorial governor in 1821, for example, he described his role as one of "administering laws that know no distinction between the rich and poor, the great and ignoble." When he ran for the presidency for the first time in 1824, Jackson identified the national debt as "a curse to a republic; inasmuch as it is calculated to raise around the administration a monied aristocracy, dangerous to the liberties of the country." All of these statements indicate Jackson's commitment to democratic ideals and his fear that the national government too often favored the upper class at the expense of the people.[2]

Jackson's loss to John Quincy Adams in the controversial 1824 presidential election cemented his dedication to the principles of democratic equality. Although Jackson won the most popular votes in 1824, Adams won the runoff in the House of Representatives when none of the four candidates (Adams, Jackson, Henry Clay, and William Crawford) secured a majority of electoral votes. Many believed that Speaker of the House Henry Clay helped Adams win the presidency in exchange for receiving appointment as U.S. secretary of state. Jackson was among those who thought that Clay and Adams had conspired to thwart the people's will. According to historian Robert Remini, the "corrupt bargain" between Adams and Clay was "the single event that drove men—Jackson especially—to a more pronounced democratic position."[3]

Once he became president, Jackson pursued his commitment to promoting democracy. The nation was "worth defending," he noted in his first inaugural address, "as long as our Government is administered for the good of the people, and is regulated by their will." To that end, Jackson removed federal office-holders whom he believed viewed government "as a means of promoting individual interests [rather] than as an instrument created solely for the service of the people." Their self-interest, Jackson explained, "divert[s] government from its legitimate ends and makes it an engine for the support of the few at the expense of the many." As president, Jackson was determined to make the national government an instrument of the many and not the few.[4]

Late in his second term, Jackson reiterated his conviction that politicians should be delegates of the people rather than insulated trustees deciding what was good for the people. He told one of his nephews that voters should ask political candidates whether they "subscribe to the republican rule, that the people are the sovereign power, the officers, their agents, and that upon all national or general subjects, as well as local, they have a right to instruct their agents & representatives, and they are bound to obey, or resign." Only candidates who accepted that they were agents of the people were "true republicans." Jackson transformed republicanism from a largely elitist worldview into an ideology that made politicians directly answerable to their constituents.[5]

Jackson called majority rule "the first principle of our system." More than any previous president, he challenged Americans to adhere to his belief that the people were sovereign and the final authority on government actions. His views presaged both the Progressives who brought democratic change at the turn of the twentieth century and the New Deal Democrats who sought to defend democracy during the Great Depression and World War II.[6]

JACKSON BATTLED THE CORRUPTION OF CONCENTRATED ECONOMIC POWER IN POLITICS

Jackson detested corruption in all its forms, and the alleged "corrupt bargain" that decided the 1824 presidential election only heightened that hatred. During his presidency, Jackson directed his suspicion of corruption at the Second Bank of the United States and its directors, who he believed had tried to influence the 1828 presidential election. Stopping the Bank's corrupting influence, he insisted, was essential to protecting Americans' liberty. Otherwise, this financial behemoth was going to "destroy the purity of the right of Suffrage" by using the people's money to buy elections.[7]

In 1832, Henry Clay and other Bank supporters pushed for the Bank's recharter four years prior to its expiration. Jackson would have none of it. When the legislation made it to his desk, he vetoed it. In his veto message, he denounced the "prostitution of our Government to the advancement of the few at the expense of the many." He blamed "the rich and powerful" for trying to "bend the acts of government to their selfish purposes." Jackson stood squarely with the 99 percent and against the 1 percent. He would not allow a privileged economic elite to control and corrupt government of, by, and for the people.[8]

Bank supporters did not take kindly to Jackson's veto, nor to his removal of government deposits the following year. Led by Clay, anti-Jackson senators succeeded in censuring the president in March 1834 by a 26–20 vote. Jackson responded with a "protest" message defending his actions. He explained that the veto was necessary because through "its money and power to control the Government and change its character," the national bank endangered the nation's democratic experiment. Combining his belief in democracy with his fight against corruption, Jackson pronounced that "the President is the direct representative of the American People . . . elected by the People and responsible to them." Jackson conceived what neither Washington nor Jefferson had ever envisioned: that the chief executive of the United States was truly the people's president.[9]

Today, we would scoff at a president who did not wield the veto power in the spirit of Jackson. Old Hickory predicated his fight against "the hydra of corruption," as he called the Bank in 1832, on his belief that it benefitted the elite at the expense of the average American. Like many presidents and presidential candidates, Jackson raised himself from marginal economic status to become a member of the elite, but unlike many modern-day politicians, Jackson looked to root out corruption instead of allowing it to ensnare him. He placed the people and their trust in a democratic interpretation of the presidency above his own personal and class interests.[10]

Jackson's claim that the president was "the direct representative of the American People" was revolutionary, endowing the office and its incumbent with both symbolic and real authority. Thanks to Jackson's model, Americans today expect the president to solve problems and to represent the people and not the special interests.

JACKSON SUPPORTED THE UNION

Jackson also deserves his place on the $20 bill for his bold actions during the Nullification Crisis of 1832–1833, when South Carolina politicians, upset over the passage of tariff legislation in 1828 and 1832, passed an ordinance of nullification that refused to allow the federal government to collect tariff revenue within the state. While the nullifiers believed that the tariff unfairly affected their region's economy, they also were concerned that the federal government was overstepping its power to collect a revenue tax since the national debt was nearly paid off. (The payment of the national debt, which had been one of Jackson's main objectives as president, occurred in January 1835—a not insignificant achievement in and of itself.) Nullifiers feared that antislavery congressmen intended to use the excess revenue to sponsor colonization efforts, which would send former slaves to Africa.

Although a slave owner and a supporter of states' rights, Jackson had no sympathy for nullification. In part, his lack of support stemmed from Jackson's own brush with a disunionist movement led by Aaron Burr in 1806. The former vice president attempted to convince several prominent southerners, including Jackson, that he needed their military support to defend the southwestern United States from Spanish invasion. Jackson was suspicious about the true motives of Burr and his fellow conspirators, warning William C.C. Claiborne, governor of the Orleans Territory, "there [is] something rotten in the State of Denmark. . . . You have enemies within your own City, that may try to subvert your Government, and try to separate it from the Union." "I will die in the last ditch before I would . . . see the Union disunited," he wrote Claiborne.[11]

Jackson's military service also reinforced his notion of nationalism. He spent nearly a decade in the United States Army, defeating Native American and British forces during the War of 1812 and neutralizing Native American and Spanish threats between the war's end in 1815 and his resignation from service in 1821. During those years, Jackson moved beyond his state and even regional allegiance to give his main loyalty to the nation. Even his much-maligned treatment of Native American groups in the 1810s stemmed, in part, from his desire to make the nation's safety paramount. In the nullification movement, Jackson recognized a significant threat to the Union's future, and he responded as any strong nationalist would.

For nearly three months, Jackson and the South Carolina nullifiers faced off in a test of wills. Following their nullification of the tariff legislation, the nullifiers began preparing for war. The president responded with his own threats of force, telling one South Carolina supporter that if his state could not quell the threatened rebellion, then it had "a right to call upon the Government for aid and the Executive will yield it as far as he has been vested with the power by the constitution and the laws made in pursuance thereof." Jackson also issued an official proclamation denouncing nullification as treason. Privately, he told fellow Tennessean John Coffee that "no man will go further than I will to preserve every right reserved to the people, or the states." However, "the union must be preserved," he told his friend. "I will die with the union."[12]

Jackson reinforced his determination to keep the Union intact by asking for congressional authorization to use his power as commander-in-chief against the nullifiers if they persisted in their planned rebellion. The message that he submitted with the "Force Bill," as this legislation was called, was unequivocal. South Carolina threatened the "Federal Union founded upon the great principle of popular representation," and Jackson expected Congress to join with him in "solemnly proclaim[ing] that the Constitution and the laws are supreme and the *Union indissoluble.*" Privately, he promised that, if needed, he would march 200,000 soldiers to South Carolina "to quell any and every insurrection, or rebellion that might arise to threaten our glorious confederacy, a union, upon which our liberty prosperity and happiness rests." He continued, "Fear not, *the union will be preserved,* and treason and rebellion promptly put down, when and where it may shew its monster head."[13]

By March 1833, Jackson's strong opposition to secession had succeeded. Congress passed a new compromise tariff that the South Carolina nullifiers accepted, dropping their threats of disunion. Henry Clay and, to a lesser extent, John C. Calhoun received much of the credit for ensuring that cooler heads prevailed, but Jackson played a significant role in keeping the Union intact. He made it clear throughout the winter months that he was willing to use force if necessary, but he also insisted that Congress pass a new tariff. The compromise tariff left Jackson less than satisfied, but he accepted it. He also did not prolong the crisis by imposing further sanctions on South Carolina. Not usually known for levelheadedness, Jackson demonstrated that trait effectively during the Nullification Crisis.[14]

Jackson's decisive stand against the nullification movement prevented civil war in 1832–1833. Arguably, his actions saved the United States (and therefore ultimately helped free the slaves) because, by pushing disunion nearly three decades into the future, it allowed the nation to be in a stronger position to defend the Union once secession finally occurred in 1860–1861. Lincoln's heroics in the Civil War and his standing as the nation's greatest president owes a great deal to Jackson's firm stance in the nullification movement.

CONCLUSION

Jackson was far from perfect. He fought duels, engaged in brawls, and held grudges. More significantly, he enslaved African Americans and killed Native Americans, taking their land in the process. While popular with many Americans during his lifetime, Jackson fails to engender much admiration given our twenty-first-century sensibilities.

Jackson, however, possessed many admirable qualities. He was a strong leader who acted in the best interests of the Union. When facing criticism for unpopular decisions, he persisted in what he believed was the best course for the nation and its people. Jackson also made crucial decisions that helped to make the United States a more democratic nation. When he came into office, the government was largely run by an insulated elite: four of the nation's first six presidents came from one state, Virginia, and the other two came from one family, the Adamses. Before Jackson, the president was not generally seen as a man of the people, but he pressed for a democratic government responsive to the people's will. Jackson also fought corruption in all its forms, including the power of wealth and organized interests to control government policy. In resisting the power of the national bank, he is a model for those reformers today who want a more equitable life for all classes of Americans. Finally, Jackson defended the Union against a serious threat to its future, establishing a model that Abraham Lincoln, no fan of Old Hickory's, emulated as the nation divided in 1860–1861. Jackson had his faults, but his positive contributions to the nation more than warrant him a place on our nation's currency.

Jackson was, of course, a man of his time. His definition of democracy—for White men—was a limited one by twenty-first-century standards. Jackson's endorsement of "rotation of office" looks like the political cronyism that so many Americans today decry as corruption. One can even criticize his Unionist stance against nullification as hypocritical, given his endorsement of Georgia's states' rights argument for Cherokee removal. Both Jackson's faults and his contributions, however, serve to remind us that our nation, our leaders, and we ourselves are flawed human beings. Two centuries from now, Americans may look at us and point out our failure to live up to our ideals. We will be judged in the same way that we now condemn Jackson, and we will be found similarly wanting. Instead of erasing him from our daily lives, we should leave Jackson on the $20 bill not only as a tribute to his role in creating American democracy but also as a reminder of his failings—and of our own shortcomings in realizing the full measure and meaning of democracy.

NOTES

PRO

1. Zachary Warmbrodt, "Lew: I have Hamilton's back," *Politico*, July 10, 2015.
2. Benedict Anderson, *Imagined Communities: Reflections on the Origin and Spread of Nationalism, Revised Edition* (New York, NY: Verso, 2006).
3. I borrow here the language of former Supreme Court Justice Sandra Day O'Connor, writing in a different context of governmental Christmas displays and how the government may impermissibly send a message to "nonadherents that

they are outsiders, not full members of the political community, and an accompanying message to adherents that they are insiders, favored members of the political community." *Lynch v. Donnelly*, 465 U.S. 668 (1984).

4. 31 USC 5114(a)

5. See Abby Ohlheiser, "Why Is Andrew Jackson on the $20 bill? The Answer May Be Lost to History," *Washington Post*, June 17, 2015; and Gene Hessler, *The Comprehensive Catalog of U.S. Paper Money* (Chicago, IL: Henry Regnery Company, 1974).

6. Thomas Jefferson, *The Writings of Thomas Jefferson*, 7: 454-463; ed. Albert Ellery Bergh, definitive edition (Washington, DC: Thomas Jefferson Memorial Association, 1907). See also Daniel J. Boorstin, *The Lost World of Thomas Jefferson* (Boston, MA: Beacon Press, 1948), esp. 204–212.

7. See Michael Paul Rogin, *Fathers and Children: Andrew Jackson and the Subjugation of the American Indian* (New York, NY: Alfred A. Knopf, 1975): 156.

8. See Daniel Feller, *The Jacksonian Promise, 1815-1840* (Baltimore, MD: Johns Hopkins University Press, 1995).

9. President Jackson's Veto Message Regarding the Bank of the United States; July 10, 1832.

10. See Richard Hofstadter, *The American Political Tradition* (New York, NY: Vintage Books, 1989 [first published 1948]). Hofstadter argues that, "Jackson's election was more a result than a cause of the rise of democracy."

11. See David Greenberg, "Keep Andrew Jackson on the $20," *Politico Magazine*, June 14, 2015.

12. Rogin, *Fathers and Children*, 13.

13. Worcester v. Georgia, 31 US 515 (1832).

14. 31 USC 5114(b).

15. Daniel Feller, quoted in Ohiheiser, "Why Is Andrew Jackson on the $20 bill?" *Washington Post*, June 17, 2015.

16. D.H. Lawrence, *Studies in Classic American Literature* (Garden City, NY: Doubleday, 1953 [first published 1923]): 93.

17. See "Louise Erdrich on Wilma Mankiller, the First Female Cherokee Chief," in *The New York Times* The Opinion Pages, Room for Debate, "If A Woman's Place Is on the 20," http://www.nytimes.com/roomfordebate/2015/03/18/putting-a-woman-on-the-20-bill/louise-erdrich-on-wilma-mankiller-the-first-female-cherokee-chief.

18. Cornel West, "Diverse New World," in Paul Berman, ed., *Debating P.C.* (New York, NY: Dell Publishing, 1992), 327.

CON

1. George Washington to John Sullivan, 31 May 1779, in *The Writings of George Washington*, ed. Worthington Chauncey Ford, 14 vols. (New York, NY: G.P. Putnam's, 1889–1893), 7:461.

2. Robert V. Remini, *The Legacy of Andrew Jackson: Essays on Democracy, Indian Removal, and Slavery* (Baton Rouge: Louisiana State University Press, 1988), 9-10; Andrew Jackson to William Dickson, [1] September 1801, Andrew Jackson to Littleton H. Coleman, 26 April 1824, in *The Papers of Andrew Jackson*, 9 vols., ed. Daniel Feller et al. (Knoxville: University of Tennessee Press, 1980), 1:256, 5:399 (hereafter *PAJ*); Andrew Jackson to John Quincy Adams, 22 November 1821, in *Correspondence of Andrew Jackson*, 7 vols., ed. John Spencer Bassett and J. Franklin Jameson (Washington, DC: Carnegie Institution, 1926-1933), 3:139 (hereafter *CAJ*).

3. Remini, *Legacy of Andrew Jackson*, 14.

4. First inaugural address, 4 March 1829, First annual message, 8 December 1829, in *A Compilation of the Messages and Papers of the Presidents, 1789-1897*, 11 vols., ed. James D. Richardson (Washington, DC: GPO, 1897), 2:438, 449.

5. Andrew Jackson to Andrew J. Donelson, 12 May 1835, Andrew J. Donelson Papers, Library of Congress, Washington, DC.

6. First annual message, 8 December 1829, in Richardson, ed., *Messages and Papers*, 2:448.

7. Andrew Jackson to John Overton, 8 June 1829, in *PAJ*, 7:271.

8. Veto message, 10 July 1832, in Richardson, ed., *Messages and Papers*, 2:590–91.

9. Censure resolution vote, 28 March 1834, "Protest" message, 15 April 1834, in U.S. Senate, *Register of Debates*, 23rd Cong., 1st. sess., 1187, 1329, 1333; Andrew Jackson to Andrew Jackson, Jr., 16 February 1834, in *CAJ*, 5:249.

10. Andrew Jackson to James K. Polk, 16 December 1832, in *CAJ*, 4:501.

11. Andrew Jackson to William Charles Cole Claiborne, 12 November 1806, in *PAJ*, 2:116.

12. Andrew Jackson to Joel R. Poinsett, 2 December 1832, Andrew Jackson to John Coffee, 14 December 1832, in *CAJ*, 4:493, 500.

13. "Force Bill" message, 16 January 1833, in Richardson, ed., *Messages and Papers*, 2:631-632; Andrew Jackson to Joel R. Poinsett, 24 January 1833, in *CAJ*, 5:11.

14. Robert V. Remini, *Andrew Jackson*, 3 vols. (New York, NY: Harper & Row, 1977–1984), 3:43.

4

RESOLVED, Congress should restore each state's freedom to set its drinking age

PRO: John McCardell

CON: James C. Fell

Important debates about public policy often encompass both an obvious and a less obvious dispute. The obvious dispute is about what the policy should be. Should casino gambling be legalized? Should tougher controls on air pollution be enacted? Should bike riders be forced to wear helmets?

The less obvious dispute is about who should decide what the policy will be. Sometimes this involves a family feud within the national government. Should Congress or the president decide when to withdraw American troops from a military commitment? Should the elected branches or the Supreme Court set public policy concerning affirmative action? At other times, the dispute is about which level of government in the federal system—the national government (usually called, a bit confusingly, the federal government), state governments, or local governments—should make public policy on welfare, education, law enforcement, and a wide range of other issues. Or, in the case of this debate, should Congress restore each state's freedom to set its drinking age?

Arguments about the powers of the federal government and the state governments run through much of American history. Could the federal government establish a national bank and exempt it from state taxes? A Supreme Court decision, *McCulloch v. Maryland* (1819), was needed to resolve that question. Could a state refuse to be bound by a federal tariff law that it considered oppressive? In 1832, President Andrew Jackson said no, Vice President John C. Calhoun of South Carolina resigned from office and said yes, and the great Nullification Crisis was born. `Could states decide to secede from the

Union? It took four years of civil war, from 1861 to 1865, to settle that one. For several decades, beginning in the late nineteenth century, additional battles were fought about the state governments' authority to regulate business and about the federal government's authority to enforce civil rights for African Americans and members of other racial and ethnic minority groups.

In the twentieth century, the federal government's efforts to expand its policy-making domain at the expense of the state governments took a new form. Instead of fighting legal battles about Washington's constitutional authority over the states, the federal government increasingly used its power of the purse to, in effect, buy the states' cooperation. Through grant-in-aid programs, Washington gave the states money to spend and clear instructions about how to spend it. The number of grant programs grew from just a few as recently as the early 1930s to several hundred today. The interstate highway system, for example, took shape when the federal government passed a law in 1956 that offered the states ninety cents of every dollar used to build highways according to Washington's specifications.

A grant is a gift that comes with strings attached. In 1984, at a time when each state still set its own drinking age without federal interference and most states had recently decided to reduce the age to under twenty-one, Congress passed the National Minimum Drinking Age Act. The act did not order the states to do anything, nor could it have done so without provoking a fierce constitutional challenge in the Supreme Court. Instead, the act stipulated that any state with a drinking age below twenty-one would lose 10 percent of its annual federal highway grants. Within a few years, every state decided to bring its legal drinking age into conformity with the new federal standard.

Laws are not passed in a political vacuum. In the Vietnam War era, many states had lowered their drinking ages because eighteen-, nineteen-, and twenty-year-olds argued persuasively that if they were old enough to be drafted to fight in the war, they were old enough to drink. A steep increase in alcohol-related traffic fatalities among younger drivers changed the political climate by spurring the formation of a new and politically savvy grassroots organization called Mothers Against Drunk Driving (MADD) in 1980. MADD lobbied vigorously for legislation to raise the drinking age to twenty-one.

In theory, disputes about who should make public policy on a particular issue are different from disputes about what the policy should be. In reality, these disputes seldom remain entirely separate. John McCardell and James C. Fell are on opposite sides of the resolution that Congress should restore each state's freedom to set its drinking age: McCardell is for the resolution, and Fell is against it. What both know, however, is that in the foreseeable future, Congress is highly unlikely to reduce the drinking age to eighteen. They also know that if the individual states were free to reduce it, some of them probably would. McCardell wants to see that change occur, and so he wants to move the decision from the federal government to the state governments. Fell supports the current drinking age, and so he wants to leave the decision right where it is, in Washington.

PRO: John McCardell

"Some may feel that my decision is at odds with my philosophical viewpoint that state problems should involve state solutions," said President Ronald Reagan in July, 1984; however, he continued, "in a case like this, where the problem is so clear-cut, then I have no misgivings about a judicious use of federal inducements to encourage the states to get moving."[1]

The "problem" that, in this case, trumped philosophy involved drunken-driving fatalities. The solution seemed as clear-cut: raise the drinking age to twenty-one. With the stroke of a pen, the president signed into law the National Minimum Drinking Age Act, in effect wresting away, seemingly for good, what had explicitly and unequivocally been a state prerogative since 1789. The bill did not, because it could not, mandate a national drinking age. Rather, it created a powerful "incentive": states would remain free to set the age, but any state setting the age lower than twenty-one would forfeit 10 percent of its federal highway funds each year.

If the president's decision ran counter to his own prostate government political instincts, it also renewed the historic debate over the limits of federalism and situated that debate in the highly charged arena of alcohol policy. Led by South Dakota, twelve states (the others were Colorado, Hawaii, Kansas, Louisiana, Montana, New Mexico, Ohio, South Carolina, Tennessee, Vermont, and Wyoming) challenged the constitutionality of the act. Eventually the case reached the Supreme Court, which in 1987, by a vote of 7–2, upheld the law. Writing for the majority, Chief Justice William H. Rehnquist noted: "We need not decide in this case whether [the Twenty-first] Amendment would prohibit an attempt by Congress to legislate directly a national minimum drinking age. Here, Congress has acted indirectly under its spending power to encourage uniformity in the States' drinking ages.... [W]e find this legislative effort within constitutional bounds even if Congress may not regulate drinking ages directly."[2] And with those words, public debate on the issue ceased.

Thus, since 1984, there has been a de facto national drinking age. The results have been sufficiently mixed to warrant a reopening of what for too long was viewed as a settled question. Yet the forces, and the "incentives," militating against any change in the status quo have for a quarter of a century successfully stifled serious discussion and debate over the consequences—intended and unintended—of this legislation. It is time for that debate to resume. It is time to change the law.

To understand the urgency for change, as well as to grasp the irony of the present condition, one needs to recognize that in many ways, history is repeating itself. America has always had an uneasy relationship with alcohol, swinging wildly over the years from periods of remarkable laxity and permissiveness to periods of prohibition. Unlike most other countries, where alcohol has generally been viewed as a food rather than as an intoxicant and as an enhancement to social and family relationships rather than as an irresponsible escape from reality, the American experience reflects an uncertain, and always unsettled, cultural attitude toward alcohol.

Federalism did little to resolve the uncertainty and contributed much to the unsettling, because the authority to set alcohol policy resides, under the Constitution, exclusively with the states. Moreover, many states carried the federal principle still further, allowing individual counties, under the rubric of "local option," to make laws reflecting the prevailing attitudes within particular localities. As a result, laws governing the production, purchase, possession, and consumption of alcoholic beverages resembled a crazy quilt of the permissible and the impermissible.

To minds more comfortable with tidiness and consistency, such an approach always seemed undesirable. To those whose attitudes were shaped by a particular set of understandings—often but not always grounded in religious beliefs—that sought to differentiate moral from immoral behavior, such an approach seemed unacceptable, a secular impediment placed in the way of realizing God's design in a fallen world.

From time to time, a prohibitionist impulse has amassed sufficient muscle to neaten the untidiness and clean up the moral squalor. During the first half of the nineteenth century, a "temperance" movement began. By 1836, the American Temperance Society claimed more than 8,000 local chapters and more than 1.5 million members. But because merely encouraging temperance did not mean outright prohibition, this movement failed to satisfy those who, moved by religious revivals to eradicate sin wherever it could be found, turned to the government for assistance.

As early as 1830, most states had some form of licensing law meant to limit the right to sell alcohol to responsible retailers. Over the next twenty years, temperance advocates pushed to strengthen these regulations by limiting the quantities that might be sold to particular individuals and by allowing a local option on whether intoxicants could be sold at all. New York enacted local option legislation in 1845, and, following the lead of Maine, which passed the first statewide prohibition law in 1846, Vermont, Rhode Island, and Minnesota Territory embraced prohibition in 1852; as did Michigan in 1853, Connecticut and New York in 1854; and New Hampshire, Tennessee, Delaware, Illinois, Indiana, Iowa, and Wisconsin in 1855.

Themes that would become familiar and recurrent continued to surface. Enforcement of prohibition proved almost impossible. Per capita consumption of alcohol increased dramatically. Public opposition to prohibition grew, especially in the rapidly growing cities. Many of the laws, having been hastily drafted and passed, proved susceptible to legal challenge. Finally, as civil war loomed, ending slavery took priority over other reform efforts.

Thus, the pattern was set: elision of temperance into prohibition; the graphic depiction of the evils of strong drink; the increasingly extreme certitude of temperance advocates; the belief that only legislation could solve the problem; acquiescence to the argument that governmental intrusion may be necessary for the public good; difficulties of law enforcement; an increase rather than a decrease in drinking; and finally, gradually, a dawning awareness that legislative intervention in private life may have more unintended than intended consequences.

In the late nineteenth century, under the leadership of the Women's Christian Temperance Union, one of the first organizations to keep a professional lobbyist in Washington, the reform impulse revived. The movement was strongest in rural, small-town, Protestant America. Unlike in the 1850s, when prohibitionists sought legislation (and discovered that what a legislature could do, it could just as easily undo), in the 1880s they sought reform through state constitutional amendments. Five states—Kansas, Maine, Rhode Island, North Dakota, and South Dakota—adopted constitutional prohibition, while New Hampshire and Vermont continued prohibition by statute. In 1893, the newly formed Anti-Saloon League joined the prohibition effort and elevated the movement's sights from the state to the national level.

There was no disputing that alcohol regulation remained entirely a state matter. But, thought Wayne Wheeler, president of the Anti-Saloon League, what if the U.S. Constitution itself could be amended? What better way to "hurl a missile at the giant wrong"?[3] The United States' entry into the Great War in 1917, coupled with the Progressive Era belief that government regulation could, by adjusting unwholesome environments, bring about social change, provided the opportunity. Joining the fervor for supporting American troops in the field, prohibitionists insisted that not a single grain of wheat or barley or a single kernel of corn should be diverted to produce alcoholic beverages. No effort should be spared to defeat the Hun (whose name was often associated with beer).

Thus, in 1917, Congress adopted, and forty-four states by 1919 ratified, the Eighteenth Amendment to the Constitution, embedding prohibition in the fundamental law of the land. A joyful leader of the Anti-Saloon League believed that "there is as much chance of repealing the Eighteenth Amendment as there is for a humming-bird to fly to the planet Mars with the Washington Monument tied to its tail."[4]

The Eighteenth Amendment's attempt to ban "the manufacture, sale, or transportation" of alcohol soon came face-to-face with a more potent law, the law of unintended consequences. By 1929, per capita consumption of alcohol was higher than it had been in 1918, a year before Prohibition became law. Criminal behavior—moonshining, bootlegging—became rampant. Enforcement of the law proved almost impossible. "Prohibition has driven the saloon off the side-walk," wrote one observer, "but has put it in the cellar, where it is out of sight."[5]

Within little more than a decade, by December 1933, the unthinkable and the impossible happened. For the first and only time in American history, two-thirds of the House and Senate and three-fourths of the state legislatures voted to repeal a constitutional amendment. With the repeal of Prohibition, the making of alcohol policy reverted to the individual states, and the untidiness and inconsistency returned as well.

Almost forty years would pass before the question of the drinking age reappeared. The catalyst was not concern over alcohol and its effects but rather the unpopular war in Vietnam—one fought mostly by young draftees deemed capable of defending their country but incapable of exercising any of the other responsibilities of adulthood. The inconsistency received its most forceful and articulate expression in a simple slogan: "Old enough to fight—old enough to vote." Persuaded by the justice as well as the logic of the argument, Congress passed and the states ratified the Twenty-sixth Amendment, which stated that "the right of a citizen age 18 to vote shall not be abridged on account of age."

The Twenty-sixth Amendment prompted a serious reconsideration of twenty-one as the age of majority. Indeed, if eighteen-year-olds were capable of voting intelligently and placing their lives on the line for their country, by what right, or logic, ought they be denied other privileges and responsibilities of adulthood? As a result, by the end of the 1970s, most states had redefined the age of majority as eighteen, and the rest had set the age at nineteen. At the same time, between 1970 and 1979, twenty-nine states lowered their drinking ages.

Once again, the law of unintended consequences held sway. In the states choosing to lower the drinking age, no provision was made to prepare those on whom a new privilege had been conferred to exercise responsibility. It was as if the privilege to drive a car were granted without any driver training or any probationary period during which new drivers could gain experience and confidence. Not surprisingly, alcohol-related traffic fatalities rapidly increased in the eighteen-to-twenty age group. The problem of drunken driving was both genuine and serious. In 1980, the mother of a thirteen-year-old girl who had been killed by a forty-seven-year-old repeat-offender drunken driver founded Mothers Against Drunk Driving (MADD), and the drinking age debate began in earnest.

As fatalities quickly reached unacceptable levels, MADD led a public call for action. In 1982, President Reagan appointed a special Commission on Drunk Driving, which brought forward, unanimously, thirty-nine recommendations. Of these, the most prominent was that "States should immediately adopt 21 years as the minimum legal purchasing and public possession age for all alcoholic beverages." Recognizing the potential constitutional conundrum, the commission added: "Legislation at the Federal level should be enacted providing that each State enact and/or maintain a law requiring 21 years as the minimum legal age for purchasing and possessing alcoholic beverages. Such legislation should provide that the Secretary of the United States Department of Transportation disapprove any project under Section 106 of the Federal Highway Act . . . for any State not having and enforcing such a law."[6]

The need for uniformity, in the view of Senator Frank Lautenberg of New Jersey, a principal sponsor of the legislation, arose from the problem posed by so-called blood borders: those places where a state with a higher drinking age bordered a state with a lower age. Too many young people, the senator argued, were driving across these borders, in his case from New Jersey into New York, to drink where the age was lower and then driving home, sometimes with fatal consequences. A uniform drinking age, he argued, would end this fatal practice. By a bipartisan vote of 81–16, the measure passed, and on July 17, 1984, President Reagan signed the National Minimum Drinking Age Act, effectively creating a national drinking age of twenty-one.

In the years since this law was enacted, states have made occasional efforts to reopen the question of the drinking age. For example, at various times the legislatures of Wisconsin, Kentucky, New Hampshire, and South Carolina have considered exempting active-duty military personnel from the twenty-one age requirement. Vermont considered a bill to educate and license eighteen-year-olds as a way of lowering the age. Missouri voters attempted a ballot initiative to lower the age. In every case, however, these efforts failed because the prospect of losing 10 percent of federal highway money loomed. If the purpose of attaching a highway fund "incentive" to the drinking age law was to end serious debate over the matter, then the measure must be adjudged a success.

Therein, however, lies a deeper problem. No public policy, however effective or worthy its supporters may deem it, should be placed, for all time, effectively outside the arena of political debate and rendered virtually impossible to change. A growing body of evidence suggests that the National Minimum Drinking Age Act has not been an unmitigated blessing. Some of that evidence serves as a reminder of the country's experience under Prohibition. The vast majority of young people between the ages of eighteen and twenty routinely disobey the drinking age law.[7] The proliferation of fake IDs reflects a determination to flout the law and risks breeding disrespect for law in general. As a result, the law has proven virtually impossible to enforce: It is estimated that of every one thousand violations only two result in arrest or citation.[8]

Not only is the law regularly violated, but the violations occur behind closed doors, in the latter-day equivalent of the "speakeasies" of the 1920s. There, out of public view and away from easy detection, young adults are consuming alcohol in quantities that are life and health threatening. The law has not eliminated drinking; it has simply displaced it from visible, public venues to clandestine locations. Assaults, date rapes, property damage, and emergency room calls attest to the persistent, intractable problem of "binge" drinking that all too often proves toxic.

It also proves unnatural, in that the drinking age law has served to split the previously concentric worlds of alcohol consumption and social intercourse into separate spheres. In the United States, young people "do shots" or "preload" before going to social events where they know alcohol will not be available. This behavior is very different from that observed in most of the rest of the world, where lower drinking ages and more open cultural attitudes toward alcohol have created very different—and healthier—environments for young people.

The law unquestionably represents an abridgment of the age of majority that young adults considered capable of voting, signing contracts, serving on juries, and fighting in the military have difficulty comprehending. In addition, the role of parents in teaching their children has been unintentionally marginalized by a law that places alcohol off limits until an individual turns twenty-one.

Finally, although drunken-driving fatalities have in fact been reduced, the reduction has occurred in all age groups; further, the reductions in the United States have been paralleled in Canada, where the drinking age has remained either eighteen or nineteen.[9] Safer automobiles, mandatory use of seat belts, and promotion of the concept of the "designated driver" have had far more to do with the downward trend than the higher drinking age.

Moreover, over the past quarter century, a fundamental shift has occurred in Americans' attitudes toward drinking and driving. As a senior official at the National Highway Traffic and Safety Administration put it: "If you look back, it's no longer acceptable to drive drunk. It's socially reprehensible, in fact, to drive drunk."

The problem of drunken driving has not been eliminated, but it has been addressed and reduced, and technology now exists, in the form of ignition interlock devices, that can keep impaired drivers of all ages off the highways.

The need to reduce drunken driving by adjusting the drinking age has been superseded by more effective and targeted methods.

It has also been supplanted by a very different sort of problem, which has at least in part been caused by the higher drinking age. Reasonable people may disagree about how closely related the drinking age and the problem of clandestine binge drinking may be, but the relationship cannot be denied. The looming public health crisis occasioned by toxic and secretive alcohol consumption in the twenty-first century may require a different set of solutions from those used to solve a very different problem in the last century. Data gathered by the College Alcohol Study, which supports keeping the drinking age at twenty-one, show that the incidence of binge drinking among college-age young adults has not budged—up or down—in the twenty-five years since the law was changed. It is hard to argue that the law has been very effective in curbing binge drinking.[10]

There is only one place where, constitutionally, the whole matter may be examined and public policy adjusted to meet a new reality, and that place is the state capitals. But the drinking age, as a part of any possible solution to the problem of binge drinking, remains off limits so long as the federal highway fund "incentive" remains on the books. If that "incentive" were removed, or, alternatively, if states were to be granted waivers for a period of time in order to try new approaches, fresh, creative ideas would surely emerge. This is the genius of federalism. Allowing each state to try something different, something appropriate for its own population, can lead to better practices, better policy, and safer environments.

This is not an unreasonable expectation. In the twentieth century, states were viewed as "laboratories of progressivism." Many things we now take for granted nationally—regulation of corporations, the secret ballot, women's suffrage—were all innovations, thought by some to be too radical to be acceptable, that were first tried on the state level. It is hard to imagine that a state might have had its highway funding reduced for allowing women to vote. But had a similar "incentive" existed one hundred years ago, would any state have had the courage to put such funding at risk?

What works in one state may not work as well in another. The federal government should not tell New Jersey what its drinking age should be; neither should New Jersey dictate to South Carolina, Vermont, or Montana. And before the concern over "blood borders" is allowed to thwart debate, it should be remembered that states bordering Canada and Mexico already have "blood borders." Even more to the point, unless legislatures enact uniform closing hours for bars, there will be "blood borders" within every community where some bars close at 1:00 a.m., others at 2:00 a.m., and still others at 3:00 a.m. State boundaries are only one form of "blood border."

It is likely that a genuine national consensus will never be reached regarding what the drinking age should be. Rather than continuing to coerce such a consensus and sustain the illusion that the question of the drinking age is settled—and that all the evidence lies on one side of the debate—let Congress restore to the states the right to do what, under the Constitution, only the states may do. Let Congress allow the states, unimpeded by federal "incentives," to make public policy that reflects the particular reality that exists within each state. Let federalism work its genius without interference. Return the right to set the drinking age to the states.

CON: James C. Fell

Perhaps no alcohol safety measure or policy has attracted more research and public attention or shown more consistent evidence for its effectiveness than the minimum legal drinking age (MLDA) of twenty-one in the United States. MLDA laws were established in the states after the repeal of Prohibition in 1933. At that time, control of alcohol was left to the states, most of which set the MLDA at twenty-one. By 1969, thirty-five states still had MLDA laws set at age twenty-one (see Map 4.1). However, when the Twenty-sixth Amendment lowered the voting age from twenty-one to eighteen in 1971, many states lowered their drinking ages to eighteen or nineteen. Consequently, by the end of 1975, only twelve states had MLDA-21 laws—that is, laws setting the drinking age at twenty-one (see Map 4.2).

Studies in the 1970s and 1980s showed significant increases in alcohol-related crashes involving youths aged eighteen to twenty in states that lowered their drinking ages. There was also anecdotal evidence that many youths under age twenty-one who resided in states with MLDA-21 laws were driving long distances to neighboring states with an MLDA of eighteen or nineteen so they could legally drink at bars. Some of these youths were involved in crashes when they were driving back to their home states in a highly intoxicated condition. Concern over these developments and other drunk-driving issues led to the establishment of Mothers Against Drunk Driving (MADD) in 1980 and the President's Commission on Drunk Driving in 1982. Both of these organizations advocated a uniform drinking age of twenty-one in all states in order to eliminate the "blood borders" and reduce drinking and driving by youth. In 1984, Congress adopted the National Minimum Drinking Age Act, which provided a substantial incentive for states to set their MLDA at twenty-one. If they did not do so by 1988, they faced losing

Map 4.1

U.S. Minimum Legal Drinking Ages as of December 31, 1969

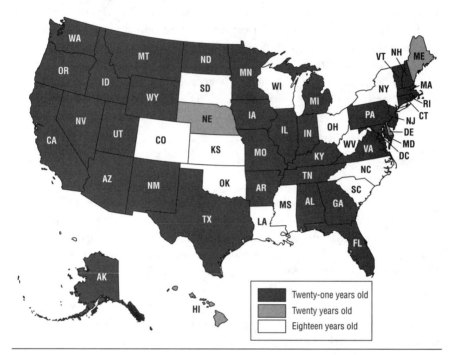

■	Twenty-one years old
▨	Twenty years old
□	Eighteen years old

Source: Data from Insurance Institute for Highway Safety.

10 percent of their federal highway construction funding. By 1988, all fifty states and the District of Columbia had set the MLDA at twenty-one.

Between 1982 and 1998, the population-adjusted rate of drinking drivers age twenty and younger involved in fatal traffic crashes decreased 59 percent.[1] MLDA-21 laws have been shown to be associated with this decline. The National Highway Traffic Safety Administration (NHTSA) has estimated that MLDA laws save approximately 800 to 900 lives a year in traffic fatalities alone.[2] Every year, new studies continue to demonstrate the effectiveness of MLDA-21. A 2011 study concluded that if the U.S. drinking age were lowered to eighteen, the result would be an estimated additional eight deaths per 100,000 person-years among eighteen- to twenty-year-olds.[3] A 2011 report to Congress by the Substance Abuse and Mental Health Services Administration noted a significant decline in binge drinking by college-bound twelfth graders.[4] A study published in 2012 found that lower drinking ages result in an elevated risk of suicide and homicide for women, and that raising the drinking age to

Map 4.2

U.S. Minimum Legal Drinking Ages as of December 31, 1975

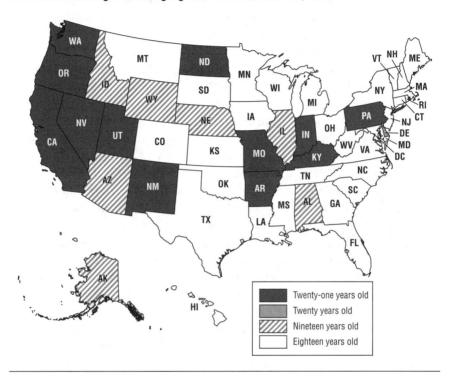

Source: Data from Insurance Institute for Highway Safety.

twenty-one may be preventing an estimated 600 suicides and 600 homicides annually.[5] However, despite strong evidence of the effectiveness of MLDA-21, there are movements in some states to lower the legal drinking age, and at least one organization is working to repeal the national uniform drinking age act.

Technically, each state still has the freedom to set its drinking age. That right was never taken away by the federal government. So far, however, no state has chosen to exercise its freedom to lower the drinking age, given that this would also mean forgoing millions of dollars in federal highway construction funding and most likely result in a significant increase in youthful traffic deaths on their highways. The use of this incentive, or sanction, is a common practice of the federal government when it wants to persuade states to adopt policies that affect the nation's public safety. This mechanism was also used to persuade all states to adopt zero-tolerance laws for drivers under age twenty-one in 1995 and to adopt the blood alcohol concentration (BAC) limit of 0.08 g/dl (grams of alcohol per deciliter of blood) for drivers age twenty-one and older in 2000. In 2011, a bill was introduced in the U.S. Senate calling for the withholding of highway construction funding for states that do not adopt laws mandating the installation of breath alcohol ignition interlock devices on the vehicles of drivers convicted of driving while intoxicated.

The National Minimum Drinking Age Act required states only to adopt statutes that made it illegal for persons younger than twenty-one to publicly possess alcohol or to purchase alcohol. It allowed states many exceptions to the law, including allowing those under age twenty-one to drink at home, in their parents' presence, or in any private residence. These exceptions were allowed, in part, so that parents who choose to do so can teach their children responsible alcohol consumption in the privacy of the home. The act said nothing about states adopting laws making it illegal to provide or sell alcohol to those under age twenty-one, hosting alcohol parties for those under twenty-one, or even using a fake ID to purchase alcohol. The states thus had considerable flexibility and could allow for many exceptions. In addition to the possession and purchase laws required by the federal act, eighteen additional laws have been adopted by some states. These include laws making it illegal for anyone younger than age twenty-one to consume alcohol as well as laws against using a fake ID to purchase alcohol and furnishing alcohol to those under twenty-one. States have also passed laws establishing twenty-one as the minimum age for selling and serving alcohol.[6] Although all states have subsequently passed laws making it illegal for a youth to use a fake ID to purchase alcohol, it is not illegal in half the states to manufacture, produce, or transfer a fake ID.

Critics of the National Minimum Drinking Age Act advance many different arguments for its repeal. For example:

- "Young people routinely disobey the law." People routinely disobey drunk-driving laws, too, but that is no reason to abolish these laws. Drunk-driving laws do not eliminate drunk driving, but they substantially reduce it, just as the drinking age of twenty-one substantially reduces underage drinking.

- "Drunk-driving fatalities involving youth have decreased by a similar amount in Canada, where the drinking age is eighteen or nineteen." True. However, in Canada drunk-driving fatalities for drivers age twenty-one and older have decreased at about the same rate as those for drivers younger than twenty-one. In the United States, in contrast, the number of drinking drivers younger than twenty-one involved in fatal crashes decreased 62 percent between 1982 and 2004, whereas fatal crashes among drinking drivers over age twenty-one decreased only 33 percent. Most of the difference in rates is attributable to the minimum drinking age law.

Below, I focus on four main themes of the critics of the National Minimum Drinking Age Act: (1) Europeans let their kids drink from an early age, yet they do not have any more alcohol-related problems than Americans do; (2) anyone old enough to be drafted into the military is old enough to drink; (3) young people are drinking anyway, so we should teach them to drink responsibly; and (4) the drinking age should be regulated by the states, not the federal government. Each of these arguments is fundamentally flawed.

THE DRINKING AGE IN EUROPEAN COUNTRIES

The U.S. MLDA of twenty-one is one of the highest in the world. In Europe, for example, the MLDAs range from fourteen in Switzerland to sixteen in France and Italy to eighteen in Ireland. European countries are often held up as examples of places where liberal drinking age laws and liberal attitudes toward alcohol foster responsible styles of drinking by young people. It is often asserted that alcohol is more integrated into European culture and that young people in these countries are introduced to moderation in drinking at early ages within the context of the family. As a result, it is said, young Europeans learn to drink more responsibly than do young Americans. The evidence suggests, however, that this is not the case.

Intoxication is a strong measure of problematic drinking and is associated with a wide variety of personal and social problems. If socialization into drinking is related to more responsible drinking, young Europeans would presumably have lower rates of intoxication than do young Americans. Figure 2-1 displays the thirty-day prevalence rates for self-reported intoxication for European and American adolescents ages fifteen and sixteen. In the 2003 Monitoring the Future survey, U.S. adolescents showed a moderate rate of intoxication (18 percent) compared with their European peers, and one that was substantially lower than in most other countries. According to the European School Survey Project on Alcohol and Other Drugs, only in Turkey and Cyprus are the intoxication rates of fifteen- to sixteen-year-olds substantially lower than in the United States.

Concern about these high rates of adolescent intoxication has prompted European nations to initiate debate about the most appropriate age for legal access to alcohol and to look to the United States' MLDA of twenty-one as a

Figure 4-1

Prevalence of Intoxication by Adolescents in the Past Thirty Days, United States and Europe

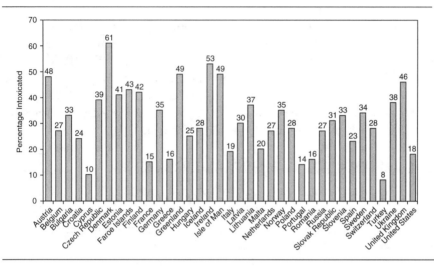

Sources: 2003 European School Survey Project on Alcohol and Other Drugs and 2003 Monitoring the Future survey.

possible model. What Europeans and others find when they examine MLDA-21 laws is that they help to keep hazardous consumption of alcohol down, save lives, reduce injuries of all types, and decrease other alcohol-related problems.

AGES OF INITIATION

"If I'm old enough to go to war, I should be old enough to drink" is another oft-heard argument for lowering the drinking age. In truth, however, many rights have different ages of initiation. In most states, a person can obtain a hunting license at age twelve and drive at age sixteen. Other rights we regulate by age include the right to sell and use tobacco, the right to gamble in casinos and buy lottery tickets, and the right to give legal consent for sexual intercourse and marriage. Vendors such as car rental facilities and hotels also have set minimum ages for the use of their services—an individual must be twenty-five years old to rent a car and twenty-one years old to rent a hotel room. The minimum age for initiation is based on the specific behaviors involved and takes into account the dangers and benefits of that behavior at a given age. The military recruits eighteen-year-olds fresh out of high school because at that point in their lives they are physically fit and highly trainable. This does not mean they are ready to drink.

Alcohol affects young people differently than it does adults. A teenager may look like an adult and even be more physically fit, but the teenager's body is still developing. According to the American Medical Association, it actually takes less alcohol to make a teenager drunk in comparison with an adult in his or her twenties. A normal adult's liver can safely process an estimated one ounce of 80-proof alcohol per hour, but a teenager's liver can process only half that amount—about one-fourth of a "light" beer.

The MLDA-21 law takes into account that underage drinking is related to numerous health problems, including injuries and deaths resulting from alcohol poisoning, car crashes, suicides, homicides, assaults, drownings, and recreational mishaps. In fact, the leading cause of death among teens is car crashes, and alcohol is involved in close to one-third of these fatalities. In 2013, 17 percent of drivers between the ages of sixteen and twenty who were involved in fatal motor vehicle crashes had a blood alcohol content (BAC) of 0.08 g/dl or higher compared to 33 percent of drivers aged twenty-one to twenty-four. The percentages of motor vehicle deaths related to drinking were much higher during the 1970s and 1980s, when many states had lower drinking ages.

There is mounting evidence that repeated exposure to alcohol during adolescence leads to long-lasting deficits in cognitive abilities, including learning and memory. Susan Tapert and Sandra Brown, alcohol researchers at the University of California, San Diego, have conducted a series of studies examining the effects of alcohol use on neuropsychological functioning in adolescents and young adults. In one study of subjects ages thirteen to nineteen recruited from treatment programs, the researchers observed that a return to drinking after the program ended led to further decline in cognitive abilities—particularly in tests of attention—over the next four years. Early onset of drinking by youth has also been shown to be related to a significant increase in the risk of future alcohol-related problems, such as addiction, getting into fights, and automobile crashes.

TEACHING RESPONSIBLE DRINKING

Some argue that the MLDA-21 law is obsolete and is actually exacerbating high-risk, hazardous drinking in clandestine locations. They say that if the drinking age were lowered, youths would learn to drink responsibly because they would get an idea of their tolerance by learning to drink under supervision at bars or at functions on college campuses, rather than at uncontrolled private parties.

The problem with this argument is that no evidence exists to indicate that young people learn to drink responsibly when they are able to consume alcohol legally at a younger age. Countries with lower drinking ages suffer from alcohol-related problems as great as or greater than those in the United States. Responsible consumption comes with maturity, and maturity largely comes only as certain protective mechanisms, such as age, marriage, and employment, begin to take hold.

Supervision does not necessarily lead to responsibility. Many bars encourage irresponsible drinking by deeply discounting drink prices and by heavily promoting specials such as happy hours, two-for-ones, and bar crawls. Many bars also serve obviously intoxicated patrons. On college campuses, fraternity and sorority members drink more frequently than their peers and are more likely to accept high levels of alcohol consumption as normal.

Some have suggested issuing special licenses to eighteen- to twenty-year-olds that allow them to drink alcohol if they complete an alcohol education course. This sounds like a good idea. However, there is no evidence that lowering the drinking age to eighteen for those who complete an education program will reduce the problem. In fact, there is strong evidence to the contrary. Take driver education programs in the high schools as an example. These programs were designed to teach young drivers about the dangers of driving and give them the skills and knowledge to drive responsibly. Yet a landmark study found "little support for the hypothesis that formal driver education is an effective safety measure." Although "driver education does teach safety skills, students are not motivated to use them"; in addition, "driver education fosters overconfidence."[7] Studies sponsored by the NHTSA have shown that young drivers who have completed driver education courses have crash rates no different from those of young drivers who have not. Based on this experience, it does not seem likely that a forty-hour alcohol education program would work to reduce underage drinking problems.

THE FEDERALISM ARGUMENT

Another argument advanced by critics of the National Minimum Drinking Age Act is that the drinking age is a matter best left to the states. The trouble with this argument is that providing for the public safety is a primary responsibility of government at all levels, including the federal government. Moreover, surveys show that 80 percent of Americans support setting the drinking age at twenty-one, with little or no variation by state in attitudes toward MLDA laws.

Despite the strong public support for MLDA-21, it is likely that if Congress had not adopted twenty-one as the national drinking age, MLDAs would still vary considerably from state to state. If the federal law is repealed, there will again be state variability in drinking ages. Highways cross state borders, and most are built with federal funds, so it is the federal government's business to ensure that we do not return to the "blood borders" for young people that were created by different drinking ages in different states.

The federal government has a special obligation to protect young people. If the minimum drinking age is lowered to eighteen, the result will be greater availability of alcohol not only to eighteen- to twenty-year-olds but also to those younger than eighteen. Studies have shown that lowering the drinking age to eighteen also increases alcohol-related crashes for fifteen- to seventeen-year-olds. The earlier young people start to drink, the greater the odds that they will be injured while under the influence, have a motor vehicle crash after drinking, or get into a fight. Youths who start drinking at age eighteen are twice as likely to get drunk as those who start at age twenty-one. Youths who start drinking at age eighteen also have a greater chance of becoming alcohol dependent.

The federal government should act when it can appreciably improve the health and safety of the nation's citizens. By creating an incentive for states to adopt MLDA-21 laws, the federal government has clearly done that. A recent study has indicated that the various MLDA-21 laws in the states save approximately 1,100 lives each year in reductions in traffic fatalities involving young drivers.[8] Medical research shows that excessive drinking by youths twenty and younger may cause brain damage as well as reduce brain function. Early onset of drinking increases the risk for future alcohol abuse, automobile crashes, and assaults, among other alcohol-related problems.

Congress enacted the National Minimum Drinking Age Act to protect the health and safety of the public. The experiences of other countries that have tried lowering their drinking ages show that the federal government's decision was a wise one. In 1999, New Zealand lowered its drinking age from twenty to eighteen. The result, according to a recent study, was a dramatic increase in automobile crashes. The rate of traffic crashes and injuries to eighteen- and nineteen-year-old males increased 12 percent, and the rate for males ages fifteen to seventeen increased 14 percent. For females, the effect was even greater—rates increased 51 percent for eighteen- to nineteen-year-olds and 24 percent for fifteen- to seventeen-year-olds.[9]

When the lives and well-being of so many young people are at stake, it is appropriate for the federal government to step in and protect the public. States, it is worth underscoring one final time, are still free to set their drinking ages lower than twenty-one so long as they are willing to accept the increase in youthful deaths and give up federal highway moneys. The federal government is not directly coercing any state to adopt twenty-one as the drinking age.

The National Minimum Drinking Age Act has been a balanced, effective, and popular tool for combatting the many problems associated with youthful drinking. Repealing it would be a grave mistake.

NOTES

PRO

1. *Time*, July 2, 1984.
2. *South Dakota v. Dole*, 483 U.S. 203 (1987)
3. John Kobler, *Ardent Spirits: The Rise and Fall of Prohibition* (New York, NY: G. P. Putnam, 1973), 180–83.
4. Quoted in David E. Kyvig, *Repealing National Prohibition* (Chicago, IL: University of Chicago Press, 1979), 2.
5. Quoted in Herbert Asbury, *The Great Illusion: An Informal History of Prohibition* (New York, NY: Doubleday, 1950), 73–74.
6. See Presidential Commission on Drunk Driving, *Final Report* (Washington, DC: Government Printing Office, November 1983), 10.
7. See, for example, the Alcohol Policy Information System's individual state profiles of underage consumption of alcohol, at http://www.alcoholpolicy.niaaa.nih.gov; Substance Abuse and Mental Health Services Administration, Office of Applied Studies, *Results from the 2007 National Survey on Drug Use and Health: National Findings* (NSDUH Series H-34, DHHS Publication No. SMA 08-4343) (Rockville, MD: Substance Abuse and Mental Health Services Administration, 2008); John Schulenberg et al., "The Problem of College Drinking: Insights from a Developmental Perspective," *Alcohol: Clinical and Experimental Research* 25 (March 2001): 473–77; and Daniel N. Allen, David G. Sprenkel, and Patrick A. Vitale, "Reactance Theory and Alcohol Consumption Laws: Further Confirmation Among Collegiate Alcohol Consumers," *Journal of Studies on Alcohol* 55 (January 1994): 34–40.
8. Mark Wolfson, A. C. Wagenaar, and Gary W. Hornseth, "Law Officers' Views on Enforcement of the Legal Drinking Age," *Public Health Reports* 110, no. 4 (1995): 428–37.
9. James H. Hedlund, Robert G. Ulmer, and David F. Preusser, *Determine Why There Are Fewer Young Alcohol-Impaired Drivers* (Final Report to the National Highway Traffic Safety Administration, Report No. DOT-HS-809-348) (Washington, DC: U.S. Department of Transportation, September 2001).
10. "College Binge Drinking Rate 44 Percent; Remains the Same Eight Years Running: Positive Trends Fail to Bring Down Binge Drinking Rate, According to Harvard College Alcohol Study," press release, College Alcohol Study, March 25, 2002, http://www.hsph.harvard.edu/cas/Documents/trends-pressRelease.

CON

1. James H. Hedlund, Robert G. Ulmer, and David F. Preusser, *Determine Why There Are Fewer Young Alcohol-Impaired Drivers* (Final Report to the National Highway Traffic Safety Administration, Report No. DOT HS 809 348 (Washington, DC: U.S. Department of Transportation, September, 2001), http://www.nhtsa.gov/people/injury/research/feweryoungdrivers/index.htm.

2. National Highway Traffic Safety Administration, National Center for Statistics and Analysis, *Traffic Safety Facts: Lives Saved in 2007 by Restraint Use and Minimum Drinking Age Laws* (DOT HS 811 049) (Washington, DC: U.S. Department of Transportation, November, 2008).

3. Christopher Carpenter and Carlos Dobkin, "The Minimum Legal Drinking Age and Public Health," *Journal of Economic Perspectives* 25, no. 2 (2011): 133–56.

4. Substance Abuse and Mental Health Services Administration, *Report to Congress on the Prevention and Reduction of Underage Drinking* (Washington, DC: U.S. Department of Health and Human Services, May, 2011).

5. Richard A. Grucza, Pamela R. Hipp, Karen E. Norberg, Laura Rundell, Anastasia Evanoff, Patricia Cavazos-Rehg, and Laura J. Bierut, "The Legacy of Minimum Legal Drinking Age Law Changes: Long-Term Effects on Suicide and Homicide Deaths Among Women," *Alcoholism: Clinical and Experimental Research* 36 (2012): 377–84.

6. James C. Fell, Sue Thomas, Michael Scherer, Deborah Fisher, and Eduardo Romano. "Scoring the Strengths and Weaknesses of Underage Drinking Laws in the United States." *World Medical & Health Policy*, 7 no.1 (2015): 28–58.

7. Daniel R. Mayhew and Herb M. Simpson, "The Safety Value of Driver Education and Training," *Journal of the International Society for Child and Adolescent Injury Prevention* 8, suppl. 2 (2002): ii, 3–8.

8. James Fell, Michael Scherer, Sue Thomas, and Robert Voas. "Assessing the Impact of 20 Underage Drinking Laws." *Journal of Studies on Alcohol and Drugs*, 77 (2016): 249–260.

9. Kypros Kypri, Robert B. Voas, John D. Langley, Shaun C. R. Stephenson, Dorothy J. Begg, A. Scott Tippetts, and Gabrielie S. Davie, "Minimum Purchasing Age for Alcohol and Traffic Crash Injuries among 15- to 19-Year-Olds in New Zealand," *American Journal of Public Health* 96, no. 1 (2006): 126–31.

RESOLVED, Congress should pass the Democracy Restoration Act restoring the right to vote in federal elections to people with criminal records

PRO: Erika L. Wood

CON: Roger Clegg

Way back in 1906, the inaugural issue of the *American Political Science Review* featured an essay titled "Negro Suffrage: The Constitutional Point of View," by John Rose, the U.S. district attorney of Baltimore. Rose began by quoting from the Fifteenth Amendment: "The right of citizens of the United States to vote shall not be denied or abridged by the United States or by any State on account of race, color, or previous condition of servitude." The words, Rose said, were "plain. Everybody understands them."[1]

The problem, Rose noted, was that although the amendment plainly prohibited restrictions on the basis of race, it left the qualifications for suffrage in the hands of the states. And while "it might be easy to show" that "colored citizens" had been "interfered with in attempting to exercise their right of suffrage," it was much more difficult to demonstrate that this interference was "on account of" their race or color. In other words, so long as states did not admit to racial motives, the amendment left them free to devise race-neutral qualification requirements that had differential effects on various racial groups.

In South Carolina, Rose pointed out, "a simple education qualification enforced with entire honesty and strict impartiality would disfranchise 60,000 or 70,000 more negroes than Whites. Under universal manhood suffrage there would be a negro majority in that State of upward of 20,000. If the right to vote was limited to those adult males who can both read and write there would be a White majority of nearly 45,000."[2]

Rose cataloged the ways in which southern states, between 1890 and 1905, had revised their constitutions or written new ones that disenfranchised African Americans. Alabama, for instance, adopted a new constitution in 1901 that assessed a poll tax of $1.50 per year, required all voters to be able to read and write, and mandated that individuals could not register to vote unless they had been "engaged in some lawful employment" during the year prior to registering. The employment and literacy requirements were waived for those who owned forty acres of land or had real or personal property worth $300. Moreover, individuals who did not meet the literacy, employment, or property-holding qualifications could still qualify to vote if they were descended from persons who had served in the U.S. or Confederate Army, a provision that enfranchised many poor and illiterate Whites in Alabama but few African Americans.

Making things still more difficult for African American voters was the discretionary power held by local election officials. Alabama's new constitution, for instance, authorized local registrars, if they chose to do so, to require potential voters to name under oath every person they had worked for during the previous five years; those whose statements were not completely accurate could be tried for perjury. Not surprisingly, African American voter turnout plummeted. In 1900, about 180,000 African Americans were registered to vote; by 1903 there were fewer than 5,000.[3]

An additional component of what Rose called the "disfranchising machinery" of the new southern constitutions was the restriction on the right to vote imposed on those men who had been convicted of crimes. There was nothing new about laws requiring disenfranchisement for persons convicted of serious crimes—the practice dated back to English and even Roman law and was commonplace in both northern and southern U.S. states in the decades before the Civil War. But the new southern constitutions expanded the numbers of crimes for which a person could be permanently disenfranchised to include those that were conceived of as "Black" crimes. Mississippi's constitution of 1890, for instance, listed burglary, theft, arson, and bigamy as permanently disenfranchising crimes. Murderers, on the other hand, were still permitted to vote. Alabama's 1901 constitution disenfranchised those convicted of a huge range of offenses, including vagrancy, miscegenation, adultery, sodomy, and any crime involving "moral turpitude."[4]

During the 1960s, the United States abolished many restrictions on suffrage that were race neutral on their face but had racially disparate impacts. In 1964, the Twenty-fourth Amendment abolished the poll tax, and the following year the Voting Rights Act outlawed literacy tests. But laws that disenfranchised criminals have largely been left in place. Today about one in seven Black males in the United States is disenfranchised because of a criminal conviction. In 1985, in *Hunter v. Underwood,* the U.S. Supreme Court did nullify a section of the Alabama constitution that disenfranchised those convicted of misdemeanors involving moral turpitude (the two individuals challenging the law, one Black and one White, had been disenfranchised for writing bad checks) because the Court found that the section had clearly been adopted with the intent of disenfranchising African American voters. However, the courts have consistently upheld bans on felons voting on the grounds that whatever their effects on different racial groups their intent is not racially discriminatory. Even Mississippi's criminal disenfranchisement law was upheld because the law had been changed—among other things, by adding murder and rape to the list of criminal offenses for which a person forfeits the right to vote. These changes, the federal court ruled, removed the "discriminatory taint" of the state's ban on felon voting.[5]

Erika L. Wood argues not just that the courts are wrong to ignore the racially discriminatory consequences of such laws but also that Congress should remedy the problem, at least for felons who have already served their time in prison. Roger Clegg disagrees, arguing that the current laws are not driven by racial animus and that society has every right and many good reasons to disenfranchise those who have been convicted of felonies.

PRO: Erika L. Wood

The right to vote is the foundation of American democracy. It gives Americans a voice in our government and in turn holds our government accountable to the American people. But it has not come easily. Our history is marked by a recurring movement to expand the franchise to include those previously excluded based on race, gender, and class. There remains one significant blanket barrier to the franchise. Nearly six million Americans are denied the right to vote because of criminal convictions in their pasts; more than four million, or 75 percent, of these people are out of prison—living, working, and raising families in our communities—yet they are denied the right to vote for years, often for decades, and sometimes for life.[1]

Criminal disenfranchisement laws differ from state to state.[2] Two states—Maine and Vermont—do not disenfranchise anyone with a criminal conviction; people in prison may vote there. On the other end of the spectrum, four states—Florida, Iowa, Kentucky, and Virginia—currently disenfranchise everyone with a felony conviction for life unless the individual is granted clemency by the governor. The rest of the states fall somewhere in between: thirteen states and the District of Columbia allow people on probation and parole to vote; five states allow individuals to vote while on probation but not while on parole; nineteen states restore voting rights once an individual has completed probation and parole; and seven states permanently disenfranchise those with certain types or numbers of convictions, unless the state approves individual rights restoration.

In recent years, there has been a movement in the states to end criminal disenfranchisement and restore voting rights to those who are living in the community. In the past two decades, more than twenty states have taken either legislative or executive action to allow more people with past criminal convictions to vote, to vote sooner, or to access that right more easily.[3] As a result of these changes, an estimated 800,000 Americans became eligible to vote between 1997 and 2010.[4]

While there has been significant reform since the 1990s, millions of U.S. citizens continue to be denied the right to vote. Congress should pass the Democracy Restoration Act (DRA) to remedy this injustice and provide a uniform federal standard across the country. The DRA would restore voting rights in federal elections to the 4.3 million Americans who are out of prison, living in the community. Specifically, the DRA states, "The right of an individual who is a citizen of the United States to vote in any election for Federal office shall not be denied or abridged because that individual has been convicted of a criminal offense unless such individual is serving a felony sentence in a correctional institution or facility at the time of the election."[5] Passage of the DRA will (1) strengthen our democracy, (2) advance civil rights, (3) protect public safety, and (4) ease election administration.

STRENGTHEN OUR DEMOCRACY

Abraham Lincoln famously described American democracy as "government of the people, by the people, for the people." After centuries of persistent struggle to expand the right to vote, our country is closer to this democratic ideal than ever before. Criminal disenfranchisement laws are one of the last remaining blanket barriers to the ballot box.

In the early days of the American republic, the right to vote was limited to White men who owned property, but over the past two centuries, Americans have fought on the battlefield, in the streets, and in the courtroom to expand suffrage. By 1860, most states had abolished the requirement that a citizen own a minimum amount of real property in order to vote. In 1870, the Fifteenth Amendment proclaimed that the right to vote "shall not be denied or abridged . . . on account of race, color, or previous condition of servitude." Many states, however, found ways to prevent former slaves from voting. Some states imposed literacy tests that required would-be voters to prove that they could read and write, creating a barrier for former slaves, who were largely uneducated. Some enacted "grandfather clauses" under which persons who were eligible to vote prior to 1866 remained eligible, and their lineal descendants were also eligible and exempted from any recent requirements. Thus, if a person's grandfather could vote, he could also vote. Many states also enacted "poll taxes," requiring any would-be voter to pay a fee to the state before being allowed to vote. In reality, these requirements perpetuated the very conditions that the Fifteenth Amendment was intended to eliminate, even though race was never mentioned as a voter qualification.

One by one, these barriers have been struck down. Grandfather clauses were declared unconstitutional in 1915. Five years later, the Nineteenth Amendment extended the right to vote to women. By the mid-1950s, most states had extended suffrage to Native Americans. In 1964, the Twenty-fourth Amendment abolished the poll tax. The following year, the Voting Rights Act outlawed literacy tests and other measures that had long been used to suppress the African American vote. After two centuries of expansion of the franchise, the continuing disenfranchisement of citizens with criminal histories stands in stark contrast to our country's increasingly inclusive vision of democracy.

The widespread policy in the United States of denying the right to vote to people who have been released from prison makes the nation an outlier among modern democracies around the world. In most European countries, people are allowed to vote while serving prison sentences. In some European countries (mainly countries of the former Eastern bloc), people are barred from voting while in prison but are reenfranchised upon release.[6] People in prison are allowed to vote in many other countries, including Israel, South Africa, Canada, and even Iraq.

ADVANCE CIVIL RIGHTS

Criminal disenfranchisement laws have deep roots in the Jim Crow era. In the late 1800s, many of these laws spread as part of a larger backlash against the adoption of the Reconstruction Amendments—the Thirteenth, Fourteenth, and Fifteenth Amendments—which ended slavery, granted equal citizenship to freed slaves, and prohibited racial discrimination in voting practices.

When slavery ended, White elites in many states, particularly—although not exclusively—in the South, sought to hold on to their political power by designing laws that excluded African Americans from the polls. African Americans who tried to register and vote were often subjected to intimidation and violence. The legal barriers discussed above—while race neutral on their face—were put in place intentionally to prevent African Americans from voting.

Felony disenfranchisement laws were a part of this effort. Between 1865 and 1900, twenty-seven states enacted laws restricting the voting rights of people with criminal convictions.[7] At the same time, states expanded their criminal codes to punish offenses that they believed targeted recently freed slaves, including vagrancy, petty larceny, miscegenation, and bigamy. Thus, targeted criminalization and felony disenfranchisement combined to produce a legal loss of voting rights that effectively suppressed the political power of African Americans for decades.

Historical records memorializing state constitutional conventions reveal some astounding rhetoric in support of these laws. During the Virginia Constitutional Convention of 1901, delegate Carter Glass (later a prominent U.S. senator) described the suffrage proposal that included felony disenfranchisement as a plan that would "eliminate the darkey as a political factor in this State in less than 5 years."[8] The strategy was not limited to southern states. In New York, African American suffrage was the subject of much debate at the 1821 and 1846 constitutional conventions. In a refrain that echoes throughout the century-long suffrage debate, New York delegate Samuel Young implored: "Look to your jails and penitentiaries. By whom are they filled? By the very race whom it is now proposed to clothe with the power of deciding upon your political rights."[9]

In an 1896 decision, *Ratliff v. Beale,* the Mississippi Supreme Court confirmed that the new state constitution narrowed the disenfranchisement provision to target crimes of which African American men were then more often convicted. The court explained:

> Within the field of permissible action under the limitations imposed by the federal constitution, the convention swept the circle of expedients to obstruct the exercise of the franchise by the negro race. . . . This race had acquired certain peculiarities of habit, of temperament, and of character, which clearly distinguished it as a race from that of the whites. . . . [C]riminal members [of the negro race are] given rather to furtive offenses than to the robust crimes of the whites. Restrained by the federal constitution from discriminating against the negro race, the convention discriminated against its characteristics and the offenses to which its weaker members were prone.[10]

Today, Mississippi's constitution still denies the right to vote based on the same "furtive offenses."

The disproportionate impact of criminal disenfranchisement laws on minority communities continues to this day. Nationwide, more than two million African American men have lost the right to vote, seven times the number in the non-African American population.[11] Three states—Florida, Kentucky, and Virginia—disenfranchise more than 20 percent of their African American voting-age population.[12]

These statistics mirror stark racial disparities in the criminal justice system. African Americans are seven times more likely than Whites to be incarcerated.[13] Proponents of felony disenfranchisement argue that these disparities are merely the result of a higher propensity among members of minority communities to commit crimes. Yet, the overrepresentation of African Americans in the criminal justice system cannot be explained solely by differing crime rates. For instance, nationwide, 44 percent of those incarcerated on felony drug charges are African American, while African Americans constitute only an estimated 14 percent of monthly drug users.[14] Whites make up only 23 percent of inmates with drug convictions but about 70 percent of monthly users.[15]

Despite this history and continuing impact, legal challenges to criminal disenfranchisement laws have been stymied, making a legislative fix all the more necessary. In 1974, the U.S. Supreme Court decided *Richardson v. Ramirez,* a challenge to California's disenfranchisement laws.[16] The majority opinion relied on an obscure clause of the Fourteenth Amendment to sanction criminal disenfranchisement laws. The Court said that Section 2 of the Fourteenth Amendment, which reduces a state's representation in Congress if the state has denied the right to vote for any reason "except for participation in rebellion, or other crime," distinguishes felony disenfranchisement from other forms of voting restrictions, which must be narrowly tailored to serve compelling state interests in order to be constitutional.

Based on current incarceration rates, three in ten of the next generation of African American men will lose the right to vote at some point in their lives. Passing the DRA is one important step in the movement to correct centuries of organized efforts to disenfranchise African American voters.

PROTECT PUBLIC SAFETY

Critics of the DRA sometimes argue that disenfranchisement is an appropriate punishment for breaking the law. But there is no credible evidence that continuing to disenfranchise people after they are released from prison serves any legitimate law enforcement purpose. To the contrary, many law enforcement officials have come to believe that criminal disenfranchisement laws do more harm than good.

Bringing people into the political process makes them stakeholders in society and helps to steer former offenders away from future crimes. Branding people as political outsiders by denying them the right to vote disrupts reentry into the community. Allowing someone to vote after release from incarceration affirms the returning member's value to the community, encourages participation in civic life, and helps to rebuild ties to fellow citizens.[17]

A number of law enforcement professionals and national organizations support the DRA. In 2010, the executive director of the American Probation and Parole Association, testifying before Congress in support of the bill, stated: "One of the core missions of parole and probation supervision is to support successful transition from prison and jail to the community. Civic participation is an integral part of this transition because it helps transform one's identity from deviant to law-abiding citizen. For this reason, the Democracy Restoration Act is an indispensable part of the re-entry process."[18]

This perspective is confirmed by the experiences of those whose voting rights have been restored following a criminal conviction. One New York resident reflected on voting for the first time in 2008 after having her rights restored: "I've never before felt like I could make a difference in terms of what happens around me. But I walked out of the polling place on Election Day feeling like I mattered, that I made a difference. And I realized how far I've come."[19] A man in Iowa described his experience this way: "The feeling [of voting] was humbling and empowering. The sense of hopelessness and questioning your self-worth seemed to vanish once I had voted. I hope everyone understands the importance of having your citizenship and voting rights restored. It instills a sense of hope and belief that if you do the right thing, society is forgiving and there will be opportunities to succeed."[20]

For all of the history and all of the politics, the right to vote is a very personal piece of empowerment. If we as a society want those who have done wrong to change and do right, then this one act can mean a life change for the half million people who leave prison every year in the United States.

EASE ELECTION ADMINISTRATION

The disenfranchisement by law of nearly six million Americans is only half the story. These laws actually disenfranchise many more eligible voters than the millions who are denied the right to vote by law. Across the country, there is persistent confusion among election officials about their states' criminal disenfranchisement policies. Election officials receive little or no training on these laws, and there is little or no coordination or communication between election offices and the criminal justice system. These factors, coupled with complex laws and registration procedures, result in the mass dissemination of inaccurate and misleading information, as well as the potential that properly registered voters will be purged from the voting rolls.

Interviews with election officials in several states from 2003 to 2008 revealed some startling results:

- Half the election officials interviewed in Colorado did not know that Coloradans on probation could vote, in a state where 46,000 people are currently on probation.[21]

- Half the officials interviewed in Arizona did not know that their state law provides a process for people with more than one conviction to have their voting rights restored.[22]

- One-third of the election officials interviewed in Ohio did not know if individuals with misdemeanor convictions could vote.[23]

- One-third of the election officials in New York, New Jersey, and Washington State said that they would require individuals with felony convictions to provide some kind of documentation before allowing them to register to vote, even though such documentation is not required by law, and in some cases does not even exist.[24]

Administering these complicated laws also creates the opportunity for erroneous "purges" of eligible citizens from the voting rolls. The most notorious example of using felony disenfranchisement laws to purge the rolls occurred in Florida in the period leading up to the 2000 presidential election. Florida's secretary of state implemented a program to purge from Florida's voter rolls any person whose name shared 80 percent of the letters of a name in a nationwide felon database. Under such a system, for example, a Californian with a felony conviction named John Michaelson would cause an eligible Floridian named John Michaels to be removed from the rolls. Not surprisingly, more than half of those who appealed the purge after the 2000 election were deemed eligible to vote, but by then they had already been illegally disenfranchised.[25]

CONGRESSIONAL AUTHORITY

There are two sources in the Constitution for Congress's authority to enact the DRA: the election clause of Article I, Section 4; and Congress's enforcement powers under the Fourteenth and Fifteenth Amendments.[26]

Congress has broad powers to regulate federal elections under the election clause, which states: "The Times, Places and Manner of holding Elections for Senators and Representatives, shall be prescribed in each State by the Legislature thereof; but the Congress may at any time by Law make or alter such Regulations." This clause has consistently been read expansively to include Congress's authority to regulate voting requirements for federal elections, including voter eligibility. In *Oregon v. Mitchell*, the U.S. Supreme Court upheld Congress's ability to lower the voting age in federal elections, and in doing so, clearly endorsed Congress's "ultimate supervisory power" over federal elections, including setting the qualifications for voters.[27]

Congress's enforcement powers under the Fourteenth and Fifteenth Amendments provide an additional basis for congressional authority to enact the DRA. Both amendments grant Congress the power to enforce their provisions "by appropriate legislation." The Supreme Court has described this enforcement power as "a broad power indeed."[28] It is long settled by the Supreme Court that Congress's enforcement powers are a grant of broad authority to eradicate racial discrimination in voting.

In order to fall within Congress's enforcement powers under the Fourteenth Amendment, legislation must exhibit "a congruence and proportionality between the injury to be prevented or remedied and the means adopted to that end."[29] That is, the legislation must be aimed at remedying past constitutional violations, and it must be "an appropriate response" to a "history and pattern of unequal treatment."[30] *Because the DRA protects the right to vote, arguably the most fundamental constitutional right, and attempts to remedy past and present racial discrimination, it meets this legal standard.*

When acting pursuant to the Fifteenth Amendment, Congress's enforcement powers are at their pinnacle because such legislation involves both the fundamental right to vote and the suspect category of race. Legislation enforcing the Fifteenth Amendment is afforded deferential review from the courts because it necessarily protects against racial discrimination and deprivations of the fundamental right to vote.[31]

CONCLUSION

The denial of nearly six million American citizens' right to vote is a national problem that calls for a national solution. Passing the Democracy Restoration Act would eliminate one of the last vestiges of Jim Crow in our country and would adopt the policy that already exists in fifteen states: If a person who was incarcerated has rejoined society, then he or she should have a voice and vote in our political system. As a resident of Tennessee explained after getting his right to vote back: "When you're afforded the opportunity to vote, you think 'I am fully vested in my city, state and country; I'm just as much a citizen as anyone else.' It presents a mindset that looks forward, not backward."[32]

CON: Roger Clegg

Congress should not pass the so-called Democracy Restoration Act (DRA) for two reasons. First, it does not have authority under the Constitution to do so. Second, even if Congress had the authority to pass this bill, it would not be good policy because the matter of felon voting rights is best left to individual states, and there are sound reasons some states may decide that at least some felons should not be allowed to vote.

The heart of the DRA is Section 3, which states, "The right of an individual who is a citizen of the United States to vote in any election for Federal office shall not be denied or abridged because that individual has been convicted of a criminal offense unless such individual is serving a felony sentence in a correctional institution or facility at the time of the election." Thus, with the exception of those currently serving time in prison for a felony conviction, the DRA would require that all persons convicted of crimes—those serving time for misdemeanors, those in "any residential community treatment center" for a felony, those on probation or parole for felonies or misdemeanors, and those who have completed their sentences for felonies or misdemeanors—be allowed to vote in federal elections. Also, since it is logistically difficult for any state to have one voting list, set of ballots, and set of voting booths for federal elections and another for state and local elections, it is likely that this bill would change who is allowed to vote in state and local elections. This is a dramatic change, because currently the vast majority of states bar from voting at least some felons not currently serving time.

LACK OF CONGRESSIONAL AUTHORITY TO ENACT FELON REENFRANCHISEMENT LEGISLATION

There are three theories under which Congress might be asserting constitutional authority for passing this bill. If Congress has authority to pass this bill under Article I, Section 4, of the Constitution, it can simply assert its conclusion that all criminals (excepting felons currently in prison) are entitled to vote. Under this theory, Congress would not rely on any claim that it is addressing racial discrimination. Under the other two theories, Congress could assert authority to pass this bill under the enforcement clause of the Fourteenth or Fifteenth Amendment, either because of the disparate impact that disenfranchisement of felons has on some minority groups or because this disenfranchisement is racially motivated.

Article I, Section 4

Article I, Section 4, of the U.S. Constitution states, "The Times, Places and Manner of holding Elections for Senators and Representatives, shall be prescribed in each State by the Legislature thereof; but the Congress may at any time by Law make or alter such Regulations." Although this section clearly grants Congress the power to regulate the "times, places, and manner" of holding federal elections, it does not give Congress the power to determine who is eligible to vote in these elections. That power is reserved to the states in Article I, Section 2, which provides that electors for the House of Representatives— and, by extension, for all federal elections—"shall have the Qualifications requisite for Electors of the most numerous Branch of the State Legislature." Thus, the Constitution gives authority for determining who can vote to the states.[1] Unless the Constitution is amended to say otherwise, Congress does not have the authority to require that felons be enfranchised.

Moreover, the framers were right to let states determine who should vote. Some states are more conservative than this bill would allow, but at least two are more liberal, and it is not clear why we should insist on a one-size-fits-all approach. The bill's advocates complain about a lack of uniformity, but it is hard to take this complaint seriously when it allows nonuniformity so long as it is in the more liberal direction.

The Fourteenth and Fifteenth Amendments

If Article I, Section 4, does not give Congress the power to trump the states' authority to determine voting qualifications, then we are left with the claim that Congress may pass the DRA under its authority to enforce the Fourteenth and Fifteenth Amendments. Laws that have disparate impact but no discriminatory intent do not violate the Fourteenth and Fifteenth Amendments. The Supreme Court has so held repeatedly with respect to the Fourteenth Amendment. A plurality so held with respect to the Fifteenth Amendment (see *City of Mobile v. Bolden,* 1980), a majority ratified this holding in *Reno v. Bossier Parish School Board* (1997), and it is difficult to see how the standard could be different for one Reconstruction Amendment than for another. When the Supreme Court in *Hunter v. Underwood* (1985) considered a claim that a state law denying the franchise to those convicted of crimes "involving moral turpitude" was unconstitutional race discrimination, it held that "official action will not be held unconstitutional solely because it results in a racially disproportionate impact. . . . Proof of racially discriminatory intent or purpose is required to show a violation of the Equal Protection Clause." Accordingly, Congress cannot assert its enforcement authority if it can point to nothing but disparate impact.

The DRA, however, does not assert that states disenfranchise criminals for racial reasons, nor could this assertion be plausibly made. To begin with, Section 2 of the Fourteenth Amendment itself contemplates disenfranchisement. It acknowledges that "the right to vote" may be "abridged . . . for participation in rebellion, or other crime." Surely this is recognition in the most relevant part of the Constitution that there are typically nonracial reasons for disenfranchising criminals.

That an overwhelming number of states have passed criminal disenfranchisement laws also indicates that something other than racial discrimination is the motive. Rather, as the Sentencing Project and Human Rights Watch—vigorous supporters of felon reenfranchisement—acknowledge, "disenfranchisement in the U.S. is a heritage from ancient Greek and Roman traditions carried into Europe." In Europe, the civil disabilities attached to conviction for a felony were severe, and "English colonists brought these concepts with them to North America."[2] Consider the following: (1) only two New England states—Maine and Vermont—allow all felons to vote, (2) thirty-one states prohibit felons who are on probation from voting, (3) thirty-five states prohibit felons who are on parole from voting, and (4) the states with lifetime voting bans are hardly the old Confederacy. Indeed, only two states in the old Confederacy (Virginia and Florida) disenfranchise all felons—and there the governors have frequently reenfranchised felons. A majority of the states in the old Confederacy do allow felons to vote so long as they are no longer in prison, on parole, or on probation. It is true that, between 1890 and 1910, five southern states (Alabama, Louisiana, Mississippi, South Carolina, and Virginia) tailored their criminal disenfranchisement laws to increase their effects on black citizens—but those laws are no longer on the books.

Writing in the *American Sociological Review,* proponents of felon enfranchisement Christopher Uggen and Jeff Manza concede that restrictions on felon voting "were first adopted by some states in the post-Revolutionary era, and by the eve of the Civil War some two dozen states had statutes barring felons from voting or had felon disenfranchisement provisions in their state constitutions."[3] That means that more than 70 percent of the states had these laws by 1861—when most blacks could not vote anyway because they were enslaved or lived in northern states that denied them the franchise on the basis of their race. In 1855, only five states, all in New England, did not exclude blacks from voting on the basis of race.[4] Historian Alexander Keyssar confirms that outside the South criminal disenfranchisement laws "lacked socially distinct targets."[5] Even in the post–Civil War South, Keyssar finds, in some states "felon disfranchisement provisions were first enacted [by] Republican governments that supported black voting rights."[6]

In *City of Boerne v. Flores* (1997), which dealt with Congress's enforcement powers under the Reconstruction Amendments, the Supreme Court declared, "There must be a congruence and proportionality between the injury to be prevented or remedied and the means adopted to that end." There is no "congruence and proportionality" between guaranteeing people the right to vote irrespective of race and a requirement that criminals be allowed to vote, just because there happens to be at any moment a racial imbalance among felons.

If there were evidence that a state's felon disenfranchisement law had discriminatory roots, it would be a straightforward matter for the well-funded organizations that oppose these laws to challenge that law in court. This has not occurred, and the reason is that the evidence is not there. If such evidence existed, there would be no reason for the DRA to be limited to federal elections.

POLICY OBJECTIONS TO FELON REENFRANCHISEMENT

Even if Congress had authority to pass the DRA, it should not. There are compelling arguments in favor of disenfranchising felons—certainly strong enough to refute a claim that Congress must intervene to prevent some sort of irrational malfeasance in the states by dictating a one-size-fits-all national policy. Conversely, the policy arguments in favor of enfranchising felons are unpersuasive.

The Arguments against Felon Voting Are Strong

Those who are not willing to follow the law cannot claim a right to make the law for everyone else. And when you vote, you are indeed making the law—either directly, in a ballot initiative or referendum, or indirectly, by choosing lawmakers.

Not everyone in the United States may vote—not children, for example, or noncitizens, or the mentally incompetent, or criminals. We have certain minimum, objective standards of responsibility, trustworthiness, and commitment to our laws for those who would participate in the solemn enterprise of self-government. And it is not unreasonable to suppose that those who have committed serious crimes against their fellow citizens may be presumed—until they have shown otherwise—to lack this responsibility, trustworthiness, and commitment. Should children be voting? The mentally incompetent? People who are not citizens? People who refuse to follow the law and harm their fellow citizens? Of course not.

The Arguments in Favor of Felon Voting Are Weak

The arguments in favor of felon voting are unpersuasive. Here are four of the most commonly heard arguments in favor of felon voting.

"Once released from prison, a felon has paid his debt to society and is entitled to the full rights of citizenship." This rationale would apply only to felons no longer in prison, of course, and would arguably not apply to felons on parole or probation. Even for these "former" felons, the argument is not persuasive. Although serving a sentence discharges a felon's "debt to society" in the sense that his basic right to live in society is restored, serving a sentence does not require society to forget what the felon has done or bar society from making judgments based on his past crimes.

For example, federal law prohibits felons from possessing firearms or serving on juries, which does not seem unreasonable. Here is a more dramatic example: Most would agree that a public school ought to be able to refuse to hire a convicted child molester, even after he has been released from prison. In fact, there are a whole range of "civil disabilities" for felons after prison release as a result of federal and state law. Society is not required, nor should it be required, to ignore someone's criminal record once that person gets out of prison.

Finally, it is unlikely that those on the other side of the aisle really take this argument seriously. If they did, then presumably they would agree that if a felon has *not* paid his debt to society, then he should *not* be able to vote. But this is frequently not the case. Marc Mauer, executive director of the Sentencing Project, for example, believes that "people in prison should have the right to vote."[7]

"Disenfranchisement is a disproportionate penalty." Common sense would dictate that some felons be allowed to vote and others not. Some crimes are worse than others, some felons have committed more crimes than others, and some crimes are recent while others are long past. At one extreme, it is hard to see why a man who wrote a bad check in 1953 and has had a spotless record since then should not be entrusted with the franchise. At the other extreme, however, it is hard to see why a man just released after serving time for espionage and treason, and after earlier convictions for murder, rape, and voter fraud, should be permitted to vote.

Yes, not all crimes are equal, even among felons, and one cannot presume that all felons are equally to be mistrusted with the ballot. But it does not follow that therefore all felons should be allowed to vote. Rather, it would be more prudent to distinguish among various crimes, such as serious crimes like murder, rape, treason, and espionage on one hand and marijuana possession on the other; between crimes recently committed and crimes committed in the distant past; and among those who have committed many crimes and those who have committed only one.

But this line drawing is precisely why the matter should be left to the states, and why it should be applied on a case-by-case basis. It would be difficult for Congress to undertake this power because, for one thing, every state has its own array of criminal offenses. Further, these offenses are constantly changing, so Congress would have to be constantly updating any statute it wrote drawing distinctions among various crimes. It would also be difficult to draft a statute drawing intelligent lines with respect to the recentness of crimes and the number of crimes committed.

"These laws have a disproportionate racial impact." Undoubtedly the reason that there is such interest in this subject is that a disproportionate percentage of felons are African Americans. But, as discussed earlier, the racial impact of these laws is irrelevant as a constitutional matter. It should also be irrelevant as a matter of policy. Legislators should determine what the qualifications or disqualifications for voting are and then let the chips fall where they may. In *The Souls of Black Folk*, W. E. B. Du Bois wrote, "Draw lines of crime, of incompetency, of vice, as tightly and uncompromisingly as you will, for these things must be proscribed; but a color-line not only does not accomplish this purpose, but thwarts it."[8]

The fact that these statutes disproportionately disenfranchise men and young people is not cited as a reason for changing them—as "sexist" or "ageist"—nor does it matter that some racial or ethnic groups may be more affected than others. That criminals are "overrepresented" in some groups and "underrepresented" in others is no reason to change the laws. This will probably always be the case, with the groups changing with time and with the country's demography. If large numbers of young people, black people, or males are committing crimes, then our efforts should be focused on solving those problems. It is bizarre instead to increase criminals' political power.

Much has been made of the high percentage of criminals—and, thus, disenfranchised people—in some communities. But the fact that the effects of disenfranchisement may be concentrated in particular neighborhoods is actually an argument in the laws' favor. If these laws did not exist there would be a real danger of creating an anti–law enforcement voting bloc in local municipal elections, for example, which is hardly in the interests of a neighborhood's law-abiding citizens. Indeed, the people whose votes will be diluted the most if criminals are allowed to vote will be law-abiding people in high-crime areas—people who are themselves disproportionately poor and members of minority groups. Somehow, the liberal civil rights groups often forget about them.

"We should welcome felons back into the community." The DRA suggests that reenfranchising felons is a good way to reintegrate them into society. This should not be done automatically, however, but rather carefully and on a case-by-case basis, once it is shown that the felon has in fact turned over a new leaf. When that has been shown, then holding a ceremony—rather like a naturalization ceremony—in which the felon's voting rights are fully restored would be moving and meaningful.

The restoration should not be automatic because the change of heart cannot be presumed. Richard Freeman of Harvard University and the National Bureau of Economic Research has found that "two-thirds of released prisoners are re-arrested and one-half are reincarcerated within 3 years of release from prison. . . . Rates of recidivism necessarily rise thereafter, so that upwards of 75%–80% of released prisoners are likely to be re-arrested within a decade of release."[9]

Felon reenfranchisement sends a bad message: We do not consider criminal behavior such a serious matter that the right to vote should be denied because of it.

CONCLUSION

In sum, Congress does not have authority to pass the DRA, and even if it did, it would be unwise to do so.

NOTES

INTRO

1.   John C. Rose, "Negro Suffrage: The Constitutional Point of View," *American Political Science Review* (November, 1906): 17.
2.   Ibid., 23–24.

3. Ibid., 24, 28, 31.

4. Ibid., 25. See also Alexander Keyssar, *The Right to Vote: The Contested History of Democracy in the United States* (New York, NY: Basic Books, 2000), 62–63, 307, Table A.15; Wayne Flynt, "A Legacy of Shame," speech delivered at the Rally for Constitutional Reform, Tuscaloosa, AL, April 7, 2000, http://www. constitutionalreform.org/archive/speeches/speech_wf.html; Alex C. Ewald, "'Civil Death': The Ideological Paradox of Criminal Disenfranchisement Law in the United States," *Wisconsin Law Review* (2002): 1090–95. Northern states were far from immune to this trend of expanding disenfranchising crimes in ways that disproportionately affected non-Whites. See Erika Wood and Liz Budnitz, *Jim Crow in New York* (New York, NY: Brennan Center for Justice, New York University School of Law, 2009), http://brennan.3cdn.net/50080b21f7f0197339_ z7m6i20ud.pdf.

5. Keyssar, *The Right to Vote*, 306, 308.

PRO

1. Christopher Uggen, Sarah Shannon, and Jeff Manza, *State-Level Estimates of Felon Disenfranchisement in the United States, 2010* (Washington, DC: Sentencing Project, 2010), 5, http://sentencingproject.org/doc/publications/fd_State_Level_ Estimates_of_Felon_Disen_2010.pdf.

2. The Brennan Justice Center at New York University School of Law provides a map that details the different felony disenfranchisement laws across the country; see http://www.brennancenter.org/page/-/democracy/usa%20map%20 3.23.2011.pdf.

3. Myrna Perez, Tomas Lopez, and Vishal Agraharkar, *The Sustained Momentum and Growing Bipartisan Consensus for Voting Rights Restoration* (Brennan Center for Justice, 2015), https://www.brennancenter.org/analysis/sustained- momentum-and-growing-bipartisan-consensus-voting-rights-restoration#_ ednref3.

4. Nicole Porter, *Expanding the Vote* (Washington, DC: Sentencing Project, 2010), 2. Three states have recently restricted voting rights. In 2011, the governors of Iowa and Florida rolled back recent reforms to their criminal disenfranchisement laws. In Iowa, Governor Terry Branstad reversed an executive order signed in 2005 by Governor Tom Vilsack that had automatically restored voting rights upon completion of sentence. See Lee Rowland, "A Dark Day for Democracy in Iowa," *Huffington Post*, January 25, 2011, http://www.huffingtonpost.com/lee-rowland/a-dark-day-for- democracy-_b_813957.html. In Florida, Governor Rick Scott reversed reforms put in place by his predecessor, Governor Charlie Crist, that had streamlined the restoration process for many individuals with nonviolent convictions. See Erika Wood, "Turning Back the Clock in Florida," *Huffington Post*, March 10, 2011, http://www.huffingtonpost.com/erika-wood/turning-back-the-clock- in_b_834239.html; and Erika Wood, "Florida Elections: How Soon We Forget,"

New York Times, April 5, 2012, http://campaignstops.blogs.nytimes
.com/2012/04/05/florida-how-quickly-we-forget. Most recently, in 2012, South
Dakota passed legislation that denied voting rights to people on probation and
parole. S.D. Codified Laws § 12-4-18.

5. Bill text, 114th Congress (2015–2016), S.772/H.R.1459, https://www.congress
.gov/bill/114th-congress/house-bill/1459.

6. Laleh Ispahani, *Out of Step with the World: An Analysis of Felony
Disenfranchisement in the U.S. and Other Democracies* (New York, NY: American
Civil Liberties Union, 2006), 3–4, http://www.aclu.org/images/asset_upload_
file825_25663.pdf.

7. Alexander Keyssar, *The Right to Vote: The Contested History of Democracy in the
United States* (New York, NY: Basic Books, 2009), Table A.15.

8. *Report of the Proceedings and Debates of the Constitutional Convention, State of
Virginia* (Richmond, VA: Hermitage Press, 1906), 3076.

9. *Reports of the Proceedings and Debates of the New York Constitutional Convention
of 1821, Assembled for the Purpose of Amending the Constitution of the State of
New-York* (Albany, NY: E. & E. Hosford, 1821), 178, 191. For a thorough
examination of the history of New York's criminal disenfranchisement law, see
Erika Wood and Liz Budnitz, *Jim Crow in New York* (New York: New York
University School of Law, Brennan Center for Justice, 2009), http://brennan.3cdn
.net/50080b21f7f0197339_z7m6i20ud.pdf.

10. *Ratliff v. Beale,* 20 So. 865, 868 (1896).

11. "Felony Disenfranchisement Laws in the United States," *Sentencing Project,*
August 2012, 1, http://www.sentencingproject.org/doc/publications/publications/
fd_bs_fdlawsinus_Sep2012.pdf.

12. Ibid.

13. Marc Mauer, *Race to Incarcerate* (New York, NY: New Press, 2006), 139.

14. Marc Mauer, *The Changing Racial Dynamics of the War on Drugs* (Washington,
DC: Sentencing Project, 2009), 6–7, http://www.sentencingproject.org/doc/dp_
raceanddrugs.pdf.

15. Ibid.

16. *Richardson v. Ramirez,* 418 U.S. 24 (1974).

17. For more information on law enforcement support for restoring voting rights, see
Erika Wood, *Restoring the Right to Vote* (New York, NY: Brennan Center for
Justice, New York University School of Law, 2009), 9–11, http://www
.brennancenter.org/content/resource/restoring_the_right_to_vote. See also "Law
Enforcement and Criminal Justice Advisory Council," *Brennan Center for Justice,*
New York University School of Law, http://www.brennancenter.org/content/
pages/law_enforcement_criminal_justice_advisory_council.

18. Testimony of Carl Wicklund, executive director, American Probation and Parole
Association, before the Judiciary Committee, Constitution, Civil Rights, and
Civil Liberties Subcommittee, U.S. House of Representative, March 16, 2010,
http://brennan.3cdn.net/047d04ef2d0893df95_t8m6y9g01.pdf.

19. Right to Vote Project, *My First Vote* (New York, NY: Brennan Center for Justice, New York University School of Law, 2009), 2, http://www.brennancenter.org/content/resource/my_first_vote.

20. Ibid., 5.

21. Erika Wood and Rachel Bloom, *De Facto Disenfranchisement* (New York, NY: Brennan Center for Justice, New York University School of Law, and American Civil Liberties Union, 2009), 3, http://www.brennancenter.org/content/resource/de_facto_disenfranchisement.

22. Ibid., 4.

23. Ibid., 3.

24. Ibid., 6.

25. John Lantigua, "How the GOP Gamed the System in Florida," *The Nation*, April 30, 2001, 11. See also Myrna Perez, *Voter Purges* (New York, NY: Brennan Center for Justice, New York University School of Law, 2008), http://www.brennancenter.org/content/resource/voter_purges.

26. For a thorough analysis of Congress's power to pass the DRA, see the testimony of Professor Burt Neuborne before the Judiciary Committee, Constitution, Civil Rights, and Civil Liberties Subcommittee, U.S. House of Representative, March 16, 2010, http://brennan.3cdn.net/d232cc12cbcdfda443_u5m6bxvto.pdf.

27. *Oregon v. Mitchell*, 400 U.S. 112, 121, 124 (1970). See also *Kusper v. Pontikes*, 414 U.S. 51, 57 N.11 (1973).

28. *Tennessee v. Lane*, 541 U.S. 509, 518, 520 (2004).

29. *Boerne v. Flores*, 521 U.S. 507, 520 (1997).

30. *Tennessee*, 541 U.S. at 509, 518, 520.

31. Some may argue that Section 2 of the Fourteenth Amendment and the Supreme Court's decision in *Richardson v. Ramirez* limit Congress's enforcement authority, but reliance on *Richardson* is misguided, because the DRA is legislation aimed at remedying past and current racial discrimination in the voting system. Even if Section 2 were found to somehow limit Congress's power, the Fifteenth Amendment's subsequent broad ban on race discrimination in voting carries no such exception.

32. Denver Schimming, Goodlettsville, Tennessee, quoted in Wood, *Restoring the Right to Vote*, 8.

CON

1. This is clearly how the framers understood these two sections of Article I. In *Federalist* No. 60, Alexander Hamilton explained that under Article I, Section 4, the national government's "authority would be expressly restricted to the regulation of the times, the places, and the manner of elections. The qualifications of the persons who may choose or be chosen . . . are defined and fixed in the Constitution, and are unalterable by the legislature." In *Federalist* No. 52, James Madison wrote of Article I, Section 2, "To have left [the definition of the right of suffrage] open for the occasional regulation of the Congress would

have been improper." Any doubt on this point was laid to rest by the Supreme Court in *Arizona v. Inter Tribal Council of Arizona* (2013), as discussed in Hans A. von Spakovsky and Roger Clegg, *Felon Voting and Unconstitutional Overreach* (Heritage Foundation, February 11, 2015), 5-6, http://www.heritage.org/research/reports/2015/02/felon-voting-and-unconstitutional-congressional-overreach.

2. Jamie Fellner and Marc Mauer, *Losing the Vote: The Impact of Felony Disenfranchisement Laws in the United States* (Washington, DC: Sentencing Project, 1998), 2, http://www.sentencingproject.org/doc/File/FVR/fd_losingthevote.pdf.

3. Christopher Uggen and Jeff Manza, "Democratic Contraction? Political Consequences of Felon Disenfranchisement in the United States," *American Sociological Review* 67 (December 2002): 781.

4. Alexander Keyssar, *The Right to Vote: The Contested History of Democracy in the United States* (New York, NY: Basic Books, 2000), 55.

5. Ibid., 162.

6. Alexander Keyssar, "Did States Restrict the Voting Rights of Felons on Account of Racism?," *History News Network*, October 3, 2004, http://hnn.us/articles/7635.html. See also Richard M. Re and Christopher M. Re, "Voting and Vice: Criminal Disenfranchisement and the Reconstruction Amendments," *Yale Law Journal* 121 (2012): 1584–1670; and John Dinan, "The Adoption of Criminal Disenfranchisement Provisions in the United States: Lessons from the State Constitutional Convention Debates," *Journal of Policy History* 19 (2007): 282–312.

7. The "paid his debt to society" metaphor is inapt anyhow. *See* Roger Clegg, "The Fox Is Guarding the Henhouse," *Center for Equal Opportunity* (May 6, 2013), http://www.ceousa.org/issues/693-the-fox-is-guarding-the-henhouse.

8. W. E. B. Du Bois, *The Souls of Black Folk* (1903; Rockville, MD: Arc Manor, 2008), 123.

9. Richard Freeman, "Can We Close the Revolving Door? Recidivism vs. Employment of Ex-Offenders in the U.S." (discussion paper presented at the Urban Institute Reentry Roundtable, New York University Law School, May 19–20, 2003), 2, http://www.urban.org/UploadedPDF/410857_freeman.pdf. It is sometimes asserted that felon reenfranchisement leads to less recidivism, but this assertion is dubious, as discussed by Clegg and Spakovsky, *Felon Voting and Unconstitutional Overreach*, 10.

RESOLVED, states should enact voter ID laws and reduce early voting

PRO: Michael Nelson

CON: Keith Gunnar Bentele and Erin O'Brien

Voter fraud has a long and colorful history in the United States. "Vote early and often" they used to say in machine-controlled cities like Chicago. So called "repeaters" were allegedly paid by New York's Tammany Hall machine to cast votes pretending to be people who had recently died. Some localities had voting rates approaching or exceeding 100 percent. Stuffing ballot boxes with fraudulent votes was undeniably an important part of the American way of democracy. Some even think that John F. Kennedy beat Richard Nixon in the 1960 presidential race through fraudulent votes in Texas.

If voter fraud is an integral part of American history, voter suppression of minority votes is even more tightly woven into the history of American democracy. Poll taxes (outlawed by the 24th Amendment in 1964), literacy tests (outlawed by the Voting Rights Act in 1965), and voter intimidation are only a few of the ways in which White Americans ensured that Black Americans did not exercise their right to vote.

Concerns about voter fraud have often been closely linked with concerns about the political influence of ethnic or racial minority voters. In the late nineteenth and early twentieth centuries, Progressive reformers concerned about corruption and the electoral strength of new immigrants pushed state laws that required citizens who wanted to vote to register prior to the Election Day. These new voter registration requirements reduced fraudulent voting, but they also contributed to a steep decline in voting rates in the early decades of the twentieth century. Voter fraud had been checked but at the expense of keeping "large numbers (probably millions) of eligible voters from the polls."[1]

For the last several decades, concerns about voter fraud have largely been voiced by Republicans. When Congress debated the National Voter

Registration Act (a.k.a., the "Motor Voter" law because it allowed citizens to register to vote at the DMV when renewing their drivers licenses), Republican Representative David Dreier denounced the NVRA as "the National Voter Fraud Act" and maintained that it would provide "cover to corrupt officials that pad the voter rolls with deceased and nonexistent officials."[2] Republican critics of the law, which was passed by a Democratic Congress and signed into law by Democratic President Bill Clinton in 1993, probably worried less about fraud than they did that the law would boost Democratic turnout, particularly because it allowed citizens to register at welfare offices.

The battle over requiring voter IDs (and how strict these should be) and allowing early voting (and how many days should be allowed) are only the latest episodes in the long and contested history of voting rights in the United States. Not surprisingly, partisan interests have never been far from this long running debate about whether we should prioritize expanding voter access or reducing the possibility of voter fraud. The battle over voter IDs and early voting, like the dispute over registration requirements in the 1890s and the NVRA in the 1990s, is strongly partisan. Believing that expanding voter access will help them, Democrats back early voting and resist strict voter ID requirements; fearing that an expanded electorate will hurt them, Republicans resist the expansion of early voting and favor establishing voter ID requirements.

Michael Nelson asks us to set aside partisanship for a moment and consider the arguments on their merits. After all, voter IDs are commonplace in Europe where turnout is much higher. Moreover, despite Democratic fears of voter suppression, he maintains that there is little evidence that voter ID requirements have reduced turnout. He also asks us to think twice about the wisdom of early voting. It may boost turnout all right but at the cost of being able to take into account new information that comes to light in the days before Election Day. More people voting in ignorance of the candidates' foibles and positions hardly seems like a plus for democracy.

Keith Gunnar Bentele and Erin O'Brien present a very different perspective. There is, they argue, no convincing evidence that voter fraud is a problem today—unlike in the late nineteenth century. Requiring voter IDs is a solution without a problem, and thus, it makes no sense to set aside the partisan motives, particularly when those motives are so closely entangled with racial ones. In their view, voter IDs have nothing to do with ensuring the integrity of the voting process and everything to do with shutting out minority voters. And it is no coincidence, they add, that Republicans have taken aim at early voting, a voting mechanism used disproportionately by African American voters. They contend that a nation committed to civil rights is a nation that should be committed to expanding early voting and rolling back voter ID laws.

PRO: Michael Nelson

S howing a driver's license or other government-issued photo identification card is an ordinary feature of modern life in the United States. Try boarding a plane without one. Or buying an M-rated video game. Or renting a hotel room. Adopting a pet. Opening a bank account. Cashing a check. Picking up a prescription. Buying Sudafed over the counter. Or, if you are poor, applying for food stamps or Medicaid. I'm sixty-seven years old, but I get carded every time I order a beer or buy a bottle of wine.

None of these things needed an official photo ID a few decades ago, but now we take the requirement for granted. Clearly every twenty-first century American needs a photo ID just to function in our society, and almost anything that encourages them to get one is good—including an obligation that you show a photo ID to demonstrate that you are the registered voter you say you are before you're allowed to cast a vote in an election.

Yet critics of requiring voters to prove their identity at the polls, as a growing number of states do, argue that it's a purely partisan effort by Republicans to disenfranchise pro-Democratic constituencies, especially African Americans and Latinos, most of whom are presumed (by Democrats) to be Democrats.

These critics constitute a loud but relatively small share of the American people. Surveys of public opinion during the past decade have consistently shown that more than 70 percent of Americans support requiring voters "to show official, government-issued photo identification" (the wording in *Washington Post* polls on the subject) when they present themselves to vote.[1] What's more, critics of the photo ID requirement represent a minority even of those for whom they claim to speak. Despite the chorus of complaint that photo ID laws are aimed at Democrats, African Americans, and Latinos, all three groups of voters support them: self-identified Democrats by about 60 percent, Latinos by about 65 percent, and African Americans by 65 percent or more.[2]

THE CASE FOR PHOTO IDS

Of course, being outnumbered on an issue doesn't always mean you're wrong. So let's look at the facts.

For starters, proposals to require voters to show photo IDs are not some partisan Republican scheme. In 2005, the *nonpartisan* Commission on Federal Election Reform, which was headed by former president Jimmy Carter, a Democrat, and former secretary of state James A. Baker III, a Republican, recommended that states legislate a photo ID requirement. According to its final report, the Commission's purpose was "to make sure that the person arriving at a polling site is the same one that is named on the registration list."

Why was this a big deal? First, the Commission argued, whether or not voter fraud is widespread, "in close or disputed elections, and there are many, a small amount of fraud could make the margin of difference. And second, the perception of possible fraud contributes to low confidence in the system." With poor people in mind, the Commission added, such an "ID should be easily available and issued free of charge" to those who need but cannot afford one.[3]

Seventeen states currently have photo ID laws in effect. In keeping with the Commission's recommendation—as well as with the general societal trend toward requiring photo IDs for more and more activities—most of these states created theirs starting in 2005. Nearly one-fourth of the photo ID-mandating states are solidly "blue"—that is, they voted for the Democratic nominee in all five presidential elections from 1992 to 2012. Another sixteen states allow voters to present a nonphoto form of identification, such as a recent bank statement that shows their name and address. Remarkably, all the other states allow people to vote without showing any ID at all.

Part of the critics' argument is that requiring people to present a photo ID before voting is unconstitutional. Not so. In 2005, Indiana passed one of the strictest photo ID laws in the country. It stipulated that the only acceptable IDs are those issued by the state of Indiana or the U.S. government and that they must display an expiration date (which, regrettably, most student IDs do not, the main reason these IDs often do not qualify). The law allowed those who could not produce proof of identification to cast a provisional ballot that would be counted if they went to their local court house no later than the following Monday with the required identification. Free IDs were available to those who wanted them.

A Democratic member of the Indiana House of Representatives named William Crawford challenged the legality of his state's new law, and the dispute went all the way to the Supreme Court. In the 2008 case of *Crawford v. Marion County Election Board*, the justices validated Indiana's law by a vote of 6 to 3. The author of the majority opinion was John Paul Stevens, one of the more liberal members of the Court. Justice Stevens wrote,

> Because Indiana's [ID] cards are free, the inconvenience of going to the Bureau of Motor Vehicles, gathering required documents, and posing for a photograph does not qualify as a substantial burden on most voters' right to vote, or represent a significant increase over the usual burdens of voting. The severity of the somewhat heavier burden that may be placed on a limited number of persons—e.g., elderly persons born out-of-state,

who may have difficulty obtaining a birth certificate—is mitigated by the fact that eligible voters without photo identification may cast provisional ballots that will be counted if they execute the required affidavit at the circuit court's office.[4]

Critics of the Supreme Court's *Crawford* decision and the Indiana law (as well as of an equally strict one implemented the same year in Georgia) predicted calamitous consequences on Election Day 2008. Black turnout would be suppressed in those states, they argued, because so many African Americans were thought to lack a valid photo ID.

What actually *did* happen in Georgia and Indiana? According to a study by the Reuters News Agency, more African Americans voted in both states than ever before.[5] In Georgia, which records the race of every registered voter, Black registration soared by 30 percent in 2008, and the percentage of registered African American voters who cast a ballot in the election rose from 72 percent (the turnout rate in 2004, before Georgia's photo ID law took effect) to 76 percent.

Well, critics said, the 2008 election wasn't a fair test because Barack Obama, the first African American ever nominated for president by a major political party, was on the ballot. That argument was plausible, but only for two years. In the 2010 midterm election, in which Obama was not a candidate, Black voter turnout in Georgia rose 7 percentage points above the previous midterm election in 2006.

Indiana does not register voters by race, but Reuters found that, as in Georgia, voter turnout in the state's most minority-intensive counties rose in 2008. As in Georgia, too, minority turnout also increased in the 2010 midterm election.

Additional examples abound of Black voter turnout rising, not falling as alarmist critics predicted, in states with new photo ID laws. Consider, in 2015, the *Washington Post* reported, "Lawyers and civil rights officials suing North Carolina speak in historic and apocalyptic terms" about the state's new photo ID law. "The striking slogan they have adopted: 'Our Selma,'" invoking the brutal beatings that law enforcement officers inflicted on peaceful voting rights marchers in Selma, Alabama, in 1965. A U.S. Justice Department lawyer participating in the North Carolina case argued in federal district court that the state's new law should be invalidated because "the discriminatory effects of [the statute] were neither accidental nor unforeseen."[6]

In truth, the effects of the statute on voter turnout were nonexistent. In the 2014 midterm election (the first election to which the new law applied), the *Post* reported, "Despite dire predictions from experts about what the changes would mean for minority turnout, African American participation actually increased from the last non-presidential election year, 2010." In an understatement, the *Post* called this "an inconvenient fact for the [law's] challengers."[7]

As for the country as a whole, in the 2012 presidential election, the first to occur after the decade-long trend toward stricter voter identification laws culminated, the turnout rate for African Americans exceeded, by 2 percentage points, that of Whites for the first time in history.[8]

THE CASE AGAINST PROLONGED EARLY VOTING

Efforts in certain states to reduce the period allowed for early voting—that is, appearing in person to vote before Election Day—have also come under fire from liberals and Democrats. Thirty-three states permit early voting in a pre-election period that lasts an average of twenty-two days (and in one state lasts forty-five days). In not a single one of these states is there a plan to eliminate early voting entirely.

Early voting—much less several weeks of it—hardly constitutes a fundamental right or a deeply rooted American tradition. Not that long ago, the practice did not even exist. One good reason for limiting the early voting period to about ten days (as a few states already have done) is that election campaigns continue and new information becomes available to voters right up until the day of the election. Voting too early means cutting oneself off from the possibility that this information might cause one to change one's mind about which candidates to support.

Nonetheless, fault finders raise the same alarms about limiting early voting as they do about requiring photo IDs: namely, that the Democrats will suffer because reducing the length of the early voting period will reduce minority turnout. One problem with this argument is that in North Carolina, Wisconsin, and Ohio—three states that actually did shorten the early voting period in advance of the 2014 midterm election—no decline in Black turnout occurred compared with 2010, the most recent previous midterm election.[9] A second problem is that of the states that allow no early voting at all, a majority are strongly Democratic, including New York, Connecticut, and Massachusetts.

MAKING VOTING EASIER DOES NOT CAUSE MORE PEOPLE TO VOTE

Two dubious premises underlie critics' arguments against recent efforts to tighten ballot security. The first is that fraudulent voting is virtually nonexistent because so few people have been caught doing it. But isn't that what one would expect when voting rules are so lax as to allow people to easily get away with, say, casting a ballot in more than one place or voting even though one isn't a citizen? What do such critics make of the recent study by political scientists Jesse Richman, Gulshan Chattha, and David Earnest, whose analysis of data from the Cooperative Congressional Election Study found that 6.4 percent of *non*-citizens voted in 2008?[10] Or of the 2012 study by the Pew Center on the States that found the following:

- Approximately 24 million—one of every eight—voter registrations in the United States are no longer valid or are significantly inaccurate.

- More than 1.8 million deceased individuals are listed as voters.

- Approximately 2.7 million people have registered in more than one state.[11]

Critics' second dubious premise is that if you make something easier—in this case, voting—you are certain to get more of it. In truth, a quarter century of making voting easier and seeing turnout drop in most states should disabuse us of this notion.

Registering to vote used to be hard. As recently as 1968, a strong majority of states insisted that one live in a state for anywhere from six months to two years (and in a county within that state for, typically, six months) in order to be eligible to vote there.[12] Once you became eligible, the act of registering always meant showing up in person and usually meant going to the county seat, where the registration office was only open on weekdays during normal business hours.

In 1993, spurred on by President Bill Clinton, Congress passed the National Voter Registration Act. Better known as "Motor Voter," the new law required states to offer registration opportunities at public assistance offices when people applied for welfare, food stamps, or Medicaid and at motor vehicle bureaus when people went in for a driver's license. It also required that states allow people to register by mail. Constitutionally, the new federal law could only apply to federal elections for senator, representative, and president, but as Congress well understood, states would find it impossible to maintain a separate registration system for their own state and local elections, which meant that, in practice, the law would apply to all contests.

The result of Motor Voter was not greater voter turnout in the next presidential election but instead the lowest turnout rate since 1924. Forty-nine percent of the voting age population participated in the 1996 election, down from 55 percent in 1992, the steepest decline in turnout from one election to the next in almost three-fourths of a century. Despite continuing population growth, the actual number of votes declined by 8 million. In time, it became apparent that the turnout rate for those who register in welfare or motor vehicle offices is considerably lower than for other registrants.[13]

Is this so surprising? Not in the United States. Some countries, including Australia, define voting as a duty of citizenship and impose fines on those who fail to cast a ballot. But, for better or worse, in American political culture and practice, voting is considered a right. Because it is a right—and therefore something that each individual can either choose to exercise or not—voting in America is a voluntary act. People have to feel a sense of personal commitment to get out and vote as a responsibility freely assumed. And what gives people that sense of commitment to this or any other practice? Their sense of personal investment—that is, the effort they put into it. No pain, no gain is more than a locker room axiom. It is a basic psychological truth.

With this understanding in mind, it's not hard to see why voter turnout rates were higher a half century ago, when registering and voting took more effort than they do now. As political scientists Raymond E. Wolfinger and Jonathan Hoffman found, "people for whom registration is costless are unlikely to exert themselves to vote."[14] Fill out a voter eligibility form when you're already at the motor vehicle bureau to get a driver's license or at the welfare office to get food stamps and there is a good chance you won't even remember doing so, much less feel that you've invested something of yourself in the act. Take time off from work to go to the county courthouse and register—or get the free photo ID that will permit you to vote—and securing that right will mean something.

Similarly, allowing people to decide when in a prolonged early voting period to vote increases the likelihood that, notwithstanding good intentions, they never will actually get around to it. Make people vote on the first Tuesday after the first Monday in November (unless they have a good excuse, such as illness, disability, or travel), and there is a good chance that, with tens of millions of fellow citizens doing the same thing at the same time, the act of voting will mean enough to them that they'll actually put their photo ID in their pocket and head to the polls.

CON: Keith Gunnar Bentele and Erin O'Brien

Voter turnout in the United States is pitiful. Only 59 percent of eligible individuals cast a ballot in the 2012 presidential election. Turnout is even worse in off-year elections, when there is no presidential contest at the top of the ticket. In 2014, national turnout was a mere 36.6 percent, a development decried by the *New York Times* as "the worst turnout in 72 years" for a federal election.[1] And when it comes to odd year municipal elections, where neither a presidential race nor congressional elections are in play, things are downright dismal. In the 2015 municipal election, 14 percent of Bostonians turned out to the polls. Houston, the fourth-biggest city in the United States based on population, saw its highest turnout in a municipal election in over a decade, with a paltry 27 percent casting a ballot, even with a controversial antidiscrimination ordinance to consider.

The United States has a voting problem all right, but it is not ineligible voters sneaking to the polls. Rather, it is that Americans do not regularly exercise their hard fought right to vote. It is only every four years during presidential contests that most eligible Americans vote and, even then, it is only by a slim majority.

Appalling turnout makes the United States fairly unique amongst advanced democracies. As the Pew Research Center reports, when it comes to electoral participation the United States ranks 31st among the 34 countries in the Organization for Economic Development.[2] Only Japan, Chile, and Switzerland do worse.

Turnout rates are so low in the United States not because Americans are uniquely lazy or less interested in politics. Rather, it is that the United States makes it more difficult to vote than do most other democratic countries. Federalism enables confusing election rules and laws that vary substantially by state and even among localities within a state. In all but three American states, the process of registering to vote and the process of voting are separated. Automatic voter registration is not the norm, and nowhere in the United States does your registration travel with you when you move. Election Day, the first Tuesday in November, is not a national holiday nor do we cast ballots on weekends when more people have time to make it to the polls. Moreover, the hours to vote are often quite limited and vary substantially by state and locality. In short, registering to vote, staying registered to vote, and actually voting in the United States is a much more laborious task than in other countries to which we regularly compare ourselves.

These policy choices in the United States—and they are choices—have repercussions: (1) low voter turnout and (2) voter turnout that does not represent the population of the United States. Even in presidential election years, those who cast a ballot are far from a demographic mirror image of the United States. The more affluent one is, the more likely that person is to vote, be active in a campaign, and donate come election season.[3] Higher socioeconomic status often provides enhanced time, resources, and civic skills that leave the more affluent better equipped to negotiate the considerable hurdles to voting in America. About 80 percent of those making over $150,000 say they voted in

2012, and 99 percent of the top 1 percent of earners did so, but only 46 percent of those making between $10,000 and $14,999 report casting a ballot.[4] According to the U.S. Census Bureau, 38 percent of 18- to 24-year-olds reported voting in 2012 compared to 64 percent of 45- to 64-year-olds and a whopping 71 percent of those aged 65- to 74.[5] In the 2012 election, 64 percent of Whites and 66 percent of African Americans voted, whereas only 48 percent of Hispanics and 47 percent of Asians cast ballots.[6] The demographic disparities are even more acute during midterm elections. The 2010 election, for instance, saw participation by almost half of White voters, 44 percent of African Americans, and only 31 percent of both Hispanics and Asians.[7]

All this would be of little concern if the affluent had the same policy interests as the poor or middle class. Or if middle-aged and older voters backed similar policy goals as the young. Or if the policy opinions and priorities of Whites were the same as individuals of color. While there is sometimes overlap across demographic groups in policy preference, these groups frequently prefer very different policies. So while the young and old may both want to strengthen Social Security, the aged place it as a top policy priority while younger voters are more apt to put college affordability at the top of the list. Differences between affluent and lower-to-middle income Americans are even more stark. The rich, for instance, are more conservative on policies relating to "taxation, economic regulation, and especially social welfare programs" and "these distinctive policy preferences may help account for why certain public policies in the United States appear to deviate from what the majority of U.S. citizens wants the government to do."[8] In short, the voices our elected officials hear from in elections are not representative of the American population, and the wants and desires of those they do hear from are most often translated into public policy.

So we should indeed be fired up about voting! Turnout is atrocious. The uniquely cumbersome hodge-podge of voting laws depletes turnout in general and most especially amongst the young, less affluent, and individuals of color. Legislators and elected officials listen to an electorate that is decidedly more affluent, older, and Whiter. The policies that follow do not approximate the wishes of the average voter and therefore threaten democratic responsiveness and equitable public policy.[9] Solutions are desperately needed.

VOTER ID AND SHORTENING EARLY VOTING: WRONG PROBLEM, BAD SOLUTIONS

Unfortunately, voter IDs and shortening early voting periods are not the solutions American democracy needs. Far from it. Evidence from states that have rolled back early voting indicate that minority turnout gets hit particularly hard,[10] class bias in turnout is further exacerbated (increasing the gap between the affluent and poor in turnout), and policies that increase economic inequality are the result.[11] Voter IDs and shortening early voting make the issues of low turnout and disparities in turnout worse.

Why then have voter ID laws and attempts to shorten early voting dominated legislative attention in the states? How has voter identification risen to the status of a major political concern among so many Americans? The answer, as professor of public policy Lorraine Minnite puts it, is the spread of the myth of voter fraud.[12] Evidence unequivocally indicates that in-person voter fraud does not exist with any frequency. Systematic investigation into all reported claims of fraud by social scientists and journalists finds that voter fraud is very, very, very rare.[13] A multiyear investigation by President George W. Bush's Department of Justice turned up "virtually no evidence of any organized effort to skew federal elections."[14]

If you have watched the 1980s movie classic *The Breakfast Club*, you already understand the absurdity of concerns over voter fraud. In one scene, the nerdy character, Brian, is questioned by jock Andy and burnout Bender as to why he has a fake ID. Brian responds, "so I can vote." The exchange gets a laugh for the sheer ridiculousness of it. No one goes to the trouble of getting a fake ID to vote. The risks of in-person voter fraud are enormous. In a federal election, in-person voter fraud is a felony punishable by up to five years and/or a fine of up to $10,000. Further, a single act of in-person voter fraud has an extraordinarily low chance of influencing an election outcome. And any attempt to coordinate a large numbers of individuals to do so is logistically improbable given the risks involved, private ballots, and the fact that a conspiracy of a magnitude sufficiently large enough to be consequential would be very unlikely to go undiscovered. People always talk!

Despite this complete lack of supporting evidence, claims that voter fraud is rampant still pack a political punch. Proponents of the fraud narrative rely on sensational anecdotal stories that "sound like fraud" and then legislate around these tall tales. It's akin to passing legislation banning green M&M's because "a friend of your second cousin heard of a person three states over who went crazy after eating green M&M's." The story is provocative, but it is neither representative nor accurate. But it might just make you worry about those green M&M's. The myth of voter fraud works much the same way. The promotion of an unsubstantiated fear creates opportunities to push for pet electoral policies to address the unfounded fear. In the case of those peddling the voter fraud myth, these policies reduce access to the franchise via strict photo ID voter laws, shortening early voting periods, eliminating same day registration laws, and introducing onerous regulations on good government groups like the League of Women Voters that make it more difficult for them to register voters. Altogether, from 2006 to 2013, 87 restrictive changes of these various types have been passed in the states, ostensibly to curtail largely nonexistent voter fraud. And getting these laws on the books has not prevented new ones from being proposed—from just January to May of 2015, 33 states proposed or carried over a proposal for restrictive access legislation from the prior legislative session.[15] Most Americans accept their necessity because of the fraud narrative. Upward of 70 percent of Americans have come to believe that voter fraud is a pressing concern,[16] and living in a state that has passed a voter ID law does not mitigate their concern![17]

WHAT DRIVES STATES TO PROPOSE AND PASS RESTRICTIVE VOTER ACCESS LEGISLATION?

If voter fraud is a nonissue, why have so many states in recent years proposed and passed restrictive voter access legislation? Conservatives maintain that restrictive voter access legislation is a reasoned response to electoral fraud in an era of close and polarizing elections. They claim that the legislation is therefore necessary to preserve electoral legitimacy. Liberals maintain that restrictive voter access legislation is a response to demographic changes unfavorable to the Republican Party. For them, these laws are a thinly veiled attempt by Republicans to depress turnout among constituencies favorable to the Democratic Party: minorities, new immigrants, the disabled, and young.

In 2013, we set out to test these claims with empirical evidence using advanced statistical techniques.[18] We found that from 2006 to 2011, states that were more likely to propose legislation that would restrict voter access were

- states with larger percentages of African American residents,

- states with higher minority turnout and increases in minority turnout in recent elections,

- states where lower-income voter turnout increased, and

- states with higher percentages of noncitizens.

Reports of voter fraud, in contrast, had no effect on where this legislation was proposed—and this was true even though the reports of fraud did not have to be proven true. The evidence we found is both consistent with and supportive of the argument that the proposal of restrictive voter access legislation in the states—including voter ID laws and shortening early voting periods—*is driven by a desire to reduce turnout among racial minorities and lower income people, groups that consistently vote Democratic.* On this count, the concerns expressed by liberals are borne out by the evidence. Turning to what drives restrictive voter access legislation to actually *pass* in the states, we analyzed all voter access legislation passed between 2006 and 2011 and later updated this analysis to include 2012.[19] In all of these analyses, the following factors were consistently associated with states being more likely to pass restrictive voter access legislation:

- Republican control of the governorship and both chambers of the state legislative body

- The state was a potential swing state in presidential elections *and* the state was controlled by Republicans

- Larger proportions of African-American residents

- Higher minority turnout in the previous presidential election

In sum, the reasons that restrictive voter access legislation have been proposed and passed appear to be rooted in partisanship and race. In all of our analyses of proposed and passed legislation, the best existing systematic count of allegations of voter fraud is significantly associated with the passage of restrictions in only one analysis. Even in this lone case, it had a much smaller substantive impact relative to the partisan and racial factors identified above. In terms of understanding why states are passing these laws, accusations of fraud are either irrelevant or only marginally significant. Based on this empirical evidence—rather than sensational anecdotes—it is clear that concerns about fraud are but convenient cover stories to justify restrictive voter access legislation. Republicans desire these suppressive legislative changes, and these changes pass more frequently when Republicans control state government. In the specific case of ID requirements, all strict voter ID legislation passed since 2006 has been passed in states under Republican control. Similarly, with one exception, all reductions in early voting since 2010 have all been passed in states with Republican majorities. Republican-controlled swing states are particularly ripe for this legislation as are states with larger proportions of African Americans and minority voters. In combination, these findings provide strong empirical support that new restrictions on voter access are intended to suppress Democratic constituencies and especially minority voters.

MORE ARGUMENTS AGAINST VOTER ID AND SHORTENING EARLY VOTING

At this point we have told you that there is no empirical evidence of widespread voter fraud and have presented evidence that suggests that partisan motives are behind the passage of this legislation. But how then to handle the intuitive appeal of the argument that "One needs an ID to buy booze, or board an airplane, or to checkout a library book. Why shouldn't you need an ID to vote?" Easy. Call it out for what it is: diversionary. Buying booze may be pleasurable, hopping on a plane allows one to visit new locales, and we're all for literacy. But the right to vote—the expansion of the franchise to those without property, to African Americans (the 15th Amendment), to women (the 19th Amendment), and to young people (the 26th Amendment)—is not the same as buying alcohol or checking out a book. The right to vote is fundamental to American democracy. Catching a flight is not.

Further, advocates of voter IDs are often skeptical that people do not have IDs or that obtaining them constitutes a real challenge. However, multiple studies have found that roughly one in ten eligible voters lack the forms of identification required to vote under these laws.[20] Racial minorities and the urban poor are greatly overrepresented among the eligible voters who lack the necessary identification. For these individuals, the fees and travel associated with obtaining IDs may constitute a genuine burden. In a recent successful legal challenge to Texas's strict voter ID law, a federal appeals court ruled that the law had a discriminatory effect. During the trial, experts testified that roughly 600,000 registered Texans lacked the necessary identification to vote, and that Hispanics and African-Americans were, respectively, 2.4 and 1.8 times more likely to lack an ID compared to Whites.[21] Multiple witnesses in this challenge described the challenges involved in obtaining the underlying documentation necessary to obtain free "election identification certificates." Depending on your state of birth the cost of obtaining the birth certificate necessary to get this "free" ID can range from $2 to $47, a cost that may be out of reach for some poor families. And those in rural Texas, who are disproportionately Hispanic, live greater distances from the relatively few locales where these "free" IDs can be obtained. College students also find having the proper ID more cumbersome. Students who live and attend college in a state different than their parents often register to vote in the state they now reside, but, under most voter ID laws, they have to change their state ID or driver's license to do so. [22] Their student ID is not considered an acceptable voter ID in many states The process is costly, cumbersome, and turns a blind eye to the unique situation of college students.

Requiring voter ID seems to serve little purpose, but the case for shortening early voting periods is even more baffling. Why would we want to reduce the window of opportunity for citizens to cast a legal ballot? Some Republicans have suggested that early voting provides more opportunities for voter fraud. But the most common argument to justify cuts to early voting is that there should be uniformity across counties in terms of the hours that polling places are open.[23] If rural counties cannot afford or cannot staff extra hours, then urban counties should not be providing these extra hours. This argument implies that uniformity in polling place hours is a more important consideration than guaranteeing citizens' access to the voting booth. We expect few American agree with this proposition. Further, the most obvious solution, and the one that promotes the political participation so fundamental to the American experiment, is to provide funds to support these extra hours in all counties. These weak justifications provided for reductions in early voting sound like another diversion once one considers the increasing popularity of early voting among African Americans. In the 2012 election, 41 percent of African Americans in the South voted early compared to 35 percent of Southern Whites.[24] In particular states, these disparities are even more dramatic—54 percent of African Americans voted early in Florida in 2008 and over 70 percent did so in both the 2008 and 2012 elections in North Carolina.[25] Studies indicate that Florida's reduction in early voting increased congestion at polls and early voting sites and that these problems were especially likely to impact African American voters.[26] Across a wide range of demographic characteristics in the 2012 election, disparities in wait times nationwide were the greatest along racial/ethnic lines with Whites, Hispanics, and African Americans facing national average wait times of 12, 19, and 23 minutes respectively.[27]

POLICIES THAT INCREASE TURNOUT AND COMBAT INEQUALITY IN TURNOUT

There is some good news. Though the balance of legislative efforts has undoubtedly been restrictive toward the ballot box, since 2012 some 23 states plus the District of Columbia have passed laws expanding voter access.[28] These include online registration systems—ideal given how much most of us do online—as well as preregistration of 16- and 17-year-olds, Election Day registration, same-day registration, and automatic registration in California and Oregon. These are victories for democracy and the concept of one person, one vote. However, although many of these policies have been found to increase turnout overall, they are less effective in reducing disparities in turnout between more and less affluent citizens.[29]

TAKEAWAYS

Following the election of Barack Obama, voter ID laws took center stage in our discussions of election practices. This attention ignores the fundamental problems of American elections: low turnout; dramatic inequality in who turns out; and the disproportionate responsiveness of our political system to older, affluent, and White voters. Voter ID laws and shortening early voting periods are part of a voter suppression movement that has swept across the American states and is driven by a complex blend of partisan and racial motives. Social science research shows that voter fraud is a red herring. Voter fraud is not associated with a state's likelihood of proposing or adopting restrictive voter access legislation. What is associated with passage of these laws is Republican control of state government and the presence of racial minorities. Where this legislation passes, minorities and low-income people are disproportionately impacted, and legislative outcomes compound economic inequality. Voter ID laws and other voter restrictions threaten the concept of one-person, one-vote and introduce costly and inefficient regulations to an already cumbersome voter maze. Liberals are right: The myth of voter fraud is propagated by those on the right to fend against demographic changes favorable to the Democratic Party. The better response to these demographic changes would be for Republicans to develop policy positions and platforms that compete for—rather than silence—minority voters.

NOTES

INTRO

1.   Alexander Keyssar, *The Right to Vote: The Contested History of Democracy in the United States* (New York, NY: Basic Books, 2000), 158.
2.   Tova Andrea Wang, *The Politics of Voter Suppression: Defending and Expanding Americans' Right to Vote* (Ithaca, NY: Cornell University Press, 2012), 65.

PRO

1.   "Fear of Voter Suppression High, Fear of Voter Fraud Higher," *WashingtonPost. com* (August 13, 2012), https://www.washingtonpost.com/page/2010-2019/ WashingtonPost/2012/08/12/National-Politics/Polling/release_116.xml?uuid=E1k PqOQZEeGJ93biOpgtBg.
2.   Ibid.; *Rasmussen Report*, "78% Favor Proof of Citizenship Before Being Allowed to Vote" (March 25, 2014): http://www.rasmussenreports.com/public_content/politics/ general_politics/march_2014/78_favor_proof_of_citizenship_before_being_ allowed_to_vote; Mario Trujillo, "70% Support Voter ID Laws," *The Hill*, May 16, 2014; and Juan Williams, "The Voter Fraud Myth," *Memphis Flyer*, July 9, 2015.

3. *Building Confidence in U.S. Elections: Report of the Commission on Federal Election Reform* (September 2005): http://www.eac.gov/assets/1/AssetManager/ Exhibit%20M.PDF. See also Jimmy Carter and James A. Baker III, "A Clearer Picture on Voter ID," *New York Times*, Feb. 3, 2008.

4. *Crawford v. Marion County Election Board*, 553 U.S. 181 (2008).

5. Colleen Jenkins, "Insight: Scant Evidence of Voter Suppression, Fraud in States with ID Laws," *Reuters News Agency*, Nov. 2, 2012, http://www.reuters.com/ article/us-usa-campaign-voterid-idUSBRE8A10UJ20121102.

6. Robert Barnes, "N.C. Case Represents Pivotal Point of Voting Debate," *Washington Post*, July 30, 2015.

7. Ibid.

8. Paul Taylor and Mark Hugo Lopez, "Six Take-Aways from the Census Bureau's Voting Report," (May 8, 2013), http://www.pewresearch.org/fact-tank/2013/05/08/six-take-aways-from-the-census-bureaus-voting-report.

9. Jay Cost, "Fighting for the Black Vote," *Weekly Standard* (June 22, 2015), 12-13.

10. Jesse T. Richman, Gulshan A. Chattha, and David C. Earnest, "Do Non-Citizens Vote in US Elections," *Electoral Studies* 36 (2014): 149-157.

11. Pew Center on the States, "Inaccurate, Costly, and Inefficient: Evidence That America's Voter Registration System Needs an Upgrade" (February 2012), http:// www.pewtrusts.org/en/research-and-analysis/reports/2012/02/14/ inaccurate-costly-and-inefficient-evidence-that-americas-voter-registration-system-needs-an-upgrade.

12. See the table on pages 40–41 of William J. Crotty, *Party Reform and the American Experiment* (New York, NY: Thomas Y. Crowell, 1977).

13. Thomas E. Patterson, *The Vanishing Voter: Public Involvement in an Age of Uncertainty* (New York, NY: Alfred A. Knopf, 2002), 132.

14. Raymond E. Wolfinger and Jonathan Hoffman, "Registering and Voting with Motor Voter," *PS: Political Science and Politics* 34 (March 2001): 85–92.

CON

1. The Editorial Board, "The Worst Voter Turnout in 72 Years," *New York Times*, November 11, 2014.

2. Drew DeSilver, "U.S. Voter Turnout Trails Most Developed Countries: By International Standards, U.S. Voter Turnout is Low," *Pew Research Center*, May 6, 2015.

3. Sidney Verba, Kay Lehman Schlozman, and Henry Brady, *Voice and Equality: Civic Voluntarism in American Politics* (Cambridge, MA: Harvard University Press, 1995).

4. Benjamin I. Page, Larry M. Bartels, and Jason Seawright, "Democracy and the Policy Preferences of Wealthy Americans," *Perspectives on Politics* 11 (March 2013): 51–73.

5. United States Census Bureau, "Voting and Registration in the Election of November 2012-Detailed Tables."

6. Thom File, "Population Characteristics: The Diversifying Electorate—Voting Rates by Race and Hispanic Origin in 2012 (and Other Recent Elections)," U.S. Census Bureau, Current Population Survey (May 2013): 1–13.

7. Mark Hugo Lopez, "Dissecting the 2010 Electorate," *Pew Research Center*, April 26, 2011.

8. Page, Bartels, and Seawright, "Democracy and the Policy Preferences of Wealthy Americans," 51.

9. Martin Gilens and Benjamin Page, "Testing Theories of American Politics: Elites, Interest Groups, and Average Citizens," *Perspectives on Politics* 12 (September 2014): 564–581.

10. David Kimball, "Evidence that Negative Views of Minority Voters Influence Public Worries about Election Fraud," Scholars Strategy Network, SSN Basic Facts (January 2014).

11. William Franko, Nathan Kelly, and Christopher Witko, "How Roadblocks to Voting Make Income Inequality Worse," Scholars Strategy Network, SSN Key Findings (January 2014).

12. Lorraine C. Minnite, *The Myth of Voter Fraud* (Ithaca, NY: Cornell University Press, 2010).

13. Lorraine C. Minnite, "The Misleading Myth of Voter Fraud in American Elections," Scholars Strategy Network, SSN Key Findings, (January 2014).

14. Eric Lipton and Ian Urbina, "In 5-Year Effort, Scant Evidence of Voter Fraud," *New York Times*, April 12, 2007.

15. Brennan Center for Justice, "Voter Laws Roundup 2015: Voting Restrictions," June 3, 2015.

16. Judicial Watch, "77% of Americans Concerned about Government Corruption; Majority See it Getting Worse," December 26, 2013.

17. David Kimball, "Evidence that Negative Views of Minority Voter Influence Public Worries about Election Fraud," Scholars Strategy Network: Basic Facts Brief" (June 2014).

18. Keith G. Bentele and Erin O'Brien, "Jim Crow 2.0?: Why States Consider and Adopt Restrictive Voter Access Polices," *Perspectives on Politics* 11 (2013): 1088–1116.

19. Ian Vandewalker and Keith G. Bentele, "Vulnerability in Numbers: Racial Composition of the Electorate, Voter Suppression, and the Voting Rights Act," *Harvard Latino Law Review* (2015), 18.

20. Brennan Center for Justice, "The Challenge of Obtaining Voter Identification," July 18, 2012.

21. Zachary Roth, "In Texas Voter ID Trail, Witnesses Describe Burden of Getting ID," *MSNBC*, September 4, 2014; Jim Malewitz, "Court: Texas Voter ID Law Violates Voting Rights Act," *Texas Tribune*, August 5, 2015.

22. Matt Apuzzo, "College Students Claim Voter ID Laws Discriminate Based on Age," *New York Times*, July 5, 2014.

23. Ari Berman, "GOP Steps Up Attack on Early Voting in Key Swing States," *The Nation*, March 28, 2014.

24. Paul Gronke and Charles Stewart III, "Early Voting in Florida," MIT Political Science Department Research Paper No. 2013-12, April 8, 2013.

25. Lloyd Dunkelberger, "Experts: Early Voting Law Could Face Legal Challenge," *The Ledger*, June 11, 2011; Samantha Lachman, "What's at Stake in the Trial Over North Carolina Voting Restrictions," *The Huffington Post*, July 10, 2015.

26. Michael C. Herron and Daniel A. Smith, "Precinct Closing Times in Florida During the 2012 General Election," *Election Law Journal: Rules, Politics, and Policy* 11(September 2012): 331–347; Paul Gronke and Charles Stewart III, "Early Voting in Florida," MIT Political Science Department Research Paper No. 2013-12, April 8, 2013.

27. Charles Stewart III, "Waiting to Vote in 2012," *Journal of Law and Politics* 28(Summer 2013), 439–463.

28. Brennan Center for Justice, "States That Expanded Voting Since the 2012 Election," June 2, 2015.

29. Elizabeth Rigby, "Do Election Reforms Promote Equal Participation?," Scholars Strategy Network, SSN Key Findings (April 2012).

RESOLVED, the United States should adopt a national initiative and referendum

PRO: Todd Donovan

CON: Richard J. Ellis

The question of which Americans are allowed to vote is an important one. So is the question of what decisions Americans get to make with their votes. The answers to both questions have changed a great deal over time and almost always in the direction of greater democracy.

The Constitution originally left it entirely to the states to decide matters of voter eligibility. Their typical decision during the founding period was to confine the franchise—that is, the right to vote—to White male property owners who were at least twenty-one years old. During the 1820s and 1830s—often called the era of Jacksonian democracy—states dropped the property qualification, thereby bringing White workingmen into the electorate. In 1870, right after the Civil War, the Fifteenth Amendment forbade states from denying African Americans the right to vote, although many southern states found ways to keep blacks from exercising this right until a very tough enforcement bill, the Voting Rights Act, was enacted nearly a century later, in 1965. The Nineteenth Amendment extended voting rights to women in 1920, and the Twenty-sixth Amendment did the same for eighteen-year-olds in 1971. Many states still bar mentally ill people and felons from voting, but apart from these significant exceptions, the franchise belongs to every American citizen eighteen years and older.

The historic spread of the franchise across boundaries of class, race, gender, and age is one measure of how the United States has grown more democratic over the years. Another is the steadily lengthening list of the matters that Americans can decide with their votes. From the beginning, voters elected members of the House of Representatives, but not until the Seventeenth Amendment was added to the Constitution in 1913 were they empowered to elect senators. (Until then, senators were elected by the state legislatures.) The president is still chosen by the electoral college, and occasionally a candidate with fewer popular votes than the opponent wins a majority of electoral votes and becomes president, as George W. Bush did in 2000. The Constitution even leaves it to each state to decide whether its voters get to choose the state's electors, although no state since South Carolina in 1860 has done things differently. Since the early twentieth century—the Progressive Era—voters have been able not only to elect officials in general elections but also, increasingly, to choose most of the candidates for those elections in party primaries.

In addition to the creation of primary elections, another reform of the Progressive Era was to allow a state's voters to weigh in on proposed laws and constitutional amendments through initiatives and referenda. Here is the difference between the two: An initiative is placed on the ballot by citizen petition, and a referendum is placed on the ballot by the state legislature. What initiatives and referenda have in common is that once they are on the ballot, the voters decide whether or not they become law.

Referenda are much more common than initiatives, both around the world and in the United States. Several democratic nations employ national referenda, but only Switzerland allows national initiatives—and even there the Swiss legislature can weigh in before an initiative actually goes on the ballot. All fifty American states allow their legislatures to place referenda on the ballot, and forty-nine of them (all but Delaware) require that amendments to the state constitution be approved by referendum. Only twenty-four states, however—the vast majority of them west of the Mississippi River—allow initiatives. In some of these states, notably California (where initiatives are called "propositions") and Oregon, the rules for qualifying an initiative to appear on the ballot are lenient, and so these states' voters decide on many initiatives. In other states the rules are so restrictive that initiatives hardly ever make the ballot.

At the national level, the United States allows neither referenda nor initiatives. Should it? The resolution that forms the basis of this debate proposes that it should. American national democracy properly values both majority rule and minority rights, argues Todd Donovan in support of the resolution, but in practice, minorities—especially those representing wealthy economic interests—have too many advantages. Reforming the system to allow national initiatives and referenda would allow the majority to rebalance the scales. Richard J. Ellis, writing in opposition, sees things differently. In states where initiatives are used frequently, he argues, the record shows that wealthy economic interests are among those best positioned to finance expensive initiative campaigns on their own behalf. Another issue on which Donovan and Ellis disagree is the effect that allowing national referenda and initiatives would have on Congress. Would Congress be hamstrung by the legislative end runs that ballot measures represent, or would it clean up its act so that ballot measures would become less necessary?

PRO: Todd Donovan

A representative legislature is the core of a democratic system, and the initiative and referendum are tools that make a legislature both more responsive and more responsible. The initiative process allows citizens to draft laws and petition to have the public vote on those proposed laws. The referendum process allows voters to decide with their ballots the fate of laws proposed by a government. Many modern democracies use referenda to resolve major political disputes, and initiatives are common in Switzerland and several American states.[1]

At times, governments find themselves in positions where the decisions they face are of such consequence that relying on regular representative institutions may be inadequate. Consider these questions: Should Ireland, a nation dominated by a Roman Catholic Church steadfastly opposed to divorce, eliminate its constitutional ban on divorce? Should Canada extend special constitutional status to the French-speaking province of Quebec? Should Denmark approve a European constitution that many Danes view as a threat to their national sovereignty? Should the U.S. Constitution be amended to provide equal rights for women? In all but the last case, these questions were answered by direct public vote.

Representative institutions are not always in a position to resolve such controversial issues. A government may hold a solid majority in parliament, or, in the case of the United States, one party might control the White House and Congress. Majority control may give a government the ability to implement major political changes. That is different, however, from having the ability to accomplish change that has widespread legitimacy.

Consider again the European Union (EU). Like the Danish government, the French government put the European constitution to a popular vote in May, 2005. President Jacques Chirac could have had the French parliament ratify the constitution. That is what governments in Italy, Germany, and many other EU nations did. Chirac, however, had promised a referendum. Accepting the EU constitution would mean greater primacy of EU law over French law in areas such as labor and human rights. French voters rejected the proposed change, slowing the long process of ratification. If Chirac and the French parliament had simply adopted the change without popular support, they may have strengthened the hand of EU skeptics by appearing to ignore the public mood.

Public votes on such matters need not be vetoes. In Spain, 76 percent of voters said yes to the EU in an advisory vote in February 2005. This set the stage for broad-based consensus when Spanish legislators met two months later to approve the constitution. Irish voters approved lifting their country's ban on divorce in 1995. The vote was close, but, contrary to opponents' predictions, the floodgates to divorce did not open, and the once controversial matter seems to have been resolved.

THE WEAK ROLE OF POPULAR MAJORITIES IN THE UNITED STATES

Democracies require a means for giving voice to popular majorities while protecting minority rights. The United States places a much greater emphasis on the latter than on the former. Once every four years, the nation elects a president. Other than that, there are no opportunities for the American public to express its collective opinion.

In contrast, the U.S. Constitution has many mechanisms to ensure that the interests of well-funded political minorities are protected, including federalism, separation of powers, a bicameral legislature, the electoral college, checks and balances, an appointed Supreme Court, and staggered elections. Senate tradition also includes the filibuster and other tools that give political minorities tremendous power to block policy change that might have majority support. By design, the system is rife with veto points. The argument for a national initiative and referendum is ultimately an argument for countering some of the power of these veto wielders by increasing the influence of popular majorities.

NEED FOR A NATIONAL INITIATIVE AND REFERENDUM PROCESS

The United States lacks any mechanism for the expression of public sentiment on matters of policy. Even presidential elections have only indirect effects on public policy.[2] As a result, controversial questions about civil rights for racial minorities, equal rights for women, and abortion policy lingered unresolved for decades. Policy changes that had the support of a national majority were blocked for many years by a political system that granted veto power to conservative southern states, most notably in the case of civil rights for African Americans. National support for civil rights legislation increased after World War II, in part because of President Harry Truman's postwar desegregation of the U.S. Army, and in 1954, 58 percent of Americans (80 percent outside the South) approved of the Supreme Court's school desegregation decision in *Brown v. Board of Education.* Yet, most civil rights legislation was blocked in Congress until 1964 by racist southern Democrats who chaired key Senate committees.[3] A national referendum could have served as an end run around these powerful committee chairmen.

The constitutional amendment process also inflated the influence of southern opposition to equal rights for women. The Equal Rights Amendment was approved by huge majorities in Congress in the 1970s: 354–24 in the House and 81–7 in the Senate. Thirty-five state legislatures (of the thirty-eight required for ratification) approved the amendment, but North Carolina's Democratic senator, Sam Ervin, attached a requirement that the ratification process conclude in seven years. No southern states ratified, and the proposal died. Had the ERA been put to a national public vote, it almost certainly would have been approved.

To this day, political controversy about abortion continues to affect American politics, just as divorce did in Ireland prior to 1995. Yet in the United States, the courts, rather than the people, have been forced to deal with abortion policy.[4] Decades of legal wrangling have failed to resolve the controversy. This is not for the lack of a public consensus, a consensus that had begun to take shape even before the Court's 1973 *Roe v. Wade* decision created a constitutional right to abortion. Since 1973, Court majorities have pulled back from the *Roe* decision, but a majority of Americans continue to support access to abortion in the first trimester of pregnancy. Opponents of legal abortion have been able to keep the controversy alive by attacking the "judicial activism" of the Court. A national referendum on abortion would disarm the extremists and provide the nation a policy with broad public support and legitimacy.

WHO INFLUENCES CONGRESS: VOTERS OR WEALTHY INTERESTS?

Decision making in Congress is decentralized among committees and subcommittees that focus on narrow, specialized areas of policy. Corporations, unions, and interest groups influence legislation by lobbying and by financing the reelection campaigns of members of Congress who have jurisdiction over the issues that the groups are concerned about. Businesses and interest groups employed nearly 12,000 lobbyists and spent $3.2 billion lobbying the federal government in 2014. Another $3.8 billion was spent to influence the 2014 congressional elections.[5] Much of this spending was by groups representing businesses and professions trying to increase their profits. Some members of Congress are explicit about expecting contributions from business interests that are seeking earmarks and other favors.[6] Given the power that a single subcommittee—or even a single senator—may have over policy, these expenditures are often a wise investment.

The products of these arrangements are issue networks, or "iron triangles," consisting of interest groups, congressional committees, and regulatory agencies, that amplify the influence of wealth in Washington while diluting the influence of the general public. Representation would be improved by a process that grants groups outside these iron triangles the ability to affect congressional agendas. In many U.S. states, and in Switzerland, the initiative process allows citizens to propose a public vote on a statute if they collect enough signatures to qualify the statute for the ballot.

PROTECTING MINORITIES?

One valid critique of the initiative process is that it threatens minority interests. There have been numerous examples of state initiatives targeting racial, ethnic, and sexual orientation minority groups.[7] However, any measure approved by voters is subject to review by an independent, unelected judiciary. At the state level, courts have been aggressive in rejecting voter-approved initiatives that violate civil rights and liberties.[8]

With this safeguard already in place, the role of minorities in politics can be considered from a different perspective. As noted earlier, the American political system grants substantial power to influential minorities by giving well-funded interest groups the ability to block popular policies and to advance unpopular policies. In Congress, the interests of only a few people often prevail. An influential theory of politics, the logic of collective action, predicts that small, well-funded economic interests are much more likely to have full-time lobbyists than are groups representing the general public.[9] Banks, telecommunications companies, pharmaceutical firms, dairy farmers, defense contractors, and many other businesses make billions of dollars by lobbying for tax breaks, subsidies, earmarks,[10] protections against risk, and bailouts. Taxpayers and consumers pick up the tab in the form of higher taxes, higher prices for cell phone service, higher credit card fees, higher prices for dairy products, and so on.

These facts are relevant to another critique of the initiative process—that it can be dominated by wealthy interests at the expense of the "grass roots."[11] But consider money and Congress. Interest groups give money to members of Congress to encourage them to do things that serve the groups' narrow self-interests. This leads to a perception of congressional corruption, if not actual corruption, that the U.S. Supreme Court says justifies regulating contributions to members of Congress.[12] Spending on initiative campaigns, in contrast, involves attempts to win the support of a majority of voters—and money spent advancing initiatives is no sure key to victory for wealthy interests.[13]

For example, in 1988 Californians rejected well-funded industry proposals for regulating car insurance but supported a rival proposal written by consumer activists,[14] and in 2006 Arizonans approved a minimum-wage increase opposed by wealthy interests while rejecting a well-funded tobacco industry proposal to open restaurants to smoking.

In contrast, consider the relationship between money and policy in Congress. Wealthy interests have been successful in spending heavily on lobbying to secure approval of unpopular bankruptcy laws, "free" trade laws, and deregulation of media ownership. It is difficult to imagine a scenario where they could have spent money to convince voters to adopt such laws. Moreover, a single U.S. senator has the power to advance laws that could never secure a majority vote by attaching "riders" to bills that assist their campaign donors. Riders are attached to important bills that the senators know a president will have to sign; for instance, Republican senators used riders to advance a host of antienvironmental measures after accepting more than $800,000 in contributions from companies that would benefit from the riders.[15] The House Appropriations Committee is known as the "favor factory" because it allows members a lucrative method of raising campaign money and setting policy by earmarking millions of dollars for favored constituents and supporters. Many relatives of members of Congress earn large salaries lobbying them for earmarks.[16]

An initiative process would give voters the opportunity to promote laws that nullify such expenditures. It would also give people who oppose such behavior the tools to promote congressional reforms by targeting lobbying and earmarks. This, in turn, could help restore public confidence in Congress.

STRENGTHENING CONGRESS WITH DIRECT DEMOCRACY

Another concern about direct democracy is that it may undermine the role of representative institutions.[17] It is difficult to imagine what is left to undermine about Congress, but it is conceivable that the initiative and referendum would actually improve how Congress functions as a representative body.

Congress has lost the ability to effectively check the president.[18] It has delegated much authority over policy to executive agencies staffed by personnel who worked (or will work) in the industries they regulate.[19] It has delegated much of its budgeting and war-making authority to the president.[20] The modern Congress is regularly rocked by scandals, routinely characterized by gridlock, and often seen as irrelevant. These factors undermine its standing with the public. Large majorities of Americans believe that government is run for "a few big interests" rather than for the benefit of "all the people." Most Americans disapprove of how Congress does its job, regardless of which party is in power. These opinions highlight an enduring crisis of our representative government.

The modern Congress, with its maze of iron triangles, allows incumbents to do a masterful job serving constituents but a poor job of acting collectively in ways that would serve the country. Incumbents in safe seats raise huge sums of money and scare off potential election challengers.[21] These incumbent advantages diminish the responsiveness of Congress to voter preferences.[22] In addition, congressional elections rarely produce representation for moderates. For these reasons, Congress may not be the optimal institution for reflecting the preferences of the mass public.[23] Nor is it well suited for advancing innovative policies, particularly if Congress and the White House are controlled by different political parties.

As Progressive Era advocates of direct democracy argued a century ago, the initiative and referendum should make representatives both more responsive and more responsible. Initiatives send representatives signals about the scope and intensity of public concerns. Regardless of whether measures qualify or pass, the process may push legislators to adopt policies that are closer to what the public wants.[24] It may serve as a sort of "gun behind the door" that organized groups could use to prompt Congress into responding to national concerns. If designed like the Swiss indirect initiative system, the process might reinvigorate Congress by encouraging the representatives to craft responses to issues that the public is concerned about. Under the Swiss model, initiative proposals that qualify for a public vote are first considered by the legislature. The legislature may adopt the proposal, modify the proposal in consultation with proponents, or suggest an alternative proposal and let voters decide between their idea and the original proposal. Absent such pressure, legislators from safe, one-party districts may have little motivation to heed national opinion.

Legislators also currently have incentives to avoid controversial decisions. For example, while popular opinion has shifted away from the 1980s "war on drugs," many in Congress and the state legislatures have not. Initiative proposals, not legislatures, have spurred policy innovation in areas such as drug policy and medical use of marijuana. Voters in several states have approved measures to allow the medical use of marijuana, and in Utah voters have approved the easing of rules that allow government to seize any property associated with drug crimes. By forcing the legislature to deal with issues that the people care about instead of those that wealthy campaign contributors care about, a national initiative process could push legislators to do a better job of representing the interests of all the people rather than just those of a favored few.

STRENGTHENING POLITICAL PARTIES WITH DIRECT DEMOCRACY

A national initiative process would likely be difficult to use. Even a relatively modest signature standard for qualifying a statutory initiative could require that a proponent collect more than six million signatures.[25] A rule requiring a distribution of signatures across a certain number of states would make the task of qualifying even more daunting. Well-heeled economic interests that are successful in lobbying Congress may find it much more difficult to convince six million Americans to put their schemes on the ballot. Think of it this way, the mining industry might be able to convince a couple of senators who need campaign funds that open-pit cyanide gold mines are a great idea. The industry would have a much tougher time convincing voters to sign a petition to put such a question on the ballot.

Certain broad-based organizations might have the resources to qualify a national initiative. These include mass-membership interest groups such as AARP, the National Rifle Association, the National Organization for Women, and the Sierra Club, as well as unions and political parties. Political parties are perhaps in the best position to take advantage of a national initiative process. Petitioning would require organized efforts in dozens of states. Unlike narrow interest groups, parties have already established grassroots organizations in every state; such organizations are among the few vehicles that exist for mobilizing campaign workers.

In many states, partisan elected officials currently work with initiative proponents to advance new policies.[26] Divided partisan control of government and veto players in the legislature often prevent the adoption of popular policies. The initiative process has allowed partisan elected officials who supported popular policies to avoid legislative roadblocks and work outside the system. In various states, parties have worked with unions and used the initiative process to advance several measures that had been held back by legislative logjams, including teacher pay raises, K–12 class-size reduction, and minimum-wage increases.

CONCLUSION

Initiatives would prompt Congress to be more responsive to the public rather than to narrow economic interests. If used to promote reforms of lobbying and earmarks, initiatives could also cause Congress to be more responsible. An indirect initiative process would mean congressional majorities would always have some say about proposals that go before voters. As for national referenda, in order to increase the influence of the legislative branch of government, the decision to have a referendum should rest with a majority in

Congress, not the president. Majorities in each chamber should be required to authorize a statutory referendum, and supermajorities of each house should be required to propose any constitutional referendum. Empowering Congress with the initiative and referendum would give representatives additional tools for making policy and restore some balance to relations between the executive and legislative branches. With these new tools, Congress could also resume its place as the primary institution in American politics.

CON: Richard J. Ellis

If democracy is good, then surely more democracy is better. And if government for the people is our aim, then surely it makes sense to establish or at least experiment with government that is truly of the people and by the people. Why should we settle for representative democracy if we can have direct democracy, real democracy, pure democracy? Sure, the framers of the U.S. Constitution, most of whom were wealthy and well-educated elites, feared the people, but why should we allow their fears to dictate our politics? The framers wanted the Constitution to erect a barrier against the envious and shortsighted passions of the poor, the debtors, and the dispossessed. But after more than two centuries of experience with democracy, isn't it time we recognize how misplaced their fears were? The masses, after all, clamor for tax cuts more than they do for soaking the rich. And the elites who run the national government seem to be notable less for their wisdom and foresight than for their extraordinary responsiveness to special interests and campaign contributors. So why not give the initiative and referendum process a try at the national level? What do we have to lose?

The answer is plenty, although much depends on the precise form that the process takes, particularly the requirements proponents must satisfy in order to qualify a measure for the ballot. Twenty-four states have an initiative process, but usage of that process varies dramatically. Voters in Oregon and California, where qualifying an initiative for the ballot is relatively easy,[1] routinely see between five and ten initiatives on each ballot and occasionally more; in 2000, for instance, eighteen initiatives qualified for the ballot in Oregon. However, voters in initiative states where qualification is more burdensome rarely see more than one or two initiatives in an election, and many see none at all.

Consider the case of Mississippi, the last state to add an initiative process. The Magnolia State does not permit statutory initiatives or popular referenda. So although voters can change the constitution through the initiative process, they cannot use initiatives to make laws, nor can they repeal laws passed by the state legislature. Mississippi's signature threshold is high—the state requires initiative petitioners to gather signatures equaling 12 percent of the number of votes in the last gubernatorial election—but even more restrictive is the requirement that one-fifth of the signatures must come from each of the state's five congressional districts.[2] In addition, Mississippi permits the legislature to place an alternative measure on the same ballot, thereby giving the voters a choice between two amendments. Moreover, every initiative that has revenue implications must identify the amount and source of revenue required to implement it, and if the initiative reduces revenues or reallocates funding, it must specify which programs will be affected. Finally, Mississippi prohibits initiatives that would modify the initiative process or that would alter either the state's bill of rights or its constitutional right-to-work guarantee. Since adopting the initiative process in 1992, the citizens of Mississippi have voted on only six initiatives.[3]

The consequences of a national initiative process, in short, depend crucially on the details. If the signature requirement is high and there is a geographic distribution requirement that requires a certain percentage of the signatures to be collected from a large number of states, then the effect on the nation's politics would likely be minimal. Conversely, if the signature requirements are low and there is no geographic distribution requirement, then the effects could be revolutionary. When proponents of a national initiative and referendum go beyond ringing declarations about the value of "real democracy" or stinging indictments of the corruptions of "repocracy" (rule by representatives) and finally get down to filling in the crucial details, they usually come down on the side of low signature thresholds. A well-publicized constitutional amendment proposed in 1977 by Senators James Abourezk and Mark Hatfield, for instance, required the signatures of only 3 percent of voters gathered from at least ten states. A signature threshold that low would virtually guarantee a very large number of initiatives.

Proponents of a national initiative often try to blunt criticisms by pointing to the Swiss experience with direct democracy. In a 1981 book, for instance, Jack Kemp, then a New York congressman and later a presidential candidate, cabinet secretary, and vice presidential nominee, lauded Switzerland as the only country in the world "that has more democracy than the United States." In Kemp's view, the existence of a national initiative and referendum process explained why Switzerland was also the one nation that was "more peaceful and prosperous than the United States."[4]

Yet, few of the people who tout the virtues of direct democracy in Switzerland seem to know much about how the Swiss system actually works. Nor do they recognize how radically different it is from the system that advocates of a national initiative process typically have in mind. To begin with, at the federal level, the Swiss initiative power—as in Mississippi—is limited to constitutional amendments; no statutory changes can be made by initiative. Moreover, initiatives at both the federal and cantonal level in Switzerland are indirect—that is, they must first be presented to the legislative assembly. Although the federal assembly cannot stop an initiative from reaching the ballot, the legislature is allowed four years to deliberate on the measure before sending it to the people. If the federal assembly approves an initiative, it is presented to the voters with the legislature's stamp of approval, but this rarely happens. Between 1891 and 2015, only about 2 percent of the more than 200 initiatives that reached the voters carried the legislature's official blessing. The Swiss assembly is not required to take a position on an initiative measure, but it almost invariably does. There have been only a small handful of initiatives on which the assembly has failed to take an official position. When sending an initiative to the voters, the Swiss assembly will typically include an explanation of why it believes the initiative should be rejected. The legislature also has the option of placing its own counterproposal on the ballot along with the citizen initiative (in which case the legislature is allowed five rather than four years to take action). The Swiss assembly has offered the voters a counterproposal about one-quarter of the time, and voters have adopted the counterproposal more often than not. In only two cases did voters approve the citizen initiative and reject the legislative counterproposal.[5]

When offered both a citizen initiative and a legislative counterproposal, voters must indicate which measure they would prefer in the event that both measures gain a majority of votes. As a result, a citizen initiative can receive a majority of votes and still not be enacted if more voters indicate a preference for the legislative alternative. A more blatant constraint on majority rule is the requirement that a federal initiative (or the legislative counterproposal) must be approved not only by a majority of those voting but also by a majority of cantons. Since the populations of Swiss cantons vary enormously (five of the twenty-six cantons contain well over half of Switzerland's population, and the largest canton, Zurich, has more than twice as many people as the ten least-populous cantons combined), an initiative can achieve a majority of the votes and yet fall short of a majority of the cantons. Not surprisingly, the percentage of federal initiatives that are successful is exceedingly small, about 10 percent.[6]

The success rate is even lower when one considers the large number of initiatives in Switzerland that are submitted to the federal assembly with the required number of signatures but are then withdrawn by the sponsors before the legislature submits the initiative to the people. In fact, almost as many qualified initiatives are withdrawn as reach the ballot. The reasons that measures are withdrawn are various, but among the most common is that the assembly has promised or taken legislative action that satisfies the initiative's sponsors. In many of these instances the objective of the sponsors in presenting the initiative is more to prompt a legislative deal than it is to take the issue to the voters. The initiative in Switzerland is thus an integral part of the legislative process and is often used as a spur to get a majority in the legislature to heed the concerns of minority groups that have previously been thwarted in the assembly. Unlike in the United States, where the initiative process is typically a confrontational, zero-sum game, in Switzerland it is often employed to arrive at a consensus by facilitating legislative deliberation and compromise. In short, the Swiss initiative system, particularly at the federal level, is radically unlike the initiative system envisioned by advocates of a national initiative and referendum process in the United States. Instead, these advocates usually have in mind the wide-open initiative process in high-use states such as California and Oregon.

So what is wrong with bringing California's style of initiative politics to the national stage? Aren't initiative skeptics really, at heart, antidemocrats, fearful of the people? Only if one holds to a crude conception of democracy. The democratic ideal is not just to mirror public preferences but to engage in reasoned debate about the public interest. The point of having selected individuals study, discuss, and debate public policy in a face-to-face forum is that they might reach a judgment that is different from the opinions or prejudices with which they began. Expert testimony might lead them to revise their beliefs, or the intense pleas of affected groups might unsettle their convictions. The rival interests of other constituencies need to be heard and considered, and compromises may need to be reached. Individual preferences are to be negotiated, not just aggregated. Grover Norquist, longtime president of Americans for Tax Reform, says that the "one big difference between initiatives and elected representatives is that initiatives do not change their minds once you vote them in."[7] That may be so, but why should we make inflexibility and imperviousness to reason a hallmark of democracy?

Of course, critics are right that the legislative process is often excruciatingly slow. Washington State's premier initiative activist, Tim Eyman, defends the initiative process as "a laxative to a constipated political process."[8] And, in small doses, perhaps there is something to this. But why should we equate more legislation with more democracy? The framers of the Constitution assumed that the political process works best when decisions are made slowly, deliberately, and with great care. In emergencies, rapid action is necessary, but in the normal way of things speed only empowers the passions of the moment and leads to ill-considered plans. Haste is the enemy of rational dialogue and effective public policy. Enduring policies are to be built through the laborious process of building consensus among diverse groups of people. Legislative inaction, from this perspective, is not necessarily a sign of failure. Instead, the legislature's reluctance or inability to act may be a wise and necessary response to the clash of profoundly different interests and values. That is, governmental inaction often reflects the fact that the people are deeply divided about what they want.

For proponents of a national initiative and referendum, democracy is largely about counting votes. It is a very simple idea: Whoever has the most votes wins, so long as the policy is not an unconstitutional infringement on the minority. No allowance is made for intensity of preference. Imagine three friends, two of whom wish to eat at McDonald's but don't feel strongly about where they eat and one of whom wishes to go to Burger King because McDonald's makes him sick. Under the initiative process or most versions of electronic direct democracy, every preference is weighted equally. The majority rules, and so the three friends go to McDonald's, forcing the one friend either to go hungry or to become physically ill. In the legislative process, however, intensity of preference matters. The two friends may possibly try to coerce the third into eating at McDonald's, but more likely they will compromise. Not feeling strongly about the matter, the two friends may defer to the third and eat at Burger King. Or they may decide to eat at Burger King one time and McDonald's the next. Or they may look for a third option, perhaps Wendy's. Although Wendy's may be nobody's first choice, it has the advantage of not making the third friend ill, and the other two friends prefer it to Burger King. By accommodating intensity of preference rather than only counting votes, democratic deliberation can produce policies that are acceptable to minorities as well as to the majority. In contrast, initiative elections promote policies that pay scant attention to the consent of the minority and thus encourage losers to take their grievances to the least democratically accountable branch of government, the courts.

Of course, legislatures do not always or even mostly operate as they are supposed to in theory. Weighing intensity of preference may be the ideal, but the mobilization of resources often owes more to organization and money than it does to the intensity with which values and beliefs are held. The polarized partisanship among political elites often seems disconnected from the apolitical middle ground occupied by many American citizens. Amendments tacked onto legislation in the closing days of the legislative session receive nothing like the critical scrutiny envisioned by the framers of the Constitution. Disinterested policy expertise is often in short supply—particularly in states such as Oregon, where legislators have minimal professional staff.

But for all their failings, legislatures have the singular virtue of being capable of identifying, correcting, and learning from errors. Citizens are accustomed to viewing legislatures as fallible, imperfect instruments, and so neither citizens nor legislatures see anything wrong or unusual in changing and improving current laws. There is nothing sacred about the status quo. Competitive elections between political parties are expected to result in changes in public policy. A government policy enacted by the legislature is treated as the law of the land, not as the godlike voice of the people.

The real problem with initiatives is not that they are more likely to produce poor public policy than are legislatures, although they may be, but rather that mistakes made by initiative are generally more difficult to correct. A successful initiative, unlike a legislative action, is widely assumed to be the authentic expression of the "voice of the people." Legislators or interest groups who dare to suggest amending or jettisoning a law enacted by initiative are vilified for attempting to violate the popular will, as if they were trying to alter one of the commandments brought down from the mountain by Moses rather than an imperfect government policy written by special interests. Even modest attempts to have voters reconsider their decisions bring howls of populist outrage.

Yet, initiatives typically reveal more about the ideologies and preoccupations of those who supply the initiatives than they do about the priorities and values of voters. Initiative sponsors, not voters, decide whether an issue will be a constitutional amendment or a statutory change. And it is the initiative sponsors who frame the issue and the choices in ways that importantly shape the answer. Voters may prefer a particular initiative to the status quo, yet, given a wider range of options, they may rank that initiative near the bottom. Take tax-cutting initiatives. In Oregon in 1996, voters were asked to vote on Measure 47, which dramatically rolled back property taxes. Voters were offered the choice between a large rollback in taxes and no change in their taxes. They were not allowed to choose between a large and a more moderate rollback or between the proposed measure and a system of rebates for low-income or fixed-income property owners. Nor was the alternative of differential tax rates for businesses and home owners put to the voters. So while the vote on Measure 47 reflected a slim majority's preference for lower property taxes (52 percent supported the measure), the precise policies (the extent of the reduction and the restrictions on future increases, the limits on new bonds and replacement fees, and the requirement that property tax levies achieve a 50 percent turnout rate) that were enacted were less reflective of the will of the voters than they were of the will of the measure's author, Bill Sizemore.

The vote on an initiative, moreover, is often powerfully swayed by the wording of the ballot title and summary. As anyone familiar with polling knows, public opinion on many issues is extremely sensitive to how questions are worded. Ask people whether they support spending for the "poor," and their responses are far more favorable than if they are asked about spending on "welfare." Question wording was central to the battle over Proposition 209, a 1996 initiative that banned state affirmative action programs in California. The sponsors were careful not to mention affirmative action; instead the initiative prohibited the state from "discriminating against, or granting preferential treatment to, any individual or group" on the basis of race or gender. Polls showed that overwhelming majorities supported this language, but support plummeted when respondents were asked about outlawing state affirmative action programs for women and minorities. Conscious of the vital difference that wording makes, Republican attorney general Dan Lungren, a strong critic of affirmative action programs, avoided any mention of affirmative action in the hundred-word title and summary of the initiative that appeared on the ballot. Opponents of Proposition 209 took the attorney general to court, and a superior court judge directed Lungren to rewrite the summary because omitting the words *affirmative action* misled voters. Upon appeal, a district court rejected the lower court's judgment. The title and summary, the court concluded, conveyed to the public "the general purpose" of the proposition. "We cannot fault the Attorney General," the court concluded, "for refraining from the use of such an amorphous, value-laden term" as *affirmative action*. The decision not to include the words *affirmative action* was a critical ingredient in the passage of Proposition 209.[9]

Moreover, passage of a measure reveals little or nothing about an issue's salience to voters. In 1996, affirmative action actually ranked near the bottom of the list of issues that most concerned Californians. Citizens expressed far greater concern about jobs, education, the environment, and taxes. In 2000, antitax initiatives dominated state ballots—appearing in Alaska, California, Colorado, Massachusetts, Oregon, South Dakota, and Washington—even though polls consistently showed that voters were far less concerned about reducing taxes than they were about improving the quality of government services. In 2004, religious conservatives qualified antigay marriage initiatives in six states—Arkansas, Michigan, Montana, North Dakota, Ohio, and Oregon; in each case, the measure defining marriage as a union between one man and one woman passed easily, yet polls showed that policies toward gay and lesbians ranked as far and away the least important issue to voters of both parties.[10] Candidates for office tend to be much more responsive to the issues that matter most to voters than are initiative advocates, for whom there is little or no incentive to select issues that are salient to voters. Candidates, unlike initiative activists, must seek out issues that are not only popular but also matter to ordinary voters.

When activists proclaim that the initiative process "belongs to the people," they obscure political reality behind a fog of populist platitudes. The initiative literally belongs to the few who write the measures, not to the many who vote. A national initiative would do little or nothing to empower the people; instead, it would provide political activists, politicians, and special interests another way to get what they want.

NOTES

PRO

1. For an overview, see Thomas E. Cronin, *Direct Democracy: The Politics of Initiative, Referendum, and Recall* (Cambridge, MA: Harvard University Press, 1989).
2. James A. Stimson, Michael B. MacKuen, and Robert S. Erikson, "Dynamic Representation," *American Political Science Review* 89 (1995): 543–65.
3. Senator James Eastland (D-MS) blocked 120 of 121 civil rights bills that came before his committee, which was known as the "burial ground" for civil rights. Robert D. Loevy, *The Civil Rights Act of 1964: The Passage of the Law That Ended Racial Segregation* (Albany: State University of New York Press, 1997).
4. For a related argument, see Mark V. Tushnet, *Taking the Constitution Away from the Courts* (Princeton, NJ: Princeton University Press, 2000).
5. See Center for Responsive Politics, http://www.opensecrets.org.
6. Tory Newmyer, "Murtha Got Payback in '08," *Roll Call,* January 27, 2009.
7. Barbara S. Gamble, "Putting Civil Rights to a Popular Vote," *American Journal of Political Science* 41 (1997): 245–69.
8. Kenneth P. Miller, *Direct Democracy and the Courts* (Princeton, NJ: Princeton University Press, 2009).
9. Mancur Olson, *The Logic of Collective Action: Public Goods and the Theory of Groups,* rev. ed. (Cambridge, MA: Harvard University Press, 1971).
10. An earmark is an appropriation of funds that can be given directly to a specific recipient, such as a business, an organization, or local government.
11. David Broder, *Democracy Derailed: Initiative Campaigns and the Power of Money* (New York, NY: Harcourt, 2000); Richard J. Ellis, *Democratic Delusions: The Initiative Process in America* (Lawrence: University Press of Kansas, 2002).
12. *First National Bank of Boston v. Bellotti* (1978).
13. Elisabeth R. Gerber, *The Populist Paradox: Interest Group Influence and the Promise of Direct Legislation* (Princeton, NJ: Princeton University Press, 1999).
14. Arthur Lupia, "Shortcuts versus Encyclopedias: Information and Voting Behavior in California Insurance Reform Elections," *American Political Science Review* 88 (1994): 63–76.
15. See Tim Weiner, "Senate Riders Put Some on the Inside Track," *New York Times,* July 7, 1999, http://www.nytimes.com/1999/07/07/us/senate-riders-put-some-on-the-inside-track.html?pagewanted=all.

16. John Fund, "Marks for Sharks," *Wall Street Journal,* January 9, 2006.

17. John Haskell, *Direct Democracy or Representative Government? Dispelling the Populist Myth* (Boulder, CO: Westview Press, 2001); Alan Rosenthal, *The Decline of Representative Democracy* (Washington, DC: CQ Press, 1998).

18. Arthur M. Schlesinger Jr., *The Imperial Presidency* (Boston, MA: Houghton Mifflin, 1973); Matthew A. Crenson and Benjamin Ginsberg, *Presidential Power: Unchecked and Unbalanced* (New York, NY: W. W. Norton, 2007).

19. Theodore J. Lowi, *The End of Liberalism* (New York, NY: W. W. Norton, 1969).

20. Louis Fisher, "Deciding on War against Iraq: Institutional Failures," *Political Science Quarterly* 118 (2003): 389–410.

21. Alan I. Abramowitz, Brad Alexander, and Matthew Gunning, "Incumbency, Redistricting, and the Decline of Competition in U.S. House Elections," *Journal of Politics* 68 (2008): 75–88.

22. Gary King and Andrew Gelman, "Systemic Consequences of Incumbency Advantage in U.S. House Elections," *American Journal of Political Science* 35 (1991): 110–38.

23. Morris Fiorina with Samuel J. Abrams and Jeremy C. Pope, *Culture War? The Myth of a Polarized America* (New York, NY: Pearson Longman, 2005); Todd Donovan, "A Goal for Reform: Make Elections Worth Stealing," *PS: Political Science and Politics* 40 (2007): 681–86.

24. Gerber, *The Populist Paradox*; John G. Matsusaka, *For the Many or the Few: The Initiative, Public Policy, and American Democracy* (Chicago, IL: University of Chicago Press, 2004).

25. This is based on requiring the collection of signatures equal to 5 percent of votes cast in the previous presidential election. In 2012, 129 million votes were cast for president.

26. Daniel A. Smith and Caroline J. Tolbert, "The Initiative to Party," *Party Politics* 7 (2001): 739–57.

CON

1. To qualify a statutory initiative for the ballot in California, petitioners must gather signatures equaling 5 percent of the number of votes cast for governor in the preceding election; in Oregon, the number is 6 percent. For constitutional initiatives, both states require 8 percent.

2. After the 2000 census, Mississippi lost one congressional district, reducing the number of districts from five to four. However, the state continues to use the five defunct district boundaries in carrying out its distribution requirement. See Citizens in Charge Foundation, "Mississippi," in *Of the People, by the People, for the People: A 2010 Report Card on Statewide Voter Initiative Rights* (Lake Ridge, VA: Citizens in Charge Foundation, 2010), http://www.citizensincharge.org/files/2010report-mississippi.pdf.

3. Until 2011, the only initiatives that had qualified for the ballot in Mississippi were two term limits measures, both of which were defeated. In 2011, however, three initiatives qualified for the ballot: a measure that defined human

personhood as beginning at the moment of fertilization (which was defeated), a measure requiring voters to present photo identification at the polls (which passed), and a third that restricted state and local governments from taking private property by eminent domain (which also passed). Four years elapsed before the next initiative reached the ballot. That measure would have required the state to provide adequate funding for public schools and empowered the judiciary to see that the funding mandate was carried out. For the first time, the legislature chose to place an alternative measure on the ballot, which would leave it to the legislature to decide the financing of the public schools—a superfluous measure since the constitution already gave the legislature that power. Voters were then asked to vote on two questions: (1) whether they preferred to leave the constitution unchanged and (2) whether they preferred the popular initiative or the legislature's alternative. Although a large majority (59 percent) preferred the citizen initiative to the legislature's plan, a small majority (52 percent) opposed changing the constitution, and as a result, both measures failed, which meant a victory for the legislature. If you are confused by that, imagine how the voters of Mississippi felt.

4. Quoted in David B. Magleby, *Direct Legislation: Voting on Ballot Propositions in the United States* (Baltimore, MD: Johns Hopkins University Press, 1984), 31.

5. The data on initiative use in Switzerland are derived from Philip L. DuBois and Floyd Feeney, *Lawmaking by Initiative: Issues, Options, and Comparisons* (New York, NY: Agathon Press, 1998), 49–57; the booklet *Modern Direct Democracy in Switzerland and the American West,* 19, available from the Swiss embassy in the United States; and e-mail communications with Bruno Kaufmann, president of the Initiative and Referendum Institute Europe, on February 5, 2012, and November 26, 2015.

6. *Modern Direct Democracy,* 19.

7. Quoted in Richard J. Ellis, *Democratic Delusions: The Initiative Process in America* (Lawrence: University Press of Kansas, 2002), 200.

8. Quoted in ibid., 201.

9. Lydia Chavez, *The Color Bind: California's Battle to End Affirmative Action* (Berkeley: University of California Press, 1998), 80, 145–46.

10. Joseph Carroll, "Economy, Terrorism Top Issues in 2004 Election Vote," Gallup, http://www.gallup.com/poll/9337/economy-terrorism-top-issues-2004-election-vote.aspx.

RESOLVED, the United States should adopt compulsory voting

PRO: Martin P. Wattenberg

CON: Jason Brennan

In the nineteenth century, Americans turned out to vote in very large numbers. Typically about eight in ten members of the voting-age male population cast a ballot in presidential elections. Even in off-year congressional elections, turnout was usually around 70 percent. Compare that with today, when turnout percentages among the voting-age population in presidential elections have averaged in the low fifties; in 2008 turnout reached 57 percent, the highest figure since 1972 (in 2012 turnout reverted closer to form, with only 53.6 percent of the voting-age population casting a ballot). In off-year elections, the contrast is even more stark: In 2014, only one in three of the voting-age population cast ballots, and only once in the past four decades has the figure edged (marginally) above 40 percent.[1]

Why don't Americans vote as much as they used to? In part, because voting just isn't as much fun as it used to be. In the nineteenth century, Election Day took place in a raucous, almost carnival-like atmosphere. People took the day off, political parties organized spectacular torchlight parades, and candidates plied voters with food and alcohol at polling places. There was no secret ballot, no quiet booth to enter or curtain to draw. Voting was a public and noisy business. Ballots were printed not by the government but by the political parties, which distributed ballots along with "a coin or two" to help get out the vote. There was no need for a voter to know how to read or write, let alone study a voters' pamphlet. Voting was a public affirmation of one's partisan (and often one's ethnic and religious) identity that was performed by dropping a preprinted "party ticket" into the ballot box.[2]

The introduction of the secret ballot (also known as the Australian ballot) in the 1880s and 1890s helped to end the carnivalesque atmosphere. It was now the government that produced the ballots and regulated how candidates and parties got on the ballot. States adopted new rules to keep polling places safe and sober—there would be no more alcohol or petty bribes. Not surprisingly, turnout dropped precipitously.

Among the new rules that contributed most to lower turnout was the establishment of voter registration and lengthy residency requirements, sometimes up to two years. The absence of registration and residency requirements in the nineteenth century certainly contributed to voter fraud; "vote early and often" was a phrase that resonated not only in Chicago but in cities across the nation. But registration and residency requirements did more than reduce fraud; they also (and not by accident) reduced turnout among recent immigrants, the poor, and the uneducated.

Today, no state is allowed to have a residency requirement of more than thirty days (courtesy of a 1972 Supreme Court ruling, *Dunn v. Blumstein*), and registering to vote has been made substantially easier than it was during most of the twentieth century. Few states now require voters to register more than three weeks before an election, and about a dozen states permit same-day voter registration. Moreover, the National Voter Registration Act of 1993 (known as the Motor Voter Law) required states (except those that allow for same-day registration) to allow citizens to register to vote when applying for a driver's license. But even a registration requirement of three weeks can be a considerable hurdle for apolitical voters who tune in to a campaign only in its final weeks. Moreover, since a voter must register in a particular voting precinct, almost any change of address requires reregistering. Those who do not habitually follow politics and who move a lot, especially the young, are particularly burdened by these registration requirements.

One solution to the problem of the large number of nonvoters, especially among the young, the poor, and the uneducated, would be for the United States to follow the example of most other advanced industrialized democracies and adopt automatic, national, permanent registration. In these nations, such as Germany, turnout is routinely in the 80 percent range, in large part because voter registration is the government's responsibility, not the citizen's.

Another solution, one advocated by Martin P. Wattenberg, is to follow the example of countries such as Australia and adopt compulsory voting. Under this scheme, all eligible voters must cast a ballot, although they need not vote for anyone on that ballot. Casting a blank ballot fulfills the voter's legal obligation in the same way that paying taxes does. Wattenberg argues that, ultimately, compulsory voting is the only way to ensure that our democratically elected government represents all the people and not just those who bother to turn out to vote—who happen to be much more affluent, older, and better educated than those who do not vote. Jason Brennan, in contrast, argues that the cure of compulsory voting is worse than the disease of low turnout. Indeed, Brennan questions whether low turnout is really a disease at all, given that higher turnout would mean more participation by those who care less and are less well informed about politics.

PRO: Martin P. Wattenberg

The United States has a turnout problem. Only about 60 percent of citizens vote in presidential elections, 40 percent in midterm congressional elections, 25 percent in presidential primaries, and even less in municipal elections. For a country that takes great pride in its democratic traditions, the fact that the United States has one of the lowest voter turnout rates in the world stands out as an embarrassment. We can scarcely hold ourselves up as a democratic model for developing countries to emulate when so many Americans regularly fail to exercise their civic responsibility to vote.

When he was president, Bill Clinton is said to have remarked that solutions to most public policy problems have already been found somewhere—we just have to scan the horizons for them. This certainly applies to increasing voter turnout. Three possible changes stand out as particularly likely to get Americans to the polls: automatic voter registration, moving Election Day to a weekend or holiday, and requiring citizens to go to the polls.

Evidence from around the world indicates that our turnout rates could be increased if we adopted a system of automatic voter registration. In many other countries, the government takes the initiative to compile lists of eligible voters, and voters do not have to face the bureaucratic task of getting registered to vote. Since many people do not vote simply because they are not registered to do so, putting all eligible individuals on the rolls would certainly help increase turnout rates. As Attorney General Eric Holder said in December 2011: "Fortunately, modern technology provides a straightforward fix for these problems—if we have the political will to bring our election systems into the 21st century. It should be the government's responsibility to automatically register citizens to vote, by compiling—from databases that already exist—a list of all eligible residents in each jurisdiction."[1] Oregon took a big step in this direction in 2015 by enacting the first automatic registration system in the country. Oregon's Department of Motor Vehicles will now transmit information about citizens to the Secretary of State's Office for purposes of registering these people to vote or updating their registration. Individuals who are automatically registered or re-registered will be sent a notice stating their new voter registration details and will have the option to opt out of being registered if they so choose. In other words, this is a revolutionary change from one that puts the onus on the individual to opt-in to one in which the individual has to take an action to not be registered. It is estimated that 300,000 more individuals will be registered in Oregon in 2016, bringing the registration rate in the state to 87 percent of its citizenry.

An even simpler lesson we could learn from other countries is to schedule our elections on convenient days. Many Americans wrongly assume that Tuesday election days must be in the Constitution. In fact, Article I, Section 4, states only that "the Times, Places and Manner of holding Elections for Senators and Representatives, shall be prescribed in each State by the Legislature thereof; but the Congress may at any time by Law make or alter such Regulations." An 1872 law established the first Tuesday after the first Monday in November as Election Day. At that point in history it made little difference whether elections were on Saturdays or Tuesdays, because most people worked on Saturdays. Only Sundays would have been days free of work, but with elections in the late nineteenth century being occasions for drinking and gambling, that option was out of the question in such a religious country. Today, moving to weekend elections or establishing a holiday for Election Day is far more feasible and could be accomplished with a simple piece of legislation.

Although both automatic voter registration and moving Election Day to a more convenient time would help increase turnout, these are by no means panaceas for America's turnout problem. People who are not motivated by political issues are not likely to vote simply because it has become easier for them to do so. To solve our voter turnout problem, we need to make a fundamental change in people's incentives to vote. The countries that have been most successful in getting virtually all of their citizens to vote have done so in the same way that democracies accomplish many other goals—namely, by requiring them to vote or face a fine.[2] This practice is commonly known as *compulsory voting*, but this term is somewhat misleading. The secrecy of modern ballots makes it impossible to tell whether an individual has actually voted as opposed to just turning in a blank ballot. Thus, all that can be required is that citizens show up for elections, not that they vote. But given that almost all people who go to the polls under this requirement do vote for somebody, and given that *compulsory voting* is the commonly used phrase, it seems reasonable to use it with this caveat.

The concept of compulsory voting may seem strange to Americans, but it is an idea that has been tried in a number of other countries. Among established democracies with advanced industrialized societies, Australia, Belgium, Greece, and Luxembourg have compulsory voting laws. In addition, Italy, Austria, and the Netherlands had compulsory voting laws on the books for at least part of the modern era, although enforcement in each of these countries was always weak. By comparison, France, Finland, and the United States are the only advanced industrialized democracies that elect presidents who play a major role in governing. Thus, presidential government is actually rarer in wealthy democracies than is the practice of requiring citizens to go to the polls.

The best argument for the adoption of compulsory voting is simply that it works extremely well. As Arend Lijphart writes, "Compulsory voting is a particularly effective method to achieve high turnout," even with low penalties and lax enforcement.[3] In particular, survey data from countries that practice compulsory voting demonstrate that such laws are effective in getting all age groups out to vote in very high numbers. The relationship between age and turnout is negligible in all four advanced industrialized countries that currently practice compulsory voting. Unlike many other democracies that are suffering from abysmally low youth turnout, these four countries have recently experienced turnout rates ranging from 89 to 97 percent among citizens ages eighteen to twenty-nine. In contrast, in the 2010 midterm elections the U.S. Census Bureau survey found that just 24 percent of American citizens under the age of thirty reported voting. With senior citizens being roughly three times as likely as these young Americans to vote in the 2010 U.S. election, the net result was the same as if everyone had voted but the votes of each elderly person had been counted three times while that of each young person had been counted just once. Such massive inequalities in electoral participation do not occur in countries that practice compulsory voting.

When one social group votes at far higher rates than another, the impact on public policy can be profound. This is particularly likely to be the case when the views of a low-turnout group are substantially different from the views of a group that votes at a relatively high rate. Take the example of young people versus senior citizens. In 2008, the American National Election Studies found that respondents under the age of thirty were significantly more likely than those over sixty-five to favor gay marriage, abortion rights, gun control, strengthening environmental protection laws, making cuts in military spending, and establishing a national health care plan. These agenda items obviously suffer whenever young people's turnout rate falls well below that of senior citizens.

Furthermore, politicians are far more likely to pay close attention to public policy issues that affect groups that vote in high numbers. Problems that high-turnout groups consider to be important are far more likely to be dealt with before they get serious, whereas those that affect low-turnout groups can be more safely left on the back burner. Hence, the issues of interest to young adults, such as the availability of student loans, are considered to be of lower priority than they would be if everyone voted. Survey data demonstrate that Australian young people are just as apathetic about politics as their American counterparts, yet Australian politicians regularly pay attention to young people, knowing that they will vote at the next election, as attendance at elections is compulsory.

HOW MUCH SUPPORT IS
THERE FOR COMPULSORY VOTING?

One of the most common arguments against the adoption of compulsory voting is that the public won't stand for it. How much truth is there to such an assertion? And how much support is there for compulsory voting in countries that mandate showing up for elections? The answers are difficult to ascertain because no cross-national survey has asked about compulsory voting. However, some country-specific data are available for Australia, Great Britain, Canada, and the United States.

The survey data from Australia demonstrate that compulsory voting is widely popular there. Among respondents to the 2013 Australian Election Study, 70 percent thought that voting at federal elections should be required, and of these people, about two out of three said they strongly favored compulsory voting. Such high levels of support have consistently been the case in Australia, with support never falling below 60 percent in data compiled by Mackerras and McAllister dating back to 1943.[4] Interestingly, even young Australians clearly favored compulsory voting in 2013. At the same time, these young respondents were also the least likely to say that they definitely would have voted had participation been voluntary.[5] Were it not for mandatory voting, there would be a significant age gap in electoral participation in Australia similar to that found in many other countries, including the United States.

Whenever I talk to political science classes in Australia, I find that many Aussie students are amazed to learn how low turnout is for American elections. They immediately ask me why the United States doesn't just emulate their country's example and fine people who fail to participate. The best response I can think of is simply that most Americans object to the government telling them to do something, even if it is good for them. American political culture is based on John Locke's views of individual rights, which differ from Jeremy Bentham's concept of the greatest good for the greatest number, which shaped Australian culture. Most Americans would probably assert that they have an inviolable right not to show up at the polls. Survey data confirm that there is currently not much support among Americans for any law requiring them to vote. Only 21 percent of Americans interviewed in a 2004 ABC News poll supported the idea of a compulsory voting law like Australia's.

Attitudes toward compulsory voting in Canada and Great Britain fall in between the strong support for compulsory voting in Australia and the clear hostility to the idea in the United States. In both countries, support for compulsory voting increases with age. A majority of senior citizens in Canada and Great

Britain support making voting mandatory, whereas a majority of those ages eighteen to twenty-nine oppose compulsory voting. Older citizens are more supportive of compulsory voting because voters are substantially more likely than nonvoters to favor compulsory voting, and of course older people have the highest turnout rates. Ironically, it is those who have the most to gain from compulsory voting (the young) who are least supportive of it.

Citizens who vote apparently do not want to monopolize political power. Roughly half of voters in both Britain and Canada support the notion that participation by everyone is so important that the government should require it. If politicians listen primarily to those who vote, then they may well start to consider compulsory voting if turnout rates continue to fall, especially among young people. Indeed, a serious rumbling in this direction could be seen after turnout fell dramatically in Britain. The leader of the British House of Commons, Geoff Hoon, publicly stated that he thought a move to compulsory voting was necessary to reinvigorate U.K. democracy, arguing that "we need to get people more engaged in political processes."[6]

Most newsworthy of all was President Obama's positive mention of compulsory voting in response to a question in March, 2015 about how to cure the "dysfunction" in Washington. Obama not only indicated that compulsory voting would be a good cure for what ails American politics but also specifically mentioned how this reform would bring more young people into the political system. His remarks on this subject are worth quoting at length:

> In Australia, and some other countries, there's mandatory voting. It would be transformative if everybody voted. That would counteract money more than anything. If everybody voted, then it would completely change the political map in this country, because the people who tend not to vote are young; they're lower income; they're skewed more heavily towards immigrant groups and minority groups; and they're often the folks who are . . . scratching and climbing to get into the middle class. And they're working hard, and there's a reason why some folks try to keep them away from the polls. We should want to get them into the polls. So that may end up being a better strategy in the short term.[7]

If the president of the United States can publically suggest that compulsory voting is an idea worth seriously considering, then perhaps it's not so unrealistic to envision this actually being adopted a couple decades from now. After all, who could have envisioned gay marriage being legalized back in the mid-1990s when Congress passed the Defense of Marriage Act by veto-proof majorities, allowing states the ability to not recognize same-sex marriages granted elsewhere?

IS TALK OF COMPULSORY VOTING REALISTIC?

When Arend Lijphart called for compulsory voting in his 1996 presidential address to the American Political Science Association, he noted: "The danger of too much pessimism about the chances for compulsory voting is that it becomes a self-fulfilling prophecy. If even the supporters of compulsory voting believe that its chances are nil—and hence make no effort on behalf of it—it will indeed never be adopted!"[8] I wholeheartedly agree. Political scientists have been far too cautious in recommending compulsory voting despite what we know about the seriousness of the turnout problem among young people and how well this solution works to correct it.

Engineering safety experts have not backed off their recommendations that motorists be required by law to use seat belts just because many people think that whether to buckle up or not should be a matter of personal choice. Nor have researchers who have examined the effects of secondhand smoke backed off on recommendations to ban smoking in public places just because many people think that such restrictions violate their individual rights. Rather, these researchers have continued to try to educate people and shift public policy, with a fair degree of success. For example, in 2010, a Gallup Poll found that 59 percent of Americans supported banning smoking in restaurants, up from a mere 17 percent in 1987.[9] As attitudes have changed, so have laws, with 38 U.S. states banning smoking in restaurants as of 2015. The campaign to increase the use of safety belts in automobiles has been equally impressive. Every state except New Hampshire now has a law requiring the use of seat belts. Data compiled by the National Highway Traffic Safety Administration on actual usage of seat belts indicate that between 1995 and 2014, the percentage of passengers using seat belts increased from 60 to 87 percent.[10] In sum, attitudes and behavior can change as people become more aware of a problem; and once such changes are put into motion, politicians feel compelled to take actions that they never would have considered a decade earlier.

Ironically, one of the obstacles to the adoption of compulsory voting is the fear of success. Some analysts have trepidations about forcing people with limited political interest to appear at the polls. Once compelled to vote, these citizens may make choices the same way some people choose lottery numbers. Or worse yet, they may be particularly susceptible to demagogic appeals by irresponsible politicians with antidemocratic tendencies. Granted, these are serious concerns. But which is the worst scenario—a low and biased turnout with the participation of only those who follow politics or a broad and representative turnout with the participation of people who follow politics as well as those who do not? Consider the situation in Italy as of 1959, when the Civic Culture

Study found that about two-thirds of Italians said they *never* followed political and governmental affairs. Italy then had a compulsory voting law, and although it was not rigorously enforced, turnout nevertheless ranged between 92 and 95 percent. Looking back, can one really make a case that it would have been better if only the one-third of the Italian population who followed politics had voted? I think not.

In his book *Culture War?*, Morris Fiorina writes that his students express outrage at the prospect of being forced to go to the polls even if they don't like any of the candidates.[11] I would ask such students to consider whether they shouldn't be more outraged that older people are running the government while their generation is ignored because of its low turnout rate. Instituting compulsory voting would serve to level the inequalities in political participation and compel politicians to be responsive to all social groups. To those who say that compulsory voting is "un-American," I respond with a question: What is more American than making sure that every adult citizen counts equally in our democracy?

CON: Jason Brennan

I magine I had a magic wand. Waving the wand would instantly make the median American voter more misinformed, more ignorant, and more irrational about politics. As a result, the quality of candidates who make it onto the ballot, and who win elections, would be worse. As a result, we would get worse policies and laws. Would waving the magic wand be good for America? This magic wand may in fact exist. Compulsory voting might be just such a magic wand.

Many who advocate compulsory voting do so because they believe it will produce better government, government that is more just and equitable. This argument may seem plausible. However, I will show that there is no good reason to believe that compulsory voting would produce better government; in fact, it might even produce slightly worse government.

Political scientist Annabelle Lever recently reviewed the empirical studies on compulsory voting and concluded that it has "no noticeable effect on political knowledge or interest [or] electoral outcomes." Moreover, she found compulsory voting to be "no guarantee of egalitarian social policies." In Australia, for instance, which has long practiced compulsory voting, there is no evidence that high turnout has led "parties to compete for the votes of the poor, the weak, and the marginalized."[1]

Despite the lack of evidence, people continue to speculate that compulsory voting would result in better government. There are two major arguments in favor of this contention. Let us call the first the *correlation argument*:

A. Compulsory voting causes high voter turnout.
B. High voter turnout and good government are correlated.
C. If high voter turnout and good government are correlated, then high turnout causes good government.
D. Therefore, compulsory voting would produce better government.

Premise A is true. Premise B is questionable. Partly, it depends on what counts as "good government." However, for the sake of argument, let us grant that B is true. After all, granting this premise helps the other side, not my side. However, even if we grant that B is true, premise C is problematic.

Even if high voter turnout and good government were correlated, we could not automatically conclude that high turnout causes good government. It may be that good government causes high turnout. Or it may be that some third factor causes both of them. The only way to know is to check with empirical studies.

In fact, political scientists have tried to check. To my knowledge, no empirical study has found that high voter turnout causes better government. Part of the problem with this is that there is no obvious, uncontroversial test of what counts as better government.[2] That said, political scientists will often assume that one marker of good government is that citizens trust the government and approve of it. In this case, however, insofar as there is much evidence at all, the causal arrow appears to point the other way. There is strong evidence that when citizens approve of and trust their governments, this causes higher turnout.[3] It seems that when citizens have warm, fuzzy feelings about their government, they are more likely to vote. The balance of evidence indicates that approval of and trust in government cause high turnout, not that high turnout causes approval and trust. So, the correlation argument fails.

A more fundamental argument for compulsory voting is what we can call the *demographic argument*:

A. Voters tend to vote in their self-interest.
B. Politicians tend to give large voting blocs what they ask for.
C. When voting is voluntary, the poor, members of minority groups, the uneducated, the working classes, and young people are less likely to vote than are rich, White, educated, upper-middle-class, and older people.

D. If this is so, then under voluntary voting, government will tend to promote the interests of the rich, of Whites, and of the old over the interests of the poor, of minorities, and of the young.

E. Under compulsory voting, almost all demographic and socioeconomic groups vote equally.

F. Thus, under compulsory voting, government will promote everyone's interests.

G. Therefore, compulsory voting causes better government.

The demographic argument also seems plausible. It seems reasonable to speculate that forcing the poor to vote will protect them from selfish rich voters. It thus seems reasonable to speculate that compulsory voting will produce fairer and more equitable government.

However, the demographic argument has major problems. First, it assumes (in premise A) that voters vote in their own self-interest. Second, it assumes (in premise F) that if nonvoters were to vote, this would tend to help them rather than hurt them. Both of these assumptions seem like common sense—but they are mistaken.

The demographic argument assumes that voters vote selfishly, yet political scientists who have conducted empirical studies of voting behavior generally agree that voters do not vote selfishly. Rather, voters tend to vote for what they perceive to be in the national interest.[4] Most voters try to promote everyone's interests, not just their own. So, proponents of compulsory voting want to force people to vote in order to protect them from a largely nonexistent threat—the threat of the selfish majority voter. In short, premise A of the demographic argument is false.

The demographic argument also assumes that nonvoters know enough about politics and economics to choose candidates who would in fact benefit them. However, there is no reason to assume that.

Imagine a character named Betty Benevolence. Betty has good intentions. She wants to make the world a better place. However, Betty is irrational and processes information in a biased, unscientific way. As a result, Betty has incorrect ideas about how best to help others. When she sees someone drowning, she throws water on his face. When she sees someone starving, she burns his remaining food. She means well, but her actions make things worse. As a voter, Betty intends to support candidates and policies that will eliminate poverty and help the downtrodden. However, she has mistaken beliefs about economics, sociology, political science, and other relevant social scientific matters. Betty votes for politicians who make things worse, not better. Betty means well, but she does us no favors by voting.

Betty is not just some fanciful thought experiment. Although few of us are like Betty in our daily lives, many of us are much like Betty when we vote. Why the difference? It has to do with incentives. If you are trying to cross a street and ignore the oncoming traffic, you die. If you vote but ignore or evade all relevant information in making your voting decisions, nothing happens. You are more likely to win millions of dollars in a multistate lottery than you are to change the outcome of a congressional election.

Social scientists have long studied voter knowledge and rationality. The results are frightening. Most voters are ignorant, misinformed, irrational, and biased about political issues.[5] The typical person who abstains from voting is even more ignorant, misinformed, irrational, and biased than the typical person who votes. That is, when it comes to politics, current voters are much like Betty, and current nonvoters are even more like Betty.

For instance, the economist Bryan Caplan shows that Americans have systematically mistaken beliefs about trade, immigration, how well markets function, and the trajectory of the economy.[6] The median American voter would fail Econ 101. When the median voter votes, he or she chooses candidates who share the median voter's mistaken beliefs about basic economics. Like Betty, the median voter thus tends to choose candidates who *undermine* his or her own goals.

While the median U.S. voter is economically illiterate, the median nonvoter is even *more* illiterate than the median voter.[7] The median voter would get an F in Econ 101, but the median nonvoter would get an even lower F. The median voter makes big mistakes about economics, but the median nonvoter makes even bigger mistakes. Thus, forcing everyone to vote would create an even more deeply misinformed and irrational electorate.

The demographic argument correctly asserts that White, affluent, and older people are more likely to vote than non-White, poor, and young people. However, it also turns out that, in general, being White, affluent, and older is correlated with political knowledge, while being non-White, poor, and young is correlated with political ignorance and misinformation.[8] The people who vote tend to be more knowledgeable than those who abstain.

The demographic argument gets the facts wrong. It assumes that voters are well-informed and rational but selfish when it comes to electoral politics. However, in fact, most voters are ignorant and irrational but altruistic. Most voters (and nonvoters) want to promote justice and the common good. That does not make them good voters. Voters have defective *knowledge* if not defective motives.

Most people who support the adoption of compulsory voting in the United States think it would produce better government. I expect that, on the contrary, it would produce slightly worse government. The law can force us to go to the polls, but it cannot force us to vote intelligently. It cannot force us to be well-informed rather than ignorant. It cannot force us to process information in a rational, unbiased way. Requiring everyone to vote would probably hurt the very people it is meant to help. The adoption of compulsory voting in the United States would cause the median level of political knowledge and rationality to drop. It would be like waving a magic wand that makes the electorate slightly dumber about politics.

So far, I have undermined one major argument (and some supporting arguments) in favor of compulsory voting. However, it is difficult to prove a negative. Fortunately, in this debate, the other side has the burden of proof. That is, those who want to force citizens to vote must produce a compelling justification. By default, we should presume that compulsory voting is unjust.

Compulsory voting is, after all, compulsory. Advocates of compulsory voting want governments to coerce people into voting. In commonsense moral thought, we presume that coercion—including coercion by governments—is wrong until it is shown to be otherwise. When the state intrudes into citizens' lives or forces them to perform a service, this is presumed unjust until it is shown to be otherwise. Anytime the state restricts citizens' liberties, this is presumed unjust until it is shown to be otherwise. In general, compulsion has to be justified; the lack of compulsion does not.

As an analogy, imagine we are debating about whether to go to war. The prowar side would have the burden of proof. Wars are presumed illegitimate. In any debate about going to war, the antiwar side does not need to prove that the proposed war is bad. Rather, the prowar side has to prove that the proposed war is just. Otherwise, the antiwar side wins by default. Similarly, in this debate, the procompulsory voting side needs to prove that compulsory voting is good and just. It has to overcome the presumption against government coercion. Otherwise, the anticompulsory voting side wins by default.

Proponents of instituting compulsory voting in the United States usually attempt to argue that compulsory voting would produce certain desirable consequences. For the sake of argument, suppose they were right. This would not be enough to justify compulsory voting.

In general, showing that compulsion produces desirable consequences is not enough to justify compulsion. For example, social scientists consistently find that regular church attendance and marriage make most people happier.[9] Making people happier is a desirable consequence, yet this would not justify the state's forcing people to attend religious services (of their own choosing) or to find spouses. Social scientists have also shown that getting sufficient sleep makes people happier.[10] Although it is desirable for everyone to be happier, that would not justify the state's forcing people to get more sleep. Americans who live in sunny areas tend to be happier than those who live in rainy areas, but that would not justify the state's forcing people to move to the Sunbelt. That coercing people would produce good consequences is not enough to justify coercing them.

The political theorist William Galston advocates compulsory voting. He agrees that compulsory voting infringes citizens' liberty, but he says, compulsory voting is only a *small* or *trivial* infringement of liberty. Compulsory voting requires little from citizens.[11] Voting takes a half hour every few years. Compulsory voting is less onerous than jury duty.

Galston is right: Forcing citizens to vote is only a small infringement of liberty. But even the pettiest violations of liberty must be justified. Suppose Congress passed the following law, the Red Scarf Mandate:

> Congress will provide a red scarf to each citizen. Each citizen must wear a red scarf for a total of two minutes per year. The citizen may choose the time most convenient for him or her to wear the scarf.

The Red Scarf Mandate is a petty violation of liberty. However, it would still be an unjust law. It would be morally wrong for Congress to pass the Red Scarf Mandate unless it had compelling reasons. We have our own lives to lead. We are presumed to be free to live as we like until shown otherwise. Congress may not push us around and tell us what to do unless it has extremely good grounds to override our freedom.

Voter participation rates are low in some countries. So what? Instead of asking how we can make them higher, we should ask instead how we could induce people to vote smarter. It is important that enough people vote and, when they do vote, that they vote well. That does not imply that we need *everyone* to vote, especially if many potential voters do not know enough to vote well. Democracy tends to be a good thing. That does not mean the state should shove it down our throats.

NOTES

INTRO

1.   If we look at voting-eligible population (that is, exclude those who are noncitizens as well as felons who are disenfranchised by state law), then the recent numbers look better. Much of the decline in turnout during the latter decades of the twentieth century was an artifact of a marked increase in the numbers of noncitizens and disenfranchised felons. However, even if we look at only the

voting-eligible population (that is, exclude noncitizens and disenfranchised felons), voter turnout in 2012 was still less than 60 percent, well below the roughly 80 percent turnout rates routinely reached in the late nineteenth-century United States and in the twenty-first century in many European nations.

2. Jill Lepore, "Rock, Paper, Scissors," *New Yorker,* October 13, 2008; Richard Franklin Bensel, *The American Ballot Box in the Mid-Nineteenth Century* (New York, NY: Cambridge University Press, 2004).

PRO

1. Eric Holder, speech delivered at the Lyndon Baines Johnson Library and Museum, Austin, TX, December 13, 2011.

2. In Australia, the typical fine for nonvoting is twenty Australian dollars. However, judges typically accept any reasonable excuse, and few people end up paying a fine for not voting. In the Australian federal election of 2004, there were about 13 million enrolled voters, 94.3 percent of whom participated. Of the approximately 740,000 nonvoters, only about 50,000 actually paid a fine.

3. Arend Lijphart, "Unequal Participation: Democracy's Unresolved Dilemma," *American Political Science Review* 91 (1997): 2.

4. Malcolm Mackerras and Ian McAllister, "Compulsory Voting, Party Stability, and Electoral Advantage in Australia," *Electoral Studies* 18 (1999): 221.

5. Of respondents ages eighteen to twenty-nine, 46 percent said they definitely would have voted in 2013 had voting been voluntary, compared to 74 percent among Australian senior citizens.

6. "Hoon Suggests Compulsory Voting," *BBC News World Edition,* July 4, 2005.

7. "Remarks by the President to the City Club of Cleveland," March 18, 2015.

8. Lijphart, "Unequal Participation," 11.

9. Lydia Saad, "Americans Want Smoking Off the Menu at Restaurants," *Gallup Poll Report,* August 6, 2010.

10. T.M. Pickrell and E.H. Choi, "Safety Belt Use in 2014—Overall Results." Traffic Safety Facts Research Note, February 2015, National Highway Traffic Safety Administration.

11. Morris P. Fiorina with Samuel J. Abrams and Jeremy C. Pope, *Culture War? The Myth of a Polarized America* (New York, NY: Longman, 2005), 111.

CON

1. Annabelle Lever, "'A Liberal Defence of Compulsory Voting': Some Reasons for Scepticism," *Politics* 28 (2008): 61–64. See also Annabelle Lever, "Compulsory Voting: A Critical Perspective," *British Journal of Political Science* 40 (2010): 897–915; Peter John Lowen, Henry Milner, and Bruce M. Hicks, "Does Compulsory Voting Lead to More Informed and Engaged Citizens? An Experimental Test," *Canadian Journal of Political Science* 41 (2008): 655–67; and Simon Jackman, "Compulsory Voting," in *International Encyclopedia of the Social and Behavioral Sciences,* Ed. Neil J. Smelser and Paul B. Baltes (Amsterdam: Elsevier, 2004), 93–97.

2. See the discussions in Loren Lomasky and Geoffrey Brennan, "Is There a Duty to Vote?," *Social Philosophy and Policy* 17 (2000): 62–86; and Alan Paten, "The Republican Critique of Liberalism," *British Journal of Political Science* 26 (1996): 25–44.

3. See Michaelene Cox, "When Trust Matters: Explaining Differences in Voter Turnout," *Journal of Common Market Studies* 41 (2003): 757–70; Margaret Levi and Laura Stoker, "Political Trust and Trustworthiness," *Annual Review of Political Science* 3 (2000): 475–507; Timothy Besley, *Principled Agents? The Political Economy of Good Government* (New York, NY: Oxford University Press, 2006), 17–20; Mark Franklin, *Voter Turnout and the Dynamics of Electoral Competition in Established Democracies since 1945* (New York, NY: Cambridge University Press, 2004), 91–118. See also Jocelyn Evans, *Voters and Voting: An Introduction* (Thousand Oaks, CA: Sage, 2004), chap. 7, for a summary of explanations of voter turnout, some of which suggest that higher-quality governance produces higher turnout, rather than vice versa. Arend Lijphart, *Patterns of Democracy* (New Haven, CT: Yale University Press, 1999), 284–86, also provides some evidence that better governance causes higher participation.

4. For example, see Diana Mutz and Jeffrey Mondak, "Dimensions of Sociotropic Behavior: Group-Based Judgments of Fairness and Well-Being," *American Journal of Political Science* 41 (1997): 284–308; Dale Miller, "The Norm of Self-Interest," *American Psychologist* 54 (1999): 1053–60; Carolyn Funk and Patricia Garcia-Monet, "The Relationship between Personal and National Concerns in Public Perceptions of the Economy," *Political Research Quarterly* 50 (1997): 317–42; Geoffrey Brennan and Loren Lomasky, *Democracy and Decision* (New York, NY: Cambridge University Press, 1993), 108–14; Bryan Caplan, *The Myth of the Rational Voter* (Princeton, NJ: Princeton University Press, 2007), 229. See also Jason Brennan, *The Ethics of Voting* (Princeton, NJ: Princeton University Press, 2011), 202n2.

5. For example, see Brennan, *The Ethics of Voting,* chap. 8; Jamie Terence Kelly, *Framing Democracy: A Behavioral Approach to Democratic Theory* (Princeton, NJ: Princeton University Press, 2012); Michael X. Delli Carpini and Scott Keeter, *What Americans Know about Politics and Why It Matters* (New Haven, CT: Yale University Press, 1996); Jonathan Haidt, *The Righteous Mind: Why Good People Are Divided by Politics and Religion* (New York, NY: Pantheon, 2012); Drew Westen, *The Political Brain: The Role of Emotion in Deciding the Fate of the Nation* (New York, NY: Public Affairs, 2008); Bryan Caplan, Eric Crampton, Wayne A. Grove, and Ilya Somin, "Systematically Biased Beliefs about Political Influence: Evidence from the Perception of Political Influence on Policy Outcomes Survey" (working paper, George Mason University, 2012).

6. Caplan, *Myth of the Rational Voter.*

7. Ibid., 255–56.

8. For example, see Scott Althaus, "Information Effects in Collective Preferences," *American Political Science Review* 92 (1998): 545–58.

9. For example, see Michael Argyle, *The Psychology of Happiness* (London, Uk: Routledge, 2002). The Pew Research Center, using data from the General Social Survey, reports that regular church attendees are about twice as likely to report being very happy as are those who never or seldom attend church. See Pew Research Center, "Are We Happy Yet?," February 13, 2006, http://pewresearch .org/pubs/301/are-we-happy-yet. That religious service attendance is strongly correlated with happiness is well-known, but researchers dispute *why* religious attendance seems to make people happier.

10. Daniel Kahneman, Alan B. Krueger, David A. Schkade, Norbert Schwarz, and Arthur A. Stone, "A Survey Method for Characterizing Daily Life Experience: The Day Reconstruction Method," *Science* 306 (2004): 1776–80.

11. William Galston, "Telling Americans to Vote, or Else," *New York Times,* November 6, 2011, SR9.

RESOLVED, Congress should remove the caps on the amount that individuals can contribute to candidates for federal office

PRO: John Samples

CON: Richard Briffault

In 1972, insurance magnate W. Clement Stone gave several million dollars to President Richard Nixon's reelection campaign. Stone said he gave the money because he admired Nixon's resilience and strength. Some critics alleged it was because he hoped to be named ambassador to Great Britain—if so, the money was in vain, though perhaps that was because the incumbent ambassador in London gave Nixon's campaign $250,000. Nixon was not the only one raking in big checks. His opponent George McGovern received $400,000 from philanthropist Stewart Mott, who four years earlier had been among a handful of wealthy individuals who bankrolled Senator Eugene McCarthy's insurgent campaign to topple President Lyndon Johnson.

Nixon would later say of Stone that no man had given him more and asked for less. Many were less sanguine about candidates' reliance on the contributions of "fat cat" millionaires and set out to reform the campaign finance system. The reformers' crusade was aided by the Watergate scandal that soon brought to light numerous transgressions by the Nixon administration, including not only the cover-up of the administration's break-in at the Democratic Party headquarters but also shaking down contributors and soliciting illegal campaign contributions. On August 8, 1974, the same day that a disgraced Nixon announced his resignation, the House of Representatives passed a series of amendments to the Federal Election Campaigns Act (FECA). These amendments, signed into law by new president Gerald Ford in October 1974, imposed strict limits on (a) the amounts that individuals could contribute to candidates for federal office, (b) independent expenditures that could be made on behalf of a candidate, and (c) the total amount candidates could spend in a campaign.

In 1976, in *Buckley v Valeo* (1976), the Supreme Court struck down much of Congress's handiwork, notably the limits it placed on independent expenditures and candidate spending. However, the Court left in place the restrictions Congress placed on contributions by individuals as well as by political action committees (PACs) set up by interest groups to contribute to campaigns. Campaign contributions, the Court reasoned, could be limited because to allow individuals or groups to donate huge sums of money to a candidate created the appearance if not the reality of corruption and therefore threatened the integrity of the electoral process. Campaign spending, however, including independent expenditures on behalf of a candidate, did not create even the appearance of corruption, and so the government did not have an interest that was sufficiently compelling to justify restricting the freedom of speech guaranteed by the First Amendment.

The Court's distinction between campaign contributions and campaign expenditures has been assailed by liberal and conservatives alike. Liberals have generally insisted that money is not a form of speech, and therefore Congress should be free to regulate the way campaigns are financed. Conservatives have been equally critical of *Buckley*, insisting that the Court should have rejected all of Congress's efforts to restrict the flow of money into politics since limiting money inevitably reduces the amount of speech.

The financing of federal elections has changed in many ways since *Buckley*, but contribution limits remain in place. In 2016, no individual can give more than $2,700 to a candidate in any election (the primary and general election count as two elections). That is nearly three times the $1,000 limit that was put in place in 1974 (in 2002 Congress doubled individual contribution limits to $2,000 and indexed them to inflation) but nothing like the amounts that donors were allowed to give before the 1974 amendments to FECA.

John Samples argues that it is time for Congress to admit that it got it wrong in 1974 (and 2002) and to abolish individual contribution limits. In Samples's view, democracy depends on candidates being able to communicate their message to as many voters as possible and thus contribution limits diminish our democracy. Contribution limits, he maintains, are a boon to incumbents because they starve challengers of funding. Moreover, such limits increase the amount of time candidates need to spend raising money—and thus reduce the amount of time for governing as well as campaigning. And far from stopping the flow of money into politics, contribution limits have fueled the rise of SuperPACs that, so long as they are independent of candidates, can raise and spend unlimited amounts of money. Lifting contribution limits would render SuperPACs unnecessary and would enable candidates to control their message.

Richard Briffault counters that lifting contribution limits is the wrong way to fix our ailing campaign finance system. The answer is not to lift contributions but to undo the damage done by Supreme Court rulings that have limited Congress's power to regulate money. For Briffault, lifting the limits is to give up altogether and allow the wealthy to call the shots and bring us full circle back to the regulatory regime that brought us the corruption of Watergate.

PRO: John Samples

Consider how two people, call them Ann and Charles, might participate in an election. Ann might give money to a candidate for office who then uses the sum along with other donations to buy television time to solicit votes. On the other hand, Charles might buy television time to solicit votes on behalf of the same candidate. Ann is contributing to a candidate's campaign. Charles is directly spending on speech to support a candidate.

Federal law limits the sums the Anns of the world may contribute. In 2015 and 2016, an individual may give no more than $2,700 to a candidate in each election. Individuals may also give up to $5,000 per election to a political action committee that in turn donates to a candidate. Other limits apply to donations to the political parties.[1]

Since 2010, government may not restrict Charles's direct, independent spending for candidates. The courts say that such spending translates directly into speech about candidates and elections. To restrict (or prohibit) such spending precludes such speech and thus abridges the freedom of speech protected by the First Amendment.[2]

Ann's contribution looks a lot like Charles's independent spending. It ends up supporting speech in favor of a candidate for office. If Ann could give more money, her candidate might buy more television time to broadcast more speech. All things being equal, limiting her contributions limits the amount of speech Americans might hear at election time.

But all things are not equal. Ann's donations to a candidate are limited, but her spending in support of that candidate is not. If she "maxes out" her contribution to her candidate, she can just start spending money independently to help her choice, as Charles did. As long as Ann has a strong desire to get involved in an election, her speech may be complicated but not ultimately limited by contribution limits. On the other hand, her speech through established channels like campaigns and parties is restricted by the limits.

Looked at another way, contribution limits push some funding for political speech away from established channels and toward relatively new institutions such as Super PACs. Many, but not all, donors would probably support speech through established institutions if they could. But the limits make that impossible. Ann's support for speech must go to "outsiders."[3]

Should federal law favor "outsiders" at a cost to "insiders"? Perhaps. Insiders might care too much about organized groups in the capital, and outsiders can force the concerns of a broader public onto the public agenda. On the other hand, compared to parties and experienced candidates, outsiders lack experience organizing and representing mass opinion. Resources may be wasted and civic-minded folks frustrated. Outsiders are also likely to be more extreme in their commitments.

However, even if one prefers giving to outsiders rather than to insiders, there are strong reasons to oppose the current regime that privileges outsiders. After all, voters are supposed to choose the government, and if government favors one group over another it helps choose itself. Election laws should be neutral toward those engaged in politics. Contribution limits are not neutral; they favor outside spending over established channels. Citizens, not public officials, should choose between insiders and outsiders. Removing contribution limits would mean that neither Ann nor Charles would have a legal reason to favor outsiders over insiders.

Neutrality might, of course, be attained in another way. The government might apply the contribution limits now obligatory for insiders to independent spending by outsiders. Ann and Charles would then have no legal reason to prefer outsiders over insiders.

This solution, however, violates the freedom of speech protected by the First Amendment. If Charles wishes to spend $1 million supporting speech, forcing him to spend only $2,700 precludes a lot of speech. Many Americans dislike electoral speech. Some dislike conflict and confrontation; others may know and dislike Charles's political views. Both groups may think less speech supported by Charles is a fine thing. But the Constitution and the Supreme Court disagree. Public distaste for verbal conflict or banality seems more like crankiness than a justification for limiting a fundamental freedom, and restrictions on political speech have long received the highest protection offered by Court.

Contribution limits might serve values as important or more important than the freedom of speech. If so, we might have a case on balance for limiting the freedom of speech through contribution limits. What are those important values, and do limits on spending serve them well?[4]

In *Buckley v. Valeo* (1976), the Supreme Court concluded that limits on contributions served two important interests. First, the limits prevented "corruption and the appearance of corruption spawned by the real or imagined coercive influence of large financial contributions on candidates' positions and on their actions if elected to office."[5] The Court defined corruption as exchange of large contributions for "a political *quid pro quo* from current and potential office holders." In Latin, *quid pro quo* means "something for something." This exchange, the Court continued, undermines "the integrity of our system of representative democracy."[6] Representatives should respond to the wishes of a majority without violating constitutional rights; *quid pro quo* arrangements imply that representatives respond to money.

What is *quid pro quo* corruption? Think first of bribery. A representative of an interest group gives a member of Congress cash so that the member will vote for a tax break for the members of the interest group. It is also bribery if the interest group provides a campaign contribution in exchange for a promise to support a tax break. Such clear cases of bribery are illegal now and when *Buckley* was decided.

What then is *quid pro quo* corruption? An implicit exchange of money for something in politics? Perhaps not. Consider an example from the 2016 Democratic primary. Sen. Bernie Sanders asked, "How many think it's a great idea that we have trade policies that lead to plants in West Virginia being shut down? How many think there should be massive cuts in Pell grants or in Social Security?"[7] Notice the effect of each policy supported by Sanders. Protectionist trade policies keep plants open and wages going to West Virginia voters. Preventing reductions in Pell grants mean West Virginia students have more money than they would if the cuts happened. The same would be true of Social Security recipients. Sanders seems to be promising money in exchange for votes. His campaign, however, is often lauded as an exemplar of representative democracy. Are political *quid pro quos* bad only if someone other than a candidate for office proposes them?

Consider another West Virginia example. The United Mine Workers (UMW) represents many of the voters sought by Sanders. Those voters and the UMW are concerned that coal companies may not be economically capable of meeting their pension obligations. If not, the federal government would be called upon to make the pensions good.[8] Senator Sanders supported a bill making sure that the government made good on those pensions.[9] Imagine that the UMW gives Sanders a large campaign contribution. The UMW contributed to a presidential candidate who promised to give money to their members. Was it a corrupt *quid pro quo*?

You might answer these questions by assessing the motivations of the people involved. Businessmen are greedy and self-interested; their spending on politics harms the common good. Sen. Sanders and the UMW stand up for the downtrodden; their contributions make for a better America. More generally, people tend to evaluate money in politics by who benefits from spending or from restrictions on spending. Put in practice, such assessments would help one side or the other win the game of politics. A good corruption standard, however, establishes how we play the political game not who wins.

The UMW's contribution suggests the complexity of these questions. The UMW would be giving money to support a candidate (and his message) who already supported their interests. The union would seem to be engaging in electoral politics rather than corrupting democracy. Scholars of campaign finance have found that individuals and groups generally give to candidates and causes that already support their views.[10]

Perhaps *quid pro quo* corruption exists when money changes a politician's mind. Public officials might alter their vote about an issue in exchange for a contribution. Scholarly studies over many years find little evidence that contributions affect policy making once other factors (partisanship, ideology, and constituency preferences) are taken into account.[11]

It is often said that politicians trade access for contributions. By that, critics sometimes mean officeholders meet with contributors to discuss their concerns and proposals. Access is said to be exchanged for contributions.[12] Let's imagine, however, that a contribution goes toward helping an officeholder rather than to getting them to support policies they would not support, absent the money. Would meeting with them be wrong? If Sanders met with advocates from the UMW, as in the example above, would it be corrupt? Or normal politics? "Access" in itself does not seem to be the problem. Rather access would become a problem if it was part of a quid pro quo relationship involving money rather than politics.

The evidence to this point that money in politics threatens representative democracy seems ambiguous, at best. Limits on spending may or may not serve representative democracy while certainly restricting the freedom of speech. We are giving up an important value for little in return. But we should look deeper into the corruption question.

Let's assume that contributions have little independent effect on policy making, as studies suggest. That does not prove that contributions above current limits (or unlimited contributions) would not cause quid pro quo corruption. A donation of $10,000 by an individual to a candidate in an election might elicit favors that a $2,700 donation would not. The same would be all the more likely if the contribution were $1,000,000.

Independent spending on candidates does rise well above current contribution limits. But such spending does not go to the candidate but rather to direct support for speech. Perhaps you could argue that public officials know about and reward such support, creating a kind of *quid pro quo*. Evidence on this point is hard to come by. Those who spend large sums devote their efforts to one party or the other; such spending seems ideological or partisan, an expression of political commitment, rather than an attempt to buy policy favors.[13]

The *Buckley* Court also said contribution limits were justified by "the appearance of corruption stemming from public awareness of the opportunities for abuse inherent in a regime of large individual financial contributions." This appearance of wrongdoing, the Court suggested, would erode public confidence in representative government.[14] By limiting contributions, Congress would support public confidence in government.

Here is a summary of the relationship of contribution limits and trust in government. The United States had no limits on individual contributions during the 1950s and early 1960s, the era of highest trust in government.[15] Trust in government declined in the decade between 1964 and the enactment of contribution limits in 1974. From 1974 until 1980, trust continued to fall. In 1980, the limits on giving to political parties were loosened: Trust began to rise until 1986 when it plateaued and began to fall about 1989. Trust then started rising again after the middle of 1994 until the end of 2001. The McCain-Feingold law banned unlimited contributions to the parties in 2002; trust in government fell until about January 2010. Citizens United effectively removed limits on spending in early 2010; since then, trust has varied in a narrow range, but the trend is flat.[16] Many factors no doubt affected public trust during these years, but both limited and unlimited campaign contributions seem consistent with rising and falling confidence in government. In the states, too, scholars have found campaign finance regulations "are simply not important determinants of trust and confidence in government."[17]

The *Buckley* Court noted that contribution limits "may to some extent act as a brake on the skyrocketing cost of political campaigns and thereby serve to open the political system more widely to candidates without access to sources of large amounts of money."[18] Compared to no limits, contribution ceilings may well constrain the sums raised and spent on elections. Contribution limits make it more difficult to raise money since more donors must be located and persuaded to give. Hence, we may expect less money to be raised. But, contrary to the *Buckley* Court, less money is not a good thing. Fewer barriers to raising (and spending) money mean challengers have an easier time taking on incumbents. High spending campaigns also lead to better-informed voters and to increases in information among the least informed.[19]

Many people believe candidates for office spend too much time fundraising at a cost to governing (if they are incumbents) and connecting to voters (if they are seeking office). Candidates already in office probably spend far less time fundraising than most people believe.[20] Nonetheless, contribution limits mean candidates must meet their fundraising goals by soliciting more potential donors than they would have to solicit if limits were removed. Absent limits, members and candidates would have more time to govern and to connect to voters.

Many people say unequal spending violates the value of equality. After all, each citizen receives one vote, not many, in elections. Let's imagine each citizen receives the same sum to contribute to a candidate or to spend on electoral speech. As long as each person spends their allotment by themselves, equality of spending is preserved. But what if they wish to pool their allotment with others? That pooling would create unequal spending in an election. The equality rationale might trump freedom of association. What if the *New York Times* published an editorial endorsing a candidate? Does not such speech (and related spending) represent unequal influence? Equality of speech would threaten not only free speech but also freedom of association and the press.

There may be a better (and weaker) version of the equality argument. Some argue that "limits serve to mute the voices of affluent persons and groups in the election process and thereby to equalize the relative ability of all citizens to affect the outcome of elections."[21] The crucial phrase is "relative ability." That is, limits put a ceiling on how much a person can spend, but some people still spend more than others. Since 1999, PACs and donors giving over $1,000 have provided between 60 and 75 percent of funding for House races and between 42 and 62 percent of funding in Senate contests. Small donors provide 10 percent or less of funding for House candidates and about 15 percent for Senate hopefuls.[22] In 2012, about half the funding for presidential campaigns came from donors giving over $1,000, and about one-third came from donors giving over $2,500.[23] Contribution limits, in short, have not brought about an equality of spending across donor groups.

Here's the real issue, though: Freedom of speech and equality of spending are not of equal weight in the American Constitution. Equality of spending or influence does not appear in the text of the Constitution. The freedom of speech has a prominent position in the Bill or Rights. The *Buckley* Court rejected equality as a rationale for campaign finance limits: "the concept that government may restrict the speech of some elements of our society in order to enhance the relative voice of others is wholly foreign to the First Amendment, which was designed to secure 'the widest possible dissemination of information from diverse and antagonistic sources,'" and "'to assure unfettered interchange of ideas for the bringing about of political and social changes desired by the people.'"[24]

"Desired by the people" is a crucial phrase. Inequalities of spending do not necessarily translate into inequalities of influence over voters unless those voters are persuaded by speech on behalf of a candidate or cause. In a representative democracy, the final judge of the value of political speech should be the people, not censors who judge the speech corrupt or unequal.

Contribution limits on individuals should be removed because they bias political spending away from established institutions and toward outsiders. Government should favor neither outsiders nor insiders. Limits should not be extended to current independent spending on speech because the values at issue (integrity of government, public confidence, equality) are either not as important as the freedom of speech or ill-served by contribution limits.

CON: Richard Briffault

Congress should retain reasonable limits on individual contributions to candidates and political parties as part of a larger program of democratic campaign finance regulation.

Contribution limits advance several goals that are crucial to a vibrant democracy. They promote competitive elections. They curb the ability of very large donors to wield special influence over our government. They strengthen the accountability of elected representatives to their constituents. They provide an incentive for candidates to increase the political engagement of people without great financial resources. Contribution limits can advance these goals without infringing on constitutional rights. To be sure, the limits on campaign contributions have been eroded by loopholes and underenforcement. The solution, however, is not to give up on limits but instead to close loopholes, address evasions, and more vigorously enforce the rules.

In 1974, in the aftermath of the Watergate scandal, Congress limited the amounts individuals may donate to federal candidates and to political parties. In addition, currently thirty-eight states place some dollar limit on campaign donations by individuals. In 1976, in the leading decision of *Buckley v. Valeo*, the Supreme Court sustained the constitutionality of contribution limits. For forty years, the Court has consistently adhered to the position that reasonable contribution limits are constitutional, although it has also invalidated restrictions it found to be unreasonably low.

The federal contribution limits are not low. The limit on individual donations to candidates for 2016 is $2,700 per election. Federal law treats the primary and general election for the same office as two separate elections, so an individual can donate $5,400 in one election cycle to a candidate for Congress. As each member of a household can give up to the limit, a married couple can give $10,800 to a single candidate in one election cycle.[1] That is a significant amount of money. The median household income of a married couple in 2014 was $81,025, so the average married couple would have to give more than 12% of their annual income—about six weeks' worth—to a single candidate before approaching the contribution ceiling. And that's 20% of *gross* income. The fraction of *net* income that could be donated is surely far higher. And that's for a married-couple household. The average household income for a single female householder was $26,673; she would have to donate more than 20% of her annual gross income before the contribution limit would bite.[2] Even for households at the top 10th percentile—with a gross income of $150,000 in 2013—giving the maximum amount to a single candidate would consume close to a month of gross income.[3]

And that's just donations to candidates. Individuals may donate to the national political parties, which in turn support candidates. An individual can donate $33,400 to a national party committee each year and as much as $300,600 per year to specialized party accounts that support national party infrastructure, finance national conventions, and pay for legal costs.[4] Even a household at the 99th income percentile does not make enough money to contribute up to the cap on donations to parties.

If these limits are so high that they affect hardly anybody, what is the point? Well, they do affect two extremely important sets of people—the very, very rich who can give above the limits and the elected officials who run our government. Federal law requires the disclosure of only those donors to federal candidates who give $200 or more. In 2014, less than one-half of 1% of American adults made a contribution of $200 or more. And four-fifths of those donors gave under $2,500. In other words, federal campaign limits affect barely one-tenth of 1 percent of the adult population. But these high-end $2,500+ donors have an outsized impact on our elections and, ultimately, on our governance. They accounted for 77% of all reported federal campaign contributions in 2014, with just shy of half of all reported donors—less than two-hundredths of one percent of the adult American population—accounting for not quite half the total. Our elections are heavily financed not by "the 1%" but by the 1% of the 1%.[5]

Very large donors can significantly affect elections. Donors give primarily for two reasons: ideology and economic self-interest. Ideological donors give to influence the outcome of an election by electing candidates who share the donor's ideology. Ideological donors tend to be more partisan and more politically extreme than average voters.[6] A study of state legislative elections found that "donors to state candidates are more ideologically extreme than those who are equally politically active yet do not contribute money."[7] Large contributions to ideological donors promote ideologically polarized elections. Conversely, limiting large individual donations "handicaps extremists who raise most of their money from ideologically polarized donors."[8]

Other donors are less interested in affecting electoral outcomes and more interested in using donations to advance their economic interests. People with a significant stake in government policies—whose businesses are directly dependent on or affected by government subsidies, contracts, tax breaks, enforcement, and other regulatory actions—contribute in order to have access to elected officials to influence government actions that affect their businesses. These donors are essentially making a business investment in politics. But their donations can also affect electoral outcomes. Investor donors most frequently give to incumbents. A meta-analysis of studies of campaign finance—that is, a review of multiple studies—found that "one of the most robust findings in the literature" is that contributions flow disproportionately to incumbents in close races.[9] This makes sense as incumbents generally have an electoral advantage and so are likely to be reelected and able to do something for donors. Large donations reinforce the incumbency advantage. Large investment-type donations are particularly likely to be given to powerful legislators like subcommittee and committee chairs and party leaders.[10] Not surprisingly, studies of state elections and election laws have found that contribution limits "are primarily binding for incumbents" and are associated with narrower margins of victory, improvements in challengers' prospects, increased electoral competitiveness, and tighter elections.[11]

Whether investors or ideologues, large donors have an impact on both elections and government decision making. Elected officials are intensely interested in being reelected or pursuing higher office. Elections are expensive and growing more so. To win, candidates need money, and they particularly benefit from large donations. Not surprisingly, they are grateful to their donors and attentive to donor interests. This is not just a matter of *quid pro quo* vote buying. There are probably few outright donations-for-legislative-votes arrangements. But as the Supreme Court put it, the justification for contribution limits is "not confined to bribery of public officials, but extend[s] to the broader threat from politicians too compliant with the wishes of large contributors."[12]

Contributions are gifts that build relationships and create in the recipient a sense of obligation.[13] As one prominent lobbyist explained, lobbyists make significant numbers of campaign contributions "to build and reinforce relationships."[14] When the recipients of these gifts are elected officials who are particularly dependent on large donations to stay in office, they reciprocate and show their gratitude by using their official powers to do things for their major donors.

Sometimes this means voting for measures that benefit donors. Studies of the relationship between donations and votes have had mixed results due to the difficulties of disentangling the overlapping influences of partisanship, ideology, and constituency from donations. Contributions may flow to a legislator not to affect his or her vote but because he or she has already demonstrated support for the donor's interest. Nonetheless, a meta-analysis of more than thirty political science studies found that 25% to 35% of the congressional roll call votes examined exhibited some impact of campaign contributions.[15] Some legislators have acknowledged that campaign money affects legislation; then-Representative and now-news-show-host Joe Scarborough flatly declared "there's absolutely no doubt in my mind that money changed votes."[16]

Certainly major donors think they have an impact on politicians. As Donald Trump explained in the summer of 2015, "I gave to many people, before this, before two months ago [when he became a candidate himself], I was a businessman. I give to everybody. When they call, I give. . . . And you know what? When I need something from them two years later, three years later, I call them, they are there for me." [17] Megadonor Charles Koch made a similar point that he spent so much money on electoral politics because "I expect something in return." [18] Another donor, noting he had given the maximum to a candidate, insisted that gave him the right to influence a campaign, asserting "I gave $2,700. I'm entitled to 2,700 opinions." [19]

The major influence of campaign contributions is not on roll call votes on controversial bills—which are highly visible and create the risk of the legislator being seen as influenced by large donations—but on low-salience measures and behind-the-scenes activity. These include actions in committee to add or subtract a few words in a lengthy bill that can have a major impact on the fortunes of a donor. Donations can affect the awarding of a government contract, the renewal of a subsidy, the modification of a tax code provision, the delay in the effective date of a regulatory change, the bottling up of a bill in committee, the granting of a waiver, or the blocking of an enforcement action. [20] A committee chair can invite his campaign donors to present expert testimony at a committee hearing. [21] The White House may give preferential treatment on an immigration issue to members of a family which has made major donations to the president's party. [22] An officeholder's action for a donor might very well be consistent with his or her political beliefs or view of the issue's merits. But his or her active engagement with the issue—actually moving a wording change in the mark-up of a bill or contacting an agency head about a waiver—may be connected to the specific interests of a contributor. Political scientists refer to this as "the mobilization of bias," [23] and there is no doubt that contributions stimulate official action. As one Congressman put it, "you just tend to listen more carefully to people who are helping you stay in office." [24]

The impact of large donations on government goes beyond these many small favors and tends more broadly to skew political priorities and government policies. Large donors have distinctive political views on a wide range of issues. Compared with other Americans, they are more likely to favor spending cuts rather than tax increases, to worry about inflation more than unemployment, and to support cutting social welfare programs. [25] Big donors simply have different goals and concerns than ordinary voters. As Senator Christopher Murphy nicely put it in referring to the fund-raising calls he made to potential big donors, "I talked a lot more about carried interest [that is, the tax treatment of the profits private equity and hedge fund managers earn in investments] inside that call room than I did in the supermarket."[26] As a number of studies have shown, big donors appear to have succeeded in aligning a host of public policies with their preferences.[27]

Members of Congress act as representatives of their big donors even though many donors are not constituents. In 2014, winning candidates for the House received on average 64% of their itemized individual donations—that is, donations of $200 or more—from nonconstituents. Thirty-five percent of elected Representatives received 75% or more of their itemized donations from outside their districts. Nor was 2014 an outlier. For two decades out-of-district donations have accounted for at least three-fifths of itemized individual House contributions. The record in the Senate is similar. In 2014, nineteen of the twenty-eight incumbents seeking reelection drew more than half their itemized donations from out-of-staters.[28] Big donors are, in effect, a distinctive and important constituency in their own right, and a constituency that can distract legislators from serving the constituency they are supposed to represent—the voters of their districts or states.

As big donors already enjoy considerable influence even with the current caps on individual contributions to candidates and parties it could be argued that these limits aren't doing much good. Critics of contribution caps can point, further, to the surge in spending by and donations to Super PACs and other nominally independent groups, which are not subject to contribution limits, and contend that current contribution limits have been rendered ineffective. There is much truth to both points.

Nevertheless, they do not undermine the case for contribution limits. The limits do operate to cap the size of direct contributions to candidates, which is the most valuable money a candidate can have. Candidates have complete control over those funds, unlike money given to Super PACs. So dollar-for-dollar a candidate will be more grateful for a direct contribution than one to a Super PAC. Moreover, federal laws require broadcasters to sell time more cheaply to candidates than to independent committees, so money given to a candidate goes further in a campaign. Finally, even though a $2,700 donation can buy the donor some influence, that is surely much less than a direct donation of $50,000 or $100,000—or $1 million—which would result from removing caps. However unequal the current system is, a system without limits would be more so.

Moreover, donation limits give candidates an incentive to widen the scope of their fund-raising by appealing to smaller donors, thereby increasing the number of people who participate in the political process. Small donations could be further increased by tax credits or matching them with public funds as some states and cities do in their elections. Increasing the role of small donations would dilute the impact of large donations on elections and public policies. But even without tax credits or matching funds, contribution limits help democratize the political process by broadening the financial base of campaigns as well as by limiting the influence of the very affluent.

Some of the circumvention of contribution limits by donations to and spending by Super PACs and other nominally independent groups could be addressed by closing loopholes and more effective law enforcement. Super PACs and other committees are not subject to contribution limits because they are supposed to be acting independently. But with former aides to candidates running Super PACs and candidates fund-raising for them, these groups are often closely allied with candidates. Appropriate regulations and enforcement could reduce the Super PAC role by enforcing the independence the law requires.

Of course, even if independence were enforced, the unlimited donations to and spending by supportive groups that current constitutional doctrine guarantees would undermine the ability of contribution limits to curb the influence of megadonors on elections and governance. Contribution limits alone cannot achieve a democratic campaign finance system. Some form of public financing may be necessary. But contribution limits help with the goals of limiting big donor influence and expanding participation. The way to address the shortcomings of contribution limits is not by eliminating them but by enforcing them and supplementing them with other measures than reduce the ability of very large donors to dominate our politics.

NOTES

PRO

1. The Federal Election Commission oversees the disclosure of donations and thus the application of the law. For all contribution limits as of February 2015, go to http://www.fec.gov/pages/brochures/contrib.shtml.
2. *SpeechNow.org v. FEC*, 599 F.3d 686 (D.C. Cir. 2010).
3. Congress also limited contributions to political parties by prohibiting "soft money" contributions in 2002. This limit and earlier limits "unintentionally put it into the hands of proto-parties disguised as independent groups run by party-affiliated political operatives." Bruce Cain, *Democracy More or Less: America's Political Reform Quandary* (New York, NY: Cambridge University Press, 2014): 167.
4. The previous sentences are a paraphrase of the Supreme Court's "strict scrutiny" test for policies that impinge on "fundamental values" like the freedom of speech.
5. *Buckley v. Valeo*, 424 U.S. 1 (1976), at 25.
6. *Buckley v. Valeo*, 26–7.

7. David Weigel, "In Rural America, a Startling Prospect: Voters Obama Lost Look to Sanders," *The Washington Post*, October 5, 2015.

8. Matt Jarzemsky and Timothy Puko, "Coal Companies Get Reprieve on Pension Costs," *Wall Street Journal*, April 22, 2015.

9. See http://www.budget.senate.gov/democratic/public/index.cfm/2015/6/sanders-brown-baldwin-bill-to-strengthen-multi-employer-pensions.

10. Scholars have long accepted this claim. See Frank J. Sorauf, *Money in American Elections* (Glenview, IL: Scott, Foresman, 1988):310.

11. Nicholas O. Stephanopoulos summarizes "there is no evidence that much of this money is traded explicitly for political favors. Proof of quid pro quo transactions is vanishingly rare, and studies that try to document a link between PACs' contributions and politicians' votes typically come up empty." "Aligning Campaign Finance Law" *Virginia Law Review* 101(2015)1426–7. A good summary of the studies may be found in Stephen Ansolabehere and James Snyder Jr., "Why Is There So Little Money in U.S. Politics?" *Journal of Economic Perspectives* 17(2003)116: "changes in donations to an individual legislator do not translate into changes in that legislator's roll call voting behavior."

12. Since contributors have access and noncontributors do not, this relationship also might be seen as offending equality, a value that will be discussed later.

13. See Stephanopoulos, 1426: "Most Americans were moderates in 2012, but most donors were staunch liberals or conservatives." Large contributions to the political parties up to 2002 also reflected ideological concerns. See John Samples, *The Fallacy of Campaign Finance Reform* (Chicago, IL: University of Chicago Press, 2006): 96–97.

14. *Buckley v. Valeo*, 28–9.

15. During the entire era discussed, the law did prohibit contributions by organizations taking a corporate form.

16. See the chart "Public Trust in Government: 1958-2014" at http://www.people-press.org/2014/11/13/public-trust-in-government.

17. Jeffrey Milyo, "Do State Campaign Finance Reforms Increase Trust and Confidence in State Government?" Presented at the annual meetings of the Midwest Political Science Association in Chicago, IL, April 2012.

18. *Buckley v. Valeo*, 26.

19. John Coleman and Paul F. Manna, "Congressional Campaign Spending and the Quality of Democracy," *Journal of Politics* 62(2000): 757–89.

20. Ezra Klein, "Wonkblog: Congress Spends too much Time Fundraising. But it's Less Time than You Think," *The Washington Post*, July 29, 2013.

21. *Buckley v. Valeo*, 26.

22. These data are drawn from two tables provided by The Campaign Finance Institute. See http://www.cfinst.org/pdf/historical/Donors_HouseCand_2000-2014.pdf and http://www.cfinst.org/pdf/historical/Donors_SenateCand_2000-2014.pdf. Self-funding candidates, hardly a contributor to equalizing contributions, explain most of the difference between House and Senate races.

23. http://www.cfinst.org/pdf/federal/president/2012/Pres12Tables_YE12_ AggIndivDonors.pdf.

24. *Buckley v. Valeo*, 48–49.

CON

1. Federal Election Commission, "Contribution Limits for 2015-2016 Federal Elections," http://www.fec.gov/info/contriblimitschart1516.pdf.

2. U.S. Census Bureau, "Income and Poverty in the United States: 2014," at p. 6 (Table 1: Income and Earnings Summary Measures by Selected Characteristics: 2013 and 2014).

3. U.S. Census Bureau, "Income and Poverty in the United States: 2013," at p. 1 (Table A-2: Selected Measures of Household Income Dispersion: 1967 to 2013).

4. Federal Election Commission, "Contribution Limits for 2015-2016 Federal Elections," http://www.fec.gov/info/contriblimitschart1516.pdf.

5. See OpenSecrets.org, "2014 Overview, Donor Demographics," http://www .opensecrets.org/overview/donordemographics.php.

6. See, e.g., Adam Bonica, "Ideology and Interests in the Political Marketplace," *American Journal of Political Science* 57 (April 2013): 294; Joseph Bafumi and Michael Herron, "Leapfrog Representation and Extremism: A Study of American Voters and Their Members in Congress," *American Political Science Review* 104 (August 2010): 519, 531-2.

7. Michael J. Barber, "Ideological Donors, Contribution Limits, and the Polarization of American Legislatures," *Journal of Politics* 78. (No.1) (January 2016): 296, 303.

8. Id.

9. Thomas Stratmann, "Some Talk: Money in Politics. A (partial) Review of the Literature," *Public Choice* 124 (July 2005) 135, 147.

10. Lynda W. Powell, *The Influence of Campaign Contributions in State Legislatures: The Effects of Institutions and Politics* (Ann Arbor: University of Michigan Press, 2012), 205.

11. Stratmann, *Some Talk*, 130-51; Thomas Stratmann and Francisco J. Aparicio-Castillo, "Competition Policy for Elections. Do Contribution Limits Matter?," *Public Choice* 127 (April 2006): 177; Thomas Stratmann, "Do Low Contribution Limits Insulate Incumbents from Competition?, *Election Law Journal* 9 (No. 2, 2010), 125, 139.

12. *Nixon v. Shrink Missouri Government PAC*, 528 U.S. 377 (2000), quotation at 389.

13. Clayton D. Peoples, "Campaign Finance and Policymaking: PACs, Campaign Contributions, and Interest Group Influence in Congress," *Sociology Compass* 7 (2013): 900, 906.

14. Robert G. Kaiser, *Too Damn Much Money: The Triumph of Lobbying and the Corrosion of American Government* (New York, NY: Knopf, 2009), 292.

15. Douglas D. Roscoe and Shannon Jenkins, "A Meta-Analysis of Campaign Contributions' Impact on Roll Call Voting," *Social Science Quarterly* 86 (March 2005): 52.

16. Quoted in Larry Makinson, *Speaking Freely: Washington Insiders Talk About Money in Politics* (Center for Responsive Politics, 2d ed., 2003), 66.

17. Quoted in Donald Trump on Government Reform, *On The Issues*, http://www .ontheissues.org/2016/Donald_Trump_Government_Reform.htm.

18. Nicholas Confessore, "Charles Koch Defends Big-Money Campaign Contributions," *New York Times*, November 3, 2015, http://www.nytimes.com/ politics/first-draft/2015/11/03/charles-koch-defends-big-money-campaign-contributions.

19. Ashley Parker, "Big Donors Seek Larger Roles in Presidential Campaigns," *New York Times*, September 29, 2015.

20. See, e.g., Kaiser, *Too Damn Much Money*, 147–48; Powell, *The Influence of Campaign Contributions in State Legislatures*, 204–10.

21. T.W. Farnam, "The Influence Industry: Campaign Donors Called Upon for Expert Testimony," *Washington Post*, March 11, 2011.

22. Frances Robles, "Ecuador Family Wins Favors after Donations to Democrats," *New York Times*, December 16, 2014.

23. See Richard Hall and Frank Wayman, "Buying Time: Moneyed Interests and the Mobilization of Bias in Congressional Committees," *American Political Science Review* 84 (September 1990): 797.

24. Rep. Rick Lazio (R-NY), quoted in Makinson, *Speaking Freely*, 60.

25. See, e.g., Benjamin I. Page, Larry M. Bartels, and Jason Seawright, "Democracy and the Policy Preferences of Wealthy Americans," *Perspectives on Politics* 11 (March 2013): 51, 55–67.

26. Paul Blumenthal, "Chris Murphy: 'Soul-Crushing' Fundraising is Bad for Congress," *Huffington Post*, May 7, 2013, http://www.huffingtonpost .com/2013/05/07/chris-murphy-fundraising_n_3232143.html.

27. See, e.g., Nicholas O. Stephanopoulos, "Elections and Alignment," *Columbia Law Review* 114 (2014): 283, 289.

28. See Richard Briffault, "Of Constituents and Contributors," *University of Chicago Legal Forum* (2015): 29, 34–38.

RESOLVED, political parties should nominate candidates for president in a national primary

PRO: Caroline J. Tolbert

CON: David P. Redlawsk

From the beginning, the Constitution offered a clear answer to the question of who should elect the president: the electoral college. Or did it? Virginia delegate George Mason was not alone in thinking that after George Washington had passed from the scene, the electoral college would seldom produce a winner. In such a far-flung and diverse country, Mason reasoned, the electoral vote would almost invariably be fractured, leaving no candidate with the required 50 percent plus one of electoral votes. Mason estimated that "nineteen times in twenty" the president would be chosen by the House of Representatives, which the Constitution charged with making the selection from among the top five (the Twelfth Amendment, enacted in 1804, changed it to the top three) electoral vote getters in the event that no candidate had the requisite electoral vote majority. In essence, Mason thought, the electoral college would narrow the field of candidates, and the House would select the president.

Mason was wrong: In the fifty-seven presidential elections since 1788, the electoral college has chosen the president fifty-five times. Not since 1824, in the contest between John Quincy Adams, Andrew Jackson, Henry Clay, and William Crawford, has the House chosen the president. And contrary to Mason's prediction, the nomination of candidates has been performed not by the electoral college but by political parties.

The framers of the Constitution dreaded the prospect of parties. Based on their reading of ancient Greek and Roman and more recent European history, they equated political parties with conspiratorial factions. But a two-party system nonetheless began to emerge while Washington was still president, and from the start, it has functioned much better in practice than the framers feared. Indeed, it is hard to imagine how the Constitution could work without parties to choose candidates, aggregate voters' preferences, and help bridge the divide between the legislative and executive branches of the national government as well as the gaps between the layers of the federal system.

Over the years, the parties have experimented with different methods for nominating presidential candidates. The resolution proposed in this debate raises the possibility of trying yet another method: a national primary. A national primary, if adopted, would be the fifth method of presidential nomination that the parties have used. The first was the congressional caucus, in which each party's members of Congress met in private to choose their candidate for president. The problem with "King Caucus," as critics called it, was that it denied a voice in the decision to every party member and activist who did not happen to be represented by a fellow partisan in Congress. To address this objection, the congressional caucus was gradually replaced during the 1830s by a second method of nomination: the national party convention, at which delegates chosen by all of the state parties conducted most of their business in public instead of behind closed doors.

Conventions are still around, but what has changed over the years is the way the delegates to the conventions are chosen. Originally, they were picked by the leaders of each state party. During the early twentieth century, most states continued to do things this way, but others began requiring that convention delegates be chosen through state primaries in which rank-and-file voters could participate. This third method of nominating presidential candidates—often called the "mixed system"—lasted through 1968, a year dominated by controversy over the war in Vietnam. Many voters were so frustrated that neither of the major-party nominees, Democrat Hubert Humphrey and Republican Richard Nixon, opposed the war that they demanded the parties create a fourth method of nomination in which every state party would be required to choose its delegates in either a primary or an open caucus.

The fourth nomination method—the one still in use—resembles each of its predecessors by involving more people and thus further democratizing the process. Like its predecessors, too, the state primary and caucus method has come under criticism. Some complain that the process takes too long and costs too much. Others argue that it gives the small states that hold their caucuses and primaries first—specifically, Iowa and New Hampshire—too much influence over which candidates have a realistic chance to win. To some, such as Caroline J. Tolbert, the logical next step is to replace the fifty state primaries and caucuses with a single national primary in which voters across the entire country cast ballots on the same day, and every vote counts equally. Others, such as David P. Redlawsk, find more advantages than disadvantages in the current nominating method and believe that a national primary would make things worse rather than better.

PRO: Caroline J. Tolbert

The way we nominate our presidential candidates today is clearly unfair. The citizens in states that hold their nominating contests early in the process get smothered with attention from candidates and media, while citizens in states that vote later in the process barely get noticed. Frequently the contest is over almost before it starts, leaving many citizens (sometimes the majority of Americans) with no role in selecting their party's nominee. Voter turnout naturally plummets in the states with late primaries. In 2008, the Republican nomination was decided soon after Super Tuesday, leaving Republicans voting in later states with no meaningful choice, and in 2012 Mitt Romney's only real rival, Rick Santorum, dropped out in early April, with voters in twenty states, including the three most populous (California, Texas, and New York), having yet to cast a ballot. The selection of presidential candidates, one of the most important decisions that American voters make, should not be determined by a few states with early nominating contests. It is time for a national primary in which the citizens of all fifty states go to the polls on the same day and have equal voice in selecting candidates for president of the United States.

A national primary would solve three problems that plague the current system: the chaotic and self-defeating race to be among the first states to hold a nominating contest, abysmally low voter turnout, and the privileged position of Iowa and New Hampshire. A national primary would boost citizen participation while also restoring order and fairness to the way we select our presidential nominees.

SOLVING THE CHAOTIC RACE TO THE FRONT

Everybody knows that the current system is broken. As Rob Richie, executive director of FairVote, expresses it: "The entire political universe, from the heights of the Washington establishment to the depths of the grassroots, agrees that our presidential nominating process needs to be reformed."[1] Every four years the parties try to fix the problems in ways that often only make things worse. Of particular concern to the parties is the phenomenon known as front-loading[2]—that is, the process by which states schedule their primaries and caucuses near the beginning of the delegate selection calendar in order to have a greater voice in the process.

As part of their ongoing efforts to address the front-loading problem, both the Democratic National Committee (DNC) and the Republican National

Committee (RNC) revised the schedules and rules in 2008 and again in 2012. In 2008, the Democrats allowed two states (Nevada and South Carolina) to join Iowa and New Hampshire in violating the official February 5 delegate selection start date. (Nevada and South Carolina were selected because of their racial diversity—Hispanic in the former case, African American in the latter case—in order to compensate for the demographically unrepresentative character of Iowa and New Hampshire.) Any state that moved its nominating contest before February 5 would lose all of its delegates at the party's national convention. The Republicans adopted less draconian rules—violators of the start date would lose only half of their delegates. Yet, these changes did little to lessen front-loading; 70 percent of all delegates were chosen by the beginning of March. Two large states (Michigan and Florida) defied both national parties and held their nominating contests before February 5.

In 2012, Florida again defied the parties, moving the state's primary up to January 31. New Hampshire and South Carolina responded by pushing their primaries earlier. All three states had their delegates cut in half by the Republican Party, but going early mattered more to the states than getting their full allotment of delegates. The front-loading in 2012 was lessened somewhat because of some unusual events. Wrangling over redistricting forced Texas to push its primary back to the end of May, and a state budget crisis led California to move its primary back to June. But there is no reason to expect that the front-loading problem will lessen in future elections. We can expect instead that states will continue to push their nominating contests earlier and earlier, because voting earlier is in their interests.

The front-loading problem is exacerbated by what is known as the "invisible primary"—that is, the period before the first nominating event during which candidates engage in extensive fund-raising.[3] As candidates increasingly opt out of public financing, early money matters even more than in the past. The concern with a highly front-loaded nomination schedule is that candidates with the most money, name recognition, and media attention early on will win their parties' nominations. As Todd Donovan and Shaun Bowler have pointed out, between 1980 and 2004 all but one of the candidates who raised the most money the year before the first primary won their parties' nominations.[4] Front-loading means that strong candidates who lack financial resources may never have a chance to compete.

The sequential nomination process was originally designed so that a wide field of candidates could compete in early nominating events, followed by a winnowing process. Those candidates who exceeded expectations in early contests were able to raise campaign dollars to compete in later contests. Those who did worse than expected dropped out of the race.[5] However, events over the past decade have undermined the logic of the sequential nomination process. Early money continues to increase in importance, regardless of the ever-changing schedule of state nominating contests. Conventional wisdom holds that retail or face-to-face politics in Iowa and New Hampshire was supposed to level the playing field among candidates, but new research finds that only candidates with sufficient financial resources are competitive, even in early nominating events such as the Iowa caucuses, which require extensive and expensive grassroots campaigning.[6]

Critics of the national primary suggest that it offers an extreme form of front-loading, and a national primary will only make things worse. They argue that a national primary would restrict the presidential nomination to candidates who are already well-known or well financed and could increase the influence of money, which is needed to purchase television ads.

This may have been a valid criticism in the 1980s and 1990s, but the rise of the new media means that candidates no longer need huge financial resources or elite endorsements to compete effectively in a national primary. Campaigning online may level the playing field. Dark-horse candidates can reach voters by using social media such as Facebook, Twitter, Tumblr, and YouTube video. They can also use candidate websites, blogs, and e-mail. The diversity of online media makes candidate campaigns more cost-effective and able to reach wider audiences because of the relatively low cost and twenty-four-hour availability of the Internet.[7]

Barack Obama's 2008 and 2012 campaigns, for example, organized his supporters online, a feat that in the past would have required an army of volunteers and paid organizers on the ground. The Internet enables campaigns to mobilize supporters at a fraction of the cost of such mobilization in the past. Obama's campaign also took advantage of free advertising on YouTube and social media such as Facebook, instead of relying exclusively on television ads. Online political videos can be more effective than television ads because viewers make a conscious choice to watch instead of having their television programs interrupted by unwanted ads. During the 2008 presidential campaign, YouTube users spent 14.5 million hours watching Obama's video ads; buying 14.5 million hours of broadcast television ad time would have cost $47 million.[8] As of 2012, Obama's Facebook page had 31 million fans, and his YouTube channel (BarackObama.com) included almost three thousand videos. Online fundraising has also become increasingly important, as Howard Dean first showed in 2004. Obama's victory in 2008 was made possible by the huge amounts of money the campaign raised online: $750 million accrued from three million contributors. New media are rapidly changing how the game of politics is played, potentially neutralizing the impact of television advertising and making a national primary more realistic.

One thing is certain: We cannot fix the current system by patching it. State legislatures, secretaries of state, and state party leaders have a vested interest in holding their states' nominating events early in the process to receive attention from the candidates and mass media and to boost their state economies. Michigan and Florida acted rationally by breaking party rules in 2008. Left to their own self-interest, states will continue to move their primaries and caucuses closer to the beginning of the delegate selection calendar, exacerbating the front-loading problem. What is individually rational for each state, however, is bad for American democracy. Instead of ineffective party rules that try to penalize states for pursuing their self-interest, we should adopt a national primary that takes away the incentive that states currently have to circumvent the rules and leapfrog other states. By requiring all states to hold their nominating contests on the same day, a national primary solves the problem of individually rational states producing a collective outcome that is preferred by nobody.

SOLVING THE TURNOUT PROBLEM

Observers often bemoan the low numbers of American citizens who turn out for elections, but turnout in the general election is positively robust compared to the turnout in primary elections, let alone caucuses. In 2000, for instance, turnout of the voter-age population was only 14 percent in the Democratic primaries and 17 percent in the Republicans primaries. In other words, less than one-third of age-eligible Americans participated in a presidential primary. In contrast, more than half of the voting-age population voted in the general election. In 2004, when President George W. Bush was unopposed for the Republican nomination, primary turnout plummeted even lower, down to 24 percent. Meanwhile, 55 percent of age-eligible voters voted in the general election contest between Bush and Democrat John Kerry. The 2008 presidential nomination saw the largest primary turnout in history (estimates put the number at 55 million people, more than double the number who voted in the 2004 primaries), but even this was far less than the roughly 130 million people who voted in the general election. Primary turnout in 2008, moreover, sunk precipitously on the Republican side after Super Tuesday, when John McCain effectively wrapped up the nomination.[9] Turnout in Republican primaries and caucuses in 2012 was even lower than in 2008, dropping to 6 percent of the eligible voter population in the Iowa caucuses (down from 12 percent in 2008) and 31 percent in the New Hampshire primary (down from nearly 50 percent). In the April 24 Republican primaries, which were held by the last states to vote before Romney formally sealed the nomination, eligible voter turnout was 2 percent in Connecticut, 4 percent in Delaware,

16 percent in Pennsylvania, and 3 percent in Rhode Island. Voters in these states had no voice in selecting the presidential nominee. This is no way to pick the next president of the United States.

A national primary would do more than any other reform to increase participation in the nominating process. Holding an election on the same day across the entire country would create intense media interest and focus voters' attention on the election. With many viable candidates contesting, candidates would have an incentive to mobilize potential voters in all fifty states. As Lonna Atkeson and Cherie Maestas argue: "A national primary would focus broad voter attention on the race as candidates compete nationally instead of locally. Because everyone's primary would be 'coming up,' all interested voters would tune in to candidate debates to assist them in making their choice."[10]

Recent experience with the current nominating process confirms what common sense tells us: Creating a competitive election on a single day will increase turnout. Over the past decade, an increasing number of states have held their primaries on Super Tuesday, inching us ever closer to a *de facto* national primary. In 2008, twenty-three states held their primaries or caucuses on Super Tuesday, and these states experienced significantly higher turnout in primaries and caucuses than did other states.[11]

SOLVING THE IOWA PROBLEM

The "Iowa problem" refers to the fact that since 1972 this small midwestern state has always gone first in the presidential nomination, followed by another small state, New Hampshire. What rational reason is there for Iowa and New Hampshire to receive this special status? The electorates of both states are highly unrepresentative of the nation. Iowa is 90 percent White and largely rural, with an economy that is mainly agricultural.[12] Having Iowa vote first is tradition—but sometimes traditions need to be changed.

The Iowa problem is made worse by the extremely low turnout of caucuses. Only 6 to 7 percent of the voting-eligible population caucused in Iowa in 2000, 2004, and 2012. Competitive contests on both the Democratic and the Republican sides in 2008 boosted turnout to 16 percent, but even this higher turnout rate is much lower than the turnout in the 2008 primary elections. In New Hampshire, for instance, more than half of the eligible population voted, and in South Carolina, 30 percent turned out to vote. Some research suggests that participation in the relatively high-turnout 2008 Iowa caucuses may not have been as biased in terms of partisanship and socioeconomic factors as is usually the case, but even high-turnout caucuses are less representative than low-turnout primaries.[13]

Low turnout means that Iowa caucus goers are unrepresentative of Iowa's rank-and-file party members. Caucus participants are better educated, older, and have higher incomes than Iowa registered voters in general.[14] They are also more committed to and active in their parties than the average citizen. Low turnout in the caucuses also makes it costly for candidates to campaign in Iowa; contacting caucus goers has been compared to finding a needle in a haystack.

Even if Iowa were not unrepresentative of the nation, and Iowa's caucus goers were not unrepresentative of Iowa's citizens, its disproportionate impact on the primary process would still be a problem. Analysis of the 2004 election found that early voters have up to twenty times the influence of late voters in the selection of presidential candidates, and that the preferences of Iowa voters were six times as influential as those of Super Tuesday voters.[15] Why should voters in Iowa and New Hampshire, two-small population states, be given wildly disproportionate influence in choosing who our presidential nominees will be?

Defenders of the Iowa caucuses and the New Hampshire primary highlight the grassroots or face-to-face politics that are made possible by the small populations of these two states.[16] As I have argued above, however, the Internet allows candidates to participate in grassroots politics without Iowa and New Hampshire always voting first. Even if we concede that a national primary would involve making some sacrifices, those sacrifices may be worth making to achieve a fairer process that gives all citizens, not just a few favored ones, an equal say in which candidates will represent their parties in the contest for the nation's highest and most powerful office.

THE PEOPLE SUPPORT A NATIONAL PRIMARY

The American people understand that the current system is unfair. Two separate surveys conducted in 2008 found that the people's preferred reform is the national primary. In both surveys, about seven in ten Americans said they favored a national primary.[17] These numbers are consistent with the findings of earlier surveys.[18] Even when proposals for a national primary are framed in terms of the costs (for example, when respondents are prompted that if a national primary is adopted, small-population states may lose influence), a clear majority of Americans still support a national primary.

Support for a national primary varies somewhat by state size. In a 2008 Cooperative Campaign Analysis Panel (CCAP) survey, respondents from states with small populations were somewhat more likely (73 percent) to support a national primary than were those from the largest-population states

(63 percent). This finding is perhaps surprising, since critics of a national primary often argue that a national primary would disadvantage small states, which would rarely get campaign visits. It suggests, however, that those who reside in small states (apart from those living in Iowa and New Hampshire) are the ones who harbor the greatest frustrations with the current process.

The 2008 CCAP survey also asked respondents about an alternative reform that would rotate the order so that "a different state goes first each time." This idea attracted much lower levels of support. Only a bare majority (51 percent) reported that they favored it. Rotation, Americans understand, is fairer than what we have now but not nearly as fair as having everybody vote at the same time.[19]

HOW A NATIONAL PRIMARY WOULD WORK

One way of implementing a national primary is to declare the candidate with the most votes the winner of his or her party's nomination. However, there are three other viable methods of implementing a national primary.

First, a national primary could be followed several weeks later by a runoff election, in which the two candidates with the most votes would compete head-to-head for their party's nomination. This would be similar to the French presidential election system. The advantage of a runoff election is that each party would be assured that the candidate with the support of a majority within the party would win the nomination. A runoff election would prevent a candidate from winning with only a plurality of the votes of rank-and-file party members. The disadvantages of this method are the cost of the additional election and the potential for lower turnout in the runoff election.

Second, the parties could use ballots to conduct instant runoff voting (IRV), which allows voters to rank-order their candidate preferences. IRV simulates a runoff election without the need for a costly second election. Here is how it works: Voters rank candidates in order of preference (first, second, third, fourth, and so on). They can rank as many or as few candidates as they want. The voters' first choices are then tabulated, and if a candidate receives a majority (not a plurality) of first-choice votes, he or she is elected. If no candidate has a majority of votes on the first count, a series of runoffs is simulated, using the voters' preferences as indicated on the ballots. The candidate who receives the fewest first-place choices is eliminated first. All ballots are then recounted. The ballots of voters who chose the now-eliminated candidate are counted for their second-ranked candidates, but all other voters continue supporting their top candidate. Candidates continue to be eliminated and voters' ballots redistributed until a candidate gains a majority of votes. A majority is defined as 50 percent of the votes plus 1.

IRV has recently been adopted in a number of American cities, including San Francisco, San Jose, and Aspen.[20] It is cost-effective, requires only one election, and allows voters to choose their favorite candidate without having to fear that their votes (say, for a Ralph Nader) will elect their least-favorite candidate (what is called the "spoiler effect"). Most important, like an actual runoff election, it ensures that the winner enjoys true support from a majority of party voters.

Third, one could design a national primary that requires the winning candidate to gain a majority of the delegates but without IRV and without a runoff election. A virtue of this approach is that it could make party conventions meaningful again. In a crowded field of candidates, no candidate would be likely to gain a majority of delegates, and therefore the nomination would have to be settled at the convention. Making party conventions meaningful again could help to strengthen political parties and party leaders.

CONCLUSION

The American people are ready for a fundamental change in the way they choose their presidential nominees. Their clear preference is for a national primary, which would treat all citizens for all states alike and make all votes count equally. In 2012, the presidential nomination race was over before citizens of twenty states—containing about half of the American population—could cast a vote. Those left out included the roughly 38 million people in California, 26 million in Texas, 20 million in New York State, 13 million in Pennsylvania, and 10 million in North Carolina. By way of contrast, Iowa and New Hampshire combined have fewer than 4.5 million people. It is not fair to exclude so many citizens in so many states from having a voice in picking the candidates for president of the United States. A national primary will give every state a meaningful, competitive contest, increase voter turnout, and eliminate the ever-changing, crazy-quilt system of primaries and caucuses. A national primary, in short, will give the nation, at long last, a nomination process that promotes popular participation and is both simple and fair.

CON: David P. Redlawsk

> It has been said that democracy is the worst form of government except all the others that have been tried.
>
> —Sir Winston Churchill, House of Commons, November 11, 1947

L et's start with a proposition. Like democracy itself, the sequential arrangement of state caucuses and primaries that makes up our presidential nominating system is about the worst system imaginable—but only until we consider the alternatives. Given our federal system, no other approach has been found to be any better, at least not by those who would have to adopt it. And a national primary? While in a 2008 survey nearly three-quarters of the American public said they want one, a national primary is the last thing on the agenda of those who actually have to live with the system: candidates and parties.[1] *The Hill* newspaper, covering inside-the-Beltway Washington, reported in 2009 that "a national primary is something everyone hopes to avoid."[2] In the article, a former Ohio Republican Party chair, Bob Bennett, was reported as saying, "If you go back and you talk to any of the presidential candidates, they will tell you they do not want to go through what they went through [during the 2008 campaign]."

Why this disconnect between the public's desire for something called a "national primary" and party leaders' preference for anything but? The reason is simple. As much as candidates, pundits, and the public like to complain about the current system, at the least it allows candidates to build their campaigns over time, to develop and hone their strategies, and possibly to build momentum as they move through the events that define the modern presidential nomination system. The process begins slowly—with the small states of Iowa and New Hampshire—and then builds through a few more states before generally exploding onto the scene with a Super Tuesday, when a large number of states hold their contests on the same day. By starting in a few places rather than nationally, even less well-known or less well-funded candidates can nurture the hope that they might break through and capture the momentum that could carry them to the nomination. In 2012, that allowed former U.S. Senator Rick Santorum to come from nowhere to challenge eventual nominee Mitt Romney, despite Santorum's lack of money and name recognition. While Romney ultimately won the nomination, he was forced to address issues that otherwise might have been ignored. U.S. Senator Ted Cruz (R-TX) managed to build a strong Iowa campaign in 2016, pushing businessman Donald Trump into second in Iowa, despite Trump's lead in polls and overwhelming media coverage.

We only need to consider the scorn heaped on Super Tuesday by academics and candidates to wonder how a national primary could be better than what we have now. Super Tuesday is a consequence of "front-loading." Front-loading means that rather than pacing the caucuses and primaries out over some reasonable period of time (say, thirteen weeks or so), states rush to go as early as possible, in order to be "relevant" and to reap whatever benefits attention might give them. The lesson of Iowa and New Hampshire is not lost; in recent years, by one measure, Iowa received 243 times the media coverage of any other state, while an analysis of candidate momentum has found the preferences of Iowa voters were six times as influential as those of Super Tuesday voters.[3] Twenty-three states voted on Super Tuesday in 2008, making it virtually a *de facto* national primary. While fewer states joined the March 6, 2012, Super Tuesday, those that did represented more than one-third of the delegates needed to win the Republican nomination. In contrast, 2016 resulted in somewhat less front-loading, as the March 1 Super Tuesday events included 11 mostly southern states totaling nearly 20% of all Democratic and 22% of Republican delegates.

Why is front-loading a problem? As William Mayer notes, front-loading "increases the amount of early fundraising required and thereby limits the number of candidates who are able to mount a credible, competitive campaign."[4] Moreover, Mayer argues, front-loading gives voters little time to learn about the candidates and forces candidates to be less substantive as they rely heavily on paid media rather than personal contact. One can only imagine the results if all fifty states (and the District of Columbia and territories) held their nominating events on the same day. Candidates would be unable to focus in any one place, media would be stretched thin trying to cover all of the states, and voters would likely end up seeing superficial media campaigns focused on six-second television news sound bites or perhaps thirty-second YouTube videos.

Neither candidates nor the parties really want to see a national primary of any type. If anything, their desire appears to be to design a system that retains the sequential nature of the process but spreads the primaries out over some period of time. In fact, Super Tuesday was smaller and less consequential in both 2012 and 2016, than in prior years, and primaries were more evenly distributed across the primary calendar. Overall, the 2016 nominating events ran from February 1(Iowa Caucuses) into early June, and for the GOP, virtually all were consequential. Since it is the states and the political parties that determine the calendar, this is additional evidence that the parties would prefer to avoid anything resembling a national primary.

The public, on the other hand, seems solidly in favor of a national primary. This might be compelling, except that the public is also in favor of rotating state primaries—about 63 percent, in a February 2008 University of Iowa Hawkeye Poll. While the public may seem to have a preference for something other than the current system, it is not clear that there is a clamor for a national primary as such. Instead, it is more likely that poll respondents are simply parroting a media-driven narrative that something is wrong with the current system. In fact, in the same survey, voters were just as likely (about 72 percent) to support a rotating system that would guarantee Iowa and New Hampshire's preeminence as they were to support a national primary.

From the voters' perspective, the question of a national primary would seem to be relatively unimportant. Most never vote in primaries anyway. And for those who do, the campaign does not start months or even years before, as it does for those in Iowa and New Hampshire, but builds up only a few weeks ahead of the vote. Voters in each state do not have time to become fatigued by the election. Who does become fatigued? The reporters and pundits who begin following candidates long before the Iowa caucuses. They find themselves listening to the same stump speeches over and over, attending too many county fairs, taking too many bus rides across the country, and otherwise becoming exhausted by it all. Their exhaustion then plays out in their commentary. For example, in 2008, the primary schedule was such that six weeks passed between the March 11 Mississippi primary and the late April Pennsylvania primary. This should have allowed both candidates and media to focus intently on Pennsylvania. The media, however, treated the campaign as if it had already happened and Pennsylvanians should already have been aware of all the issues. This became clear in the debate between Hillary Clinton and Barack Obama, during which the debate moderators, Charles Gibson and George Stephanopoulos, focused on trivia, failing to ask good questions on important issues. No doubt part of the reason is that while the campaign was new to Pennsylvania voters, who were likely paying close attention for the first time, it was very old to the press and the pundits, who assumed everyone else had also heard it all before.

Although the exhaustion of a cynical media would not be a problem with a national primary, whether the media are tired of the process is not the point. A national primary might make things easier for the media—including saving them money by shortening the campaign coverage period—but it would cause more harm than good to the broader political system.

Let's consider what a desirable system would look like. We should evaluate reform on its ability to promote four goals: candidate quality, voter information, voter participation, and state equality. A presidential nomination system should choose *quality candidates,* not simply those who are the most well-known or the best financed. The system should allow voters to *learn* by providing them with appropriate information. Moreover, the nomination system should encourage voter *participation,* so that voters become interested and involved. Finally, it should strive for *equality* among the states in terms of allowing all Americans to cast meaningful votes.

A true national primary—a system in which all states' primaries are held on one day—is likely to fail these tests. We can already see this in what happens during the general election. Candidates focus on a few "swing" states, pouring resources into them while ignoring most states as uncompetitive. Candidates spend much of their money on thirty-second television ads that seem designed to confuse rather than to explain. And few voters ever actually see a candidate in person, unless it is for fifteen minutes on an airport tarmac as the candidate flies in, gives a canned stump speech, and flies out to the next stop. This country is simply too large to allow candidates to campaign effectively across all states if the states' primary elections are all held on the same day.

Defining what makes a "quality" presidential candidate is difficult. Political scientists say a quality congressional candidate is one who has held previous elected office and who can raise enough money to contest the election.[5] But most presidential candidates have held public office, and at least at the beginning, it is difficult to tell who will be most effective at raising campaign funds.

It is clear, however, that a national primary would advantage certain types of candidates at the expense of others. Those with ready access to very large sums of money very early—certainly at least in the year before the primary—would be able to buy the advertising time needed to contest the whole country at the same time, while others who might also be good candidates but cannot initially raise large sums would be locked out. The simple math of a national primary is that money would speak even more loudly than it does today. And it would speak through massive media campaigns rather than personalized grassroots campaigns. Instead of building their campaigns over time, most potential candidates would have to opt out. It is already quite difficult for underdogs to come out on top, but at least they have a fighting chance. In 2008, had a national primary been in place, it is likely that the largest money raisers of 2007 would have been the leading candidates—Mitt Romney and Hillary Clinton. Barack Obama and John McCain might have remained afterthoughts. And while in 2012 Romney secured the Republican nomination after a bruising primary fight in which he was again the early money leader, a national primary would have squelched the voices of the many conservative Republicans who harbored doubts about Romney. The sequential process allowed a host of challengers to contest Romney's position, forcing him to address issues that many Republicans felt were important. For the 2016 Democrats, a similar dynamic arose, as the initial frontrunner Hillary Clinton found herself challenged by VT Senator Bernie Sanders, who would never have had a chance to get traction in a national primary.

Moreover, and much more important, the sequential nature of the current system tests candidate campaigns in complex ways that would not happen otherwise. Caucuses, for example, require extensive organization. It is harder for candidates to reach caucus participants because there are fewer of them. Lower turnout in caucuses means that grassroots mobilization ("retail politics") is critical, in contrast to the mass-media campaigns that would prevail in a national primary. And grassroots campaigning tests a candidate's ability to build an organization, to create something that directly connects with voters. This ability to build, manage, and connect is an important skill for any would-be president and one that would not be well tested in a national primary.

Candidates learn from a sequential process; they take lessons learned in one state and apply them to the campaign in the next. Few, if any, candidates really know how to run a national campaign before they start. Few, if any, have had experience that would qualify them to head a massive bureaucracy and to lead the nation. Building what amounts to a half-billion-dollar business from the ground up is not easy, and our current system allows candidates to learn how to do this over time. This means the quality of candidates can be improved by the nature of the sequential campaign season.

Just as candidates can learn from campaigning from one state to the next, so too do voters learn over time. One major advantage and unique feature of sequential voting is that voters later in the process have more information about candidates, including information on election outcomes, delegate totals, candidate traits, ideology, and policy positions.[6] This may give later voters the opportunity to make more informed decisions than they would otherwise, while earlier voters may actually be slightly disadvantaged. But early states make up for this by the greater amounts of attention they get from the candidates and the media, enhancing their voters' political interest and knowledge. The book *Why Iowa?*, examining the 2008 campaign, finds exactly that. Early nominating events shaped perceptions of whether candidates could win the nomination and presidency (viability and electability) and in turn shaped candidate choice in later primaries and caucuses. Early voters were mobilized, and later voters became more aware and involved as long as the campaign remained competitive.[7]

As voters learn from a sequential system they are also encouraged to participate, especially with candidates on the ground holding events that are open and accessible. Granted, this is much more likely in smaller early states than in larger later states, but the counterexample of Pennsylvania in 2008 is instructive. Because there was a period before the Pennsylvania primary during which no other primaries were scheduled, candidates had time to hold events, build the grass roots, and encourage participation. And Pennsylvania voters responded. While the same cannot be said of most of the states on Super Tuesday, this is a problem of front-loading rather than of a sequential system. A properly spaced sequential process enhances voter participation in ways a national primary cannot. Voters are encouraged to participate when candidates can build an organization and are discouraged when candidates rely primarily on media campaigns. Political operative Dan Leistikow, who worked for both John Edwards and Obama, made this point in talking about Iowa:

In Iowa, regular people can look candidates in the eyes, size them up, and ask tough questions. Changing the schedule to favor larger states where TV commercials matter more than face to face contact with voters might be good for the frontrunner, but it isn't good for our democracy.[8]

Finally, the fact that some states seem less important and others more important in a sequential system is hard to overlook. Obviously, some state must go first. And because we generally know the dates of our elections in advance, both candidates and the media will flock to the earliest states as early as they can. This is unavoidable in a sequential system and certainly one area where a national primary might fix a perceived problem. But why should we expect that candidates will treat all states equally in a national primary? Treatment of states in a national primary would likely depend heavily on how the votes are aggregated. If the system proposes simply counting votes nationally and awarding each party's nomination to the candidate with the most votes, then candidates will focus on the largest vote-rich states, to the detriment of the majority of states. Perversely, moreover, Democrats will focus on the most Democratic states, and Republicans will focus on the most Republican states. Not only will some states be ignored, but the process is also likely to reinforce the current dichotomy between red states and blue states. Perhaps, instead, the national primary should award delegates state by state, as is now the case. But this would do nothing to solve the problem for Republicans, since the largest states get the most delegates, and historically, many of these states have awarded delegates on a winner-take-all basis. If anything, this could cause Republican candidates to focus even more intently on the largest, most Republican states. Democrats, because they do not use winner-take-all for delegate selection, would focus on a mix of the largest Democratic states and ones in which a given candidate might think he or she has a particular advantage. So while Iowa and New Hampshire would clearly lose their privileged place in a national primary, it does not follow that voters in all states would become equal in their influence on the nomination.

These points lead to an interesting problem with the national primary idea: Who gets to decide how the individual states run their contests? Most national primary proposals envision a single set of rules—using a primary election—that would apply to all states. While in theory this sounds reasonable, in practice our federal system leaves wide latitude to states to run their own elections; in fact, there is no constitutional basis for any imposition of a national primary, leaving it unclear who could impose it in the first place. Even the parties themselves do not have complete control over the timing or nature of their contests, since many states pay for the elections and legislate their dates and forms. In addition, those states that prefer caucuses would be overridden by a national primary.

Any proposal that mandates that all contests be held on the same day but leaves the mechanism to the states is problematic as well. Problems even arise with as simple an issue as aggregating the votes nationally. Democratic state caucuses, for example, generally report delegate counts, not actual votes. And even where actual vote counts are reported, the lesson of the 2012 Iowa Republican caucus—in which former U.S. Senator Rick Santorum and Mitt Romney essentially tied—is that variations in vote counting across states may cause serious problems. Democrats saw the same thing in the 2016 Iowa Caucuses, where Sanders and Clinton ended in a virtual tie, with Clinton barely edging out Sanders in the delegate count. Any system that imagines tallying up the vote across all states will quickly run into problems unless the form of voting is mandated and regularized across all states, which again may lack any constitutional basis. A lack of consistency would doom any attempt at a national primary.

And then there is the problem of determining who wins. Both parties currently require that a candidate win an outright majority of delegates to the national convention to win the nomination. Would this translate into requiring a majority of votes? Would that then mean a runoff if no one gets a majority, as is likely? Alternatively, one could imagine a voting mechanism that would allow voters to specify first and second choices (generally known as instant runoff voting), but this then moves us back into the challenge of setting the same rules nationwide. Probably the biggest single problem with a national primary is that no one quite knows what form it would take and what its unintended consequences might be.

In defending the current system, I should make one thing clear: It has its problems. The incentive structure for the states usually causes them to rush to the earliest possible date, hoping to get the attention of both candidates and media. The campaigns seem to start earlier every four years. The parties could solve this problem, however, by establishing some basic rules and sticking to them. An attempt was made to do so in 2012, when only the Republican nomination was contested. States that violated the rules had their delegations cut in half, but this did not seem to make much difference. And in 2008, states that violated the rules were threatened with the same punishment, but in the end, the national parties caved in once the nomination had been secured. Thus, the lesson is that the rules can be violated with relative impunity. Nonetheless, the 2016 cycle had both parties establish just four "carveout" states—Iowa, New Hampshire, South Carolina, and Nevada—which were allowed to hold their events before the official start date of March 1, 2016. This seemed to work: No other state tried to violate the rule by going earlier, but as noted above, many states did bunch up on March 1 itself.

Beyond this front-loading problem, the other problem that gets the most complaints is that nominees are usually decided well before the end of the primary season, resulting in some (maybe many) states becoming irrelevant. Obviously, this was not a problem for the Democrats in 2008, when the contest came down to the very last primary in June, nor in 2016 when both parties' contest came down to the wire before only one candidate was left standing. Likewise, in 2012, Romney did not lose his last major challenger until late April, after more than thirty contests had been held. Even in 2008, when McCain wrapped up the nomination by the end of February, more than 60 percent of states had voted, owing to massive front-loading that year. Recent contests suggest that worries that a candidate will win long before most states have their chance to vote are misplaced.

The early twentieth-century development of the primary election system was part of a series of reforms championed by the progressives of the era, designed for the most part to take power from political bosses and machines and place it in the hands of the rank and file. Primaries were seen as a way to break the control of the bosses in the smoke-filled rooms, allowing voters a direct say in who would be their parties' nominees. As primaries developed at the state level, interest began growing for a national presidential primary. Theodore Roosevelt offered to use a national primary in the 1912 Republican nomination, but incumbent president William Howard Taft declined.[9] Numerous national primary bills have been introduced in Congress since that time, but none has come close to passing. Putting aside the question of whether Congress actually has the constitutional power to mandate a national primary, it is interesting that, despite a long list of complaints about the current system, a national primary has not come to pass.[10] Yet, as has become typical, calls came again to change the system in 2015, with Reince Priebus, chair of the Republican National Committee, informing Iowa and New Hampshire that there are no "sacred cows" and they should not always expect to be first.[11] This is all well and good, but since 1972, the system has operated as is, and at least until now, no one has come up with a better approach. It is unlikely that this will change in the foreseeable future. And, in fact, it never should. While the current system may not be perfect—few if any human institutions are—the law of unintended consequences should be carefully noted. A national primary of any type—forcing all states to hold nominating events on the same day—simply does not offer significant improvement over the sequential nomination process we have today, which has served us reasonably well despite the complaints that have been lodged against it.

NOTES

PRO

1. See "Primary Power to the People," FairVote, http://www.fairvote.org/?page=27& pressmode=showspecific&showarticle=256. See also Caroline J. Tolbert and Peverill Squire, "Editors' Introduction: Reforming the Presidential Nomination Process," *PS: Political Science and Politics* 42 (2009): 27–32.

2. William G. Mayer and Andrew E. Busch, *The Front-Loading Problem in Presidential Nominations* (Washington, DC: Brookings Institution Press, 2004).

3. Marty Cohen, David Karol, Hans Noel, and John Zaller, *The Party Decides: Presidential Nominations Before and After Reform* (Chicago, IL: University of Chicago Press, 2008). See also John Aldrich, "The Invisible Primary and Its Effects on Democratic Choice," *PS: Political Science and Politics* 42 (2009): 33–38.

4. Todd Donovan and Shaun Bowler, *Reforming the Republic: Democratic Institutions for the New America* (Englewood Cliffs, NJ: Prentice Hall, 2004).

5. John H. Aldrich, "A Dynamic Model of Presidential Nomination Campaigns," *American Political Science Review* 74 (1980): 651–69.

6. David P. Redlawsk, Caroline J. Tolbert, and Todd Donovan, *Why Iowa? How Caucuses and Sequential Elections Improve the Presidential Nominating Process* (Chicago, IL: University of Chicago Press, 2011).

7. Karen Mossberger, Caroline J. Tolbert, and Ramona S. McNeal, *Digital Citizenship: The Internet, Society, and Participation* (Cambridge, MA: MIT Press, 2008).

8. Claire Cain Miller, "How Obama's Internet Campaign Changed Politics," *New York Times*, November 7, 2008.

9. For these and other data on voter turnout, see Michael P. McDonald's United States Elections Project website, in particular, "2008 Presidential Nomination Contest Turnout Rates," http://elections.gmu.edu/Turnout_2008P.html and "2012 Presidential Nomination Contest Turnout Rates," http://elections.gmu.edu/Turnout_2012P.html. See also Larry J. Sabato's Crystal Ball website, http://www.centerforpolitics.org/crystalball; and Nonprofit Voter Engagement Network, "America Goes to the Polls: A Report on the Voter Turnout in the 2008 Presidential Primary," http://electionlawblog.org/archives/011185.html.

10. Lonna Rae Atkeson and Cherie D. Maestas, "Meaningful Participation and the Evolution of the Reformed Presidential Nominating System," *PS: Political Science and Politics* 42 (2009): 59–64.

11. Brian Knight and Nathan Schiff, "Momentum and Social Learning in Presidential Primaries" (National Bureau of Economic Research, Working Paper No. W13637, November 2007).

12. See Hugh Winebrenner, *The Iowa Precinct Caucuses: The Making of a Media Event*, 2nd ed. (Ames: Iowa State University Press, 1998).

13. David P. Redlawsk, Daniel C. Bowen, and Caroline J. Tolbert, "Comparing Caucus and Registered Voter Support for the 2008 Presidential Candidates in Iowa," *PS: Political Science and Politics* 41 (2008): 129–38.

14. Walter J. Stone, Alan I. Abramowitz, and Ronald B. Rapoport, "How Representative Are the Iowa Caucuses?," in *The Iowa Caucuses and the Presidential Nominating Process,* ed. Peverill Squire (Boulder, CO: Westview Press, 1989).

15. Knight and Schiff, "Momentum and Social Learning," 18.

16. Christopher Hull, *Grassroots Rules: How the Iowa Caucus Helps Elect American Presidents* (Stanford, CA: Stanford University Press, 2007).

17. Caroline J. Tolbert, David P. Redlawsk, and Daniel C. Bowen, "Reforming Presidential Nominations: Rotating State Primaries or a National Primary?," *PS: Political Science and Politics* 42 (2009): 71–79.

18. See Steven S. Smith and Melanie J. Springer, eds., *Reforming the Presidential Nomination Process* (Washington, DC: Brookings Institution Press, 2009); Bruce E. Altschuler, "Selecting Presidential Nominees by National Primary: An Idea Whose Time Has Come?," *Forum* 5, no. 4, art. 5 (2008), http://www.bepress.com/forum/vol15/iss4/art5.

19. Tolbert et al., "Reforming Presidential Nominations."

20. See "Where Instant Runoff Is Used," FairVote, http://www.fairvote.org/where-instant-runoff-is-used.

CON

1. University of Iowa Hawkeye Poll, February 2008, reported in Caroline J. Tolbert, David P. Redlawsk, and Daniel C. Bowen, "Reforming Presidential Nominations: Rotating State Primaries or a National Primary?," *PS: Political Science and Politics* 42 (2009): 71–79.

2. Reid Wilson, "RNC Poised to Begin Altering Its Primary Calendar for 2012," *The Hill,* June 15, 2009, http://thehill.com/homenews/campaign/20126-rnc-poised-to-begin-altering-its-primary-calendar-for-2012.

3. Christopher C. Hull reports on media coverage of the 2004 Iowa caucuses in his book *Grassroots Rules: How the Iowa Caucus Helps Elect American Presidents* (Stanford, CA: Stanford University Press, 2007); and Brian Knight and Nathan Schiff carry out multivariate analysis of the influence of early versus late states in "Momentum and Social Learning in Presidential Primaries" (National Bureau of Economic Research, Working Paper No. W13637, November 2007).

4. William G. Mayer, "An Incremental Approach to Presidential Nomination Reform," *PS: Political Science and Politics* 42 (2009): 65–69.

5. Gary C. Jacobson and Samuel Kernell, *Strategy and Choice in Congressional Elections* (New Haven, CT: Yale University Press, 1981).

6. Marco Battaglini, Rebecca Morton, and Thomas Palfrey, "Efficiency, Equity, and Timing of Voting Mechanisms," *American Political Science Review* 101 (2007): 404–29.

7. David P. Redlawsk, Caroline J. Tolbert, and Todd Donovan, *Why Iowa? How Caucuses and Sequential Elections Improve the Presidential Nominating Process* (Chicago, IL: University of Chicago Press, 2011).

8. Quoted in Iowa Caucus Digest, *Globe Gazette*, Des Moines Bureau, October 9, 2007, http://globegazette.com/news/article_d5ed7066-b4c0-5d6b-a9f8-fcbc9cb1f3c4.html.

9. Bruce E. Altschuler, "Selecting Presidential Nominees by National Primary: An Idea Whose Time Has Come?," *Forum* 5, no. 4 (January 2008).

10. William G. Mayer and Andrew E. Busch, *The Front-Loading Problem in Presidential Nominations* (Washington, DC: Brookings Institution Press, 2004).

11. Alan Rappeport, "New Hampshire and Iowa Not Assured First Contests, Top Republican says," *The New York Times*, September 29, 2015. http://www.nytimes .com/politics/first-draft/2015/09/29/new-hampshire-and-iowa-not-assured-first-contests-top-republican-says.

RESOLVED, Congress should bring back earmarks

PRO: Scott A. Frisch and Sean Q Kelly

CON: Jeffrey Lazarus

Arizona Senator John McCain, the Republican nominee for president in 2008, disagreed with his Democratic opponent, Illinois Senator Barack Obama, about many things during their general election campaign—but not about earmarks. "Earmarking is a gateway drug . . . to out-of-control spending and corruption," said McCain during their first debate, citing "$3 million to study the DNA of bears in Montana" as an example. "Senator McCain is absolutely right," Obama replied, "which is why I suspended any requests for my home state, whether it was for senior centers or what have you."

McCain and Obama were members of Congress at the time they were running against each other for president, which is one reason both were so familiar with earmarks. Earmarks are provisions of laws—or, more commonly, of the committee reports accompanying the enactment of those laws—that direct the federal government to spend money on specific projects. In 2008, Congress appropriated an estimated $17.2 billion to be spent on 11,620 earmarks. By one estimate, the extent of earmarking had tripled since 1994.

Earmarking became a growth industry in Congress during the 1990s and 2000s for two main reasons. First, community organizations, universities, hospitals, business firms, and state and local governments decided that instead of relying on the usual process of competing for federal funds from executive branch agencies, they could guarantee success by being named and funded in congressional laws or committee reports. Second, members of Congress realized that by helping these constituent groups they could win their loyalty, not to mention getting the rest of the country to spend money on projects that would benefit the states or districts they represented.

No one, including earmarking opponent Jeffrey Lazarus, argues that earmarks constitute a major portion of the federal budget deficit. Lazarus argues instead that decisions such as which hospital gets a grant should depend on which community needs the money the most and which hospital submits the best application, not on who happens to have the most influential senator or representative in Washington.

The conservative tea party movement that arose during Obama's first year as president focused public attention on earmarks as a symptom of government run amok. Liberal groups such as Common Cause also stepped up their campaigns against the impropriety of earmarks. President Obama responded by insisting that his $787 billion economic stimulus bill, enacted by Congress in 2009, contain no earmarks. After Republicans took control of the House of Representatives in 2010, the House enacted a ban on earmarks, and Obama announced he would not sign any bill that contained earmarks. Several months later, the Democratic-controlled Senate agreed to a moratorium on earmarks for the duration of the 112th Congress (2011–2012).

That ban remains in place today, much to the chagrin of Scott A. Frisch and Sean Q Kelly who call on Congress to bring back earmarks. Earmarks, they argue, ought instead to be cherished for the crucial role they play in well-functioning legislative process. Certainly abolishing earmarks doesn't seem to have improved things in Washington, DC. Lazarus, in contrast, views earmarks as a symptom of what is wrong with Congress—and bringing back earmarks as precisely the wrong direction to take if we are to clean up the way we legislate in the nation's capital.

PRO: Scott A. Frisch and Sean Q Kelly

"I hate to puncture the purist bubble of our political science professors, but the Congress can't function without the ability to appropriate resources for congressional districts through negotiation."

—Former Representative Jim Moran[1]

Congressional earmarks have become a symbol of all that is wrong with American politics. A national obsession with earmarks has developed, stoked by "watchdog groups," a handful of congressional opponents of earmarks (such as Senators John McCain and Jeff Flake), and a compliant media. Together they have woven a narrative populated with greedy lobbyists and members of Congress who "deliver the goods" in exchange for campaign contributions or, even worse, outright bribes.

Anyone unfamiliar with the term *earmark* got an education during the 2008 presidential election. Opposition to "wasteful earmarks" was a centerpiece of John McCain's presidential campaign. McCain referred to earmarks as a "gateway drug" leading to out-of-control federal spending and deficits. Tea party activists made eliminating earmarks a high priority, and after the Republican takeover of the House of Representatives in the 2010 election, momentum to ban earmarks reached a fevered pitch. A moratorium on earmarks was put in place in the first days of the 112th Congress in early 2011.

Contrary to the narrative that dominates the contemporary debate, we argue that earmarks are good for American democracy. Earmarks make sense in the context of American politics. They are not the cause of our national debt, nor are they more susceptible to corruption than any other form of federal spending.[2] In fact, since the earmark moratorium was imposed, none of the alleged problems that critics claim are associated with earmarks have been eliminated or even improved, yet negative consequences abound. Congress has become more gridlocked, the national debt continues to grow, the American people trust Congress less, and the belief that Congress wastes taxpayer money has increased since earmarks were eliminated.

Earmarks reflect the exceptional nature of American democratic institutions. The framers of the Constitution intentionally invested the power of the purse (that is, the power to spend money) in Congress. Article I, Section 9, states, "No money shall be drawn from the Treasury, but in Consequence of Appropriations made by Law." In *Federalist No. 58*, James Madison called the power of the purse "the most complete and effectual weapon with which any constitution can arm the immediate representatives of the people, for obtaining a redress of every grievance, and for carrying into effect every just and salutary measure." By keeping the power of the purse close to the people, through their representatives, Congress would remain responsive to the needs and wishes of the sovereign people, thus enabling the national government to adapt policies to local needs. And the representatives of the people could be held democratically accountable at the ballot box for their spending.

Madison also argued that it was the power of the purse that would protect Congress from the "overgrown prerogatives of the other branches of the government." Madison and the other framers of the Constitution maintained a healthy distrust of executive power. They bestowed the power of the purse on the Congress to enable Congress to resist the advances of the executive into the prerogatives of the legislative branch. The founders understood that investing the power to make war and the power to spend money in the same institution was a blueprint for tyranny. Stripping Congress of the power to earmark—thereby undermining one of Congress's institutional prerogatives—represents an immense shift in the balance of power between Congress and the executive that allows for dramatically increased executive power, precisely what the founders sought to avoid.

The U.S. Congress was designed to be a forum for the competing demands of interests that exist in American society. Representatives would bring the narrow interests of their constituencies to the House and Senate. Concerned about reelection, they would doggedly pursue the interests of their voters, and those who were successful were more likely to be reelected. Representatives would compete within the institution to have the interests of their constituents incorporated in legislation. Their ability to do that successfully depended on their ability to build support among their fellow members of Congress. Members would need to navigate their priorities through both chambers of Congress. Success would require compromise, and the founders trusted that legislation that successfully passed through this process (and survived a presidential veto) would serve the interests of the entire nation. Considered this way, the legislative process is like Darwin's conception of natural selection. Just as only those organisms that adapt to environmental conditions will survive, only those ideas that are worthy, that serve the interests of the greatest number, will survive the brutally competitive environment in Congress. Competition between interests, combined with the legislative machinery, creates a legislative ecology that favors compromise.

Truly bad earmarks are unlikely to survive. In any particular district, there are more demands for support than can be accommodated by a member of Congress. Proposed projects compete for the support of members of Congress; members and their staffs consider the qualities of each project, the needs of their districts, and the likelihood of success for earmarks in the legislative process and promote only a few of those requests. The vast majority of project requests are winnowed out through this process. Once inside the legislative machinery, earmark requests are subject to additional scrutiny from appropriations subcommittee staff, administrative agencies, committee leaders, and the legislative process (subcommittee, committee, floor, and conference). Reforms enacted before the moratorium required the listing of all earmark requests and their sponsors on a publicly available website subjecting those requests to more public scrutiny than any other form of government spending receives.

Members of Congress have a strong incentive to prevent bad earmarks from seeing the light of day. Media scrutiny of earmarks is intense, and those that are potentially embarrassing pose electoral threats to members of Congress. Congressional staffers are aware of the attention that watchdog groups and journalists devote to earmarks. Many staffers have told us that they take great pains to oppose projects that may turn out to be embarrassing. One staffer we interviewed put it this way: "At the end of the day my boss is going to make a decision based on my recommendation, and it is my job on the line, and hers too."

Congress has the power to direct spending; on that the Constitution is clear. The Constitution does not require that Congress appropriate money responsibly; that is a function of constitutional design, in the juxtaposition of interests in such a way that the judgment and responsibility of each member and the intersection of all members' collective interests produce appropriations that reflect the interests of both constituencies and the nation. Members of Congress provide a valuable service to their constituents by using federal programs to respond to local needs in a way that faceless bureaucracies are incapable of doing. Members of Congress bring local problems to the attention of the government. In this regard, the Congress causes government to adapt generic programs to local conditions. By using earmarks, Congress overcomes the one-size-fits-all solutions that are convenient for executive bureaucracies in Washington, DC, but are unresponsive to local conditions.

Earmarks sometimes advance the national interest. Even if a member of Congress pursues an earmark because he or she has narrow, district-centered concerns, the result can be a project of national significance. The basic logic of the framers of the Constitution parallels that of the economist Adam Smith, who believed that the selfish decisions of individual actors in an economic market result in outcomes that build the "wealth of nations," that is, that serve the common good. Likewise, the founders believed that the narrow, self-interested behavior of members of Congress—in the context of the competitive legislative "marketplace of ideas"—could produce policies that would serve the interests of the country. One project in this category is the Human Genome Project, which began as an idea promoted by a senator seeking to protect the science-dependent economy of his state as it adjusted to the realities of the post–Cold War world. Senator Pete Domenici's (R-NM) support for the project through earmark spending had a catalytic impact that resulted in one of the most important scientific advances in recent years.

Using earmarks, Congress has pressed the executive branch to pursue programs and technologies that otherwise might have gone unrecognized by the executive bureaucracy. One program that began life as an earmark resulted in the development of the Predator drone, a weapon that has revolutionized modern warfare through its ability to strike at terrorist targets with little risk to American personnel. The Predator drone was developed with funding from an earmark that was created over the objections of the U.S. Air Force leadership, who did not originally see the value in pilotless aircraft. Earmarks can originate in the "selfish" concerns of legislators or come from the "better angels" of those interested in promoting good policy. Either way, the end result can be something of immense national importance.

Critics of earmarks argue that spending decisions should be based on "objective criteria" employed by the executive bureaucracy. But bureaucratic program managers can steer contracts and grants toward favored vendors and recipients, and they regularly do so away from the watchful eyes of the media, watchdog groups, and the public. Shifting the power of the purse to the executive branch undermines the delicate balance developed by the framers. Giving the executive branch additional power to determine the locations of grant and contract spending shifts the power of the purse to unelected bureaucrats, who are not democratically accountable. The federal bureaucracy is famously opaque, and the potential for corruption in the executive bureaucracy is enormous.

Since the publication of our book *Cheese Factories on the Moon: Why Earmarks Are Good for American Democracy,* Congress has embarked on an experiment in life without earmarks. In November 2010, when Congress was rapidly moving toward an earmark moratorium, we warned that such a moratorium would make legislating much more difficult. As political scientist Diana Evans and others have pointed out, earmarks are the grease that lubricates the wheels of the legislative process. Perhaps it is no coincidence that the 112th Congress will be forever known for its lack of legislative accomplishments. The 113th Congress was even less productive. Demonstrating that the earmark moratorium is responsible for the precipitous decline in legislative activity is difficult, but there is no doubt that earmarks have eased the way for the passage of important legislation in the past. Lyndon Johnson, both as Senate majority leader and later as president, kept a list of legislators and their key (earmark) project desires in his breast pocket and famously used that list when seeking to secure difficult votes for landmark legislation. More recently, the fate of the controversial fiscal year 2006 spending bill in the House of Representatives for the Departments of Labor, Health and Human Services, and Education demonstrates the role that earmarks play in securing difficult votes. The conference report on the bill was defeated after eighty-five members who had previously supported the bill in the House changed their votes when the bill returned from conference. The likely explanation for the defection of so many members was that $1 billion in earmarks was stripped out of the bill between House passage and the conference stage. It is extraordinarily easy for members of Congress to vote against a bill when there are no consequences for them or their constituents—that is, when they have "no skin in the game."

District-specific projects have been a part of the legislative process since the founding of our country. In fact, the ninth bill passed by Congress in 1789 contained an earmark for a lighthouse to be built at Cape Henry, Virginia, which was part of a political deal to lure southern representatives to vote for the Lighthouses Act. The bill also contained a provision designed to appeal to another local constituency by providing federal government support for piers, an earmark supported by Philadelphia's merchants. The deal-making aspect of the legislative process may not appeal to those who find transactional politics to be vulgar; however, it is the nature of the uniquely American system of governance designed by the framers. Our constitutional system makes it difficult to pass laws. Earmarks are a means, discovered early in our history, to overcome the systemic bias toward inaction; they can be the sweetener that helps cut the bitter taste of compromise.

Granted, the federal budget is fundamentally out of balance today, but the roughly $18 billion spent on earmarked projects in 2009, the high point of earmarking, is hardly to blame for that. If Congress had not spent a single penny on earmarks, the 2009 budget deficit still would have been $1.4 trillion. Rather than focusing on earmarks, which are simply congressional decisions about what projects to fund and the geographic locations of those projects, critics of government spending should focus on the creation and expansion of government programs. That happens through the annual budget resolutions that establish annual spending amounts and revenue levels and the congressional authorization process that creates new government programs and periodically reauthorizes them. Earmarks simply provide zip codes for previously determined spending priorities. For example, after legislators determine that government will spend a certain amount of money in a given year on military construction, earmarks determine which bases should be given priority for new construction funding.

Earmarks are not to blame for excessive federal spending. Reforms enacted to improve the earmark process in recent years make them less susceptible to corruption than are many grants distributed by the executive branch behind a veil of secrecy. Excessive attention to the supposed ills of earmarks detracts from the larger dynamics that drive the federal budget out of balance: rapidly increasing entitlement spending and an unwillingness to either increase revenues or decrease spending. The federal deficit was less than $500 billion in fiscal year 2008, when earmarks exceeded $18 billion. The deficit increased to approximately $1.3 trillion in fiscal year 2011, the first year of the ban on earmarks. In short, getting rid of earmarks will do nothing to reduce budget deficits. The national debt was $14.1 trillion in January 2011; in spite of the ban on earmarks, it now stands at more than $19.2 trillion.

Earmarks have now been banned for more than five years. It is naïve to think that eliminating earmarks somehow reduced the corrosive impact of campaign money on Congress. If the link between earmarks and campaign contributions is as strong as opponents claim, then getting rid of earmarks should have resulted in a precipitous decline in donations to members of Congress running for reelection. However, according to OpenSecrets.com, campaign contributions to representatives and senators running for reelection actually increased between 2010 (the last election before the moratorium) and 2014. If donors gave money in exchange for earmarks, why are they still giving now that earmarks have been eliminated?

Opponents of earmarks argued that eliminating earmarks allowed the Appropriations Committee to focus more attention on how government money was being spent. Using data from the Policy Agendas Project and from the House Appropriations Committee, we calculated that there was an average of 62 oversight hearings per year before the ban and 29 hearings per year once the ban was in place. Ironically, the earmark ban led to *less* oversight. Why? Attention to earmark spending provided an incentive for committee members to pay close attention to government spending. In the absence of earmarks, there are fewer incentives to engage in the dreary work of oversight.

Finally, congressional gridlock has reached new heights in the absence of earmarks. The number of bills signed into law has declined dramatically since the moratorium was imposed. Congress passed only 72 laws in 2013; that is the lowest number of bills enacted in 20 years. Without the incentives to support bills described above, even an ardent opponent of earmarking, former House Speaker John Boehner, remarked to Texas colleague Ralph Hall: "It's not like the old days, Ralph. . . . Without earmarks to offer, it's hard to herd the cats."

Debating the value of earmarks distracts from weightier questions that Americans must resolve: What should the policy priorities of the country be?

Can funding for Medicare, Social Security, and other entitlement programs be made sustainable? What is the correct level of revenue needed to support government spending? Legislation to address some of these questions may require earmarks to lubricate the legislative machinery for the votes ahead. Earmarks, as we have seen, have been an integral part of the legislative process since the founding of the country, and they have played an important role in building coalitions needed to pass landmark legislation. Many earmark projects have not only served local interests but achieved national priorities too. In short, earmarks should be reintroduced.

CON: Jeffrey Lazarus

I magine you are a member of Congress and you need some money for your reelection campaign. Your job gives you control over a lot of money: You and your colleagues set the federal budget every year, after all, and that potentially gives you access to hundreds of billions of dollars. But unfortunately for you, that is the taxpayers' money, and taking it for your campaign would be illegal. But wouldn't it be nice if there were a way to get around those pesky laws, perhaps by exchanging some of that federal budget money for campaign cash? Well, fortunately for you, there is a way! Or at least there used to be. It's called an earmark. It's easy, and if Congress members do it right, it's perfectly legal. Using earmarks, members of Congress can virtually buy campaign donations—and sometimes even personal goodies—with taxpayer money.

What, exactly, is an earmark? Different people have different definitions, but basically an earmark is a provision in a bill that sends the government's money to a specific person, organization, or corporation. Earmarks are placed directly into bills by individual Congress members acting almost on their own, and this makes earmarks different from every other form of government spending. With other forms of spending, there needs to be agreement among a number of people before money gets spent: A committee made up of Congress members might have to vote, or the entire chamber (House or Senate) would have to vote. Or a bureaucratic agency might have to sign off on the spending. But none of these things has to happen with an earmark. Instead, an ordinary Congress member (with the help of certain other, more powerful members) just places the earmark into the bill. As a result, an earmark is almost a private transaction between a member of Congress and a private citizen.

This changes the way money flows through our government. Using earmarks, members of Congress can fund their personal projects without having to worry about whether other members of a committee, the chamber, or anyone else thinks the project is a good idea. This allows members to reward campaign donors—or themselves!—in remarkably specific and lucrative ways. On the other side of this coin, private citizens who benefit from an earmark can very easily identify which member of Congress was responsible and reward the member accordingly. In combination, these two things make it very easy for Congress members to trade earmarks—paid for with your money—for campaign contributions.

Right now, neither the House nor the Senate allows members of Congress to place earmarks in bills. Earmarks were an important part of the legislative process for several decades before they became a divisive political issue. However, in the decade of the 2000s several politicians—Republicans in particular—began arguing that they are unhealthy for American democracy. When Republicans took control of the House of Representatives after the 2010 elections, they changed House rules to ban the practice. The Senate followed suit soon after, and as a result, earmarks are not currently part of the legislative process.

That's a good thing, because when earmarks were widely used, the kind of corruption I described above happened all over Congress—in both the House and the Senate and among both Democrats and Republicans. The Center for Responsive Politics (CRP) kept track of the connection between earmarks and campaign donations and makes the information available on its website, OpenSecrets.org. According to CRP, in 2008 and 2010 more than half of all members of Congress received donations from organizations for which they had personally secured earmarks. A lot of members received pretty small amounts, but a few raised a lot of money this way: In 2008, five members of Congress each received more than $100,000 from people who benefitted from their earmarks; in 2010, six did.[1] The only member in the six-figure club both times was Democratic congressman Jim Moran of Virginia, who got an extra perk—the corporations receiving his earmarks also kicked in more than $100,000 for his brother Brian's campaign for governor of Virginia.[2]

Actually, the numbers reported by CRP are low estimates of the amount of campaign donations earmarks brought to members of Congress. First of all, the numbers do not include donations made to members by the lobbying firms that helped recipients get the earmarks. Lobbying firms donate a lot of money to members of Congress because firms need to keep their lines of access to members open. Second, CRP does not report money donated by individuals who might be more loosely affiliated with the earmark recipients. Third and most important, CRP does not report money that comes to members through the "bundling" efforts of earmark recipients or the involved lobbyists. In this practice, a private citizen asks the people he or she knows to donate money to a member of Congress and then delivers to the member—often personally—the resulting "bundle" of checks worth tens or hundreds of thousands of dollars. As long as the bundlers' friends are donating their own money, this is also legal. All told, earmarks brought members of Congress a lot more money than even the CRP accounted for; academic studies estimate that each earmark was worth about $30,000 in campaign donations.[3] With individual members sponsoring several dozens of earmarks, the whole system quickly got members several hundreds of thousands of dollars.

The undisputed king of the earmark was Democratic congressman Jack Murtha of Pennsylvania. For more than twenty years, Murtha was a high-ranking member of the House subcommittee that decides how to spend federal money related to defense. In that position, he had more control over how to distribute earmark money than almost every other member of Congress. Over those twenty years, Murtha raised millions of dollars in campaign funds from corporations benefiting from his earmarks. Eventually, one of Murtha's staff members left Murtha's office to form a lobbying firm that specialized in helping companies get earmarks from Murtha and other high-ranking members. This firm, the PMA Group, grew into one of the biggest and most influential lobbying firms in Washington. But it could only do that because it was playing a fixed game. Every PMA client had to donate money to Murtha's campaign before they could get PMA's help securing earmarks. And nobody got an earmark from Murtha without going through PMA first. PMA even would help its clients set up fake companies and organizations so that they could get around campaign finance laws that limit how much an individual can give to a member of Congress—so they could donate more money to Murtha. All of that is, of course, illegal, and the former staff member who ran PMA Group, Paul Magliocchetti, was convicted and sentenced to more than two years in prison. Murtha himself died of complications following gallbladder surgery in 2010, while under investigation.

Murtha aside, it's worth asking if this confluence of campaign donations and earmarking was just a coincidence. Maybe these earmarks just *happened* to go to people who just *happened* to give campaign money to members of Congress. After all, hundreds of thousands of people and organizations donate money to Congress members every year—surely some of these donors are going to get earmarks just by happenstance, right? Probably not. Beyond anecdotes about members such as Murtha and Moran, there is a lot of evidence that members of Congress systematically traded earmarks for campaign cash. For one thing, for several years, high numbers of donations went to members' campaigns in March. Why March, if elections are not held until November? Well, March is when earmarks get placed into spending bills—if you are giving a campaign donation in exchange for earmarks, that would be the time to do it.[4] Also, researchers who have investigated the link between earmarks and campaign donations have conducted very careful analyses, with the goal of ruling out precisely these types of coincidences. They have examined many other factors that might explain why a donor would give to a certain member of Congress, including the economic makeup of the state or district and what committees the member serves on. Even after all these things are taken into consideration, the story is still the same: Earmarks go hand in hand with campaign cash.[5]

If members of Congress used earmarks only to secure campaign donations, that would be bad enough—how would you like to be a candidate for Congress and know that you have to run against an incumbent who can trade the public's money for campaign funds? But it gets worse than that. Several members of Congress have been caught using earmarks not only to raise money for their reelection campaigns (which under certain conditions was legal, even if it is unethical) but also to enrich themselves and their acquaintances (which usually is illegal). The list of members of Congress involved in earmarks-related scandals could go on for pages.[6] Here is just a small sampling of the types of things members did with earmarks:

- In 2005, Randy "Duke" Cunningham (R-CA) conspired to take $2.4 million in bribes from defense contractors who received up to $80 million dollars in earmarks that Cunningham steered through Congress. When the scheme was uncovered, Cunningham resigned from Congress. Both Cunningham and those who attempted to bribe him pled guilty and served prison sentences.[7]

- In 2008, Darrell Issa (R-CA) bought a $16.6 million office building in Vista, California, on West Vista Way. Why is the name of the street important? At the same time as he was making the purchase, he earmarked more than $1 million in funding to widen, add bus stops on, and add parking adjacent to West Vista Way, right where his new office building was located. These improvements greatly increased the value of his building.[8]

- Over the years, Florida developer Dennis Stackhouse did a lot of favors for Kendrick Meek (D-FL) and Meek's mother, former congresswoman Carrie Meek (D-FL). After Carrie Meek left Congress, Stackhouse hired her as a "consultant," paying her $90,000 and giving her free use of a Cadillac Escalade. He spent $5,000 on a birthday party for Kendrick Meek and even gave Meek's chief of staff $13,000 for a down payment on a house. In exchange, Meek requested a $4 million earmark for Stackhouse's development firm and arranged other federal funding, including a smaller earmark, worth more than $1 million. (The big earmark never came through, but the other funding sources did.)[9]

A reasonable person might wonder if this type of corruption would go away if we could just limit earmarks to nonprofit organizations, such as universities, hospitals, and museums. Maybe taking profit out of the equation would reduce earmarks' corrupting effect on campaign finance. In fact, Congress attempted to do just that before they got rid of earmarks entirely. In 2010, leaders changed the rules so for-profit corporations could no longer receive earmarks. But the reform attempt failed because people just found a way around the rules. Private, for-profit corporations joined with nonprofit organizations to jointly receive earmarks and split the proceeds. Some corporations could not find nonprofits to join with, so they formed sham organizations that could get the money under the new rules and then the corporations took the money for themselves. One company in Ohio created a nonprofit at 9:30 a.m. the day after the ban was announced, used the nonprofit to request earmarks, and then donated tens of thousands of dollars to its member of Congress, Marcy Kaptur (D-OH), to make sure the earmarks came through.[10] With earmarks, it seems, where there's a will there's a way—even if the way skirts the law.

To be sure, earmarks are not the root of all evil. Many of the projects funded by earmarks probably deserved to be funded. Earmarks often payed for things such as new two-way radios for a county's emergency dispatch center, new diagnostic equipment for a hospital, or fixing up the aging housing at an army base. These are things the government should be spending money on, by most people's reckoning. However, because of the way earmarks get funded—each individual member was out to fund his or her own projects—there was no way to judge the worthiness of these projects against each other. Hundreds of counties across the nation might need new radios, probably every hospital wants the most up-to-date diagnostic equipment, and at any given time, dozens of military bases need repairs made to their housing units. When the funds for these types of projects are distributed via earmarks, nobody looks at all of the requests to see which counties, hospitals, or military bases need the money the most. Instead, the most well-connected and powerful members of Congress get the most spending every time, regardless of who needs the money.[11] So if you run a hospital in need of some new equipment, you better hope your member of Congress is in with the right crowd.

Another point that people make in earmarks' favor is that they were not the only way members of Congress use their positions improperly or illegally to enrich themselves. There are plenty of examples throughout history of corrupt members of Congress doing all the things discussed in this essay and more without the help of earmarks. Finally, it is important to make clear that even though earmarks do spend taxpayers' money, they are not the reason the United States has a budget deficit. The amount of money going to earmarks is a drop in the bucket compared to the money that goes every year to defense spending, Social Security, Medicare and Medicaid, and interest on the federal debt.

But neither of these points rehabilitates earmarks. The amount of money being spent is not what's important—what's important is that the money is being *exchanged*. Members of Congress steer taxpayer dollars to private citizens, who then reward the members with campaign donations. This makes corruption easy and (in most cases) legal. With earmarks, members do not need to search for ways to enrich their campaign donors—the process is laid out right there in front of them, complete with preprinted forms. All a member has to do is fill in the name of the recipient and the amount of money. With earmarks, members don't need to cover their tracks or worry about getting caught. In fact, they can advertise! Members would go into their districts looking for someone who is willing to trade a $10,000 campaign contribution for an earmark worth potentially millions of dollars in federal funds. With that kind of return on an investment, who wouldn't donate to his or her Congress member?

Earmarks allow members of Congress to directly trade federal taxpayer money for campaign money. They also make it easy for members to—sometimes legally, sometimes not—use the public office voters entrusted them with to enrich themselves and their friends. Members of Congress are not supposed to do that, and there is no reason to have a system in place that makes it easy for them.

NOTES

PRO

1. Quoted in Wright, Austin, and Jeremy Herb, "The Rise of the 'zombie' earmark: Lawmakers find stealthier ways to get around ban on Pentagon projects," *Politico* (2015), http://www.politico.com/story/2015/10/zombie-earmarks-defense-spending-pet-projects-214938#ixzz3qIYheYy1 10/20/15.

2. For an extended presentation of our argument for earmarks, see Scott A. Frisch and Sean Q Kelly, *Cheese Factories on the Moon: Why Earmarks Are Good for American Democracy* (Boulder, CO: Paradigm, 2011).

CON

1. Center for Responsive Politics, "111th Congress Earmarks," http://www
.opensecrets.org/bigpicture/earmarks.php?cycle=2007&type=HC.
2. David D. Kirkpatrick and Ron Nixon, "Brother's Role in Congress Carries Weight
in Race," *New York Times,* April 17, 2009, http://www.nytimes.com/2009/04/17/
us/politics/17moran.html?_r=2.
3. Jeffrey Lazarus, Jeffrey Glas, and Kyle T. Barbieri, "Earmarks and Elections to the
U.S. House of Representatives," *Congress and the Presidency* 39 (2012): 254–69.
4. "Murtha Fundraiser Missed Donor Pal," *Washington Times,* March 24, 2009,
http://www.washingtontimes.com/news/2009/mar/24/murtha-fundraiser-
missed-donor-pal.
5. Stacy Gordon and Michael Rocca, "Earmarks as a Means and an End: The Link
between Earmarks and Campaign Contributions in the U.S. House of
Representatives" *Journal of Politics* 75 (2013): 241-253; Jeffrey Lazarus, Jeffrey
Glas, and Kyle T. Barbieri, "Earmarks and Elections to the U.S. House of
Representatives," *Congress and the Presidency* 39 (2012): 254–69.
6. Tom Finnigan, *All about Pork: The Abuse of Earmarks and the Needed Reforms*
(Washington, DC: Citizens Against Government Waste, May 3, 2006), http://
membership.cagw.org/site/DocServer/PorkFinal.pdf?docID=1621.
7. Special Counsel for the Cunningham Inquiry, "Report of the Special Counsel for
the Cunningham Inquiry: Executive Summary," U.S. House of Representatives
(2005), http://www.fas.org/irp/congress/2006_rpt/harman101706.pdf.
8. Lee Fang, "Exclusive: Issa Secured Nearly $1 Million in Earmarks Potentially
Benefiting Real Estate That He Owns," *ThinkProgress,* March 30, 2011, http://
thinkprogress.org/politics/2011/03/30/151097/issa-earmark-property.
9. David Ovalle and Scott Hiaasen, "U.S. Rep. Kendrick Meek Tied to Failed
Poinciana Park Project Fraud Case," *Tampa Bay Times,* May 15, 2010, http://
www.tampabay.com/news/politics/national/article1095113.ece.
10. Eric Lipton and Ron Nixon, "Companies Find Ways to Bypass Ban on Earmarks,"
New York Times, July 5, 2010, http://www.nytimes.com/2010/07/05/us/
politics/05earmarks.html?_r=2.
11. Jeffrey Lazarus, "Giving the People What They Want? The Distribution of
Earmarks in the U.S. House of Representatives," *American Journal of Political
Science* 54 (2010): 338–53; Steven J. Balla, Eric D. Lawrence, Forrest Maltzman,
and Lee Sigelman, "Partisanship, Blame Avoidance, and the Distribution of
Legislative Pork," *American Journal of Political Science* 46 (2002): 15–25; Frances
E. Lee, "Geographic Politics in the U.S. House of Representatives: Coalition
Building and Distribution of Benefits," *American Journal of Political Science* 47
(2003): 714–28; Scott A. Frisch, *The Politics of Pork: A Study of Congressional
Appropriation Earmarks* (New York, NY: Garland, 1998).

12

RESOLVED, proportional representation should be adopted for U.S. House elections

PRO: Douglas J. Amy

CON: Brendan J. Doherty

In the nineteenth century, Americans typically looked upon European politics with smug disdain. They regarded American political institutions as the greatest in the world, and certainly far superior to the corrupt and autocratic regimes of the Old World. In the twentieth century, however, educated Americans began to look at Europe with a more envious eye. During the Progressive Era, some American reformers viewed European nations as a model for more humane social welfare policies. During the 1950s, American political scientists expressed admiration for the "responsible parties" of Great Britain, where the government governed, the opposition opposed, and the voters knew which party to reward when things went well and which to blame when things went badly. Britain's parliamentary system seemed free of the divided government and diffused responsibility of America's system of checks and balances and separation of powers. Today, the responsible party model has fallen out of fashion, and the European import to which American students of politics seem most attracted is proportional representation.

Under a system of proportional representation, legislators are elected in multimember districts based on the percentage of vote their party receives. If, for instance, in a district with ten seats a party gets 40 percent of the vote, then it is allotted four seats. In a closed party list system, the voter casts a ballot for the party, and which of the party's representatives gets seated depends on the order in which the party slates its nominees. If a party wins four seats, then the top four candidates from the party list are elected. In an open list system, voters are able to indicate their candidate preferences as well as their party preference; the party vote determines the number of seats a party gets, but the winners from each party are determined by the candidate preferences of that party's voters. The American system, in contrast, is a single-member plurality system in which one legislator is elected to represent each district, and the winner is the candidate who gets the most votes.

Interest in proportional representation in the United States emerged at the end of the nineteenth century and the beginning of the twentieth. The Proportional Representation League was founded in the United States in 1893. Between 1915 and 1950, more than twenty cities in the United States adopted proportional representation, but in every city except Cambridge, Massachusetts, proportional representation was repealed. In all but a few cases, the repeal was accomplished by a direct vote of the people. Ironically, one Progressive Era reform—the citizen initiative—was used to abolish another.

In 1908, the voters of Oregon approved an initiative that empowered the legislature to adopt proportional representation in multimember legislative districts. Its passage was fueled by popular outrage at the gross inequities that had been produced by single-member districts in state legislative races in the previous election. In 1906, fifty-nine Republicans and one Democrat were elected to the Oregon House of Representatives, even though Republicans had gained only 57 percent of the statewide popular vote. The rest of the vote was split among Democrats (32 percent), Socialists (7 percent), and Prohibitionists (5 percent). Since Republicans earned a plurality in every district but one, they won 98 percent of the House seats. The legislature, however, never used the power bestowed on it by the 1908 initiative, and attempts to require the legislature to change to proportional representation failed three times at the ballot box and once in the legislature.

The recent revival of interest in proportional representation among Americans owes much to the frustration people feel regarding the large number of uncompetitive and often uncontested legislative races as well as the blatant gerrymandering of districts to protect incumbents or to advance one party at the expense of another. Douglas J. Amy gives voice to this frustration in advancing the case for proportional representation. Proportional representation, Amy argues, is more just and more democratic than our winner-take-all, single-member district system. Brendan J. Doherty, however, cautions us to beware of attractive-sounding foreign imports. Proportional representation, he warns, would weaken the connection between legislators and constituents, empower party insiders at the expense of ordinary voters, give more power to parties with narrow ideological appeals, and make gridlock in government an even greater problem than it is today.

PRO: Douglas J. Amy

Proportional representation is the best political reform that most Americans have never heard of. If you ask most people if they think we should adopt proportional representation elections for the U.S. House of Representatives, you will probably be greeted with blank stares. They have little idea what proportional representation (PR) is or what the considerable advantages of this reform would be.

That's because most of us don't often think about electoral systems—the methods we use to cast votes and elect our leaders. We don't usually question the way we elect members of the House or consider whether there might be a better way. Our traditional system is what political scientists call a single-member plurality (SMP) system. House members are elected one at a time in single-member districts, with the winner being the candidate who gets the most votes—the plurality.

This is the usual way we elect the members of our legislative bodies in the United States, so most of us just take for granted that this is the only logical way to do so. But a large part of the rest of the world would disagree. Most Western industrialized democracies long ago abandoned SMP elections in favor of proportional representation.

Why have they done that? Should we follow in their footsteps and adopt this reform? To understand the answers to these questions, we need first to understand what PR is and then to understand how it solves many of the serious problems that afflict our current election system.

WHAT IS PROPORTIONAL REPRESENTATION?

Proportional representation comes in several varieties, but there are two basic ways that all PR systems differ from our current winner-take-all election system. First, all PR systems use multimember districts. Instead of electing one member of the legislature in each district, PR uses much larger districts in which several members are elected at once. Figures 12.1, 12.2, and 12.3 illustrate districting maps for a hypothetical state that elects twenty members to the U.S. House. Figure 12.1 shows our current single-member district system, Figure 12.2 shows a PR system that uses four five-member districts, and Figure 12.3 shows a PR system with two ten-member districts. Each party nominates a slate of candidates equal to the number of seats at stake—five candidates in a five-member district.

The second way that PR differs from our current system is in the way that winners are chosen. Instead of a winner-take-all approach, winners of seats are

Figure 12.1	**Figure 12.2**	**Figure 12.3**
Twenty Single-Member Districts	Four Five-Member Districts	Two Ten-Member Districts

determined by the proportion of the vote that a party receives. So if 40 percent of the voters in a ten-member district cast their votes for Democratic candidates, that party would receive four of the ten seats, and those seats would go to the four Democratic candidates receiving the most votes. If candidates for the Green Party or the Libertarian Party win 10 percent of the vote, that party would receive one seat, and so on.[1]

Since PR requires multimember districts with at least three or four seats to divide up among the parties, it would not be appropriate for some very small states that elect only one or two members to the U.S. House. However, PR would be perfectly feasible for larger states, and there is no constitutional barrier to its adoption. The Constitution allows states to choose their own methods for electing representatives to the House.

Proportional representation was invented to correct what were seen as serious deficiencies in winner-take-all systems such as single-member plurality and to produce election results that are fairer and more representative. So what exactly are the problems with our current system, and how does PR solve them?

UNREPRESENTATIVE ELECTIONS

The basic flaw with our single-member district voting system is that it does a terrible job representing the American public. All Americans should have a say in government, but this is impossible under our current system. It is intentionally designed to represent only one part of the public—those who vote for the winning candidate in a district. Everyone else gets no representation. So if you are a Republican in a predominantly Democratic district (or vice versa), an African American in a White district, or a minor-party supporter in any district, then you are usually shut out by our current election system. Your candidate is unlikely to win, and you will have no one to represent you and speak for you in the legislature.

Typically, in U.S. House elections, about a third of all votes are wasted—cast for candidates who lose. This means that more than thirty million Americans usually come away from the voting booth with no one to represent them in the House. It's no wonder that many Americans feel little connection with their members of Congress—they are represented by someone they voted against.

Proportional representation eliminates this problem. Wasted votes are virtually eliminated, and nearly all voters are able to elect someone to represent them. Even if you vote for a party that gets only 20 percent of the vote, you still win some representation. In PR elections, 90 to 95 percent of voters elect someone to represent them, in contrast to only 60 to 65 percent in current U.S. House elections. Instead of a winner-take-all system, PR is an all-are-winners system, which is one reason it is so popular in other democracies.

Wasted votes also tend to create unfair distortions in representation. Some political groups get more representation than they deserve, and others get less. On the district level, for instance, the party with 51 percent of the vote gets 100 percent of the representation. On the legislative level, the result is that parties often receive many more or many fewer seats than they deserve based on their proportion of the vote. For example, all nine members of the Massachusetts delegation to the U.S. House are Democrats, even though more than one-third of Massachusetts voters cast their ballots for the Republican candidates. Sometimes the misrepresentation is so egregious that the party that comes in *second* in the popular vote is actually able to secure the *majority* of seats in the legislature. In 2012, the GOP won a majority in the U.S. House, despite the fact that Democratic House candidates garnered 1.3 million more votes than Republican candidates nationwide. Such unfair and undemocratic outcomes would be eliminated by PR. For example, if Massachusetts adopted PR, Republican voters would be able to win three of that state's nine seats. The idea behind PR is that all parties should get the representation they deserve—no more and no less.

BREAKING THE TWO-PARTY MONOPOLY

Imagine that you log on to iTunes and discover that it now offers only the two most popular genres of music: pop and country. No rap, no dance or jazz or electronic or world or classical. Just the big two. You would probably be outraged—along with millions of others. But Americans run into this very same situation every time they enter the voting booth. The only real choice we have is between Republicans and Democrats, even if we think of ourselves as Green, Libertarian, or independent. Only about 25 percent of Americans strongly identify with the Republican or Democratic Party, and yet the House is made up of representatives from only those two parties. This is hardly democratic.

The main reason for this two-party monopoly is our single-member plurality system. In this system, only large parties that can receive a majority or plurality of the vote stand any chance of victory. A popular third party may pick up 20 percent or 30 percent of the vote but still fail to elect anyone. This discourages people from even voting for third-party candidates. Worse yet, if people do vote for a third-party candidate, they may actually help elect the candidate they like the least. This is the classic "spoiler" problem. Voting for a Green candidate only takes away votes from the Democratic candidate and helps the Republican to win. In the 2000 election, votes for the Green Party candidate, Ralph Nader, allowed George W. Bush to win Florida—and the presidency. In short, our current electoral system discriminates against minor parties and often punishes people who dare to vote for them.

PR would break up this two-party monopoly and eliminate the spoiler problem. Under PR, all parties that get over the minimum required percentage of the vote—usually around 5 percent—are guaranteed their fair share of seats and representation. A minor party that receives 20 percent of the votes would receive 20 percent of the seats—one seat in a five-seat PR district. Voters could support the candidates and parties they really believe in without fear of wasting their votes or aiding their opponents.

Americans want more choices at the polls. Two-thirds say they want to see other parties seriously challenge the Democrats and Republicans for office, but this is very unlikely to happen unless we adopt proportional representation. And only with PR will we be able to have a multiparty U.S. House that truly represents the diversity of political opinion in this country.

ELIMINATING GERRYMANDERING

Another problem that plagues American elections is gerrymandering. This is the manipulation of district lines to produce an unfair advantage for one party or another. The dominant party in a state often redraws district lines to favor its own candidates. Republicans, for instance, might divide up a large mass of Democratic voters and incorporate them into two predominantly Republican districts—thus ensuring that all the Democratic votes are wasted, and only Republicans are elected.

Gerrymandering creates uncompetitive districts where only one candidate stands a real chance of being elected. If a district is drawn so that it is 70 percent

Democratic, the Republican candidate has virtually no opportunity to win. So while voters think they are deciding who represents them when they go to the polls on Election Day, often that decision has already been made for them many years before by the politicians who drew their district's lines.

Thanks largely to gerrymandering, more than 95 percent of House members now reside in uncompetitive districts and get reelected as a matter of routine. Real competition—and real voter choice—is largely absent from these elections. In a recent election in Florida, 43 percent of the U.S. House seats were not even contested by one of the major parties. And gerrymandering predetermines not only who wins a specific seat but also, often, who controls the House itself. That is why the parties fight so viciously over the redistricting process—they know that a favorable outcome can ensure a majority of the seats in the House even if that party doesn't get a majority of the votes. Gerrymandering helped Republicans to win a majority of the seats in the House between 1996 and 2004, even though they never received more than 50 percent of the nationwide vote.[2]

Gerrymandering would be eliminated overnight in most states if we were to adopt PR for House elections. This is not simply because there would be fewer district lines to draw. Studies have shown that gerrymandering is virtually impossible in large multimember districts with at least five seats.[3] No matter how the lines of these large PR districts are drawn, they have no effect on who gets elected. Every party—even the smaller ones in the district—is able to win its fair share of seats. And every district is competitive because all parties can win some seats. With PR, the voters, not line-drawing politicians, decide who is elected.

BETTER REPRESENTATION OF WOMEN AND MINORITIES

Adopting PR would also greatly improve the representation of women and racial and ethnic minorities, adding important new voices and new perspectives to the House of Representatives. Right now, these groups are substantially underrepresented. For example, in 2015, non-Whites (Blacks, Hispanics, Asians, and Native Americans) made up over 38% of the U.S. population but had only 23% of the seats in the U.S. House. And that body remains 81% male, even though most Americans are female. These groups tend to be much better represented in countries using proportional representation. For instance, most PR countries do better—often dramatically better—than the United States at ensuring fair gender representation. In Sweden, 44 percent of the lower house is made up of women—compared to 19 percent in the

United States. In Norway, the figure is 40 percent; in the Netherlands, 37 percent; and in Germany, 36 percent.

What accounts for this? PR tends to increase the representation of women and minorities because more of them tend to be nominated under this system. The reason is that candidates are nominated in slates in PR elections. In a five-member district, each party puts up a slate of five candidates. With a slate system, parties can institute quotas, something that is not practical in an SMP system. Some European parties, for instance, require that at least 40 percent of the candidates on the slate be women. And because more women are nominated, more tend to get elected.

Some Americans would balk at such quotas. But even without quotas, adopting a PR system would still encourage the nomination and election of more women and minorities. In our current single-member district system, it does not seem odd if the sole party nominee is a White male. With a slate of five candidates, however, it would seem decidedly odd if all the nominees were White males. This creates pressure that encourages parties to include some female and minority candidates on their slates voluntarily.

If we want the U.S. House to be more inclusive and democratic—to be a true mirror of the U.S. population—then we need PR to ensure that voices of women and minorities are heard and acted on in this important policy-making body. Imagine how different the House would be with 30 to 40 percent female representatives.

PRODUCING POLICIES THAT REFLECT PUBLIC PREFERENCES

Ultimately, PR's ability to produce more accurate representation for voters, groups, and parties is important because it makes legislatures more responsive to the demands of the public. Many Americans think that politicians do not listen to them, and that public policies often represent what wealthy special interests want, not what the public wants. Studies show that PR is more likely to produce a legislature that pursues policies that the public wants. In one such study, G. Bingham Powell looked at twenty-two democracies and compared how well the policy positions of legislators reflected the positions of the general public.[4] He found that policy makers in PR countries tended to have political positions that more closely resembled those of the public than policy makers in SMP countries. If the point of democracies is to enact policies that closely reflect the will of the public, then it would be better to have the U.S. House elected by PR.

Having a House of Representatives that is more responsive to the general public could significantly change policy in many areas. For example, most Americans would like to see a reduction in our high level of economic inequality. Studies have shown that countries with PR tend to have lower rates of poverty and lower economic inequality than countries with SMP elections.[5] This is because their multiparty systems are more likely to have a leftist party that strongly promotes the interests of the poor and the working class. When these parties are part of ruling coalitions, they help enact policies—for example, higher minimum wages, more generous public pensions and unemployment programs, and government support for unions—that promote the interests of the less well off.

CONCERNS ABOUT PROPORTIONAL REPRESENTATION

With all of these advantages of PR, it is easy to see why most other industrialized Western democracies have switched to this system. Nevertheless, some Americans worry about the potential disadvantages of PR. For example, one common fear is that a multiparty House of Representatives would be a recipe for chaos and gridlock. If it is difficult to get legislation passed in a two-party House, imagine how much harder it would be with three, four, or five parties. However, if we look at the multiparty legislatures in Europe, we find that such gridlock rarely occurs. In fact, most of them pass legislation much more efficiently than does our Congress. How can this be? It is simple: Each party does not go its own way. Parties typically join together in two large coalitions, a center-right coalition and a center-left coalition, one of which has the majority of votes needed to pass legislation.

In the con essay, Brendan Doherty claims that PR routinely allows a party to rule without a broad public mandate—when it only gets 30 to 40 percent of the vote. But this is misleading. Such a party would not rule by itself but share power with one or more smaller parties in a coalition that represents over 50 percent of the voters—a majority mandate. In fact, ruling coalitions often represent considerably more than a slim majority. It is not unusual for parties in a ruling coalition to represent 55 to 60 percent of the voters. The parties in the current "grand coalition" in Germany got over 67 percent of the vote. The ruling party in the U.S. House often gets barely over 50 percent of the vote and sometimes less. The Republicans won majorities in the House in 2012 and 2014 by gaining 48 percent and 52 percent of the vote respectively. So in practice, PR usually creates a much broader public mandate for the ruling majority.

Doherty also argues that having the largest party share power with smaller parties is bad because it gives very small extremist parties "tremendous influence." But this rarely happens. One of the few instances of this is the example in Israel that he cites—a country that uses a form of PR that is unusually open to these very small parties. Typically, the smaller parties in a coalition are not extremist at all and exert only a modest influence on public policy. And this kind of moderate small party influence is desirable because it gives some power to legitimate political minorities that are completely powerless in SMP systems. Small parties in ruling coalitions help to create a more inclusive democracy.

Some Americans are also concerned that they would have to give up their small, single-member districts to adopt PR elections. They like having an elected official that represents the interests of their local geographic area. However, there is a form of PR that does not require voters to give up their small local districts. In this "mixed-member PR," half the legislature is elected from small, single-member districts and the other half by PR, so that all parties are represented accurately. This system has proved very popular among recent adopters of PR, such as New Zealand and the new parliaments in Scotland and Wales. In the United States, states with large delegations of House members could easily adopt this form of PR and have the best of both worlds: small districts and fair representation.

Another common misconception about PR is that voters would be able to vote only for parties, not for individual candidates. But this is true of only one form of PR—the closed party list system. Most PR systems allow voters to cast their votes for the individual candidates they prefer. For example, in the open list system, a voter casts a vote for an individual candidate on a party's list of candidates. That vote counts two ways. First, it helps determine the party's portion of the overall vote and the number of seats it wins. Second, it counts for the individual candidate. Those candidates with the most votes go to the top of the list and are the first ones chosen to occupy any seats that are won by the party.

Interestingly, most critics of proportional representation do not even try to deny the many serious shortcomings of SMP elections or the numerous substantial advantages of PR. Instead they focus on trying to identify some disadvantages of PR. But as we have seen, most of these alleged disadvantages of PR are exaggerated or simply mistaken. PR's benefits clearly outweigh its drawbacks. That is why, over the last 100 years, the strong trend in advanced Western democracies has been to switch from SMP to PR elections—with almost no countries going the other way.

PR: TOWARD A BETTER DEMOCRACY

Ask yourself these questions: Do you believe that all citizens should have a voice in government, that all parties should compete on an even playing field, that both minorities and majorities deserve representation, and that our legislatures should reflect the true diversity of political views among the public? If you answered yes, then you should be in favor of proportional representation.

In the end, the choice between PR and SMP is not simply about deciding between two different voting systems. It is about choosing between having more or less democracy in the United States. Changing to PR elections in this country would be a major step toward creating a fairer, more representative, more inclusive, and ultimately more democratic political system. That is why proportional representation is a reform that deserves much greater attention in the United States. In the two other major Western democracies that still cling to the SMP system, Great Britain and Canada, large and active citizens' movements are promoting a change to PR. We need that same kind of movement in this country.[6]

CON: Brendan J. Doherty

At first glance, defending the current system that gives us the U.S. House of Representatives does not appear to be an appealing task. Congress's approval ratings are at record lows, and many Americans might be predisposed not only to throw the bums out, as the old saying goes, but also to throw out the system that brought us the bums in the first place. Douglas Amy is correct that the American people don't know much about proportional representation (PR), and he does an admirable job of making the case for PR's benefits. But no aspiring reformer should jump on board without giving serious consideration to its shortcomings as well.

Politics is the process through which we fight out disagreements over national priorities. It is, in Harold Lasswell's famous formulation, "who gets what, when, how."[1] No electoral system is neutral. The various systems distribute power and influence in different ways. And the ways in which a system of proportional representation would distribute power should give us pause. Such a system would allow political parties to take power without a clear mandate from the people. It would lead to disproportionate influence for small political parties on the ideological fringes, since such parties are often needed to form a governing coalition. In our governmental system of shared powers that was designed to make lawmaking difficult, this would lead to even more legislative gridlock, especially given the lack of a mechanism in the U.S. Constitution to resolve a deadlock if no majority coalition can be formed. A PR system would give more power to party insiders and lessen the ability of Americans without political connections to win high office. And it would undermine the connection of individual Americans to individual legislators by weakening the geographic ties essential to good representation. In short, the cure of proportional representation might be worse than the disease.

TAKING POWER WITHOUT
A MANDATE FROM THE PEOPLE

When Republicans expanded their margin of control of the House of Representatives in the 2014 elections, they won 247 seats, 29 more than was needed for a clear majority, and John Boehner was again elected Speaker of the House. Similarly, when Democrats took power eight years earlier, they won 233 seats, 15 more than the 218 needed for a majority in the chamber, and Nancy Pelosi claimed the Speaker's gavel.[2] So it is after each biennial congressional election. Having won a majority of seats in the chamber, one party assumes the speakership and control of the chamber. The winning party's popular mandate flows from the decisions of the people, who every two years empower one of our two big-tent parties to pursue its vision of a more perfect union. In order to win the necessary majority of seats, each party must be inclusive enough to nominate candidates with a range of ideological views who can win a sufficient number of races in politically diverse parts of the country.

Similar mandates would be lacking under a system of proportional representation. While many hail the salutary benefits of smaller parties flourishing if PR were adopted for the U.S. House, the emergence of those smaller parties would lead to parties governing with a much weaker mandate from the people. Would a Democratic or Republican Party that claimed the Speaker's gavel but held only, for example, 22 percent or 38 percent of the seats in the chamber be able to claim a popular mandate in support of its policy priorities? Hardly.

How likely is the scenario in which a party heads the government despite winning far less than a majority of the seats? Very likely. All one needs to do is look at parties that have headed governments in PR systems around the world. In Germany, Angela Merkel won a second term as chancellor in 2009 after her Christian Democratic Union/Christian Social Union Party won only 239 of the 622 seats in the parliament, the Bundestag—a mere 38.4 percent.[3] Merkel retained the chancellorship even though more than 60 percent of the seats in parliament were won by other parties. In Israel, Benjamin Netanyahu became prime minister in 2009 after his Likud Party won 27 of the 120 seats in the Knesset, the Israeli parliament.[4] The 22.5 percent of seats held by Netanyahu's party makes Merkel's mandate seem sweeping in comparison.

The most striking historical instance of a party heading a government without majority support from the people under a system of proportional representation is that of the Nazis in Germany, who never commanded majority support in the course of their rise to power. Adolf Hitler was named chancellor in early 1933 after the Nazi Party had won 196 of 584 legislative seats (33.6 percent) in the November 1932 elections. He then illegitimately assumed dictatorial powers and suppressed the political opposition, leading his country down the road to World War II.[5] This is an extreme example but one that illustrates the potential worst-case outcome of a system that can empower a party that wins only one-third of the seats in the legislature.

In each of these instances, the party that took power did so after a clear majority of the people voted for other parties. How do parties that win only 22.5 percent, 33.6 percent, or 38.4 percent of the seats in a legislature take power in that legislature? They need the help of other parties that join with them to form a coalition government. This arrangement can give disproportionate influence to small parties that boast relatively small levels of public support.

PARTIES ON THE IDEOLOGICAL FRINGES AND THE POTENTIAL FOR GRIDLOCK

A party that wins a plurality but not a majority of seats needs other parties to align with it to form a coalition government. Amy portrays these as "center-left" or "center-right" coalitions, and the use of the word *center* in both formulations offers the comforting notion that these coalitions will be mainstream ones, with a tendency to follow policies that can be reassuringly characterized as more or less centrist.

But because a party that wins a plurality but not a majority of the seats *needs* other parties in order to form a government, the smaller parties can wield disproportionate power, since without their support the government would fall. These parties are often fringe or extremist parties whose positions are not supported by the majority of the public. Nevertheless, they can make demands for their party members to hold powerful posts within the government and for their policy positions to be adopted.

Take the example of the coalition formed in Israel following elections for the Knesset in 2009. The Kadima Party, headed by Tzipi Livni, won 28 of the chamber's 120 seats, one more than the Likud Party's 27 seats. But Likud, headed by former prime minister Benjamin Netanyahu, was able to put together a governing coalition, while Kadima was not. How did Likud do it? After taking well over a month after the elections to craft backroom deals, Likud brought three other parties into its coalition that had won 15, 13, and 11 seats, respectively, resulting in an alliance that held a majority of the seats in the Knesset. Avigdor Lieberman, who headed the Yisrael Beitenu Party, which held 15 of the Knesset's seats—just 12.5 percent—was described in the press as the "kingmaker" in the new government. In exchange for bringing his party into the coalition, Lieberman was named foreign minister. A profile described Lieberman this way: "An immigrant from Moldova who was once a marginal political player, he will serve as foreign minister and Israel's face abroad[,] an almost unthinkable proposition just a few months ago for a polarizing politician widely criticized as a racist."[6] Thus, the system of proportional representation gives tremendous influence to smaller parties, which can extract policy promises and positions of power in exchange for their support in a coalition government. Amy acknowledges this when he offers the example of leftist parties as influential coalition members. Such coalitions could just as readily depend on far-right parties; in either scenario, a PR system gives disproportionate power to more ideologically extreme factions.

What happens if disparate parties are not able to find common ground and form a majority coalition? In parliamentary systems, mechanisms exist to call new elections in such circumstances. The elections held in Greece on May 6, 2012 yielded just such a result. The four leading parties won only 18.9 percent, 16.8 percent, 13.2 percent, and 10.6 percent of the vote that day, with three other parties winning between 6.1 and 8.5 percent of the vote. After more than a week of negotiations, no majority coalition could be formed, and new elections were then scheduled for the following month.[7] No similar mechanism for calling new elections exists under the U.S. Constitution. Elections to the House of Representatives are held every two years. What would happen if six different parties each won a sizable portion of the vote in, say, November 2016, but no majority coalition could be formed by party leaders trying to cut deals in smoke-filled rooms? With no means of resolving the deadlock, how could the House of Representatives function effectively and meet the needs of the nation? In the absence of a mechanism to trigger a second round of nationwide elections, as the Greeks did—a chaotic and suboptimal course of action in any event—the small extremist parties necessary to form a majority coalition and avoid perpetual deadlock would wield all the more disproportionate influence.

And if deals were struck to form a coalition, would the government then function smoothly? Amy contends that there is less gridlock in multiparty European legislatures. To the extent this is true, it is due not to any natural tendency of party coalitions to work in concert but instead to the fact that most of these European governments have parliamentary systems that are designed to facilitate the efficient enactment of legislation. The situation in the United States is quite different. Our government was designed with many veto points built into the system that make it far easier to block than to enact legislation. This institutional tendency toward gridlock would be exacerbated by, not ameliorated by, a PR system if it were grafted onto our current constitutional structure.

Many commentators decry the influence of far-left and far-right members of the Democratic and Republican Parties in the U.S. House of Representatives. If these legislators formed splinter parties under a PR system, they would have even more power. Amy contends that the Israeli example is an outlier, and that "Typically, the smaller parties in a coalition are not extremist at all." In the case of the United States, the smaller parties would include the Socialist Party on the left and the Tea Party on the right. Parties like these would be kingmakers within the House, and Democrats and Republicans would be even more beholden to lawmakers on the ideological fringes. Would giving disproportionate power to these factions improve the functioning of our government, or would it lead to more dysfunction and gridlock?

POWER TO PARTY INSIDERS, NOT THE PEOPLE

Who are the individual people who run for the House of Representatives under the banner of a political party? In our current system, they can be just about anyone who, on his or her own initiative, decides that something must be done and that he or she is the one to do it. The ability of teachers, small business owners, police officers, and other regular people to stand for office regardless of the support of party insiders is one of the strengths of our current system.

In a system of proportional representation, the entrepreneurial ability of party outsiders to run for and win seats in Congress would be severely limited. Who chooses who gets to run for office in a system of proportional representation? Party leaders choose, not the people. Amy contends that open list elections in a PR system give people the power to vote not just for parties but for specific candidates, and that the candidates with the most votes within a party are the first to claim the seats that the party wins. This seems appealing only when compared to the closed list elections in some countries that use PR, in which the people vote only for parties and not for specific candidates. Amy claims that, "With PR, the voters, not line-drawing politicians, decide who is elected," but even in an open list system, the candidates who compose the lists are chosen by party insiders, not by the people.

Over the past hundred years, American politics has progressed away from party insiders making decisions in smoke-filled rooms toward a political system in which everyday Americans can choose their elected representatives. In 1913, we moved from the selection of U.S. senators by state legislatures to the direct election of senators by the people. In the 1970s, we discarded the practice of party leaders choosing presidential nominees at national conventions in favor of having the people select the nominees through a series of primaries and caucuses. Adopting proportional representation for elections to the House of Representatives would take us backward by trading candidate initiative for control by party insiders.

WEAKENING LOCAL REPRESENTATION

The connection between a citizen and a legislator is at the heart of American politics. Members of Congress are elected from particular places to represent the people who live in those places. This geographic representation manifests itself in both legislative priorities and constituent services. Adopting a system of proportional representation would dramatically weaken the quality of this representation in Congress.

Each district has its own member of Congress who looks out for the legislative concerns of the folks back home. For instance, the people who live in the Sixteenth District of California, which in 2016 stretched along the state's San Joaquin Valley and boasted a largely agricultural economy, have different interests and thus different legislative priorities than those in the state's Fifty-third District, which encompassed parts of San Diego and its suburbs. The Sixteenth District was represented by Jim Costa, who served on the Agriculture and Natural Resources Committees. The biography on his congressional website described him as "a third-generation family farmer" and used the word *agriculture* or a variant of *farm* ten times. It also boasted of his efforts on water issues critical to the district and on legislation governing the prices of dairy products, and touted his winning the American Farm Bureau's "Friend of the Farm Bureau award." Costa clearly devoted a great deal of effort to representing the interests of his district.[8]

Representative Susan Davis demonstrated a similar commitment but in a manner tailored to her San Diego–based district, which was known for its substantial connection to the U.S. Navy. Davis served on the Armed Services Committee, and in the biography on her congressional website she described herself as a "military spouse" and the daughter of a World War II veteran, using the word *military* twelve times and *veteran* or *veterans* an additional nine times. Her biography emphasized her commitment to the issues important to her district by declaring that "Susan has been a strong advocate for military families. . . . [S]he has been at the forefront on issues that directly impact service members and their families, such as increases in pay and benefits, improved housing and a health care system worthy of their service and sacrifice."[9] Her biography made no mention of agricultural issues, just as Representative Costa's did not reference military or veterans' issues. Both Californians dedicated themselves to looking out for the substantially different concerns of the people they represented.

Proportional representation would degrade the ability of people to be represented effectively by weakening the critical connection between individual citizens and their legislators. In California, a state with more than 38 million people, it is a substantial challenge for the two U.S. senators, Barbara Boxer and Dianne Feinstein, to represent the diverse interests across the state.[10] In contrast with the biographies of Representatives Costa and Davis, neither senator's website biography uses the words *farm, agriculture,* or *veterans,* and each mentions the word *military* only once.[11] But the member of the House from each of California's fifty-three congressional districts looks after the particular interests of the folks back home. This is still a tall order, though, as each district in California contains more than 700,000 people. A pure PR system would sever the local geographic ties between the people and their representatives. If each of California's fifty-three House members represented all of the more than 38 million people across the state, who would look after the specific interests of the good people in cities and towns such as San Diego, Fresno, and Truckee?

Amy argues that this concern can be addressed through the use of a "mixed-member PR system," in which half of a state's representatives would be elected according to proportional representation, and the other half would still be elected from single-member plurality districts. If this were applied in California, then just twenty-six or twenty-seven of the state's members of the House would be elected from specific districts, which would each need to be double the population of current districts. At the beginning of the Republic, the Constitution established that there should be no more than one representative for every 30,000 people.[12] Today, House districts average about 700,000 people. In a mixed-member PR system, each of California's twenty-six or twenty-seven House members tied to specific districts would represent about 1.4 million people. Surely this would result in *worse* representation, not better. Most Americans already feel that their government does not represent them well—why adopt a system that would further weaken the ties between the people and their legislators?

WHY WE SHOULD KEEP THE CURRENT SYSTEM

Choosing between adopting proportional representation and maintaining the current method of electing members of the House is not, as Amy argues, "choosing between having more or less democracy in the United States." Rather, it is a choice between two systems that allocate power and influence in different ways. Our current system is not perfect, and in a time in which people trust the institutions of power in our country much less than they used to, it makes good sense to think about whether reforming some of those institutions would lead to better outcomes.

Let us briefly review what our current system does well. Political parties win majorities in the House of Representatives and can claim a mandate from the people when they do so. This mandate helps the majority party to overcome the many veto points built into our constitutional system that make it difficult to get things done and to pass legislation to deal with the pressing needs of society. The parties that control the House are two big-tent parties; the ideologically extreme members of the parties wield some influence, but this is tempered by the need for the parties to be inclusive enough to support candidates with a range of ideological views in order to win a majority of seats in parts of the country where different political views prevail. In our system, regular citizens can run for and win seats in the House without the blessing of party insiders. And when they get to Congress, the single-member district system provides them with the incentive to look out for the interests of the people back home.

The American political system is far from perfect, but proportional representation would not make it better. PR would lead to control of the House by parties that had received far less than majority support across the country. It would give disproportionate power to the smaller political parties on the ideological fringes that would be needed to form a governing coalition, which in turn would make legislative gridlock more likely. It would empower party insiders, not the people, to decide who could serve in the Congress. And it would make it all the more difficult for people across the country to have their interests represented by a member of Congress. This would yield not more democracy but instead a democracy in which parties would govern with less legitimacy, extremist parties would be kingmakers, party insiders would gain power at the expense of the people, and the quality of representation would be degraded. We should not adopt a system that might cause more problems than it would solve.

NOTES

PRO

1. For more details on the workings of specific PR systems—what the ballots look like and so on—see the Proportional Representation Library at http://www .mtholyoke.edu/acad/polit/damy/prlib.htm. See also Douglas J. Amy, Real Choices/New Voices: How Proportional Representation Elections Could Revitalize American Democracy (New York, NY: Columbia University Press, 2002); and David Farrell, Electoral Systems: A Comparative Introduction (New York, NY: Palgrave, 2001).

2. Republicans did win more votes than Democrats in each of these elections, but in 2012 they won a majority of seats despite failing to win even a plurality of the vote. For the two parties' percentage of House votes and House seats won between 1946 and 2012, see Table 2.2 in http://www.brookings.edu/~/media/ Research/Files/Reports/2013/07/vital-statistics-congress-mann-ornstein/Vital-Statistics-Chapter-2--Congressional-Elections.pdf?la=en.

3. Arend Lijphart and Bernard Grofman, Eds., *Choosing an Electoral System: Issues and Alternatives* (New York, NY: Praeger, 1984), 7.

4. G. Bingham Powell, *Elections as an Instrument of Democracy: Majoritarian and Proportional Visions* (New Haven, CT: Yale University Press, 2000).

5. Alberto Alisena and Edward Glaeser, *Fighting Poverty in the U.S. and Europe: A World of Difference,* (Oxford: Oxford University Press, 2006).

6. Currently, the main organization promoting PR in the United States is FairVote in Washington, DC; see the organization's Web site, http://www .fairvote.org.

CON

1. Harold Dwight Lasswell, *Politics: Who Gets What, When, How* (New York, NY: Peter Smith, 1950).

2. "Party Divisions of the House of Representatives," House of Representatives website, n.d., accessed April 1, 2016, http://history.house.gov/Institution/Party-Divisions/Party-Divisions.

3. "Official Result for the 2009 Bundestag Election," German Bundestag, n.d., accessed October 28, 2015, http://www.bundestag.de/htdocs_e/bundestag/ elections/results/index.html.

4. Amy Teibel, "Israel's Livni Cool to Deal with Netanyahu," *Associated Press,* February 15, 2009.

5. Richard J. Evans, *The Coming of the Third Reich* (New York, NY: Penguin Press, 2005), 229–308; "Elections in the Weimar Republic," *German Bundestag,* April 2014, http://www.bundestag.de/blob/189774/7c6dd629f4afff7bf4f962a45c110b5f/ elections_weimar_republic-data.pdf.

6. Teibel, "Israel's Livni"; Mark Lavie, "Centrist Labor Joins New Israeli Government," *Associated Press,* March 25, 2009; "A Look at Key Members of Israel's New Government," *Associated Press,* March 31, 2009.

7. "Greece Election Results *Mapped,*" Guardian, May 7, 2012, http://www.guardian. co.uk/news/datablog/interactive/2012/may/06/greece-elections-results-map; "New Greek Elections as Coalition Talks Fail—Venizelos," *BBC News,* May 15, 2012, http://www.bbc.co.uk/news/world-europe-18076757.

8. "About Jim Costa," U.S. Congressman Jim Costa website, n.d., accessed October 26, 2015, https://costa.house.gov/about/full-biography.

9. "Full Biography," U.S. Congresswoman Susan Davis website, n.d., accessed October 26, 2015, https://susandavis.house.gov/about/full-biography.

10. "State and County QuickFacts: California," *U.S. Census Bureau,* n.d., accessed October 26, 2015, http://quickfacts.census.gov/qfd/states/06000.html.

11. "Biography," U.S. Senator Barbara Boxer website, n.d., accessed October 26, 2015, http://www.boxer.senate.gov/about/biography.html; "Biography," U.S. Senator Dianne Feinstein website, n.d., accessed October 26, 2015, http://www.feinstein .senate.gov/public/index.cfm/biography.

12. "Constitution of the United States: A Transcription," n.d., accessed October 26, 2015, http://www.archives.gov/exhibits/charters/constitution_transcript.html.

13

RESOLVED, the redistricting process should be nonpartisan

PRO: Elaine C. Kamarck

CON: Justin Buchler

The U.S. Constitution clearly vests the power of apportionment—the number of House seats each state receives—with Congress and specifies that the number of representatives a state receives must be proportional to its population.[1] The Constitution is silent, however, about redistricting, the drawing of the boundaries of congressional districts. The Constitution does not say who should draw the boundaries or how they should be drawn, and the task has largely been left to state legislatures. Occasionally in the nineteenth century, Congress did provide the states with some general rules. In 1842, for instance, Congress specified that districts should be contiguous (that is, territorially connected), and that each district should elect only one member (some states in those days still used multimember, at-large districts rather than single-member districts). In 1872, Congress legislated that House districts should be made up of "as nearly as possible an equal number of inhabitants." However, Congress generally refrained from involving itself in redistricting, both out of a belief that the Constitution did not grant it that power and because the members thought that exercising such power, even if it were constitutional, would be unwise. As a House report from 1901 explained, allowing Congress to redistrict would open up the prospect of partisan gerrymandering on a national scale. Of course, it was true that state legislatures carried out partisan gerrymandering, "but the division of political power is so general and diverse that notwithstanding the inherent vice of the system of gerrymandering, some kind of equality of distribution results." That is, although drawing boundaries to advantage one party at the expense of another was to be regretted, it was safer to distribute that power to the states so that one party's gain in some states would be counterbalanced by another party's advantage in other states.

The trouble with leaving redistricting to the states, however, was that states varied widely in their practices, particularly in their toleration of population discrepancies between districts. In 1946, these population discrepancies were brought before the U.S. Supreme Court in *Colegrove v. Green*. Kenneth Colegrove, a professor of political science at Northwestern University, filed suit against the state of Illinois because the congressional district in which he lived was made up of 914,000 people, while the nearby Fifth District included only 112,000 people. His vote was thus worth only one-eighth as much as the vote of a citizen in the Fifth District, and he insisted that this inequity was a violation of the Fourteenth Amendment's equal protection guarantee. The Supreme Court disagreed, however, insisting that redistricting was "of a peculiarly political nature and therefore not meant for judicial interpretation." It was the responsibility of Congress or the state legislatures, not the courts, to ensure equal representation.

Sixteen years later, however, the Court famously reversed course in *Baker v. Carr* (1962) and entered the "political thicket" that it previously warned against. *Baker* was precipitated by a challenge to Tennessee's state legislative boundaries, which had not been redrawn since the turn of the century. This was not an isolated problem. Delaware and Alabama had also neglected to redraw state legislative boundaries for the past sixty years, and nine more states had gone three decades since last adjusting their district lines. In some states, the population discrepancy between the largest and smallest state legislative districts was as much as one hundred to one. In Tennessee, the ratio was about ten to one, with urban residents the big losers. The Supreme Court decided in *Baker* that, contrary to its opinion in *Colegrove,* such matters were in fact justiciable—that is, decidable by courts. Two years later, in *Reynolds v. Sims* (1964), the Court ruled that the "one person, one vote" principle required that state legislative districts, including those constituting the upper house, must contain roughly equal populations. That same year, in *Wesberry v. Sanders,* the Court ruled that the same principle applied to districts drawn for the U.S. House of Representatives. The courts have been heavily involved in the redistricting process ever since, particularly in policing the use of race in the drawing of legislative boundaries.

The courts have been reluctant, however, to referee politically motivated gerrymandering that either advantages one party over the other (a partisan gerrymander) or protects incumbents of both parties (a bipartisan gerrymander). In *Davis v. Bandemer* (1986), for instance, a sharply divided Court set the plaintiff's threshold so high that it seemed nearly impossible to find a redistricting plan that would not pass constitutional muster. In *Vieth v. Jubelirer* (2004), the Court heard a challenge to a Republican gerrymander of congressional districts in Pennsylvania and again was sharply divided, with the four most conservative justices arguing that partisan gerrymanders were nonjusticiable and the four most liberal justices arguing that they were justiciable. The critical swing vote in the case was provided by Justice Anthony Kennedy, who agreed with the Court's conservatives that there could be no judicial remedy in this case but held out the possibility that the Court might someday discover a workable standard that would allow for judicial review of political gerrymanders.

These and other court cases have given states a relatively wide berth in redistricting, so long as they adhere to strict population equality and do not unconstitutionally dilute the votes of racial and ethnic minorities. Political gerrymandering may not violate the U.S. Constitution, but the question remains as to whether it is a problem that we should seek to remedy. Elaine C. Kamarck argues that it is and recommends nonpartisan redistricting as a way to take the partisan politics out of the drawing of district lines and help make elections more competitive. Justin Buchler disagrees, arguing that politicians have an incentive to avoid partisan gerrymanders, and that the bipartisan gerrymanders that politicians do have an incentive to craft actually benefit voters.

PRO: Elaine C. Kamarck

The current method of redistricting undermines the intentions of the Founding Fathers and threatens American democracy. As it stands, the process produces a very large number of congressional districts in which only one political party has a chance of winning. Take, for example, the 2010 midterm elections, in which sixty-three seats changed party. The election was historic, viewed as a major political event and an upset for President Barack Obama, yet the sixty-three seats that changed hands constitute only 14 percent of the House of Representatives.

The fact is that the current system of redistricting creates very few competitive districts, and therefore, even in a "big" election year such as 2010, less than one-seventh of the seats change hands. In recent years, Congress has had abysmal approval ratings, sometimes as low as 9 percent, and yet, incumbent reelection rates have remained high at 90 percent in 2012 and 95 percent in 2014. Districts are drawn in ways that make it impossible for voters to register their displeasure with the record of one political party or the other. And if voters cannot use the electoral system to express their opinions of the way Congress is working, there is a major flaw in the democratic process.

When the Founding Fathers created Congress they created two houses, each with a particular purpose. The Senate was intended to be one step removed from the whims of the people. For that reason, senators were chosen by state legislatures, not by the people. In addition, longer terms of six years helped the Senate to serve as a brake on short-term and perhaps ill-advised actions of "the mob." On the other hand, the House of Representatives was supposed to reflect the will of the people in an immediate way. That is why the Founding Fathers declared that House members would be elected directly by the people every two years. The House was to be the place where the people were supposed to rule and where government was supposed to be directly and immediately affected by the people's demands.

Today, however, the intentions behind the Founding Fathers' creation of the House of Representatives have been lost. The reason is that congressional districts are drawn so that it is virtually impossible for one or the other party to win. This practice is known as gerrymandering. The term originated in Massachusetts in 1812, when the incumbent governor, Elbridge Gerry, signed into law the new state senate districts. Among the districts created was a weirdly shaped one that political cartoonists of the day rendered as a creature with wings and some observers likened to the shape of a salamander. The district had been created to ensure the election of a person from a specific party.

The word *gerrymander*, combining Gerry's name and the word *salamander*, came to be used to refer to the intentional drawing of congressional district boundaries in such a way that they create districts that are almost impossible for a given party to win—or lose.

With the assistance of computerization and block-by-block census and voting data, the creation of congressional districts has moved from an art to an exact science. Congressional district lines are drawn every ten years after the nation's census is taken. In most states they are drawn by state legislatures, and whichever political party has the most votes in a state's legislature is the political party that draws the districts. Not surprisingly, the party in power tries to draw district lines in ways that will guarantee more "safe" districts for it than for the other party. Today it is not at all unusual to find congressional districts that look every bit as weird on a map as the original district that Governor Gerry signed into law. Take a look at the bizarrely shaped districts in Figure 13.1: Arizona's Second Congressional District, North Carolina's Twelfth Congressional District, and Illinois's Fourth Congressional District.

Figure 13.1

Most Gerrymandered Congressional Districts: (a) Arizona's Second, (b) North Carolina's Twelfth, and (c) Illinois's Fourth

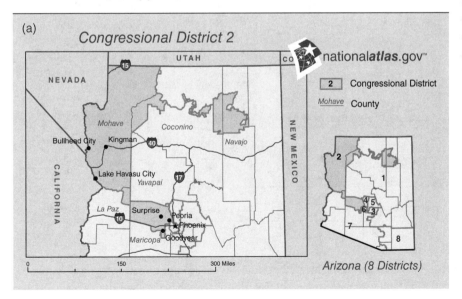

(Continued)

(Continued)

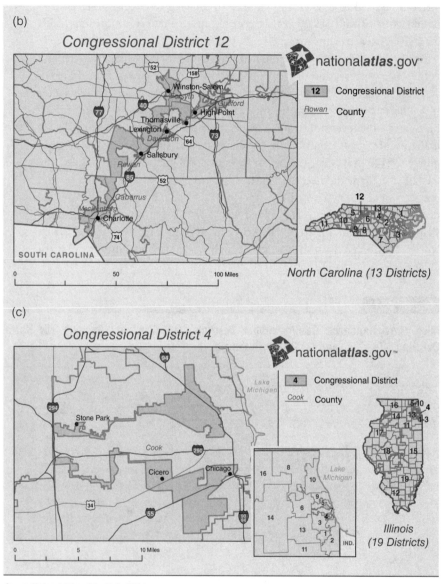

Source: National Atlas of the United States.

Over the past century, the number of safe congressional districts has increased, and the number of competitive House seats has declined dramatically. At the beginning of the twentieth century, the House of Representatives had an average of 187 "swing" or competitive seats. By the end of the century, that number had

Table 13.1

Incumbents Winning with at Least 60 Percent of the Vote

Decade	Average percentage of House incumbents winning with at least 60 percent of the major-party vote
1960s	64
1970s	73
1980s	78
1990s	71
2000s	80

Sources: Data from Norman J. Ornstein, Thomas E. Mann, and Michael J. Malbin, *Vital Statistics on Congress 2008* (Washington, DC: Brookings Institution Press, 2008), Table 2.12; and tabulation from William A. Galston, "Can a Polarized American Party System Be 'Healthy'?," *Issues in Governance Studies* (Brookings Institution) 34 (April, 2010).

fallen to a mere 58 seats. The 2010 midterm elections came close to the record set in 1948 for the number of incumbent House members defeated in a general election: 54 in 2010 compared to 68 in 1948. But these sorts of elections are rare. More common is an election such as that in 2008, in which only 19 incumbents lost in the general election. In the vast majority of congressional elections since 1950, more than 90 percent of House incumbents held on to their seats.

In addition, over time safe seats have gotten even safer. Table 13.1 shows that the number of safe seats (defined by incumbents winning with more than 60 percent of the two-party vote) has increased substantially since the 1960s.

Members of Congress in safe districts can still be defeated in primary elections. For many members of Congress, then, the election most feared is the primary, and they pay particular attention to the policy desires of their primary electorates. People who vote in primaries are a tiny subset of the larger electorate. Average turnout in the 2002 congressional primaries was a mere 5.4 percent of the voting-age population, and average turnout in the 2006 congressional primaries was 4.6 percent of the voting-age population. Even in 2010, despite the much-publicized mobilization of the so-called tea party, turnout reached only 7.5 percent of the voting-age population.[1] This small slice of the electorate is made up of the hard-core ideologues of each political party, and since members of Congress can be defeated by these ideologues in primaries, the members pay an inordinate amount of attention to these voters' concerns. No wonder so many Americans feel left out of the system and believe that politicians ignore the issues that matter most to the American people.

As the result of gerrymandering, more and more congressional districts are safe seats and more and more members of Congress pay attention to their primary voters. The effect of this is to mute the voices of moderate voters and increase political polarization. Of course, other factors have also contributed to the creation of safe seats. In *The Big Sort: Why the Clustering of Like-Minded America Is Tearing Us Apart,* Bill Bishop shows how Americans have been moving, voluntarily, into geographic communities where they find others who are like them—economically, culturally, and politically.[2] Given these trends, there is a limit to the number of competitive congressional districts that could be created if redistricting were removed from the control of self-interested state legislators.

Some states have been so dismayed by the partisan gridlock and the lack of competitive districts resulting from gerrymandering that they have decided to take the redistricting process out of the hands of their state legislators and turn it over to nonpartisan bodies. The number of independent state redistricting commissions has grown over time, albeit slowly. The first four were established in the 1980s in Hawaii, Iowa, Washington, and Montana. They were followed in the 1990s by Idaho, New Jersey, and Arizona. In 2008, nonpartisan redistricting was introduced in California after voters approved Proposition 11, which established the California Citizens Redistricting Commission.

In five other states, Alaska, Arkansas, Colorado, Missouri, and Pennsylvania, there are bipartisan or nonpartisan commissions for the drawing of state legislative lines only. The most recent addition to this group is Ohio. In November, 2015, Ohio voters passed a ballot measure creating a seven-member Ohio Redistricting Commission. It requires that for a 10-year redistricting plan to pass, at least two members from each major political party must agree. It, too, does not apply to the drawing of congressional district lines.

Earlier in 2015, the U.S. Supreme Court ruled, in a challenge brought by Arizona legislators, that the independent redistricting commission was constitutional—clearing the way for more Commission-type approaches to redistricting.

Nonetheless, in most states, redistricting is still done by the leadership of the state legislature, and exquisite attention is paid to packing as many Democrats or Republicans (as the case may be) into one district. In contrast, in Iowa, the nonpartisan Legislative Service Agency uses a computer to draw the districts, taking into account *only* population and disregarding *any* political information. In addition, the agency has to keep county lines intact. The result? In Iowa, where redistricting has been bipartisan since 1981, two of the four congressional districts in 2014 were decided by margins of 5 percentage points or less, and the third was decided by 10.5 percent, a level of competition between Democrats and Republicans that is unheard of in other states.[3]

In California, the newly created Citizens Redistricting Commission consists of three Democrats, three Republicans, and two people who have no partisan affiliation. In creating the commission, state legislators had the authority to eliminate twenty-four names from a pool of sixty presented to them by the Auditor's Applicant Review Panel, which sought out nominees who had the relevant skills and background to engage in the redistricting process. The commission only recently established new lines for state elections and for congressional elections, so it is too early to say whether or not more competitive districts have been created in California, but that was clearly the intent of the reform. (After the commission members finished their work, the California legislature defunded the commission, and the state government refused to house it anywhere in existing state government—thereby casting doubt on whether the commission will be able to do its job again in 2020.)

U.S. states' experience with independent redistricting commissions is still too limited to enable us to draw definitive conclusions about whether districts drawn this way are more competitive. However, there is some suggestive evidence from earlier experiments in California, which has been at the center of redistricting battles for the past forty years. In 1971 and again in 1991, Republican governors blocked gerrymandering efforts on the part of the state's Democrats. The issue ended up in the courts and resulted in the creation of three-judge panels serving as "special masters" in charge of redistricting. Because of this, the Rose Institute in California was able to carry out a sort of controlled experiment. Figure 13.2 shows the results of the Rose Institute's study. In the two decades in which the redistricting process was in the hands of a nonpartisan panel of judges, the number of competitive districts increased substantially. And in the two decades in which redistricting remained in the hands of politicians, very few competitive districts were created.

Taking redistricting out of the hands of state legislatures will not cure all the current ills of American democracy. The evidence from California and Iowa, however, suggests that it will increase the number of competitive congressional districts, and any such increase will make our biennial national elections more responsive to the will of the people. More members of Congress from competitive districts will mean more members beholden to a broader swath of the electorate than the very small numbers who vote in congressional primaries.

Responsiveness to the people is what the Founding Fathers intended for the House of Representatives. In *Federalist* No. 52, Alexander Hamilton explained,

> As it is essential to liberty that the government in general should have a common interest with the people, so it is particularly essential that the [House of Representatives] should have an immediate dependence on, and an intimate sympathy with, the people.

Figure 13.2

Competitive Districts in the California Legislature, by Decade

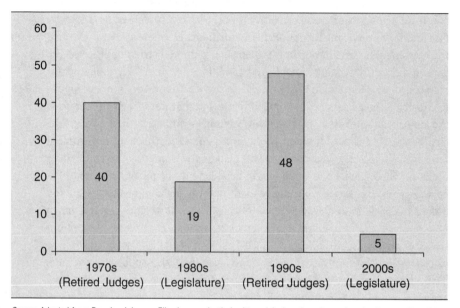

Source: Adapted from Douglas Johnson, Elise Lampe, Justin Levitt, and Andrew Lee, *Restoring the Competitive Edge* (Claremont, CA: Rose Institute of State and Local Government, Claremont McKenna College, September 26, 2005), 10.

Note: Districts counted as competitive are those that elected at least one Democrat and one Republican in the decade or, alternatively, those in which, although there was no party turnover, either the average margin of victory during the decade was less than 10 percent or more than half of the elections during the decade were decided by less than 10 percent.

Gerrymandering, especially in recent decades, has been undermining this original vision of the House of Representatives. Rather than creating opportunities for "immediate dependence on, and an intimate sympathy with, the people," gerrymandering protects the vast majority of members of Congress *from* the people. One step toward making the House a more representative and responsive body would be to remove the redistricting process from partisan state legislatures and place it in the hands of impartial, nonpartisan redistricting commissions.

CON: Justin Buchler

R eform advocates argue that partisan elected officials should not be permitted to redraw district lines because they face a conflict of interest. Clearly, partisan officials do have an *interest* in how district lines are drawn. However, that does not mean that they have a *conflict* of interest, which occurs only when an agent charged with carrying out a task has incentives to carry out that task in a way that is detrimental to the principal, which in this case is the voting public. So, in order to determine whether or not there is a conflict of interest, we must examine partisan officials' incentives, voters' interests, and the degree to which they conflict. While partisan gerrymanders are harmful to voters, partisan officials have incentives not to attempt them. Instead, they have incentives to enact bipartisan gerrymanders. That bothers many reform advocates because bipartisan gerrymanders prevent competitive elections. However, a bipartisan gerrymander, by promoting partisan and ideological representation, serves voters' interests more effectively than a plan that promotes competitive elections. Thus, partisan officials face no conflict of interest because they have strategic incentives to do precisely what is in voters' best interests.

PARTISAN OFFICIALS' INCENTIVES

Broadly defined, a gerrymander is a redistricting plan aimed at achieving a political objective. Given that all redistricting plans have political objectives, any plan can be called a gerrymander. Three types of gerrymanders warrant attention here: the partisan gerrymander, the bipartisan gerrymander, and the competitive gerrymander. A partisan gerrymander is a plan in which one party attempts to maximize the number of seats it wins. In a bipartisan gerrymander, the two parties agree to create safer seats for each party by making Democratic districts more Democratic and Republican districts more Republican. A competitive gerrymander maximizes the number of districts in which there are equal numbers of Democratic and Republican voters to promote competitive elections.

Consider, first, the partisan gerrymander. Suppose an electorate has twenty-one Democrats and twelve Republicans, and that they must be divided into three districts of eleven people each. If the Republicans were to attempt a partisan gerrymander, they would group the voters as follows: District 1, eleven Democrats; District 2, six Republicans and five Democrats; and District 3, six Republicans and five Democrats. By giving themselves majorities in two districts, the Republicans can theoretically win two out of three seats, even though they have only roughly one-third of the population. This plan, if successful, would distort the electorate's preferences. However, note the words *theoretically* and *if successful*. If just two voters switch their allegiance for some reason, Democrats can win all three seats because the Republican majorities in Districts 2 and 3 are so narrow. This is more than just a hypothetical danger. In 1974, the Watergate scandal caused an attempted Republican partisan gerrymander in New York to backfire dramatically by allowing Democrats to win seats that were supposed to be narrow Republican majorities.[1] When a party attempts a partisan gerrymander, a small shift in public opinion can cost many seats, and partisan elected officials are sufficiently risk-averse that self-interest prevents egregious partisan gerrymandering.

Perhaps the most vilified modern redistricting plan was the one passed by Texas in 2003 under the guidance of Tom DeLay, which reformers use as an exemplar of why partisan officials should not be allowed to redraw district lines. However, even that plan is far from an egregious partisan gerrymander. After the 2000 U.S. Census, the Democratic-controlled Texas state legislature and Republican governor failed to agree on a plan, so a panel of judges essentially maintained the previous plan, giving the Democrats seventeen out of thirty-two U.S. House seats from the state. The 2002 election gave the Republicans control of the state legislature for the first time in years, and they capitalized by redrawing district lines in a notorious mid-decade procedure. Under the new plan, the 2004 election gave the Republicans twenty-one out of thirty-two House seats. The process of passing that plan was unusual, not merely from a timing perspective but because it involved such amusements as Democratic state legislators literally fleeing the state in order to deny a quorum in the legislature, thereby postponing passage of the plan in a poor-man's filibuster. While the procedure that produced the plan was difficult to defend, the plan itself was another matter. The 2002 district lines gave the Democrats 53 percent of the House seats, even though the Texas electorate was majority Republican. The DeLay plan ultimately gave the Republicans 66 percent of the U.S. House districts from Texas. Which was a better representation of the Texas population? Consider the statewide election results from the years preceding the DeLay plan, which can be used to measure the partisan composition of the state.[2] As Table 13.2 shows, the DeLay plan had a Republican bias, but by most measures, that bias was smaller than the Democratic bias of the court-drawn plan. Using the 2002 Senate race as a baseline, the DeLay plan and the court plan were essentially equally biased, and using the 2002 lieutenant governor race as the baseline, the DeLay plan had a stronger bias than the court plan. However, by every other measure, the bias of the DeLay plan was smaller than that of the court plan. While it was procedurally unusual to redraw district lines mid-decade, thus understandably angering Democrats, the result of having partisan officials redraw the lines was a *reduction* in partisan bias. This is to be expected because the risks of attempting partisan gerrymanders are sufficiently high for the dominant party that, contrary to the fears of reform advocates, partisan officials rarely attempt to create an egregious bias.

Instead, since partisan elected officials are risk-averse, they are more likely to draw bipartisan gerrymanders, as they did in California after the 2000 U.S.

Table 13.2

Bias and the Texas Redistricting of 2003

Year	Office	Republican two-party vote (%)	Democratic two-party vote (%)	Court plan bias	DeLay plan bias
2000	President	64	36	17 points	2 points
2000	Senate	67	33	20 points	1 point
2002	Governor	59	41	12 points	7 points
2002	Senate	56	44	9 points	10 points
2002	Lieutenant Governor	53	47	6 points	13 points
2002	Attorney General	58	42	11 points	8 points

Source: Texas Secretary of State.

Census. In the 2000 election, Democrats won thirty-two out of fifty-two U.S. House seats in California, and the 2000 U.S. Census gave California an additional seat. However, despite the fact that Democrats controlled both houses of the state legislature and the governor's office, they made no attempt at a partisan gerrymander. Instead, they passed a bipartisan gerrymander that eliminated competitive districts, made Democratic and Republican seats safer, and left the partisan ratio essentially unchanged. In 2000, George W. Bush and Al Gore were separated by less than ten points in the two-party vote in fifteen of California's U.S. House districts. In 2004, Bush and John Kerry were separated by less than ten points in only five districts. However, the partisan ratio remained essentially unchanged. In 2002, the Democrats won thirty-three out of fifty-three House seats, which is essentially the same proportion they won before redistricting. Partisan officials rarely attempt serious partisan gerrymanders. They are more likely to attempt bipartisan gerrymanders because they don't want to run the risk of losing too many seats for their parties, they want to make their own seats safer, and those with progressive ambitions want to create safe House seats for which they will eventually run.

VOTERS' INTERESTS

Partisan officials have incentives to draw bipartisan gerrymanders. That constitutes a conflict of interest only if voters have an interest in a different type of plan. Reform advocates believe that voters' interests would be better served by a competitive gerrymander. If so, then partisan officials face a conflict of interest. So do bipartisan gerrymanders really hurt voters? Reformers such as Samuel Issacharoff ask us to imagine a situation in which Coke and Pepsi carve up the country into districts in which only Coke is sold and districts in which only Pepsi is sold, based on the strange idea that elections are like markets. Issacharoff suggests that allowing partisan officials to redraw district lines knowing that they will create bipartisan gerrymanders is no different.[3] Of course, a bipartisan gerrymander is more like placing Coke drinkers into one set of districts and Pepsi drinkers into another set, then allowing districts to choose collectively what they drink. It would seem odd to suggest that Coke drinkers in this system are prevented from drinking Pepsi just because they prefer Coke, but that is precisely what this market analogy does. For this and similar reasons, attempting to draw analogies between elections and markets is deeply misleading.[4] The fact that an election, unlike a market, is a single collective choice suggests that we should group people in ways that will allow them to make collective choices that satisfy the maximum number of people.

So what specific interests do voters have in a redistricting plan? Consider the following two interests. Voters have a collective interest in a state delegation with a partisan balance that reflects the partisan balance of the state electorate, and they have an interest in giving as many voters as possible a representative whose opinions reflect their own. Competitive gerrymanders undermine both interests.

If a state is 60 percent Democratic, a redistricting plan that produces a 60 percent Democratic delegation is better than a plan that produces a 60 percent Republican delegation. So what type of redistricting plan minimizes partisan bias? Empirically, the more competitive districts there are, the greater the partisan bias.[5] Bipartisan gerrymanders do a much better job of ensuring proportionality than do competitive gerrymanders, although this may seem counterintuitive. To understand why, consider a state evenly split between Democrats and Republicans, divided into two districts. The competitive gerrymander would be to make each district a microcosm of the state. The bipartisan gerrymander would be to create a homogeneously Democratic district and a homogeneously Republican district. If an evenly divided district has a 50 percent chance of electing a candidate of either party, then the competitive gerrymander has a 25 percent chance of electing two Democrats, a 25 percent chance of electing two Republicans, and only a 50 percent chance of producing a delegation that actually reflects the state's preferences. On the other hand, the bipartisan gerrymander would deterministically give the state the fifty-fifty delegation that it should have.[6] Bipartisan gerrymanders ensure partisan representation; competitive gerrymanders undermine partisan representation.

The second interest voters have is in electing representatives whose opinions match their own. Advocates of competitive elections argue that bipartisan gerrymanders cause two related problems: They create legislative polarization and foster discrepancies between the opinions of voters and their representatives. There is an intuitively appealing theory underlying such claims. A competitive general election might pull the candidates toward the ideological center of the district. In a district dominated by voters of one party, there won't be a competitive general election, so candidates in such districts may simply move to the extremes to win the primary. Thus, it has become a mantra for reform advocates to blame the increase in congressional polarization on bipartisan gerrymanders. Furthermore, if we assume that voters are not themselves polarized, then that polarization is a distortion of voters' preferences, so by promoting polarization, bipartisan gerrymanders foster discrepancies between the positions of voters and their representatives.

However, the data do not support such claims. Consider the histograms presented here, showing the ideologies of representatives to the U.S. House in

Figure 13.3

DW-NOMINATE Scores for the 83rd Congress (1953–1954)

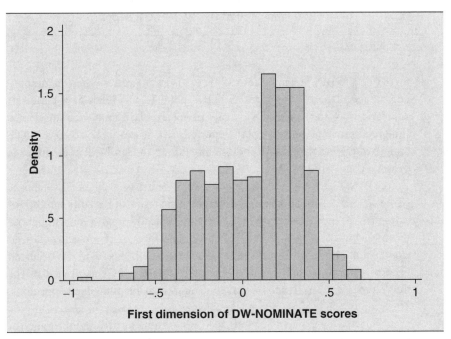

Source: DW-NOMINATE scores are compiled by Keith Poole and available at http://www.voteview.com.

Figure 13.4

DW-NOMINATE Scores for the 113th Congress (2013–2014)

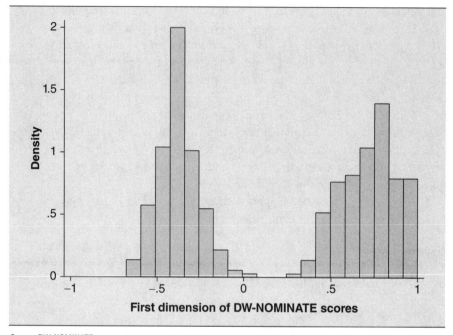

Source: DW-NOMINATE scores are computed by Keith Poole and available at http://www.voteview.com.

the 83rd (1953–1954) and 113th (2013–2014) Congresses. There is nothing unique about these Congresses. Scholars point to the 1950s as a period of depolarization and the 2000s as one of hyperpolarization, and these two Congresses are representative of their periods. The scores are DW-NOMINATE scores, where negative scores indicate liberalism and positive scores indicate conservatism.

The 83rd Congress had a large number of centrists, as Figure 13.3 shows. However, the 113th Congress had very few centrists and a large number of extremists, as shown in Figure 13.4. There was a steady progression throughout the post–World War II period that produced the now famously polarized Congress. If reform advocates are to be believed, then this trend has occurred because partisan officials have systematically eliminated competitive districts, thus removing incentives for anyone in Congress to adopt moderate positions. This proposition is false,[7] and it is relatively easy to see why.

If bipartisan gerrymanders had been responsible for the disappearance of moderates, then representatives from marginal districts in the 113th Congress

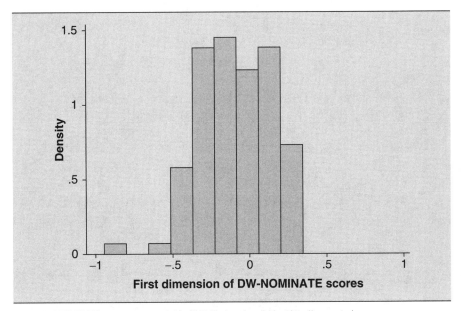

Figure 13.5

DW-NOMINATE Scores for Members in Marginal Districts, 83rd Congress

Source: DW-NOMINATE scores are computed by Keith Poole and available at http://www.voteview.com.

would be just as moderate as representatives from marginal districts in the 83rd Congress—there would simply be fewer of them in the 113th Congress. However, as we can see in Figures 13.5 and 13.6, that is not the case. Figures 13.5 and 13.6 are histograms exactly like Figures 13.3 and 13.4, except that they show the ideological scores of only those members of Congress from marginal districts, meaning those in which the presidential candidates were within 10 points of each other. These figures show that just like the rest of Congress, members from marginal districts have become more polarized. So we cannot blame polarization on the presence of fewer marginal districts. In fact, marginal districts haven't even been disappearing! Figure 13.7 shows the proportion of U.S. House districts in each presidential election that were marginal based on the definition previously used.

The number of competitive districts fluctuates over time, but Figure 13.7 hardly paints a picture of partisan officials systematically destroying competition through bipartisan gerrymanders. In fact, there were nearly as many marginal districts in 2012 as in 1952, yet polarization was much more pronounced in the 113th Congress than in the 83rd. While bipartisan gerrymanders do

Figure 13.6

DW-NOMINATE Scores for Marginal Members, 113th Congress

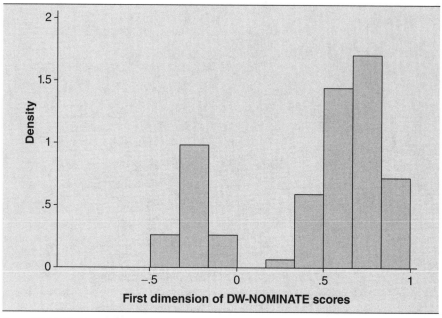

Source: DW-NOMINATE scores are computed by Keith Poole and available at http://www.voteview.com.

occur, as they did in California after the 2000 U.S. Census, their frequency and effects have been dramatically overstated by reform advocates. Marginal districts have not been disappearing, and even if they had, members of Congress from the remaining marginal districts are more polarized now than were members from marginal districts in the 1950s. Therefore, while there are many reasons to be troubled by the increasing polarization in Congress, we cannot blame that polarization on bipartisan gerrymanders.

So allowing partisan officials to redraw district lines is not responsible for polarization. We now move on to the second part of the competition-ideology argument. Proponents of competitive elections argue that competitive elections yield legislators who are more ideologically representative of their constituents than are legislators who win by landslides. There are several related problems with that line of reasoning. First, even in competitive districts, candidates must win a primary before getting to the general election, so even in competitive districts, candidates don't just appeal to the median voter because of the wide gap between the preferences of primary voters and general election voters. Second,

Figure 13.7

Percentage of House Districts that Are Marginal, by Presidential Election

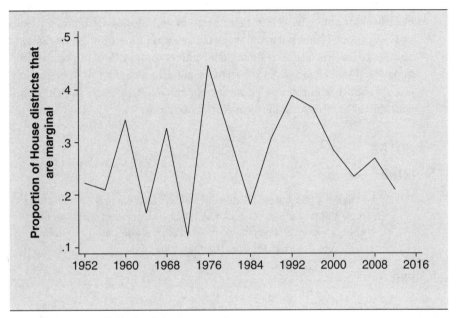

Source: Election data provided by Gary C. Jacobson.

remember that a bipartisan gerrymander requires drawing homogeneous districts, and a competitive gerrymander requires drawing politically diverse districts. When districts are politically diverse, that is precisely when we see the biggest gap between the preferences of the primary voters and those of the general election voters. Since bipartisan gerrymanders involve homogeneous districts, they ensure that the gap between the primary and general electorates is as small as possible. Thus, bipartisan gerrymanders force candidates to adopt policy positions that are as similar as possible to as many constituents as possible.[8] Furthermore, a politically diverse district ensures that no matter which candidate wins, and no matter what platform the winner proposes, a large number of constituents will disagree with it. Thus, it should be no surprise that, empirically, it is in competitive districts that voters are most likely to disagree with the platforms of their representatives.[9] Bipartisan gerrymanders, by definition, create more homogeneous constituencies, so bipartisan gerrymanders are more likely than competitive gerrymanders to elect representatives who are ideologically similar to their constituents.

A CONFLUENCE, NOT A CONFLICT, OF INTEREST

Partisan elected officials have strategic incentives to enact bipartisan gerrymanders. A bipartisan gerrymander is also the type of redistricting plan that most benefits voters by giving them partisan and ideological representation, and we cannot blame polarization in Congress on bipartisan gerrymanders. Thus, partisan officials have strategic incentives to draw lines in precisely the same way that benefits voters.[10] They do not face a conflict of interest; they face a confluence of interest, because competitive elections are in neither the constituents' interests nor partisan officials' interests.

NOTES

INTRO

1. In the original Constitution, population was calculated not only on the basis of "the whole Number of free Persons" and indentured servants but also on the number of slaves, each of whom was counted as three-fifths of a person. "Indians not taxed" were also excluded from the population count.

PRO

1. William A. Galston and Elaine C. Kamarck, *The Still-Vital Center: Moderates, Democrats, and the Renewal of American Politics* (Washington, DC: Third Way, February 2011), http://content.thirdway.org/publications/372/Third_Way_Report_-_The_Still_Vital_Center.pdf.
2. Bill Bishop, *The Big Sort: Why the Clustering of Like-Minded America Is Tearing Us Apart* (New York, NY: Houghton Mifflin, 2008).
3. See Grant Schulte, "Redistricting Sets Stage for Competitive Races in Each of Iowa's 4 Congressional Districts," Associated Press, June 6, 2012, http://www.therepublic.com/view/story/e7211957076c4d70b5367ecf78c60254/IA--Iowa-General-Election. See Real Clear Politics, http://www.realclearpolitics.com/epolls/2012/house/2012_elections_house_map.htm.

CON

1. Howard Scarrow, "The Impact of Reapportionment on Party Representation in the State of New York," *Policy Studies Journal* 9 (1981): 937–46.
2. Looking at the total number of votes each party wins in congressional elections across the state is problematic because so many incumbents face weak challengers who cannot maintain even the support of voters in their own parties.
3. Samuel Issacharoff, "Gerrymandering and Political Cartels," *Harvard Law Review* 116 (2002): 592–648.

4. Justin Buchler, *Hiring and Firing Public Officials: Rethinking the Purpose of Elections* (New York, NY: Oxford University Press, 2011).

5. David Butler and Bruce E. Cain, *Congressional Redistricting: Comparative and Theoretical Perspectives* (New York, NY: Macmillan, 1992).

6. For elaboration, see Justin Buchler, "The Statistical Properties of Competitive Districts: What the Central Limit Theorem Can Teach Us about Election Reform," *PS: Political Science and Politics* 40 (2007): 333–37.

7. Alan I. Abramowitz, Brad Alexander, and Matthew Gunning, "Incumbency, Redistricting, and the Decline of Competition in U.S. House Elections," *Journal of Politics* 68 (2006): 75–88; Seth Masket, Jonathan Winburn, and Gerald C. Wright, "The Limits of the Gerrymander: Examining the Impact of Redistricting on Electoral Competition and Legislative Polarization" (paper presented at the annual meeting of the Midwest Political Science Association, 2006); Eric McGhee, *Redistricting and Legislative Partisanship* (San Francisco: Public Policy Institute of California, 2008); Justin Buchler, "Redistricting Reform Will Not Solve California's Budget Crisis," *California Journal of Politics and Policy* 1, no. 1 (2009).

8. Justin Buchler, "Competition, Representation, and Redistricting: The Case against Competitive Congressional Districts," *Journal of Theoretical Politics* 17 (2005): 431–63.

9. Thomas Brunell and Justin Buchler, "Ideological Representation and Competitive Congressional Elections," *Electoral Studies* 28 (2009): 448–57.

10. Some might object to allowing partisan elected officials to redraw district lines because they may attempt to lock minor parties out of the process. However, we have a two-party system because of Duverger's law—a simple plurality-rule electoral system tends to produce a two-party system, so even if partisan officials had incentives to eliminate marginal districts, that would have little effect on the prospects of third parties because they are unlikely to win regardless of how district lines are drawn.

RESOLVED, the Senate should represent people, not states

PRO: Bruce I. Oppenheimer

CON: John J. Pitney Jr.

Not every high school student takes a class in civics or government anymore, but even those who don't seldom graduate without hearing words to this effect somewhere along the line: "The framers of the Constitution created the House of Representatives to represent the people and the Senate to represent the states." Students who do take classes in government may delve into *The Federalist Papers,* a series of newspaper articles that Alexander Hamilton, James Madison, and John Jay wrote to persuade the country to ratify the Constitution in 1787 and 1788. They may even read *Federalist* No. 62.

In that essay, which was published in New York's *Independent Journal* on February 27, 1788, Madison explained and defended the Senate's place in the proposed constitutional system as "giving to the State governments such an agency in the formation of the federal government as must secure the authority of the former." Not only was each individual state empowered by the Senate to defend its sovereignty, Madison added, but so were the states as a whole. For that reason, "the equal vote allowed to each State" in the Senate "ought to be no less acceptable to the large than to the small States; since they are not less solicitous to guard, by every possible expedient, against an improper consolidation of the States into one simple republic" ruled exclusively by a national government.

The truism that the House represents the people and the Senate represents the states has more than *Federalist* No. 62 going for it. After the first census in 1790, the most populous state, Virginia, had nineteen representatives, and Delaware, the least populous, had only one. After the 2010 census, Delaware still had one representative, and California had fifty-three. All of these representatives—then and now—have been elected by the people. In contrast, until the Seventeenth Amendment was added to the Constitution in 1913, senators were chosen by their state legislatures. Since 1913, senators have been chosen by voters, but Virginia, Delaware, California, and all other states still have two senators each.

This is strong evidence for the proposition that the Senate is there to represent the states—but is it strong enough? Consider the following: If that was the framers' intention, then why did they give each state two senators instead of one—that is, why did they risk the possibility that a state's two senators would cancel each other out (as in practice they often do) by voting against each other on important issues? And why didn't the Constitution authorize each state to instruct its senators how to vote on issues that came before Congress? Or to recall senators when they voted their own minds instead of giving them six-year terms designed to insulate them from pressure? For that matter, why did the framers provide that senators' salaries would be paid by the federal government, not by their own state governments? And why did the Constitution give the Senate unique responsibilities in making important national decisions—whether to ratify treaties and to accept or reject Supreme Court nominees—that have nothing to do with the states?

Questions such as these make plain that the framers designed the Senate with multiple purposes in mind, which included but were not confined to representing the states. The question presented in this debate, however, is about the Senate's present and the future, not its past—that is, *should* the Senate represent people, not states?

To this resolution, Bruce I. Oppenheimer says yes, and John J. Pitney Jr. says no. Both acknowledge the unusual constraint placed on a wide-ranging consideration of this issue by the "equal suffrage" clause in Article V of the Constitution, which says that "no State, without its Consent, shall be deprived of its equal Suffrage in the Senate." Interestingly, Pitney, who favors equal suffrage, sees a possible way around this clause, and Oppenheimer, who opposes equal suffrage, is resigned to its immutability.

PRO: Bruce I. Oppenheimer

The resolution defining this debate assumes something that has not been accurate since the adoption of the Seventeenth Amendment in 1913 and may never have been accurate. The Senate does represent people, not states. Arguably, it always has represented people, not states. But it represents them in a skewed, inefficient, and unequal manner because two senators represent the residents of each state, regardless of the state's population.

The extent of the inequality of representation of people residing in the different states has increased over the history of the Republic, just as James Madison predicted at the Constitutional Convention when he opposed apportioning the Senate by giving equal representation to each state. In 1790, a majority of the Senate could be elected from states with 30 percent of the nation's population. Today it requires less than 18 percent. And, ironically, the nine most populous states hold a majority of the population but hold only 18 percent of the seats in the Senate. Based on 2010 census data, California's two senators represent a state with a population of over 37 million. By comparison to their Senate colleagues from Wyoming, the smallest population state, they have sixty-six times the number of constituents. No powerful democratic legislature is as malapportioned, judged by the "one person, one vote" standard, as the U.S. Senate is.

In the course of this essay, I argue the following: first, the Senate may always have been meant to represent people, not states; second, the Seventeenth Amendment removed any doubt about whether the Senate represents people or states; third, the problems that equal representation of residents in states with highly varied populations creates are numerous and undesirable; fourth, the population-based House of Representatives does not compensate for the biases that the Senate creates; and fifth, little, if anything, can be done to correct this significant shortcoming of American constitutional design.

IS SENATE APPORTIONMENT A SYMBOL OF FEDERALISM?

Many people accept the idea that the Senate represents states because it is apportioned with an equal number of senators for each state. Senate apportionment is thereby assumed to function as a symbol of federalism. Accordingly, the apportionment scheme must have been designed to institutionalize a position for states in the national government.

There is some support for this view in statements articulated at the convention describing the composition of the Senate as an acknowledgment of the sovereignty of the states. And in *Federalist* No. 62, Madison argues that it makes sense for the legislature to represent both individuals and states, with the House of Representatives and the Senate, respectively, performing these functions. (Madison, however, was arguing for ratification of the Constitution, not because he believed in the apportionment basis of the Senate.) In fact, however, the delegates in Philadelphia rejected a number of proposals to link senators more closely to their states, including having them be paid by the states and subject to recall by the states. If anything, the delegates' expectation was that senators would be "national" legislators, not parochial like House members, and not responsive to state interests. The primary parameters for the Senate were that it be a small, elite body, insulated from the impulse of popular majorities. Equal representation of all states was as much, if not more, a consequence of the delegates' desire to limit the Senate's size as it was a result of an intention to provide the same representation for each state. Awarding additional Senate seats to more populous states would have resulted in a larger body than the framers thought desirable.

In the mid-1960s, the Supreme Court ruled that all state legislatures must be apportioned on the basis of population but excepted the Senate from this population-based apportionment requirement because of its linkage to the principle of federalism.[1] However, there are several reasons to doubt the Court's interpretation of why the Senate has equal apportionment for all states. First, it is unnecessary for federal systems of government to provide for equal representation of units within the national legislature. Representation can be given to the units without any requirement of equal representation. Indeed, that is what occurs in most other federal systems that have bicameral legislatures. Subnational governing units are the basis on which representation is assigned, but all units do not receive the same number of representatives. Second, the claims that states possess some residual sovereignty that requires equal representation status in one chamber of the national legislature and that the original federal compact gives states a sacrosanct status are flawed. Aside from the original thirteen states, none of the others have prior independent existence apart from territorial status as defined by the U.S. government. Often, the establishment of states was the subject of political bargains and partisan advantage, not some prior governing community of interest or geography. Even the borders of several of the original thirteen states have been altered since the adoption of the Constitution. Kentucky and West Virginia were once part of Virginia, and the area that became Maine was part of Massachusetts. Preserving preexisting sovereignty in the representational basis of the U.S. Senate because of prior attachment to these governing units is hardly supported by the historical record of the formation of states.

THE SEVENTEENTH AMENDMENT

Suppose we concede for the sake of discussion that the Senate was originally designed to represent states, not people, and that the equal representation of all states and the indirect election of senators by state legislatures, and not by the people, is sufficient evidence to substantiate that claim. The Seventeenth Amendment clearly undercuts the continuing basis of the contention. If indirect election by state legislatures provided the proof that the Senate represented states, not people, then the change to direct election of senators means that since 1913 the Senate has represented the people of the states and not the state governments. The Seventeenth Amendment formally transferred electoral accountability from state legislatures to the people.

The problem is that the apportionment basis of the Senate and the distribution of population across the states have resulted in grossly unequal representation that has far-reaching and undesirable effects not just in terms of representation but also in terms of Senate elections, influence within the Senate, and the way the Senate makes public policy. Moreover, the framers could not have envisioned how skewed Senate representation would become. Living in a country with a population of three million people, the delegates to the Constitutional Convention did not imagine that little more than two centuries later a single state would have a population twelve times greater than that. And, as mentioned above, the magnitude of the deviation of Senate representation from a one person, one vote standard has increased markedly over the years and continues to do so. Accordingly, my concern is less with the untenable claim that the Senate represents states, not people, than with how unequally it represents people and with the empirical and normative consequences that Senate apportionment has for governing.

THE NEGATIVE CONSEQUENCES
OF SENATE REPRESENTATION

The obvious starting point for examining the unfairness of Senate representation is a quantitative one. I have already alluded to the contrast between residents of Wyoming and California. As the political theorist Charles R. Beitz has maintained, "The meaning of quantitative fairness has become a settled matter: it requires adherence to the precept 'one person, one vote.'"[2] It is not merely that the Senate deviates from this standard, it is the extent of the deviation. The differences from state to state are not a few residents or votes, or even a few thousand or a few hundred thousand, but millions. And these differences have consequences. Residents in small states receive quantitatively and qualitatively better representation than do residents in large states. Although residents in

U.S. House districts in different-sized states all have roughly equal access to their representatives, those in small states have much better access to their U.S. senators than do those in more populous states. It was only a slight exaggeration during the 2008 presidential campaign to say that every resident of Delaware had met Senator Joe Biden and felt that they knew him personally. The close to 37 million residents of California could not make a similar claim about their two senators. Moreover, what is true for residents is also true for interest groups within the states and their access to their senators.

This difference in access leads to a normative concern with fairness. It is not just that the votes of individuals in small states count more in determining the composition of the Senate. The bigger problem is that Senate apportionment carries with it inequality in access. Individuals and groups in small-population states find it easier to communicate their preferences to their senators, to meet with them, and to have personal relationships with them. Importantly, because racial and ethnic minority populations are concentrated in the populous states, those demographic groups are among those that the unequal representation of the Senate affects most negatively.

As Frances E. Lee and I have demonstrated in our book *Sizing Up the Senate,* Senate apportionment also affects Senate elections in unequal ways.[3] Senators in small-population states tend to win by larger margins, need to raise far less money, and are free from electoral accountability on more issues because their states are less diverse. Large-state senators must raise money constantly and in much greater amounts. They have less time to focus on the concerns of their constituents and to pursue influential positions within the Senate. It is no accident that Senate floor leadership positions since the 1970s have been dominated by senators from small-population states: Robert Byrd of West Virginia, Robert Dole of Kansas, George Mitchell of Maine, Trent Lott of Mississippi, Tom Daschle of South Dakota, and Harry Reid of Nevada. They are the senators with the time to seek and exercise the power that leadership positions provide.

Perhaps the antidemocratic effects of Senate apportionment would be an acceptable cost of U.S. constitutional design if they were limited to representation, access, the expense and competitiveness of elections, and the influence of senators. But the effects go beyond these to the very basis of politics: who gets what, when, and how.[4] One of the major consequences of requiring all states to have two senators regardless of population is that the people in smaller states receive more funds per capita from the federal government than do those in larger states. When the Senate passes legislation that establishes a formula for distributing federal funds to the states, the formula in program after program gives small states a disproportionate share of funding, even when one controls for state program need. Whether it is transportation, community development, environmental quality, housing, education, or employment, small states receive a disproportionate share of federal dollars primarily because of the influence the U.S. Senate has over the design of those programs. Of course, any apportionment method will have biases. Even the fairest set of rules is never neutral. Some benefit more than others, even when the same rules are applied to all players. The one person, one vote standard that governs the apportioning of the House of Representatives and the state legislatures is no exception. But the apportionment scheme of the Senate, unlike the one person, one vote standard, does not meet the test of fairness.

WHY HOUSE REPRESENTATION DOES NOT COMPENSATE FOR SENATE INEQUALITY

Some might argue that the beauty of the U.S. Constitution, with its checks and balances, is that the House of Representatives—which is apportioned on the basis of one person, one vote—countervails the unequal effects of Senate representation. A careful examination of that argument quickly uncovers its flaws. In terms of access, elections, and internal influence, the House cannot compensate for the Senate. Should we expect that a House member from California, who has roughly the same number of constituents as the single House member from Wyoming, will be able to compensate in terms of representational access for the fact that California's two senators have so many more people to represent than the two senators from Wyoming do? And how can House members do anything about the fact that Senate campaigns in populous states are so much more expensive and are on average more competitive than those in small states? Nor is the House or its members likely to have much sway over which senators have the time to compete for positions of leadership.

Even when it comes to the design of legislation, the idea that the House will correct for the biases that Senate apportionment causes is not borne out by the facts. It is incorrect to assume that the House offsets Senate policy decisions that favor residents in the less populous states. After all, no bill can become law unless it is first passed in identical form by both the House and the Senate before being sent to the president. One might think that the population-based House would not allow the Senate to design formulas that give disproportional funding to small-population states and underfund the most populous states. But House members are more concerned about federal dollars going to their individual districts than they are about the overall distribution of program funding to states. In bargaining with the Senate, many House members are willing to accept the biases of Senate funding formulas in exchange for including individual projects for which they can claim credit in their districts.

Moreover, even though the House normally passes programs with population-based funding formulas, it must then bargain with the Senate in conference. At best, House conferees get the Senate to adjust its formula so that the small-state bias is not as great as in the Senate version of the legislation. But that still leaves the final version of the bill with a formula that rewards residents in the small states at the expense of those in the populous states. In fact, the Senate wins nearly three-quarters of the time when it negotiates with the House over formulas. Frequently, this type of legislation contains a minimum guarantee provision that entitles every state to at least one-half of 1 percent of the total funds. This provision alone means that the thirteen least populous states will receive more than their fair share of funds. And the minimum guarantee is just one feature that the Senate writes into legislation that results in the skewed distribution of funds.

In sum, it is a myth that through the brilliance of constitutional design the House of Representatives will automatically correct for the biases that result from Senate apportionment.

WHAT CAN BE DONE?

The good news contained in this essay is that the Senate represents people, not states. The bad news is that it does so unfairly and that the magnitude of the unfairness is increasing. That leads us to even worse news: Very little can or is likely to be done about the situation. Unlike the decision to amend the Constitution to provide for direct election of senators, the apportionment basis of the Senate is not subject to change through the normal amending process. Article V of the Constitution, which addresses the amending process, says that "no state, without its consent, shall be deprived of equal suffrage in the Senate." It is hard to imagine circumstances in which any state that benefits from the current scheme would grant that consent. Also, despite its obvious lack of fairness, Senate representation is hardly the type of issue that is likely to result in a great public outcry. (Ironically, the electoral college's deviation from the one person, one vote standard is quite modest compared with that of Senate apportionment, but there is nearly continuous public concern about the electoral college's lack of fairness.) Even if the American public were better educated about the unequal consequences of the Senate's representational scheme, one would not expect the American people to protest what many view as the most undemocratic feature of the Constitution.

Perhaps the only means available to ameliorate the degree to which Senate representation deviates from the one person, one vote standard would be to divide some of the most populous states into several states. And one can only imagine the controversies that such a move might engender.

The Senate, as it has since 1913 if not before, will continue to represent the people, not the states. But it will continue to do so unequally and with negative consequences for the people and for the ideal of American democracy.

CON: John J. Pitney Jr.

"**N**othing is either good or bad save alternatives make it so," said economist Procter Thomson. To show that the Senate should represent people instead of states, one cannot merely point out shortcomings of the current system. It is also necessary to compare that system with alternatives. That is where the case for fundamental change runs aground. To paraphrase Winston Churchill, having two senators per state is the worst possible arrangement except for all the others.

The question of alternatives has a whiff of improbability, since Article V of the Constitution forbids any amendment that would deprive any state of equal representation in the Senate without its consent. Some legal writers, however, have suggested ways around the equal suffrage clause, such as a two-part amendment that would first abolish the clause and then restructure the Senate.[1] For the sake of argument, then, let us assume that radical reform is possible. What forms could it take?

The first is simply to do away with the Senate, as a few progressives have suggested.[2] This sentiment is understandable because the chamber's procedures have sometimes enabled a minority of members to thwart liberal measures. At other times, however, the Senate has thwarted conservative ambitions. When the 2010 midterm elections resulted in a Republican majority in the House and a Democratic majority in the Senate, many progressives saw the virtue of bicameralism. "I used to rail against the Senate," said Representative Corrine Brown (D-FL), during committee markup of a GOP highway bill. "But now I thank God for the Senate."[3] Bicameralism aids in policy deliberation. The presence of two chambers may complicate the lawmaking process, but it also provides more chances to debate the merits of legislation. A relevant argument or datum that goes unnoticed in one chamber may get a look in the other. The scrutiny of a second set of eyes makes it more likely that troublesome provisions will come to light. One Senate staffer told legal scholars Victoria F. Nourse and Jane S. Schacter: "Sometimes no one is focusing on the text. Thank God for a bicameral legislature. Things can happen quickly, in the dark, in the long bills where no one has seen it."[4] In this light, it is not surprising that there is scant support for a unicameral Congress. Assuming that the Senate stays, we must now ask how it could represent population. Weighted voting would be the simplest approach. Under this system, each state would still elect two senators, but each senator's vote would equal half the state's population. Instead of having one vote each, a California senator would have 19.4 million (half the state's population) while a colleague from Wyoming would have about 292,000. Weighted voting would give the bigger states more say without requiring changes in state election laws or even the addition of any desks in the Senate chamber.

Although it may sound appealing at first, weighted voting would involve great problems. One is that it would enable a small number of senators to rule the chamber. According to the 2010 census, the nine largest states comprise more than half the nation's population, meaning that a weighted voting scheme could give control of the chamber to a mere eighteen senators. Under a cloture procedure requiring a 60 percent vote, it would still take only twenty-six senators (from thirteen states) to overpower their colleagues. These figures represent an extreme case, since the eighteen or twenty-six senators would not always have a common interest. But even under other scenarios, a minority of senators would typically prevail, and a large number would seldom have a chance to affect the outcome of a vote. This arrangement would exclude much of the country from the coalitions and compromises that create the law.[5] Another problem is that weighted voting would do nothing to change the Senate's composition.[6] One criticism of the institution is that members of historically disadvantaged groups have had difficulty winning Senate races. At the time of his election to the presidency, Barack Obama was the only African American senator. By contrast, African Americans made up 9 percent of the membership of the House and held key positions of power there. Under weighted voting, Senator Obama would have had more power in roll calls, but he would not have had more African American colleagues.

If weighted voting is out of the question, then people-based representation would entail an enlargement of Senate membership, with the size of each state's delegation corresponding to its share of the national population. A key practical question is how many more seats would be necessary. A modest increase (say, 50 more) would do little to meet a one person, one vote standard and would hardly justify the great trouble it would take to amend the Constitution. A serious expansion would require the Senate to grow to about 435 members, or as big as the House has been for nearly a century. And even that number would fall short of the reformers' ideals. Although the courts mandate that all House districts *within* a state have roughly equal populations, there are large disparities *among* the states. Because each state must have at least one House member, and because state populations vary so widely, it is impossible to devise

435 equal districts.[7] Montana has nearly twice as many people as Wyoming, yet each has one member. California's population is sixty-six times greater than Wyoming's, yet its House delegation is only fifty-three times larger. A smaller chamber would have even more severe anomalies, so for the Senate to be adequately representative of people instead of states, it would have to be at least as large as the current House—and preferably larger.

There are several reasons a bigger Senate would not be a better Senate. First of all, deliberation would suffer. Granted, the quality of debate in today's Senate is often mediocre, leading many observers to sneer when they call it "the world's greatest deliberative body." Nevertheless, in their authoritative analysis of congressional deliberation, Gary Mucciaroni and Paul J. Quirk find that floor debates in the Senate are better informed than those in the House, with more substantiation of claims and rebuttals.[8] This difference stems from the relative sizes of the two bodies. The Senate can afford to let each of its hundred members speak at length about the merits of policy. With more than four times as many members, the House must ration floor time much more stingily. In the House, Mucciaroni and Quirk find, "most speeches are very brief, ranging from one to five minutes in length; speakers generally do little more than state their positions and recite their side's scripted talking points. For the most part, speakers do not respond directly to other speakers—for example, to make and answer criticisms."[9] If the Senate doubled, tripled, or quadrupled in size, it would have to abandon its tradition of extended debate, substituting recitation for deliberation.

Second, expanding the Senate would make it more rancorous. Although the ideological differences between Republican and Democratic senators have widened, and their debates have sometimes taken on a hard edge, the Senate remains a more civil place than the House. The shouting matches and walkouts that have marred House politics in recent years have not been a part of Senate life. Once again, size helps account for the difference. Senators are much more likely to know a given colleague in their chamber than are House members. Personal relationships thus temper policy conflicts. In the House, as Ross K. Baker says, social distance loosens political restraint: "House members, like air crews dropping bombs on an enemy they cannot see, take a more cold-blooded view of partisan warfare. . . . The rules of engagement in the Senate are largely personal; in the House they are distinctively partisan."[10] Third, and most important, increasing Senate membership would have the paradoxical effect of reducing the number of senators who really matter. Among one hundred senators, power is widely dispersed, and each can play a meaningful role. The more members a chamber has, however, the harder it is to give everyone free rein, and the more likely it is that a small subset will take charge. As James Madison put it: "[In] all legislative assemblies the greater the number composing them may be, the fewer will be the men who will in fact direct their proceedings."[11] In the middle of the twentieth century, the House put great power in the hands of key committee chairs, or "barons." During the 1970s, the focus of influence shifted to the leaders of the majority party.

When ideological gaps are wide and rancor runs hot, this concentration of power means that members of the minority party have little say. In 1986, when Democrats were in their fourth straight decade of control, Representative Henry Waxman (D-CA) said, "If we have a united Democratic position, Republicans are irrelevant."[12] Specifically, the majority's leaders can use procedural rules to block the minority from offering amendments or otherwise influencing the content of legislation. In 1993, Representative Gerald Solomon (R-NY) grumbled, "Every time we deny an open amendment process on an important piece of legislation, we are disenfranchising the people and their Representatives from the legislative process."[13] When Republicans controlled the House for a dozen years after the 1994 election, Democrats complained that they had become the voiceless minority. After party control switched again in 2006, incoming Rules Committee chair Louise Slaughter (D-NY) said of the outgoing GOP majority, "They really had disenfranchised about half of the American citizens."[14] Although it may have been a stretch to speak of "disenfranchisement," members of the minority party could plausibly argue that their status had left their constituents with much less effective representation than people in majority-party districts enjoyed.

Despite pledges of change, the new majority acted just like the old one, only more so. In the 110th Congress, a Brookings Institution study found, a "pattern of tighter, more centralized control—which began more than two decades ago under Democratic rule and then intensified under Republican majorities, especially after the 2000 election—continues unabated."[15] With Slaughter now chairing Rules, Republicans lodged the same complaint that Democrats had made a few years before. Representative Tom Price (R-GA) expressed the Republican lament: "We all represent essentially the same number of people. When the majority does not allow a certain Member or Members to offer amendments or to offer their best ideas, what they do is disenfranchise nearly half of the American people."[16] When control switched yet again at the start of 2011, Republicans eased up on the restrictive rules for a while but eventually reverted to form.[17]

If the Senate were larger, it would have to tighten its procedures, enabling the majority to overpower the minority. As with the House, some Americans would have legislators who could actually legislate, while others would not.

In addition to the sheer number of senators, we must also consider the manner of their selection. At-large elections, in which Senate candidates would run statewide, could not work in the larger states. California has fifty-three House seats, and if it chose that many senators on a statewide basis, its voters would have a preposterously difficult task: Few would be able to name them all, much less appraise their performance. As a practical matter, then, population-based representation would mean dividing all but the smallest states into Senate districts. Accordingly, Senate elections would come to resemble House elections, a development that would damage the Senate's accountability.

In this context, accountability means that officials are subject to serious review by the electorate, and that they can lose their jobs if they perform poorly. Accountability hinges on two conditions. First, voters must have access to full and accurate information about what the officials are doing. Second, they must have real choices in the next election among credible challengers who can get their messages out and who have a chance of defeating the incumbent.

Voters can currently gain more information about their senators than they can about their House members. National publications and broadcast news organizations frequently run stories about senators, sometimes from a critical perspective. Individual House members are much less likely to make the national news. Reporters regard the average senator as more important and newsworthy than the average House member because each is 1 in 100 instead of 1 in 435.

Senators also tend to receive more scrutiny on their home turf. True, scholars have found that a senator generally gets only a little more coverage from a typical local newspaper than does a House member.[18] But, except in the states with a single House member, Senate constituencies include more media organizations. A New York senator must deal with the state's dozens of daily newspapers and broadcast news outlets. House members work in a different media environment. The New York City market includes many congressional districts, so while the *Times, Post,* and *Daily News* amply cover their senators, they give little space to average local House members. Elsewhere in the state, House districts may encompass just a handful of newspapers and broadcast stations. Most of these local news shops do not have Washington bureaus.[19] As a result, much local coverage of House members' Capitol Hill activity comes from press releases. In such cases, the only other major sources of information are the members' own newsletters and websites.

In aggregate, then, senators face a greater volume of scrutiny from their state press than House members get from their district press. Many of the stories about senators are puff pieces, but some are hard-hitting, and, thanks to the Internet, a voter anywhere in a state can access this coverage. If the Senate were more like the House, senators would find it easier to duck.

House members often escape the genuine competition that accountability requires. They consistently enjoy a higher reelection rate than senators, and districting explains at least some of the difference. There has long been controversy about gerrymandering, the practice of drawing districts so as to favor one party or the other. When it works, gerrymandering can provide safe districts to the dominant side. And even without gerrymandering, many House seats would still be uncompetitive. Certain locales tend to have high concentrations of Republicans or Democrats, rendering those districts virtually unwinnable for the other party.[20] Moving the Senate to a district system would thus take a large number of seats out of play.

It would also hurt the quality of Senate challengers. In each election, dozens of House districts go uncontested; in 2014, thirty candidates won election to the House without a bona fide opponent.[21] Of the House challengers who do emerge, many are weak candidates with little experience and few resources. Senators are much less likely to run for reelection unopposed (only one did in 2008) and are more likely to face credible challengers. Why? Constituency size is part of the answer. States with more than one House district will have a bigger pool of potential candidates. (Under the Constitution, any qualified resident of a state may run for any of its House seats, but in practice it is usually hard to win without local roots.)

Personal calculation is another reason for the difference. Running for office, especially against an incumbent, is a tough, costly venture. No sensible person will do it lightly. When deciding whether to enter the race, potential candidates must weigh both their chance of victory and the value of the office. (Notwithstanding Governor Rod Blagojevich's infamous description, I define "value" as power and prestige, not dollars and cents.) If the chance of victory is too remote, or if the office does not seem worth the effort, good potential candidates will probably bow out. As we have seen, a district system would mean a number of uncompetitive seats, which would draw few serious contenders. Moreover, expanding the Senate would dilute the value of each seat. Instead of being 1 of 100 members in an institution with widely dispersed power, a senator would now be just 1 of 435 in an institution where power rests with the top leaders and where minority-party members scarcely matter. A diminished prize would mean a diminished field of contestants.

So let us review. Restructuring the Senate to represent the people rather than states would render the institution less deliberative, less civil, and less accountable. It would make Senate elections less competitive. It would also tend to give greater power to the majority party, thus depriving minority-party senators of the leverage they currently have and leaving their constituents without an effective voice. In short, it would make the Senate less democratic, not more.

NOTES

PRO

1. *Reynolds v. Sims,* 377 U.S. 533 (1964).
2. Charles R. Beitz, *Political Equality: An Essay in Democratic Theory* (Princeton, NJ: Princeton University Press, 1989), 141.
3. See Frances E. Lee and Bruce I. Oppenheimer, *Sizing Up the Senate: The Unequal Consequences of Equal Representation* (Chicago, IL: University of Chicago Press, 1999).
4. Harold Lasswell, *Politics: Who Gets What, When, How* (New York, NY: McGraw-Hill, 1936).

CON

1. Scott J. Bowman, "Wild Political Dreaming: Constitutional Reformation of the United States Senate," *Fordham Law Review* 72 (March 2004): 1017–51.
2. Dylan Matthews, "The Senate's 46 Democrats Got 20 Million More Votes Than Its 54 Republicans," *Vox,* January 3, 2015, http://www.vox.com/2015/1/3/7482635/senate-small-states.
3. Quoted in Ben Goldman, "Senate Transit Bill Clears Committee with Unanimous Bipartisan Support," *DC.StreetsBlog,* February 2, 2012, http://dc.streetsblog.org/2012/02/02/senate-transit-bill-clears-committee-with-unanimous-bipartisan-support.
4. Quoted in Victoria F. Nourse and Jane S. Schacter, "The Politics of Legislative Drafting: A Congressional Case Study," *New York University Law Review* 77 (June 2002): 593.
5. See the similar argument about other weighted voting systems in Keith R. Wesolowski, "Remedy Gone Awry: Weighing in on Weighted Voting," *William and Mary Law Review* 44 (March 2003): 1907.
6. Richard Briffault, "Who Rules at Home? One Person/One Vote and Local Governments," *University of Chicago Law Review* 60 (Spring 1993): 410.
7. Jeffrey W. Ladewig and Mathew P. Jasinski, "On the Causes and Consequences of and Remedies for Interstate Malapportionment of the U.S. House of Representatives," *Perspectives on Politics* 6 (March 2008): 89–107.
8. Gary Mucciaroni and Paul J. Quirk, *Deliberative Choices: Debating Public Policy in Congress* (Chicago, IL: University of Chicago Press, 2007), 194.
9. Ibid., 195.
10. Ross K. Baker, *House and Senate,* 4th ed. (New York, NY: W. W. Norton, 2008), 80.
11. James Madison, "Federalist No. 58," in Alexander Hamilton, James Madison, and John Jay, *The Federalist Papers,* ed. Clinton Rossiter (New York, NY: Signet, 2003), 358.
12. Quoted in Janet Hook, "House GOP: Plight of a Permanent Minority," *Congressional Quarterly Weekly Report,* June 21, 1986, 1393.
13. *Congressional Record* (daily), March 3, 1993, H975–76.

14. Quoted in Carl Hulse, "With Promises of a Better-Run Congress, Democrats Take on Political Risks," *New York Times*, December 27, 2006.

15. Sarah A. Binder, Thomas E. Mann, Norman J. Ornstein, and Molly Reynolds, "*Assessing the 110th Congress, Anticipating the 111th*" (Washington, DC: Brookings Institution, Governance Studies, January 2009), http://www.brookings .edu/~/media/Files/rc/papers/2009/0108_broken_branch_binder_mann/0108_ broken_branch_binder_mann.pdf.

16. *Congressional Record* (daily), October 2, 2007, H11142.

17. Don Wolfensberger, "Why Are Restrictive Rules Ratcheting Up?" *Roll Call*, July 23, 2015, http://blogs.rollcall.com/beltway-insiders/restrictive-rules-ratcheting-procedural-politics.

18. R. Douglas Arnold, *Congress, the Press, and Political Accountability* (New York, NY: Russell Sage Foundation, 2004), 59.

19. Graham Vy Se, "Covering Washington for Those Outside the Beltway: A Lost Art?" Investigative Reporting Workshop, April 5, 2013, http:// investigativereportingworkshop.org/ilab/story/covering-washington.

20. John S. Horn, "The District Connection: Competitive Districts and Candidate Quality" (PhD diss., Claremont Graduate University, 2009).

21. "Uncontested Governor's Chairs, Senate, and House Seats up for Election on 4 November 2014," The Green Papers, August 14, 2015, http://www .thegreenpapers.com/G14/uncontested.phtml.

15

RESOLVED, Senate Rule XXII should be amended so that filibusters can be ended by a majority vote

PRO: Steven S. Smith

CON: Wendy J. Schiller

Thomas Jefferson was not at the Constitutional Convention; he was in Paris serving as the American minister to France. According to a famous story, when Jefferson returned, he had dinner with his fellow Virginian, George Washington, and asked him why the convention had created the Senate. Washington answered Jefferson's question with a question of his own: "Why did you pour that coffee into your saucer?" "To cool it," Jefferson replied. "Even so," said Washington, "we pour legislation into the senatorial saucer to cool it."

The story is almost too good to be true, and some scholars doubt its veracity. But Washington's reputed description of the Senate as a patient, deliberative, "cool" body in contrast to the impulsive, rapid-response, "hot" House of Representatives is consistent with certain constitutional features of the two chambers. The Senate is less than one-fourth the size of the House of Representatives (100 members, compared with 435), so fewer rules are needed to organize its work. Senators serve six-year terms, three times longer than the two-year terms of representatives, so most of them feel less pressure to rush through their work in time for the next election.

For these reasons, students of Congress have always thought it appropriate that the rules of the House favor focused, organized debates on proposed legislation, and the rules of the Senate favor diffuse, individualistic debates. In the 109th Congress, for example, 84 percent of all bills that were considered by the House came to the floor under closed rules (that is, rules that allowed for no amendments). In contrast, any Senate bill is open to amendment during floor debate, even if the subject of the amendment is "nongermane"—that is, it deals with a subject different from that of the bill itself.

The House also restricts the length of debate on each bill, sometimes to no more than an hour or two, with those favoring and opposing a piece of legislation often given no more than a few minutes each to make their case so that others who wish to be heard can also have their say. The Senate places no restrictions at all on how long a senator may speak. One use—or, some would argue, abuse—of this privilege is the filibuster. A senator who strongly opposes a bill but lacks the votes to defeat it is free to speak for a long while and then yield the floor to another senator who shares the same views—and so on until the bill is almost literally talked to death without ever being voted on.

In 1917, the Senate created Rule XXII in an effort to limit filibusters. The rule provided that the Senate could invoke cloture—that is, bring an end to the debate on a bill and clear the decks for it to be voted on—by a two-thirds vote of those voting on the motion. Perversely, senators began filibustering more than ever, especially southerners when bills involving civil rights were debated. South Carolina senator Strom Thurmond spoke against the Civil Rights Act of 1957 for twenty-four hours and eighteen minutes—the all-time record. (Yes, Thurmond thought of that—he spent the morning in the Senate steam room to purge himself of water.)

Summoning a two-thirds vote to invoke cloture was not impossible—for example, the Senate voted for cloture after a fifty-seven-day filibuster against the Civil Rights Act of 1964—but it was harder than most senators thought it should be. In 1975, the Senate reduced the vote needed to invoke cloture to three-fifths of all senators. Yet, use of the filibuster soared once again, from an average of one every couple of years in the 1950s to more than fifteen per year in the 2000s. Threats to filibuster have become so common that they seldom need to be carried out to be effective. If opponents of a bill can prove in advance that they have enough votes to block cloture, then those in the majority won't even bring the bill to the floor lest the other business of the Senate go undone. Although Senate rules provide that a bill passes if a simple majority of the senators voting on it say aye, the filibuster-based reality is that any important bill needs sixty votes.

Arguing for the resolution that Rule XXII should be amended, Steven S. Smith makes the case for lengthy but not unlimited Senate deliberation. Specifically, he proposes that the three-fifths rule be modified so that after every day or two of debate, the size of the majority needed to invoke cloture would be reduced. Wendy J. Schiller, citing both the constitutional mission of the Senate and the positive ratio of benefits to costs in the way filibusters actually have functioned, opposes modifying Rule XXII.

PRO: Steven S. Smith

In 2014, a majority of U.S. senators supported a bill that would place the decision to prosecute a sexual assault charge in the military in the hands of an experienced commissioned officer who is not in the alleged perpetrator's chain of command. The bill was intended to prevent retaliation for reporting an assault and to ensure a fair prosecution of the accused. The bill, authored by Senator Kirsten Gillibrand (D-NY) was supported by both Democratic and Republican floor leaders and by senators as widely different in their ideological outlooks as Bernie Sanders (I-VT), Rand Paul (R-TX), and Ted Cruz (R-TX). It died on a 55-45 cloture vote, five votes short of the three-fifths majority, or sixty votes, required to close debate and move to action on the bill.

The 2014 experience is commonplace. A Senate majority supported the bill, all the requirements for enacting legislation anticipated by the framers of the Constitution. The bill died because of a Senate rule and practice that has emerged in the more than two centuries since ratification of the Constitution and the first Congress. Throughout the Senate's history, bills have died by the hand of a Senate minority despite the support of congressional majorities and the president, but using the filibuster to kill legislation has become much more common in recent decades.

In this essay, I contend that filibusters undermine democratic accountability and are inconsistent with the Constitution. Senate Rule XXII should thus be reformed so that minorities can no longer indefinitely thwart majorities.

THE EXPANDED USE OF FILIBUSTERS AND CLOTURE

The problem of obstructionism by filibuster has in recent years become much more severe than at any time in the Senate's history. Counting filibusters is not easy. The filibustering senators often deny that they are filibustering. Moreover, newly started filibusters and many threatened filibusters kill or delay action on a bill without senators having to appear on the floor of the Senate to debate the bill. Majority-party leaders merely move on to other legislation. Moreover, majority leaders sometimes use cloture motions to prevent nongermane amendments that would be in order otherwise. Nevertheless, the number of cloture motions, shown in Figure 15.1, gives a fairly clear measure of the prevalence of filibustering as an obstructionist strategy.

Cloture petitions—and filibusters—moved from being rarities to commonplace in the 1970s, and the numbers have continued to grow since then. Once the major civil rights battles of the 1960s were over and southern Democrats

Figure 15.1

Number of Cloture Petitions in the Senate, 1961–2014

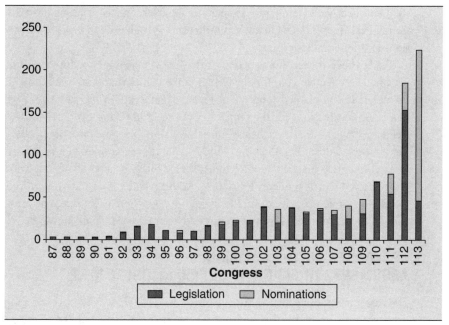

Source: U.S. Senate (http://www.senate.gov).

began to join Republicans more frequently against the expanded bloc of liberal Democrats in the early 1970s, filibusters (usually by the conservative bloc) and cloture motions (usually offered by the Democratic majority leader) became common. At nearly any time in the past two decades, some measure was being held up by a filibuster or threatened filibuster; in recent Congresses, it was likely to be several measures or nominations that were being delayed or blocked by minority obstruction. Particularly troublesome for the majority party Democrats was the frequency that President Barack Obama's nominations to executive and judicial positions were blocked during his first term in office (111th and 112th Congresses, 2009–2012). This produced a sharp increase in the number of cloture petitions that were filed and provoked the Democrats to restrict the use of the filibuster to block nominations.

In November 2013, then-Majority Leader Harry Reid (D-NV) acquired enough support from his fellow Democrats to support his point of order that a simple majority may invoke cloture to overcome a filibuster on a presidential nomination to executive and judicial branch posts, with the important exception of nominations to the Supreme Court. This reform by parliamentary ruling violated at least the spirit of Rule XXII, which requires a two-thirds majority to force a vote on a resolution to change the rules, but was seen by Reid and nearly all Democrats as necessary to overcome continuing obstruction of President Barack Obama's nominations to high executive branch positions and federal judgeships.

Reid's move rocked the Senate. For the first time, simple majority cloture became the effective rule for the Senate for an important class of business. Republicans complained loudly and forced Democrats to invoke cloture on nearly all nominations for the remainder of the 113th Congress (2013–2014), as Figure 15.1 shows. Nevertheless, after they gained a Senate majority in 2015, Republicans did not overturn the "Reid rule" and even appointed a task force to extend simple majority cloture to legislative business after struggling with Democratic filibusters on key legislation. At this writing, they have not moved to extend simple majority cloture to legislation, but there is considerable pressure on them from conservative groups and even House Republicans to do so.

RESPONSES TO THE COMMON ARGUMENTS IN FAVOR OF SUPERMAJORITY RULE

The case for retaining the right to filibuster under Senate rules rests on four propositions. The first is that minorities have interests that would be trampled by majorities without the special supermajority threshold established under Senate Rule XXII. The second is that the delay and compromise required to obtain supermajority support for legislation produces better legislation with broader support. The third is that rules should be difficult to change, and the current rule ensures that. The fourth is that the Senate was intended to protect minority rights, and the hard-earned experience of more than two centuries confirms the wisdom of that plan. I will respond to these four propositions in reverse order.

History

It is easy to assume that the Senate's current rules and practices are the product of careful deliberation and represent the current opinion of the Senate about how the institution should operate. That view is badly mistaken.

The framers of the Constitution and its principal defenders in *The Federalist Papers* emphasized the different terms of office, methods of selection, and formal powers of the Senate and the House of Representatives but said nothing about the two houses operating under different parliamentary procedures.

They were silent on the subject of the filibuster. The Constitution provides that each house can determine its own rules; the rules that the two houses might develop were not discussed.

The Senate filibuster practice is the by-product of historical accident and brass-knuckle politics, not careful consideration and deliberate choice. In the House of Representatives and most parliamentary bodies, there is a motion on the previous question. In those institutions, the motion is in order at most times and, if adopted, forces a vote on the issue at hand. The motion allows a majority of legislators to end debate, act on the issue, and move to other business.

Until 1806, the Senate had a previous question motion that was seldom used, but in that year, the Senate overlooked the motion when codifying its rules for the first time. With no recorded discussion of the previous question motion, the motion disappeared from the Senate's rules. Thus, without so much as a question or comment, the Senate lost the rule that allowed a majority to get a vote on a bill.

The absence of a rule limiting debate was not a problem for the Senate at first, but within a couple of decades, it became obvious that the absence of a debate limit facilitated obstruction by extended debate. The filibuster emerged during debates over slavery and prompted calls from many prominent senators, including Daniel Webster, Henry Clay, and later Henry Cabot Lodge, for a rule that would allow a Senate majority to bring a matter to a vote. Southern senators, seeking to block antislavery and later pro–civil rights legislation, came to defend the filibuster as vital to minority rights and continued to do so until late in the twentieth century.

On several occasions in the nineteenth and twentieth centuries, a Senate majority sought to modify the rules to create a means for limiting debate but was blocked by a filibuster or threatened filibuster. Only on two occasions, in 1917 and in 1975, did the minority relent to pressure to allow a significant reform of the standing rules with respect to filibusters. In 1917, the first cloture rule was adopted so that two-thirds of senators voting could close debate. The 1975 rule reduced the threshold to three-fifths of senators duly sworn, except for measures affecting the Senate rules, for which the two-thirds threshold was retained. In 2013, as noted, the Senate majority took the extraordinary step of modifying the plain meaning of a Senate rule through a parliamentary ruling.

Plainly, a rationale for a supermajority threshold for limiting debate cannot be found in the Constitution, in *The Federalist Papers,* in early Senate practice, or even in the views of the most prominent senators of the eighteenth and nineteenth centuries. To be sure, the framers of the Constitution and the authors of *The Federalist Papers* addressed the issue of minority rights. The protection of minority rights was to be found in creating a bicameral Congress and a separate presidency and judiciary, all selected by different means and for different terms, so that it was unlikely that any faction or party would dominate all branches of government. At no time during the early years of the Republic did the Senate's internal rules figure in thinking about how to limit the ability of majorities to act. To the contrary, both the House and the Senate were assumed to act by simple majority rule.

The lesson of hard-earned experience of the Senate is not that a supermajority threshold is in the interest of the Senate or the nation. Rather, the real lessons are that (1) it is unreasonable to expect minorities to concede parliamentary advantages to the majority voluntarily, and (2) senators can rationalize both simple- and supermajority rules with alacrity. Upon a change in party control of the chamber, senators appear to exchange their speeches on the pros and cons of majority rule across the center aisle. Only a few die-hards seem to be able to maintain a consistent attitude about majority and minority parliamentary rights. I can think of no current senator whose party has been both majority and minority who has done so.

Rules

Defenders of supermajority cloture under Rule XXII sometimes argue that the Senate's rules should be hard to change and that is what is intended. This is a good thing, it is argued, because it protects a minority of senators from arbitrary changes in procedure that any current majority might want to impose. It helps to preserve, among other things, the super-majority threshold for cloture. This view of Senate rules is not fully accurate.

The Senate certainly has made its standing rules difficult to change, at least under the terms of the standing rules. Two features of those rules are particularly important. First, the current Senate rule requires a two-thirds majority of senators present and voting to close debate on a resolution to change the Senate's standing rules. This provision means that it is more difficult to invoke cloture on a change in the rules than on regular legislation, for which only a three-fifths majority is required. Second, the Senate considers itself to be a continuing body that does not have to approve its rules at the start of each new Congress. This is a by-product, it is argued, of the fact that two-thirds of the Senate continues to serve from one Congress to the next. Because the standing rules merely continue from one Congress to the next, the parliamentary advantage rests with senators seeking to preserve old rules. Any proposed change can be filibustered, and the two-thirds threshold for overcoming a filibuster is always a potential obstacle to changing the rules.

On the face of it, then, Senate rules are hard to change. In fact, the Senate changes its rules much less frequently than the House, where the rules must be approved at the beginning of every new Congress, the majority party often makes changes when considering the approval of the rules, and, a simple majority can get a vote on the rules. In the Senate, because a resolution to reform filibustering can be filibustered, Rule XXII appears to be self-perpetuating.

The 2013 episode called into question this view of the Senate rules. The parliamentary move by Reid that gave a simple majority an opportunity to change a rule or practice was always a technical possibility. It was not an approach to changing a rule or its application that all senators approved. In recent decades, the Senate minority, when faced with a threat of "reform by ruling," threatened to bring Senate action to a crawl by demanding cloture on everything if the majority took that step. In fact, the Republican minority did stand in the way of more nominations after Reid moved in late 2013. Even a handful of Democrats objected to Reid's method, and others expressed discomfort with it because it appears to undermine the explicit cloture standard provided in Rule XXII for changing the rules. Thus, there remains a barrier to imposing simple majority cloture for legislation by a simple majority even if a simple majority can in practice impose an interpretation of the rules as it sees fit.

If a simple majority can change the meaning of a rule at will, does this mean that the Senate is actually just like the House in the ability of the majority to change the rules and process legislation? No. As Reid discovered, the Senate minority still can exact a price when it dislikes the behavior of the majority, which creates a strong disincentive for the majority to run over the minority. The minority can slow proceedings even with simple majority cloture. If a minority is obstructing action and cloture is required, the majority must still file a cloture petition, wait two legislative days—if the cloture motion is made on Monday, the Senate cannot vote on it until Wednesday, assuming it was in session daily. If the motion passes with the required supermajority, 30 hours of debate are allowed, which can consume two or three days if insisted upon by senators. This is a slow process that guarantees a right to some debate and amendments, but the minority can force repeated use of this process and impose heavy political costs on the majority. Scarce time is consumed that eventually limits how much legislating the majority party can do. The public may even blame the majority party for its ineffectiveness at governing. And, in the case of delays in acting on nominations, the work of the administration and the courts may be harmed.

Thus, while the Reid strategy shows how a simple majority can force a change in the rule, the 2013 episode also shows how the minority make the majority pay a high price for doing so. The argument that it is difficult to change the rules in the Senate is still true, but it is not simply a matter of the supermajority requirement for cloture on resolutions to change the rules.

Large Majorities and Compromise

Sometimes we get lucky and acquire good rules despite the short-term political calculations that produced them. In the case of the cloture rule, some of its advocates insist, we got lucky because the supermajority threshold forces the development of a broader consensus on controversial matters, which is good for maintaining a peaceful society. This argument is a stronger one than an alternative defense of the filibuster—that filibusters have killed much bad legislation. Both arguments ignore a very ugly history.

Race-related legislation—antislavery bills, civil and voting rights bills, antilynching measures, and many others—has been the single most common target of filibusters, particularly before the 1970s. If the filibuster serves minority rights, it is only in the narrow sense of a Senate minority. For 150 years, the filibuster protected a policy status quo that suppressed basic human rights in the most fundamental ways. It is hard to see how to weigh the bad bills on other subjects that were killed by filibuster against that horrific legacy on race.

While race-related bills have been the most common targets of filibusters, they constitute less than one-seventh of all filibustered bills. Many other important bills have been killed by filibuster or threatened filibuster. The 1917 rule change was precipitated by a filibuster of the "armed ship bill," legislation favored by the president that would have allowed American merchant vessels to arm themselves in defense against German U-boats.

The effects of the filibuster, and threats of filibuster, are so pervasive in the Senate that they are hard to quantify. Rather than being reserved for matters of "constitutional" significance, as was sometimes argued in the mid-twentieth century, filibusters now are used regularly to block legislation. Moreover, rank-and-file senators threaten to filibuster bills in order to get leverage with leaders, committee chairs, and other colleagues on otherwise unrelated legislation. In fact, filibusters have become all-purpose hostage-taking devices.

Protecting Minorities

There is no doubt that the Senate's cloture rule protects Senate minorities. There are three responses to this argument.

First, it plainly is not true that the substantial *Senate* minority required to obstruct action is necessarily a substantial *national* minority. In principle, senators from the twenty-one smallest states, constituting just over 11 percent of the U.S. population, can prevent a three-fifths majority from closing debate on regular legislation. Senators from the seventeen smallest states, constituting just over 7 percent of the population, can prevent achievement of the two-thirds majority required to invoke cloture on legislation affecting the rules. These percentages have been shrinking as larger proportions of the U.S. population have moved to urban areas in the largest states.

Second, important political minorities *within* states, including demographic minorities identified by race, occupation, age, or some other division, do not win protection from minority rights in the Senate's parliamentary rules unless elected senators represent their interests. There is nothing in the way that we elect senators—plurality, statewide elections—that gives us any reason to think that a Senate minority is any more likely to represent those interests than a Senate majority. In practice, such demographic minorities may be integral to the political coalitions for either majority or minority factions and parties in the Senate.

Third, because senators from the same state frequently represent different parties and political views, there is nothing in the protection of Senate minority rights that preserves the rights of a minority of states. It is true, of course, that antislavery legislation in the nineteenth century was opposed by southern senators, who feared that their states would hold a minority of Senate seats and needed the filibuster to protect their region. In modern America, senators from the same state often are divided on issues and cloture motions. Very seldom are the rights of states of concern in cloture motions.

Perhaps most perniciously, the filibuster and threatened filibuster have become the everyday tools of the minority party. Because the majority party seldom has three-fifths, let alone two-thirds, of Senate seats, the minority party is able to block much of the majority party's legislative program. Indeed, most cloture votes in recent decades have produced partisan divisions, with majority-party senators voting for cloture and minority-party senators voting against cloture. Rather than encouraging consensus building, the filibuster has contributed to sharpened partisanship and legislative stalemate. The protection of minority rights has withered to the protection of temporary Senate minority parties.

DO SENATE RULES REFLECT THE WISHES OF THE MAJORITY?

The ultimate argument in favor of the current Rule XXII is that super-majority rule is favored by most senators. If so, whatever the arguments against the filibuster might be, it might be argued that a majority of senators should have the right to structure their rules as they please. The record, however, does not justify this argument.

First, and most obvious, a majority of senators showed support for doing away with super-majority cloture on most presidential nominations. In 2013, that was a Democratic majority, but the new Republican majority elected in 2014 has not tinkered with the Democrats' handiwork.

Second, on several classes of legislation—budget measures, trade agreements, and many others—the Senate has accepted rules written into statutes that limit debate to a specified number of hours. That is, for some important legislation, the senators have allowed a special rule that prevents filibusters. In most cases, these statutory rules were adopted without serious objections from minority party senators.

A reasonable inference is that senators are fickle and not wedded to a strict principle of protecting minority rights super-majority cloture. They have proven quite willing to accept limits on debate, although they have accepted super-majority cloture as their default rule.

The most important problem in assessing support for reform of Rule XXII is that reformers cannot obtain a direct vote on a reform resolution if cloture cannot be invoked first. Without the vote, which senators would have supported a reform resolution remains in doubt. Nevertheless, it is clear from journalists' and senators' accounts that at various times a majority of senators have favored reducing the threshold but were blocked by a determined minority and a majority was not willing to use a Reid-like move to overcome the minority. Indeed, even when a majority of senators seemed eager to change Rule XXII, a few of them did not want to use the Reid approach to accomplish the reform.

REFORM

This is confusing, isn't it? Imagine how the average American is confused about the Senate. The jumble of simple- and super-majority rules makes it difficult to assign credit and blame for Senate outcomes. As a result, a basic feature of democracy, holding policy makers accountable, is undermined.

Rule XXII should be amended so that it secures lengthy deliberation while still allowing action on a bill by a determined majority. Specifically, I favor a cloture procedure that provides for a sliding scale of votes, starting with the threshold of three-fifths of senators voting (sixty if all are voting) and ratcheting down the threshold every day or two, so that after a week or two, the majority could obtain a vote on the legislation or rules change. This would allow plenty of time for debate and for minority senators to persuade the public and their colleagues of the virtue of their position. If they fail to persuade, then the majority would be able to rule, as the framers intended and as democracy requires.

CON: Wendy J. Schiller

> When a Senator desires to speak, he shall rise and address the Presiding Officer, and shall not proceed until he is recognized, and the Presiding Officer shall recognize the Senator who shall first address him. No Senator shall interrupt another Senator in debate without his consent.
>
> —Rule XIX of the Standing Rules of the Senate, Section 1(a)

Amazing as it seems, any of the one hundred U.S. senators can use their right to be recognized on the Senate floor to delay legislation in the U.S. Congress indefinitely or permanently. The "right" to filibuster is not actually written anywhere in the Senate rules themselves; rather, it comes from the strategic use of the right to speak on the Senate floor. U.S. senators realized early on in the nation's history that if they objected to a measure, whether it was a piece of legislation or even a change in the Senate rules, they could simply stand up, be recognized, and talk for as long as they wanted to prevent the Senate from taking a vote on the measure. The existence of the filibuster has given rise to the practice of seeking unanimous consent to move forward on any legislation in the Senate. The Senate majority leader goes to the Senate floor and asks for unanimous consent to proceed to the consideration of a bill, amendment, or executive nomination. Based on the power to speak, any senator has the right to object to the motion to proceed and, in doing so, delay the business of the Senate.

If a majority of the members of the House of Representatives passes a bill, and a majority of the Senate supports the bill, it makes logical sense that the bill should pass. Because a filibuster stands in the way of majority rule, one could argue that it is undemocratic and unfair. However, I maintain that the filibuster is an essential part of the democratic functioning of the Senate and should be preserved, albeit with stronger enforcement.

THE CONSTITUTIONAL MISSION OF THE U.S. SENATE

Congress was created as a bicameral (two-chamber) legislature whose mission was to represent all the people. The reason the framers of the Constitution created a legislative branch consisting of two parts was to maximize representation but minimize the probability that a majority could sweep through Congress and pass harmful or irresponsible legislation. They allowed the House of Representatives to grow in size as the nation's population grew, by adjusting the number of members apportioned to each state after every census.

More members produce more bills, speeches, and motions, and so in the 1920s, the House decided it was necessary to limit the number of members to 435. The House adjusted to its growing size by organizing itself into a majority-party, committee-based institution. Key to controlling business on the House floor has been the ability to move the previous question—that is, to effectively close debate with a majority vote. With the growth of political parties and partisanship, this device essentially allows the majority party to ride roughshod over the members of the minority party, who have little to no power.

In contrast, the framers did not allow the number of senators apportioned to each state to change with population growth; the only way the Senate grew in size was with the admission of new states into the Union. The framers were aware that with this permanent limitation of two senators for each state, the Senate would remain a small chamber in which senators would be forced to face each other to deliberate the merits of every bill. James Madison wrote a letter to George Washington on April 16, 1787, in which he explained that senators should stay in office longer than House members, that they should be reelected at different times to make sure to leave a majority of continuing members in office after each election, and that, as a result, "the negative on the laws might be most conveniently exercised by this branch."[1] Madison elaborated on this argument in *Federalist* No. 62, where he wrote that there is a tendency for "single and numerous assemblies, to yield to the impulse of sudden and violent passions, and to be seduced by factious leaders into intemperate and pernicious resolutions."[2] By keeping the Senate small and making sure that a majority of senators were never up for reelection at the same time, the framers gave the Senate the task of slowing down the legislative process.

The combination of small chamber size and equal apportionment gave senators the sense that they were all equal to one another, as opposed to the feeling in the House, where members from larger states had a sense of power over their smaller-state colleagues. In the early part of the nation's history, the Senate dealt mostly with issues of land expansion, commerce, and trade, and although there was conflict, it rarely rose to the level where filibustering was deemed necessary. The onset of the conflict over slavery brought with it far more contentious debate, along with more delay and obstruction. After the Civil War ended, the issues of Reconstruction, industrialization, and trade politics gave rise to more frequent and extended use of the filibuster tactic.

It was not until 1917 that the public demands on the Senate, and on Congress more generally, led senators to adopt some restrictions on debate. The filibuster had defeated a bill that was important to President Woodrow Wilson, so he campaigned across the country for the Senate to adopt "cloture," a procedure for shutting off debate. He argued that having the right to shut off debate and allow legislation to be voted on by a simple majority was a matter of national security. The Senate responded by passing a rule that allowed sixteen senators to file a cloture motion to terminate debate; if two-thirds of senators voting approved the motion, then debate would be limited to one hour per senator. For opponents of the filibuster, the first cloture reform was a hollow victory because the high bar it set (two-thirds of the Senate) was very difficult to meet. But in 1975, after decades during which the filibuster had been used to prevent or slow the passage of civil rights legislation, the Senate refined the cloture rule to require the votes of only three-fifths of the Senate to shut off debate.

The three-fifths number (sixty senators) is a supermajority threshold. There are two reasons the Senate requires this high number. First, majority-party control of the Senate is achieved when fifty-one senators agree to caucus together as a party. Typically, a majority party has between fifty-one and sixty members, and therefore the sixty-vote requirement means that the majority party must win over some members of the minority party in order to end debate. By setting the bar higher than a simple majority, the Senate guarantees that cloture can be achieved only when there is genuine national consensus on a proposal. Second, the House of Representatives is a simple-majority institution, and in order to slow the House down, or even block its actions, the Senate needs to preserve the power of the minority. Setting the number of votes required to shut down a filibuster considerably higher than a simple majority accomplishes this goal.

THE FILIBUSTER AS A TOOL FOR ADVOCACY

The strongest argument against preserving the filibuster is that it can be used for antidemocratic purposes. Even James Madison conceded as much in *Federalist* No. 62, in which he wrote that the Senate's power to slow down the legislative process might be "injurious."[3] Certainly, when southern senators filibustered civil rights legislation in the 1930s, 1940s, and 1950s (before finally losing their obstructionist battle in the 1960s), they were using the filibuster to deny fundamental human rights. However, at the same time, those southern senators were giving voice to what they perceived to be a majority of their constituents' views. In other words, southern senators were using the filibuster to represent their constituents. It should be noted, moreover, that powerful southern committee chairmen in the House of Representatives were using their majority committee power to stall or block the same legislation. The division over civil rights was deep and profound, and it is not at all clear that it was only the procedural mechanism of the filibuster that stood in the way of civil rights legislation.

Opponents of the filibuster seek out the most offensive examples of its use to argue that it should be eliminated. But where there is a clear majority position in Congress and the public, filibusters generally do not succeed. In fact, the goal of a filibuster is not always to kill a bill, amendment, or nomination. Frequently, senators use the power of delay to draw attention to local issues in their states or to raise ideological issues, present the minority-party viewpoint, or extract some benefit from the president. The filibuster has been used in a wide variety of ways by senators seeking to assert their own power as well as represent their states and constituents. For example, in 1988, Nevada's freshman senator Harry Reid began his campaign to filibuster any bill that appropriated funds to allow the Department of Energy to initiate a suitability review for dumping nuclear waste at Yucca Mountain. A year earlier, Congress passed a law that designated Yucca Mountain as a possible repository for nuclear waste, but Senator Reid prevented the program from being implemented by filibustering every bill that appropriated funds for it.[4] For nearly thirty years, Reid used the threat of a filibuster—and between 2007 and 2014 his position as Senate majority leader—to stall the Yucca Mountain project. With Reid's retirement in 2016, proponents of storing the nuclear waste there see an opening to do so, but with the designation of the Basin and Range national monument on the direct railway route to Yucca Mountain, there will be the need to find an alternative route that opponents believe will be very difficult. As of April 2016 no nuclear waste material had been deposited in Yucca Mountain.[5] Granted, there is a compelling national interest in finding somewhere to house the waste that is generated by nuclear power plants and military facilities, but Senator Reid justly argued that the residents of Nevada are being unfairly singled out, and since they are outnumbered in the House of Representatives, the Senate is their only venue to resist the plan. Without the filibuster, Nevada would have no way of protecting its interests.

Even beyond the profound responsibility that U.S. senators have to protect their home states' interests, which may require using the filibuster, senators also use the filibuster to slow down or halt legislation that they believe will be harmful to individual rights. For example, when the Patriot Act was up for reauthorization in 2005, both Democratic and Republican senators used the filibuster to obtain more protections against government intrusion on privacy and surveillance of individuals.[6] In 2013, Senator Rand Paul (R-KY) used the filibuster to delay the nomination of John Brennan to be the Director of the CIA in order to draw attention to the possibility of government use of drones against U.S. citizens on U.S. soil. [7]

If it were not for the power to filibuster, how could ordinary citizens, companies, or states stand up for their own interests in a majoritarian system of government? In the House of Representatives, the majority party grants the minority permission to present its alternative legislation on the floor only if the majority is certain it has the votes to defeat the minority's proposal. And in today's atmosphere of unprecedented partisan polarization, there is virtually no consideration of the minority position on any bills that are passed by the House of Representatives. In the Senate, the majority party has the power to bring to the floor the bills it wants to pass, but any senator from either the majority or the minority party can object to the consideration of that bill or, in the extreme, filibuster it. The filibuster in the Senate provides a crucial opportunity for senators in the minority to represent the views of their constituents and to persuade the majority to consider their alternative policy ideas. In short, the filibuster acts as a crucially important vehicle for the minority to influence national policy making.

THE PARTISAN ABUSE OF THE FILIBUSTER

One of the consequences of the increased partisanship in Congress is that senators from the minority party sometimes use the filibuster to score political points rather than to take principled stands based on individual beliefs or constituents' interests. So the pressure to reform or limit the filibuster has ebbed and flowed over time depending on the level of partisan conflict in politics, and this is especially true when it comes to judicial nominations. The filibuster has been used frequently to block judicial nominees based on their perceived ideological positions rather than their judicial qualifications. To some, this use of the filibuster violates the principle of an independent federal judiciary and treads on the president's constitutionally based appointment power. Senators from both parties are guilty of this abuse of the filibuster, and it has occurred under both Democratic and Republican control of the Senate.

In 2005, then majority leader Bill Frist (R-TN) announced a proposal to abolish the right to filibuster judicial nominees by changing the Senate rules. Senator Frist made the case that senators had been abusing the right to filibuster and violating the principle of separation of powers by obstructing Republican president George W. Bush's right to appoint members of the federal judiciary. In response, a group of fourteen senators—seven from each party— joined together to object to any limitation on the right to filibuster. The Senate eventually agreed to a compromise that formally protected the right to filibuster, but, informally, senators agreed that they would not filibuster judicial nominees except in "extraordinary circumstances."[8] This incident shows that senators are cognizant of the value and power of the filibuster and also that they understand it is not a tool to be used lightly or capriciously.

In 2012, Republican senators were accused of blocking a number of President Obama's judicial nominations, and majority leader Harry Reid became so frustrated that he took the unprecedented action of filing cloture motions on seventeen judicial nominations and scheduling roll-call votes on each nomination, one after the other.[9] The cloture votes were designed to expose what Reid argued was an abuse of the filibuster by Republicans. On the day voting was to commence, the Republicans, in the face of significant adverse publicity, agreed to allow up-or-down votes on fourteen nominees over the subsequent two months.[10]

However, this "filibuster truce" did not last long. In November 2013, Reid and the Democratic majority took the action that Frist had suggested eight years earlier, lowering the minimum number of votes necessary to invoke cloture from sixty to fifty-one on presidential nominations and judicial nominations for district and appeals court judges. They did so to clear the way for President Obama to get his nominees confirmed. Not since 1975 had the Senate altered the number of votes needed for cloture.[11] However, the Democrats left untouched the sixty vote requirement to filibuster legislation and Supreme Court nominations.

When the Republicans took back control of the Senate in 2014, the new majority leader Mitch McConnell (R-KY) retained the limitations that the Democrats had imposed on the filibuster. He had to grapple with a fractured Republican majority and faced filibusters from his own members, most notably Senator Rand Paul (R-KY) and Ted Cruz (R-TX) on issues such as national security and government spending, as well as opposition from the Democrats. In the first ten months of the 114th Congress (2015–2016), McConnell filed 61 cloture motions, and cloture was invoked 27 times. That is a greater number of cloture motions than Harry Reid filed in the same time period in the first ten months of 2013, before the Democrats changed the rules to make it harder to filibuster.[12] The key takeaway here is that even with the limitations that the Democrats imposed in the preceding Congress, and under a different party, U.S. senators still view the filibuster as an important legislative tool.

MAKING THE FILIBUSTER A MORE COSTLY ENDEAVOR

The solution to the abuse of the filibuster lies not in abolishing it but in enforcing the basic requirements of extended debate. Senator Strom Thurmond, then a Democrat from South Carolina, held the record for the longest filibuster ever recorded; in 1957, he talked for twenty-four hours and eighteen minutes against Republican president Dwight Eisenhower's civil rights bill. His filibuster required the expenditure of an enormous amount of time and energy.

With the exception of Senators Paul and Cruz, how many stories do you hear today of senators pulling all-nighters to filibuster a bill or amendment? Instead, senators can merely raise the threat of objecting to a bill to signal that they *might* actually talk long enough to delay it, and their demands are considered by their colleagues. Given that the filibuster has now been reduced to a mere sentence or two voicing an objection to a motion, it is no wonder that we have come to believe it is at the heart of all legislative delay. In fact, the abuse of the power to filibuster stems from the failure of the Senate as a whole, and the majority-party leadership specifically, to enforce the basic requirement that a filibuster consist of *extended speech.*

The U.S. Senate today has a legislative workload that is unparalleled in its history. Moreover, in addition to their legislative responsibilities, senators are expected to meet with government officials and key constituents as well as raise funds for their next reelection campaigns. In 2014, incumbent senators who ran for reelection spent an average of $11 million: Democratic incumbents spent over $13 million, and Republican incumbents spent nearly $8 million; those numbers were expected to increase in the 2016 Senate election cycle.[13] Senate incumbents who hope to defend their seats no longer have the time to stand on the Senate floor and talk, much less listen.

An upside to the high cost of running for reelection is that it could serve as a great disincentive to spend time abusing the right to filibuster. If a senator could filibuster a motion only by coming to the Senate floor, standing up, getting recognized to speak by the presiding officer, and then proceeding to talk without stopping, we would certainly see a dramatic drop in the number of supposed filibusters. Senators would engage in filibustering only when the issues at hand are of vital importance to their constituents or themselves. Opponents of the filibuster argue that trying to enforce the extended speech aspect of the filibuster is unrealistic. They argue that the majority leader is elected by the senators from his or her party, and no majority leader would be willing to risk the wrath of fellow senators by forcing them to stand up and talk indefinitely. But that answer does not hold up well in light of history; plenty of majority leaders have enforced the filibuster and kept their jobs. If the cost of filibustering were higher, then senators would be less likely to use this tactic to delay the Senate's business, and that would both make the job of majority leader easier and increase the productivity of the U.S. Senate.

Therefore, I recommend that the right to filibuster a bill, or an amendment, be preserved in the U.S. Senate under one condition: that any senator who claims to have an objection be forced to come to the floor and speak openly and publicly to his or her colleagues. From the time that the majority leader makes a motion to proceed with a bill, a senator shall have two legislative days to come to the floor; that window shall be reduced to one legislative day in the case of an amendment. (These windows of time are necessary to allow senators who are traveling to return to the Senate to make their case.) If the senator does filibuster, the standing sixty-vote threshold to invoke cloture and shut off debate on legislation shall remain in effect. If the senator fails to appear on the Senate floor to voice his or her objection, the Senate majority leader should be free to move forward with the legislation, without requiring unanimous consent or a Senate vote to do so.

The Senate was designed to be a bulwark against hasty and rash decision making by the federal government. The framers of the Constitution knew that they were taking a risk by giving a centralized government ultimate power over each state; they split the legislative branch into two chambers in order to maximize the venues where citizens could have their voices heard and their interests addressed. In the House, the voice of the majority carries the day, but in the Senate, all senators have equal power to voice dissent. The filibuster provides an essential incentive for Congress to reach a compromise among the competing interests, opinions, and ideologies that characterize American democracy.

NOTES

CON

1. Quoted in Marvin Meyers, *The Mind of the Founder: Sources of the Political Thought of James Madison* (Waltham, MA: Brandeis University Press, 1981), 68.
2. James Madison, *Federalist* No. 62, in Alexander Hamilton, James Madison, and John Jay, *The Federalist Papers,* ed. Charles R. Kesler and Clinton Rossiter (New York, NY: New American Library, Penguin Group, 1999), 377.
3. Ibid., 376.
4. Susan F. Rasky, "Accord Is Reached on Nuclear Dump," *New York Times,* December 18, 1987, http://www.nytimes.com/1987/12/18/us/accord-is-reached-on-nuclear-dump.html.
5. Scott Lucas, "Beatty Waste Fires Sparks Fear Among Yucca Opponents," *Las Vegas Sun,* October 28, 2015, http://lasvegassun.com/news/2015/oct/28/beatty-waste-fire-sparks-fears-among-yucca-opponen; Staff, "Current Press News." April 4, 2016, http://www.yuccamountain.org/new.htm.
6. Eric Lichtblau, "Extension of Patriot Act Faces Threat of Filibuster," *New York Times,* November 18, 2005, http://www.nytimes.com/2005/11/18/national/18patriot.html.
7. Philip Ewing, "Rand Paul Pulls the Plug on Nearly 13-Hour Filibuster," *Politico.com,* March 16, 2013, http://www.politico.com/story/2013/03/rand-paul-filibuster-john-brennan-cia-nominee-088507.

8. David Nather, "Senate Races Against the Nuclear Clock on Judges," *CQ Weekly Online,* May 30, 2005, 1441–43, http://library.cqpress.com/cqweekly/weeklyreport109-000001700754.

9. "Cloture Filed on 17 Judicial Nominations," United States Senate Democrats website, March 12, 2012, http://democrats.senate.gov/2012/03/12/cloture-filed-on-17-judicial-nominations.

10. Humberto Sanchez, "Senate Reaches Deal on 14 Judicial Nominees," *Roll Call,* March 14, 2012, http://www.rollcall.com/news/senate_reaches_deal_on_14_judicial_nominees-213114-1.html.

11. For more details on the cloture rules and recent changes, see Valerie Heitshusen, Congressional Research Service, "Majority Cloture for Nominations: Implications and the 'Nuclear' Proceedings," December 6, 2013, R43331, http://www.fas.org/sgp/crs/misc/R43331.pdf.

12. In the first 10 months of 2013, Harry Reid filed 49 cloture motions, and cloture was invoked 30 times. Staff, "Senate Action on Cloture Motions," http://www.senate.gov/reference/clotureCounts.htm.

13. 2014 Election Overview. OpenSecrets.org, Center for Responsive Politics, http://www.opensecrets.org/overview/index.php?cycle=2014&display=A&type=R; Ian Vandewalker, "Senate Election Spending: What to Watch for," March 8, 2016, Brennan Center for Justice, https://www.brennancenter.org/blog/senate-election-spending-what-watch.

RESOLVED, the electoral college should be abolished

PRO: George C. Edwards III

CON: Gary L. Gregg II

When James Madison crafted the Virginia Plan as a rough draft of a new plan of government on the eve of the Constitutional Convention, he proposed that the "National Executive" be elected by the "National Legislature" but said nothing about whether the executive would be an individual or a committee. When the delegates to the convention began debating what the executive should look like, they were confident where Madison was uncertain and uncertain where he was confident. The convention quickly decided that the executive should be a single person—the president of the United States. But they went around and around on the issue of how that person should be elected. In political scientist Robert A. Dahl's description, "The Convention twisted and turned like a man tormented in his sleep by a bad dream as it tried to decide."[1]

Madison's idea that the national legislature—that is, Congress—should choose the president had many champions. In fact, throughout most of the convention, which lasted nearly four months, from May 25 to September 17, 1787, the delegates held to the idea that Congress would elect the president with a one-term limit. But two problems with this idea emerged from the debates. One was that many delegates wanted the president to be eligible for more than one term but did not want Congress to both elect and reelect the president. The desire for reelection, they feared, would give the president every incentive to bribe members of Congress to support him for a second—and perhaps a third, fourth, and fifth—term. The other problem was more practical: How would Congress actually elect the president? Delegates from the larger, more populous states wanted to see members of the House of Representatives and Senate vote for president as one body, which by definition would be dominated by large-state representatives. Delegates from the small states wanted the

House and Senate to vote separately until they agreed on the same candidate, who at a minimum would have to be acceptable to the small states.

Not surprisingly, other ideas for presidential selection also were advanced. One proposed that the governors of the states, as fellow chief executives, should choose the president. Another was that each state should put forward its best citizen and Congress should elect one of them. Still another proposal was to entrust the choice to a small group of legislators chosen by lot. Another was to let the voters choose the president in a direct national election. That one was dismissed with particular contempt by Virginia delegate George Mason, who said, "It would be as unnatural to refer the choice of a proper character for chief Magistrate to the people, as it would to refer a trial of colours to a blind man."[2]

In early September, just days before the convention ended, an eleven-member committee of delegates proposed a solution that was nobody's first choice but that most delegates decided they could live with: the electoral college. Every four years, each state would choose presidential electors equal in number to its delegation of representatives and senators in Congress. If a candidate received support from a majority of electors, he would become president. If no candidate received majority support, then the House would choose the president from the ranks of the leading electoral vote recipients, with each state delegation in the House casting one vote.

Over the years, few provisions of the Constitution have proven more controversial than the electoral college. More constitutional amendments have been proposed in Congress to replace it than have been proposed concerning any other subject. In the 1950s, the leading alternative was a proportional plan, under which each state's electoral votes would be cast in proportion to the candidates' shares of the state's popular vote. A more recent idea has been to bypass the Constitution entirely and get each state to agree to cast its electoral votes for whichever candidate receives the most popular votes across the country, regardless of how the voting goes in the state. Two states, Nebraska and Maine, exercise their constitutional option to assign their electoral votes so that the candidate who carries the state gets two (corresponding to the state's two senators) and the remaining votes are assigned according to who carries each House district—the so-called district plan.

The reform proposal that has received the most support for the longest period of time has been the one that Mason dismissed at the 1787 convention: Do away with the electoral college and replace it with a direct presidential election by the people. George C. Edwards III defends this proposal in his essay, and Gary L. Gregg II opposes it, preferring to keep the electoral college as it is. Although this is an old debate, Edwards and Gregg bring fresh vigor and new arguments to the table.

PRO: George C. Edwards III

Political equality lies at the core of democratic theory. It is difficult to imagine a definition of democracy that does not include equality in voting as a central standard. Because political equality is at the core of democratic government, we must evaluate any mechanism for selecting the president against it.

The percentage of electoral votes received by a candidate nationwide rarely coincides with the candidate's percentage of the national popular vote for several reasons, the most important of which is the winner-take-all system.[1] All states except Maine and Nebraska use the winner-take-all system, in which *every* electoral vote is awarded to the candidate who receives the most popular votes in the state. In effect, the system assigns to the winner the votes of the people who voted *against* the winner.

The operation of the winner-take-all system effectively disenfranchises voters who support losing candidates in each state. In the 2000 presidential election, nearly three million people voted for Al Gore in Florida. Because George W. Bush won 537 more votes than Gore, however, he received *all* of Florida's electoral votes. A candidate can win some states by very narrow margins, lose others by large margins, and so win the electoral vote while losing the popular vote. Because there is no way to aggregate votes across states, the votes for candidates who do not finish first in a state play no role in the outcome of the election.

African Americans, who constitute the nation's most distinctive minority group, are concentrated in the Deep South. They rarely vote for the Republican candidates who win their states. Thus, their votes are wasted because they are never added up across the country. It is not surprising that presidential candidates have generally ignored these voters in their campaigns.[2]

In contests with significant third-party candidates, such as the ones in 1992, 1996, and 2000, the winner-take-all system may suppress the votes of the majority as well as those of the minority. In 1996, for example, in twenty-six states, less than half the voters determined how all of their states' electoral votes were cast.

The winner-take-all system also allows even small third parties to siphon more votes from one major-party candidate than from the other and thus determine the outcome in a state, as Ralph Nader did in both Florida and New Hampshire in 2000. Indeed, by taking more votes from Gore than from Bush, Nader determined the outcome of the entire election. The results distorted the preferences of the voters, because the preferred candidate in both Florida and

New Hampshire in a two-person race was Al Gore, not George W. Bush, who ultimately won both states.

One result of these distorting factors is that there is typically a substantial disparity between the share of the national popular vote a candidate receives and that candidate's percentage of the electoral vote. In 1876, 1888, 2000, and, arguably, 1960,[3] the candidate who finished second in the popular vote won the election.

If no candidate wins a majority of the electoral votes, as happened in 1800 and 1824, the House of Representatives chooses the president. Here, each state delegation receives one vote, allowing the seven smallest states, with a total population of about 5.5 million, to outvote the six largest states, with a total population of about 131 million. It is virtually impossible to find any defenders of this constitutional provision, which is the most egregious violation of democratic principles in American government.

The electoral college violates political equality. It favors some citizens over others, depending solely upon the state in which they live, and at times, denies the people their preferred choice for president. What good reason is there to continue such a system in a nation in which the ideal of popular choice is the most deeply ingrained principle of government?

CONSTITUTIONAL CONSISTENCY

Some defenders of the electoral college argue that its violations of majority rule are just an example of constitutional provisions that require supermajorities to take action. For example, it takes the votes of two-thirds of the senators present to ratify a treaty. The framers designed all such provisions, however, to allow minorities to prevent an action. The electoral college is different. It allows a minority to take an action—that is, to select the president. As such, it is the only device of its kind in the Constitution. Thus, defenders of the electoral college have a fundamental misunderstanding of the Constitution.

PRESIDENTIAL LEGITIMACY

Do the inflated numbers of the electoral college results provide a new president extra legitimacy? There is no evidence at all that winning a majority in the electoral college provides an additional element of legitimacy for new presidents who did more poorly in the popular vote. Even after two and a half years in office and the rally focused on the war on terrorism, 38 percent of the American public, including a majority of Democrats and half the Independents, did not consider George W. Bush the legitimate winner of the 2000 presidential election.[4]

DEFENDING STATE INTERESTS

Advocates of the electoral college often argue that allocating electoral votes by state and having states cast their votes as units ensure that presidential candidates will be attentive to and protective of states' interests, especially the interests of states with small populations. They base their argument on the premises that (1) states have interests as states, (2) these interests require protection, (3) interests in states with smaller populations both require and deserve special protection from federal laws, and (4) candidates focus on state interests, especially the interests of smaller states.

States Do Not Have Interests as States

States do not have coherent, unified interests. Even the smallest state has substantial diversity within it. That is why Alaska may have a Republican governor and one or more Democratic senators and why "conservative" states such as Montana and North and South Dakota vote Republican for president but sometimes send liberal Democrats to the U.S. Senate. As historian Jack Rakove argues, "States have no interest, as states, in the election of the president; only citizens do."[5]

State Interests Do Not Require Additional Protection

The Constitution places many constraints on the actions a simple majority can take. Minorities have fundamental rights to organize, communicate, and participate in the political process. The Senate greatly overrepresents small states, and within that chamber the filibuster is a powerful extraconstitutional tool for thwarting majorities. Moreover, more than a simple majority is required to overcome minority opposition by changing the Constitution.

With these powerful checks on simple majorities already in place, do some minority rights or interests require additional protection from national majorities? If so, are these minorities concentrated in certain geographic areas? (Because it allocates electoral votes on the basis of geography, the electoral college protects only geographically concentrated interests.) Does anything justify awarding interests in certain geographic locations—namely, small states—additional protections in the form of extra representation in the electoral system that citizens in other states do not enjoy?[6]

Two of the most important authors of the Constitution, James Wilson and James Madison, saw little need to confer additional power on small states through the electoral college. "Can we forget for whom we are forming a government?" Wilson asked. "Is it for *men*, or for the imaginary beings called

States?"[7] Madison declared that experience had shown no danger of state interests being harmed by a national majority,[8] and that "the President is to act for the *people* not for *States*."[9]

Congress, whose members are elected by districts and states, is designed to be responsive to constituency interests. The president, as Madison pointed out, is supposed to take a broader view. When advocates of the electoral college express concern that direct election of the president would suppress local interests in favor of the national interest, they are in effect endorsing a presidency that is responsive to parochial interests in a system that already offers minority interests extraordinary access to policy makers and many opportunities to thwart policies they oppose.

Supporters of the electoral college almost never specify what geographically concentrated rights or interests need special protection through the electoral college. They certainly have not developed a general principle to justify additional protections for some interests rather than others.

There Are No Distinctive Small-State Interests

Do the states with small populations that receive special consideration in the electoral college have common interests to protect? The great political battles of American history—in Congress and in presidential elections—have been fought by opposing ideological and economic interests, not by small states in opposition to large states.

A brief look at the seventeen states with the fewest electoral votes (that is, three, four, or five) shows that they are quite diverse.[10] Maine, Vermont, New Hampshire, and Rhode Island are in New England; Delaware and West Virginia are in the Middle Atlantic region; North and South Dakota, Montana, and Nebraska are in the Great Plains; New Mexico is in the Southwest; and Nevada, Wyoming, Utah, and Idaho are in the Rocky Mountain region. Alaska and Hawaii are regions unto themselves. It is not surprising that their representatives do not vote as a bloc in Congress and that their citizens do not vote as a bloc for president.

Even if small states have little in common, are there some interests that occur only in states with small populations? Most farmers live in states with large populations. The market value of the agricultural production of California, Texas, Florida, and Illinois alone substantially exceeds that of all seventeen of the smallest states combined.[11] For that matter, agriculture does not lack for powerful champions, especially in Congress, which has taken the lead in providing benefits, principally in the form of subsidies, for agriculture. Rather than competing to give farmers more benefits, presidents of both parties have attempted to restrain congressional spending on agriculture. The electoral college has not turned presidents into champions of rural America.

It is difficult to identify interests that are centered in a few small states. Even if we could, however, the question remains whether these few interests out of the literally thousands of interests in the United States deserve special protection. What principle would support such a view? Why should those who produce wheat and hogs have more say in electing the president than those who produce vegetables, citrus, and beef? Is not the disproportionate Senate representation of states in which wheat and hogs are produced enough to protect these interests? There is simply no evidence that interests such as these deserve or require additional protection from the electoral system.

Candidates Ignore State Interests

Ultimately, the argument that the electoral college protects state interests rests on what candidates actually do. Do they pay particular attention to small states, and do they focus on state-based interests that would otherwise be neglected under direct election of the president?

The most direct means for candidates to appeal to voters is to visit their states and address them in person. We know that when candidates appear at campaign events, they do not focus their remarks on what we might view as state-based interests as opposed to issues of national concern.[12]

But where do they appear? The 2012 election followed a typical pattern.[13] All four of the major presidential and vice presidential candidates avoided each of the nine smallest states and visited only New Hampshire, Nevada, Iowa, and Colorado among the 29 smallest states. A single visit by vice presidential candidate Paul Ryan to Minnesota and visits by all the candidates to Wisconsin rounded out the candidates' visits to the 38 smallest states. Barack Obama visited only eight states during the entire general election, and Mitt Romney visited only ten. The states the candidates did visit were competitive states, especially large competitive states. Similarly, only ten states accounted for nearly 100 percent of all general election television advertising by campaigns and their allies.

In the course of overlooking most states, candidates also avoid entire regions of the country. Democrats have little incentive to campaign in the heavily Republican Great Plains and Deep South, and Republicans have little incentive to visit most of Democratic New England.

In sum, the electoral college provides no incentive for candidates to pay attention to small states and take their cases directly to their citizens. Indeed, it is difficult to imagine how presidential candidates could be *less* attentive to small states than they are. Candidates go where the electoral college makes them go, and it makes them go to competitive states, especially large competitive states. In addition, they do not compensate for their lack of visits to small or noncompetitive states by advertising there.[14]

Thus, the fundamental justification of the electoral college—that it forces candidates to be attentive to particular state interests, especially those concentrated in small states—is based on faulty premises. In reality, the electoral college *discourages* candidates from paying attention to small states and to much of the rest of the country as well.

PRESERVING FEDERALISM

Defenders of the electoral college sometimes assert that it is a key underpinning of federalism. However, it is unclear what federalism has to do with the presidency, the one elective part of the government that is designed to represent the nation as a whole rather than as an amalgam of states and districts.

The founders did not design the electoral college on the federal principle. Neither the existence nor the powers and responsibilities of state governments depend in any way on the existence of the electoral college. Moreover, the founders expected electors to exercise their individual discretion when casting their votes. They did not expect electors to vote as part of any state bloc. No delegate at the Constitutional Convention referred to the electoral college as an element of the federal system or even as important to the overall structure of the Constitution. Indeed, the electoral college was "an anti-states-rights device," designed to keep the election of the president away from state politicians.[15]

Federalism is deeply embodied in congressional elections, in which two senators represent each state just because it is a state and in which members of the House are elected from districts within states. Direct election of the president would not alter these federalism-sustaining aspects of the constitutional structure.

PROTECTING NON-STATE-BASED MINORITY INTERESTS

Some observers claim that the electoral college ensures a "proper distribution" of the vote, in which the winning candidate receives majority support across social strata, thus protecting minority interests. This claim is nonsense. In 2000, George W. Bush did not win a larger percentage than Al Gore of the votes of women, African Americans, Hispanics, and Asian Americans; voters ages eighteen to twenty-nine or those sixty or older; the poor; members of labor unions; those with less than $50,000 annual household income; those with a high school education or less and those with postgraduate education; Catholics, Jews, and Muslims; liberals and moderates; urbanites; or those living in the East and the West.[16]

It strains credulity to claim that Bush's vote represents concurrent majorities across the major strata of American society. What actually happened in 2000 was that the electoral college imposed a candidate supported by White male Protestants—the dominant social group in the country—over the objections not only of a plurality of all voters but also of most "minority" interests in the country. This antidemocratic outcome is precisely the opposite of what defenders of the electoral college claim for the system.

ADVANTAGES OF DIRECT ELECTION

Direct election of the president would provide the incentive for candidates to encourage all of their supporters, and not just those strategically located in swing states,[17] to go to the polls, because under direct election, every vote counts. Thus, direct election would increase voter turnout and stimulate party-building efforts in the weaker party, especially in less competitive states.

Moreover, candidates would find it easy to spread their attention more evenly across the country. Because the cost of advertising is mainly a function of market size, it does not cost more to reach ten thousand voters in Wyoming than it does to reach ten thousand voters in a neighborhood in Queens or Los Angeles. Actually, it costs less to reach voters in smaller communities because larger markets tend to run out of commercial time, increasing the price of advertising. Since there are more swing voters in the smaller markets, and it costs less to reach them than it does to reach swing voters in the large metropolitan markets,[18] only candidates wishing to lose an election would ignore rural areas. Unsurprisingly, candidates do not ignore smaller markets when they campaign within states.[19]

It is possible that some candidates would find it more cost-effective under direct election to mobilize votes in urban areas or to visit urban areas where they would receive free television coverage before large audiences. Such actions would do nothing to undermine the argument against the electoral college, however. Small states receive almost no attention now. Instead, direct election would provide increased incentive for candidates to campaign in most small states, as well as increased incentive for them to campaign in many large and medium-size states. Direct election would disperse campaign efforts rather than deprive small states of them, as we saw in the battle for one of Maine's electoral votes in 2004 and that for Nebraska's Second Congressional District in 2008.

Some critics of direct election mistakenly claim that it would splinter the two-party system. This assertion is based on the premise that direct election would require a runoff between the two leading candidates, but in reality it would not. Under the electoral college, victorious presidential candidates—including, most recently, John F. Kennedy (1960), Richard Nixon (1968), Bill Clinton (1992 and 1996), and George W. Bush (2000)—have received less than a majority of the national popular vote about 40 percent of the time since 1824, and there is no relation between the vote they received and their later success in, say, dealing with Congress. Some of our strongest presidents, including James K. Polk, Abraham Lincoln, Grover Cleveland, Woodrow Wilson, Harry S. Truman, and Kennedy, received a plurality, but not a majority, of the popular vote.

Nor is the electoral college the basis of the two-party system. Single-member districts and plurality election are, and the nation would be one electoral district under direct election. Thus, direct election would not splinter the party system.

By contrast, direct election would protect the country from the mischief of third parties. The electoral college's winner-take-all system encourages third parties, especially those with regional bases, because by winning a few states they may deny either major-party candidate a majority of the electoral vote. Such a result was certainly the goal of Strom Thurmond in 1948 and George Wallace in 1968. Imagine giving these racist candidates leverage to negotiate with the leading candidates before the electoral votes were officially cast. Moreover, even without winning any states, Ralph Nader inadvertently distorted the vote and determined the outcome of the 2000 election.

To examine this relationship in another way, consider two third-party candidates, one contemplating running in a system of direct election and the other running under the electoral college. A potential candidate in a system of direct election risks his or her political future by running against the official party candidate. And there is no compensation. Such a candidate can win nothing at all coming in third, even taking a significant portion of the vote. So there is little incentive to run. Under the electoral college, however, a candidate finishing, say, third, might win some electoral votes and have leverage in determining the winner of the election. There is much more incentive for third-party candidates to run under the electoral college than under a system of direct election.

It is important that we not fall into a logical trap. It is circular reasoning to argue that direct election will produce a plethora of candidates, which in turn will force a runoff, which in turn will encourage candidates to run. In fact, direct election will not produce more general election candidates than does the electoral college, and there is no need for a runoff. There is a reason critics of direct election do not cite peer-reviewed studies to support their claims about the fragmentation of the party system: there aren't any.

CONCLUSION

There is no question that instituting direct election of the president will be difficult. Making this change will require amending the Constitution, a complex and time-consuming task. Although the public and many states and organizations support direct election, there are obstacles to change. Principal among them are officials who believe that their states or the members of their organizations benefit from the electoral college. We now know that these officials are wrong. They have reached their conclusions on the basis of faulty premises. Understanding the flawed foundations of the electoral college is the critical first step on the road to reforming the system of presidential selection. The culmination of this effort should be allowing the people to directly elect the presidents who serve them.

CON: Gary L. Gregg II

In *Federalist* No. 68, Alexander Hamilton contended that the electoral college was "almost the only part of the system, of any consequence, which has escaped without severe censure or which has received the slightest mark of approbation from its opponents."[1] How things have changed!

The electoral college has long been one of the least understood and most unappreciated aspects of the American constitutional order. Its opponents have campaigned against it in academe, on the op-ed pages, and in Congress. More amendments have been proposed to abolish the electoral college than have dealt with nearly any other aspect of the Constitution. Through it all, however, the electoral college has endured and continued to serve American democracy. Why?

IT WORKS

The electoral college survives because it works. It has served to elect forty-four presidents, many of them good, some great, only a few disasters. Washington and Jefferson, Lincoln and Teddy Roosevelt, Franklin Roosevelt and his admirer Ronald Reagan were all the products of our system of electing presidents. Our political system is democratic and stable. Our elections are free and honest. Our fights can be bitter, but when they are decided at the ballot box, they end with legitimate presidents and governable regimes. This long experience is the reason that even after a controversial election such as the one we had in 2000, opponents of the electoral college have not been able to advance their agenda in Congress.

Because of the electoral college's successful history, the burden of proof must be on those seeking to change the rules of the game. If they cannot demonstrate how their alternative would produce better presidents and a more stable and successful political order, then their arguments must fall.

POLITICAL EQUALITY

Opponents of the electoral college would trade this successful record for an abstraction, namely, the idea of "political equality." This is the idea that all American voters must be counted equally.[2] Critics of the electoral college tell us this is the foundation stone of the American experience, and all other considerations must give way to this ideal. Our experience with the Constitution does not support such a contention.

Political equality is an important value in the American political system, but our constitutional order does not treat political equality as the preeminent, let alone only, value. In fact, our system violates this principle in many ways. The U.S. Senate treats all states as equal, which necessarily means that voters are not treated equally. Connecticut voters have far more say in the Senate than do the voters of California, for instance. Even congressional districts are not uniform in size, leaving some members of Congress to represent more constituents than others. In Montana, for instance, the single congressional district consists of 900,000 people, whereas in Wyoming the sole congressional district contains 560,000 people. The states that are home to the majority and minority leaders in Congress have considerably more influence than do other states. The Supreme Court is far from representative, and its ability to overturn popular legislation is a clear violation of pure popular sovereignty and political equality. Our system balances a variety of sometimes competing goods in ways that produce a stable, prosperous, and free political order.

But even if political equality should trump all other concerns, the electoral college is not as bad as its opponents contend. Our presidential elections are open, free, and fair. Each is a race to win more votes than the other person. And each is based on every vote being counted and all votes counting equally. The Constitution simply tells us to count the votes on a state-by-state basis rather than as one giant political entity that elects nothing else and legally does not even exist as a constituency. Each presidential election, then, is based on political equality within the states, and in every election, the candidate with the most votes in a state wins that state.[3] That is political equality.

REFORM ATTEMPTS AND THE NEW NATIONAL VOTE PLAN

Opponents of the electoral college have proposed hundreds of amendments to the U.S. Constitution but have never been successful in passing such a measure. They have now largely moved beyond the legitimate constitutional amendment process laid out in Article V and are attempting to implement their plan through a stealthy state-by-state campaign outside the amendment process. Called the National Popular Vote (NPV) plan, the new scheme is the brainchild of computer engineer John R. Koza, best known for coinventing the scratch-off instant lottery ticket. State legislatures that sign on to the National Popular Vote Interstate Compact agree to pledge all their states' electoral college votes to the winner of a national popular vote, no matter how their own citizens voted. Once enough states enact the legislation, they need to join in the compact—enough to comprise the 270 electoral votes required to become president—the scheme would be enacted, and the American election system would be fundamentally transformed.

Having given up on the amendment process, these reformers are attempting a de facto amendment to the Constitution by going outside the amendment provisions of the Constitution. Some proponents have been bold enough to admit this. Political commentator E. J. Dionne has written in support of the plan in the *Washington Post*: "This is an effort to circumvent the cumbersome process of amending the Constitution. That's the only practical way of moving toward a more democratic system."[4]

As of 2015, the NPV plan has passed in ten states plus the District of Columbia with a combined total of 165 electoral college votes, which puts its backers halfway to their goal of de facto abolition of the electoral college. So far, however, only reliably Democratic states, such as California and Vermont, have signed on. Nonetheless, this is as serious a threat as the electoral college has faced since 1970, when a proposal to abolish the electoral college had the support of a majority of U.S. senators but fell five votes short of the number needed to end a filibuster.

COUNTING HAS CONSEQUENCES

In order to come to grips with what the abolition of the electoral college would mean for the United States, we must consider the dynamics the electoral college system has created and how they would change. Keep in mind that every presidential election since the Twelfth Amendment was added in 1804 has been run according to the rules of the game created by the electoral college. Change the rules, and you change the game. All general election campaign decisions at the presidential level have been made using electoral college math. Changing the way votes are counted will therefore have profound consequences on the way campaigns are conducted and will likely transform the entire American political system in ways that are difficult to anticipate fully.

There is no perfectly neutral method of counting votes or conducting elections. For instance, it is commonly assumed that the electoral college has "failed" to produce the same presidential winner as the winner of the national popular vote on three occasions (1876, 1888, and 2000). However, each of those races was run under the electoral college rules, with no candidate attempting to maximize his own popular-vote totals. Instead, the candidates were attempting to win a majority in the electoral college. If George W. Bush and Al Gore had been trying to maximize their popular-vote totals in 2000, the outcome might well have been that Bush rather than Gore would have won the national vote. Of course we can only speculate about this, but it should lead us to question whether the electoral college really "failed" to capture majority sentiment in these three races. We cannot know who would have won had the rules been different.

What would likely happen if we were to abandon the electoral college's way of counting votes? Senator Daniel Patrick Moynihan (D-NY) looked at this question very carefully during the 1970s and concluded that such a change would radically alter American politics and undermine the nation's constitutional stability.[5] The former senator considered it all again after the 2000 race and called the abolition of the electoral college "the most radical transformation in our political system that has ever been considered." Why would Moynihan, one of the most brilliant political figures of the late twentieth century, find the prospect of such a change "so radical and so ominous" as to demand "solemn, prolonged, and prayerful consideration"?

Quite simply, he had come to the conclusion that the electoral college is "the basic institution that has given structure to American politics." It protects the core principle of the American system, which is not political equality—as valuable as that might be—but instead the idea "that power is never installed save when it is consented to by more than one majority." This principle is evident throughout our political system, from federalism to the structure of Congress to judicial review. A bill requires majorities in two very different houses of Congress before it can be sent to the president, who must also consent to sign it into law. If the law is then challenged, the courts consider its constitutional legitimacy. Even in simple form, we have at least four majorities acting on each piece of legislation. The establishment of a simple national plebiscite at the center of our constitutional order would undermine the delicate system of concurrent majorities, Moynihan ominously warned, because it would weaken us in the face of "the ever-present threat of an overwhelming issue, an overpowering person, and the end of liberty."

Moving to a simple national popular vote would radicalize our politics in several ways. Because whoever won a plurality nationally would now win the presidency, the most extreme elements in both parties would be empowered. Under the winner-take-all system we have now in all but two states, a candidate whose support is not concentrated within states (and populous ones at that) has no incentive to enter the race. This electoral college math creates an incentive for the more conservative elements of the Republican Party to cooperate with the more moderate elements of the party and for the more liberal elements of the Democratic Party to cooperate with the party's more moderate elements. The various wings of each major party rally to their party's standard-bearer rather than push more ideological candidates and give the American people a choice between a relatively left-leaning and a relatively right-leaning candidate. The result is a clear choice and a legitimate winner.[6]

Without this system, the more extreme elements of each party would be less likely to compromise and more likely to feel empowered to run, splitting the two-party system into four or more parties or blackmailing the major-party candidates into adopting their narrower, more radical issue positions. One can envision a Ralph Nader emerging on the left, demanding, "Make me director of the EPA, or I will run and siphon off enough votes to cost you the presidency!" Or perhaps it would be a libertarian Ron Paul who says to the Republican candidate, "Make me chairman of the Federal Reserve, or I will run and take 10 percent of your vote." In a divided nation, as we have today, one candidate with the power to draw just a few percentage points of the vote nationally could completely change the outcome of the election. Corrupt bargains would be routine and our politics radicalized.

PROTECTING GEOGRAPHIC DIVERSITY

Our politics would also be moved out of the center, particularly on the Democratic side, as the path to the presidency would become one where the values and interests of smaller states and rural areas could be ignored with impunity. Currently, urban politicians who seek the presidency are forced to travel to rural areas and hear the concerns of the people who live there, concerns that might otherwise be alien to them. By forcing candidates to take part in activities such as visiting state fairs, speaking with coal miners, bowling with average citizens, and attending small-town churches, the electoral college system serves to give candidates some appreciation for the great diversity of the nation and helps to moderate their policy voices.

Without the electoral college, candidates would be able to seek the presidency by campaigning exclusively in major metropolitan areas, since they would only have to worry about winning more votes than any other person in the race, regardless of where those votes come from. A county-by-county electoral map of 2000 showed that even though Al Gore won the national popular vote, he could fly from Pittsburgh, Pennsylvania, to Los Angeles, California, without passing over a single county that he won. A campaign waged around the goal of maximizing voter turnout in and around urban areas would be tilted toward liberal or leftist policy goals and would lead to narrower and less ideologically balanced public policy after the election.

Some opponents of the electoral college have argued that it does not really serve to protect small states. They are wrong. Without the electoral college, what candidate would ever visit small states such as Nevada, New Mexico, New Hampshire, or Colorado? Yet, each of these states received visits and attention from presidential candidates in recent elections. So long as the election is close, and most presidential elections are, candidates are required to get out into the country instead of focusing only on major urban areas. This is one of the great virtues of the electoral college. No direct national election, no matter how close, will provide candidates with an incentive to visit or pay attention to small states.

Not only have a significant number of American presidents come from the most elite schools in the northeastern corner of the nation, but the last four were all graduates of at least one of the same two schools—Harvard or Yale. Most presidents have counted large cities as their homes. The great bulk of the money that pays for presidential campaigns comes from the richest zip codes of the biggest cities. And the media organizations that dominate television and newspaper coverage of presidential races are all centered in large metropolitan areas. In other words, the entire general election playing field is tilted toward catering to urban interests and urban cultures. Only the electoral college, with its slight representational bonus to rural cultures and interests, provides any balance to our presidential system. Does that matter? In contemporary America, few divisions are deeper than that between rural and urban Americans. Dismantling the electoral college would mean the effective disenfranchisement of those who live in rural America and result in an unbalancing of the political system.

RECOUNTS AND LITIGATION

Advocates for abolishing the electoral college often point to the election of 2000 as evidence that radical reform is needed. Just the opposite lesson should be drawn, however. The recounts in Florida were ugly, but because of the electoral college, they were centralized in one state and produced a president that the vast majority of Americans accepted as legitimate.

Now, imagine an election that close but without the electoral college. Imagine two candidates being separated by only a few hundred thousand votes. Lawyers would descend on every precinct in every county in every state of the nation. If just a few votes per precinct could be disqualified or "found," the results of a close national popular vote could be overturned. Recounts would be nationwide, fought in county courthouses and in front of state and federal benches across the land. The abolition of the electoral college would result in a lengthy national nightmare that would make Florida 2000 look tame by comparison.

HOW LOW WILL WE GO?

Abolishing the electoral college would make the American presidential election system a version of a Jamaican limbo dance. Most abolition proposals, like the National Popular Vote plan, do not provide for a *majority* vote winner; rather, they require only that a "national popular vote winner" be certified by the participating states. A great contribution of the current electoral college system of winner-take-all in the states is that it serves to funnel our votes into two candidates with relatively broad bases of support; it also serves to exaggerate the margin of victory for the winner, no matter how close the national popular vote is.

Our current system has a significant disincentive built in against third-party or ideological candidates. It forces the various wings of both major parties to come together in the hope of winning the White House. If a potential candidate's support is spread thin throughout the country but not concentrated in any particular states, that person has no incentive to run for president. Without the electoral college, however, ideological candidates with broad but thin support across the nation would have fewer incentives to give up the race and support a less ideologically pure candidate. As the incentives for runner-up and third-party candidates grow under the abolition plans, we have to ask, How low will we go?

Remember that with third-party candidate Ross Perot in the race in 1992, Bill Clinton won the presidency with just 43 percent of the popular vote (but 68 percent of the electoral college vote). Will we be satisfied if our president-elect wins only 40 percent of the national vote? How about 30 percent in a five-person race? Will such a president be accepted as legitimate by the other 70 percent of the people who chose someone else? Will such a president have the political strength to deal with the nation's problems and conduct business with the rest of the world? When pressed, many proponents of the direct popular vote admit that such a scenario is likely to be an unfortunate result, and they combine their proposals with runoff election provisions. But do we really want to add yet another expensive, controversial, lengthy, and lawyered leg to our presidential elections?

SUMMATION

For more than two hundred years, the electoral college has worked reasonably well to produce American presidents. It has helped create balance in our political order. It provides some small protection to rural cultures and interests that otherwise would be neglected because of a combination of urban wealth, urban media, and big-city votes. It protects the American political system from extremes, both left and right. It serves to centralize any legal battles and possible recounts into a few areas, rather than opening up every precinct in the nation to electoral challenges. And, despite contentions to the contrary, it does all of this without violating any basic principles of American government. We cannot expect much more than that, and we should not gamble what we have in chasing after abstract dreams and ideological agendas. As it has for more than two hundred years, the electoral college should continue to serve as the basic counting method of electing our presidents.

NOTES

INTRO

1. Robert A. Dahl, *Pluralist Democracy in the United States: Conflict and Consent* (Chicago, IL: Rand McNally, 1967), 84.
2. Max Farrand, ed., *The Records of the Federal Convention*, 3 vols. (New Haven, CT: Yale University Press, 1911), 2:500.

PRO

1. See George C. Edwards III, *Why the Electoral College Is Bad for America*, 2nd ed. (New Haven, CT: Yale University Press, 2011), Chap. 3.
2. Darshan J. Goux and David A. Hopkins, "The Empirical Implications of Electoral College Reform," *American Politics Research* 36 (November 2008): 860–64.
3. For a discussion of the 1960 election, see Edwards, *Why the Electoral College Is Bad for America*, 48–51.
4. CBS/*New York Times* poll, May 9–12, 2003.

5. Jack Rakove, "The Accidental Electors," *New York Times*, December 19, 2000, A35.

6. See Robert A. Dahl, *How Democratic Is the American Constitution?* (New Haven, CT: Yale University Press, 2001), 50–53, 84.

7. Max Farrand, ed., *The Records of the Federal Convention of 1787*, rev. ed., vol. 1 (New Haven, CT: Yale University Press, 1966), 483.

8. Ibid., 447–49.

9. Max Farrand, ed., *The Records of the Federal Convention of 1787*, rev. ed., vol. 2 (New Haven, CT: Yale University Press, 1966), 403.

10. I have omitted Washington, DC from this analysis; unlike the least populous states, the District of Columbia is not overrepresented in the electoral college.

11. U.S. Department of Agriculture, 2012 Census of Agriculture, vol. 1, chap. 2, table 2. (This census occurs every five years.)

12. Edwards, *Why the Electoral College Is Bad for America*, 101–3.

13. Robert Richie and Andrea Levien, "How the 2012 Presidential Election Has Strengthened the Movement for the National Popular Vote Plan," *Presidential Studies Quarterly* 43 (June 2013): 353–376; Stanley Kelley Jr., "The Presidential Campaign," in *The Presidential Election and Transition, 1960–1961*, ed. Paul T. David (Washington, DC: Brookings Institution, 1961), 70–72; Daron R. Shaw, "The Effect of TV Ads and Candidate Appearances on Statewide Presidential Votes, 1988–96," *American Political Science Review* 93 (June 1999): 359–60; Edwards, *Why the Electoral College Is Bad for America*, 103–9.

14. Edwards, *Why the Electoral College Is Bad for America*, 109–14.

15. Martin Diamond, *The Electoral College and the American Idea of Democracy* (Washington, DC: American Enterprise Institute, 1977), 4.

16. Voter News Service Exit Polls; Gallup News Service, "Candidate Support by Subgroup," news release, November 6, 2000 (based on six-day average, October 31–November 5, 2000).

17. See Eric R. A. N. Smith and Peverill Squire, "Direct Election of the President and the Power of the States," *Western Political Quarterly* 40 (March 1987): 29–44.

18. Goux and Hopkins, "Empirical Implications of Electoral College Reform." See also Daron R. Shaw, *The Race to 270* (Chicago, IL: University of Chicago Press, 2007).

19. Michael Hagen, Richard Johnston, and Kathleen Hall Jamieson, "Effects of the 2000 Presidential Campaign" (paper presented at the annual meeting of the American Political Science Association, August 29–September 1, 2002), 3.

CON

1. Alexander Hamilton, *Federalist* No. 68, in Alexander Hamilton, John Jay, and James Madison, *The Federalist*, ed. George W. Carey and James McClellan (Indianapolis, IN: Liberty Fund, 2001), 351.

2. See George C. Edwards III, *Why the Electoral College Is Bad for America*, 2nd ed. (New Haven, CT: Yale University Press, 2011).

3. The only exceptions to this rule are the states of Maine and Nebraska, which split their electoral college votes among the congressional districts and then give their remaining two votes to the statewide winner. Within the districts, as in congressional races, votes are counted equally, and the elections are run democratically.

4. E. J. Dionne Jr., "Bypassing the Electoral College," *Washington Post*, April 2, 2007, http://www.nationalpopularvote.com/pages/columns/washpost_20070402 .php?vm=r&s=1.

5. Daniel Patrick Moynihan, "The Electoral College and the Uniqueness of America," in *Securing Democracy: Why We Have an Electoral College*, ed. Gary L. Gregg II (Wilmington, DE: ISI Books, 2008), 87–101.

6. See Michael Barone, "The Electoral College and the Future of American Political Parties," in Gregg, *Securing Democracy*, 79–86.

RESOLVED, the Twenty-Second Amendment should be repealed

PRO: David A. Crockett

CON: Michael J. Korzi

Soon after the Constitutional Convention of 1787 was over, James Madison sent a copy of the proposed plan of government to Thomas Jefferson, who was serving as the American minister to France. Jefferson found much to approve in the document, but he complained in a letter to John Adams, the American minister to Great Britain, that "Their President . . . may be reelected for 4. years to 4. years for life. I wish that at the end of the 4. years they had made him for ever ineligible a second time."

The absence of a term limit on the president was not an oversight on the part of the convention. Gouverneur Morris and other delegates were convinced that "the great motive to good behavior" for a president was "the hope of being rewarded with a re-appointment." In *Federalist* No. 72, Alexander Hamilton argued that even a president who was motivated by "ambition," "avarice," or "the love of fame" would do a good job in order to hold on to the office that could fulfill those desires.

As the nation's third president, Jefferson managed to temper his concern about presidential reeligibility enough to seek and win a second term in 1804. But, in 1807, when several state legislatures petitioned him to run for a third time, he demurred, arguing that although a term limit was not "fixed by the Constitution," one should be "supplied by practice." Settling on two terms as the unwritten maximum, Jefferson invoked "the sound precedent" established by the nation's first president, George Washington.

In truth, Washington did not intend to set a precedent when he retired after his second term ended in 1797. But largely because of Jefferson's distortion of Washington's example, the two-term tradition took root in American political practice. For a century and a half, no president actively sought, much less was elected to, a third term. In 1940, however, citing the need to keep an experienced hand in the White House at a time of great international danger, Democrat Franklin D. Roosevelt ran for and was elected to a third term. In 1944, with the United States involved in World War II, he won a fourth time.

Roosevelt's death in 1945 and the election of a Republican Congress in 1946 set the stage for the enactment of the Twenty-second Amendment. The amendment took the recently violated two-term tradition "supplied by practice" and made it something "fixed by the Constitution." The amendment states that "no person shall be elected to the office of the President more than twice." Nor can anyone who succeeds to the presidency with more than two years left on the term be elected more than once.

Since the Twenty-second Amendment took effect in 1951, five presidents have served two terms but been denied the opportunity to seek a third: Dwight D. Eisenhower, Ronald Reagan, Bill Clinton, George W. Bush, and Barack Obama. Most of them would have done so if eligible. Preparing to leave the White House after eight years, Reagan pledged to campaign for repeal of the amendment, but his declining health kept him from doing so.

Polls show continuing support for the Twenty-second Amendment, but David A. Crockett argues that it should be repealed with arguments that the framers of the Constitution would recognize as well as for more contemporary reasons. In his essay opposing the resolution, Michael J. Korzi defends the two-term limit and its place in the Constitution.

PRO: David A. Crockett

> There is an excess of refinement in the idea of disabling the people to continue in office men who had entitled themselves, in their opinion, to approbation and confidence, the advantages of which are at best speculative and equivocal, and are overbalanced by disadvantages far more certain and decisive.
>
> *Federalist* No. 72

Alexander Hamilton was right. Term limits are an undemocratic limitation on the public's ability to reward or punish presidential performance. They do not constrain presidential power, and they may be responsible for weakening it in a second term. Their sole virtue, guarding against the debilitations of age, can be accomplished more effectively by other means. In short, they contribute nothing to the important functions of the American constitutional order and may even detract from some of them.[1]

THE PRESIDENCY IN THE CONSTITUTIONAL ORDER

Before addressing the value of term limits, it is important to remind ourselves about the important functions that the three branches of government perform in the American separation of powers system. Congress is a plural institution designed to represent the people and enact policies in response to the popular will through a complex deliberative process. The federal court system is composed of small bodies of experts who have job security that enables them to interpret the law and protect the rights and liberties of the people. And the presidency is a unitary institution designed to ensure the security and stability of the nation by acting energetically to set goals, respond to crises, and provide for the steady administration of the law.[2]

Any analysis of constitutional features, such as term limits, must begin with a clear understanding of their effect on the offices they target. The architects of the American constitutional order were quite clear about the role of the presidency. According to Hamilton, the president's job consists of "the execution of the laws and the employment of the common strength, either for this purpose or for the common defense."[3] The Constitution charges the president to "take Care that the Laws be faithfully executed." His power to "give to the Congress Information of the State of the Union," to recommend "necessary and expedient" measures, and to veto legislation gives the president an agenda-setting role as well. Finally, the unitary structure of the office—inhabited by just one person—provides the president with such qualities as "decision, activity, secrecy, and dispatch," which constitute "the bulwark of the national security."[4] Indeed, the president's oath of office includes the explicit duty to "preserve, protect, and defend the Constitution of the United States." The framers constructed the presidency so that the office-holder would be particularly effective serving both as a national leader and an executor of the laws passed by Congress.

If term limits strengthen or reinforce these functions and duties of the presidency, they are a positive addition to the Constitution. If they detract from these functions, they are a detriment. If they have no effect on them, they are at best superfluous.

JEFFERSON'S ARGUMENT

Thomas Jefferson provided a philosophical justification for a two-term limit in an 1807 letter to the Vermont legislature in which he outlined two major concerns. First, he articulated the common American fear of excessive executive power, arguing that unlimited reeligibility would cause the presidency to become monarchical and degenerate "into an inheritance." Second, Jefferson expressed concern for the effect of age on the body and the mind, fearing the "decline which advancing years bring on."[5] In short, Jefferson's twin concerns were the potential for tyranny and the health and vitality of the chief executive. Absent term limits, the president's leadership function might be corrupted in monarchical directions, while advancing age might weaken the office if the president no longer had full strength and capacity.

The architects of the Twenty-second Amendment relied primarily on the first of Jefferson's arguments. There was surprisingly little substantive deliberation in Congress on the measure, but Republicans and conservative Democrats, agitated by the "dictatorship" set up by Franklin Roosevelt, referred to Jefferson's fear of executive tyranny.[6] However, the structure of tenure in the three branches of government demonstrates that democratic accountability was not the only goal treasured by the framers. The House of Representatives, with its two-year terms, is the most responsive of federal institutions. Longer terms in the presidency and the Senate enable these institutions to resist popular opinion when necessary, while tenure during good behavior in the judicial branch allows justices to protect the integrity of a limited constitution against encroachments by more popular branches. Forced rotation in office is not a top concern for a branch focused on security and stability.

Having said that, the president's unitary nature makes him distinctly accountable to the people, who know precisely who to credit and blame for good times and bad. Term limits reduce that sense of accountability as the president realizes he no longer has to face the public in a performance evaluation. This point can be exaggerated, for presidents always want to establish a legacy by ensuring the election of a successor from their party, but the very attempt to secure that legacy can run counter to the interests of the heir apparent, who may have his or her own vision of what the incumbent should be doing to help secure his or her election.

Term limits also do nothing to address Jefferson's concern about the office degenerating into an inheritance. Only a few presidents in American history have had the opportunity to set the long-term agenda for the nation by redefining politics for a generation. That is why entire eras are named for Jefferson, Andrew Jackson, Abraham Lincoln, Franklin Roosevelt, and Ronald Reagan. Those who follow in their footsteps are forced to operate in their shadow, their leadership goals constrained by a policy agenda already established.[7] In a metaphorical sense, presidents like Jackson, Roosevelt, and Reagan establish political dynasties, and their partisan heirs then "inherit" a set of issues and definitions that channel their efforts in directions determined by these dynastic leaders. Thus, all Democratic presidents following Roosevelt work to complete the New Deal agenda, and all Republican presidents following Reagan work to complete the Reagan revolution. Although term limits succeed in preventing a genetic dynasty (the Bush presidencies notwithstanding), they do not prevent the establishment of political dynasties that constrain policy options despite rotation in office. President Truman's administration represented a continuation of Roosevelt's just as both Bushes were extensions of Reagan.

Jefferson's concern about age is more interesting, especially in light of Roosevelt's history. It was a Republican-controlled Congress that pushed term limits in a partisan attack against Roosevelt's four straight presidential victories, but it is Roosevelt's own age and debilitated status in his run for his fourth term that raise more questions about protecting energy and vitality in the office. Once Roosevelt broke precedent, it is logical to assume that later presidents would have been more willing to do so absent the Twenty-second Amendment, making health an increasingly important factor in nomination decisions. However, it is not clear that term limits do a better job than media scrutiny in this area. The intense media focus on the president's life includes both public responsibilities and private concerns, including medical issues. Covering everything from routine annual physicals to colonoscopies, it seems unlikely that the press would allow age-related infirmities to go unnoticed. Something like Franklin Roosevelt's deteriorating health in 1944 would never escape attention in the current media climate.

HAMILTON'S ARGUMENT

In *Federalist* No. 72, Alexander Hamilton presents the most powerful case against term limits. In contrast to Jefferson, Hamilton argues that term limits work against all the major objectives of the presidency. And while Hamilton argues against a one-term limit, his argument can be applied to the two-term rule.

First, term limits adversely affect the agenda-setting function of the presidency. All new presidents have an incentive to reverse the policies and change the personnel of their predecessors. Their need to establish their own legacies results in "a disgraceful and ruinous mutability in the administration of the government."[8] Hamilton has no complaint about change engendered by national elections. What he calls "the restraints of public opinion" work to prevent presidents from engaging in misconduct that would damage their reputations and to provide incentives to pursue worthy measures for the public good. Forced change in office, however, may cause presidents to ignore worthy projects, since they will not be around to take credit for them. Whether that motivation is truly lost—presidents are always interested in their legacies—the most common criticism of term limits is that they make presidents instant lame ducks in their second term, thus reducing their power and influence as policy leaders and agenda-setters. We knew well in advance that on January 20 in the years 2001, 2009, and 2017 Presidents Clinton, Bush, and Obama would leave the presidency. It did not take long into their second terms for them to experience a diminished ability to shape the policy agenda. Since 1952, congressional support scores for the president's agenda average 83 percent in the first year of an administration. That contrasts to a score of 61 percent in the first year of a second term and 54 percent by the final year of a two-term presidency.[9] Certainly once presidents hit the six-year mark the political class begins to look forward to the next election, a process that begins two years in advance of the inauguration. With more media attention devoted to the election, the term-limited president has little power to start new projects. Oddly enough, a president is most powerful as an agenda-setter early in his first term, when he is least experienced and knowledgeable. Once he starts his second term, when he has acquired significant knowledge and experience, his political capital only diminishes.[10] This means that as much as 25 percent or more of a two-term presidency is effectively neutered in terms of advancing an ambitious policy agenda.

Second, term limits might prompt a president who lacks the necessary civic virtue to abuse power. Although Hamilton is thinking of illegitimate and tyrannical seizure of power, it is not difficult to see how the constraints of term limits can provoke presidents to act in ways they might otherwise forego if they knew they would have to face the voters again. The modern presidential toolkit includes all sorts of devices, including executive orders, memoranda, and proclamations, in addition to an extensive personal staff that has centralized operational power in the Oval Office, all designed to help the president pursue unilateral policy making. But while the president's four-year term length is designed to protect him from rapidly changing popular opinion, the point of having elections in the first place is to encourage presidents to perform their job well. If a president cannot stand for reelection because of term limits, popular judgment will no longer constrain his behavior. If presidents feel free from the constraints of electoral politics in their second terms, they are free to use executive power for their own purposes—precisely the concern Jefferson warned about when he cautioned *against* multiple terms. It is hardly a desirable thing to have presidents completely free of the constraints of public opinion. Yet, studies show that outgoing presidents issue more executive orders when being replaced by opposite party successors—a unilateral action that runs contrary to the election results.[11] It is also not uncommon for presidents to save more controversial pardons for the lame-duck period of their term. Whether it was George W. Bush spending his reelection capital in a failed effort to revamp social security or Barack Obama choosing to govern more through executive action than the traditional legislative process, second terms seem to give presidents a greater sense of freedom to be adventurous.

Third, term limits rob the nation of the service of the most experienced individuals, all for the sake of mere change. This may be a good thing if the president is not sufficiently vigorous to continue in office—one has only to think of the deteriorating health of Presidents Dwight Eisenhower and Reagan to see why two terms were enough, not to speak of Roosevelt's fourth effort. But more recent two-term presidents have left office relatively young (by political standards), and Bill Clinton departed with very healthy public approval ratings. If the public judged these individuals to be worthy of a third term, why force change where change is neither required nor desired? For partisans, the one salutary effect of term limits is that they force out of office a popular president from the opposing party, giving their preferred party's candidate a shot at an open race. That hardly seems like an exalted purpose for a constitutional provision.

Fourth, in addition to eliminating from consideration the most experienced individuals, term limits may serve to remove them from office during a national emergency, threatening the security of the nation. To be fair, the nation has changed hands before in the middle of wars, to no ill effect. The constraints term limits place on the president's agenda-setting function in the domestic arena seem to dissipate in the national security and foreign policy fields, where the president's power to lead is less encumbered. The question has less to do with whether new presidents can act in times of crisis as it does with forcing change in the middle of a crisis whether the country desires that change or not. Roosevelt played the national security card to justify running for a third term in 1940.[12] And although his reelections to third and fourth terms came by increasingly smaller margins, he continued to win strong victories, and the judgment of history remains satisfied with his wartime leadership. If one is worried about accountability, the experiences of Truman, Lyndon Johnson, and George W. Bush demonstrate that popular disapproval of crisis management will lead to a change in leadership.

Finally, term limits force change in the administration of the law where stability is the preferred quality. No president can do the job alone, and modern presidents have a vast array of bureaucratic tools to assist them. But cabinet chiefs and presidential aides eventually experience burnout and exhaustion. If advisors stay, they may not be as sharp. If they depart, they may not be replaced by equals. It is very common for an administration to witness significant turnover in advisory positions, but term limits exacerbate this dynamic.[13] With sure knowledge that the boss is leaving at a certain point in time, many cabinet members and advisors exit the stage in search of more lucrative employment. Some of this change would unquestionably take place even with presidents seeking third terms, but the prospect of continued service and influence might draw higher quality personnel with a long-term commitment to the president's program, instead of prompting them to jump ship and write their tell-all memoirs or position themselves for the next step on the ladder of success. The certain knowledge that an administration is coming to an end makes it difficult to recruit quality replacements for aides who depart.

CONCLUSION

To summarize, barring a compelling reason it is better to maintain stability and avoid unnecessary change in the administration of laws. It is good to keep experienced people in power and give them an incentive to pursue good works. Such a provision should foster strong leadership and steady administration on the part of the president. By contrast, term limits provide little to the political system. They introduce the element of forced rotation where the original design of the office was biased in favor of stability, assuming competent performance. They hamper the president's agenda-setting function in the second term, prompting presidents to compensate through the use of unilateral executive tools. They allow a president to pay less attention to "the restraints of public opinion," since they know they have won their last victory. Other than a mandated rotation in office, the only thing term limits do is protect the nation from a president whose ambition may prompt him to serve beyond the limits of his physical and mental abilities.

Thus, the Twenty-second Amendment does little for the constitutional system. While it promises to give us the opportunity to redirect our politics through forced rotation in office, larger cyclical forces typically prevent that from happening. Jefferson's fear of dynastic politics has in fact been a constant feature of presidential politics, as far back as his own Virginia dynasty. Term limits are precisely what Hamilton said they were at the end of his argument against them in *Federalist* No. 72—"an excess of refinement." Most importantly, they rob the nation of experienced leaders when the population would prefer to keep them on the job. Driven by partisan animus, they should be removed from the constitutional order.

CON: Michael J. Korzi

The partisan origins of the Twenty-second Amendment unfairly taint its historical reputation. Advanced by Republicans in Congress, albeit with the help of Southern Democrats, the Twenty-second Amendment was enacted in response to the third and fourth terms to which Democratic president Franklin Delano Roosevelt (FDR) was elected in 1940 and 1944. The congressional debates over the proposed amendment in 1947—the amendment was passed by Congress in 1947 and was ratified by the requisite number of states in 1951—reflected the partisan acrimony. Republicans likened Roosevelt's long tenure in office to the dictatorships of Europe, while Democrats came close to canonizing the late president (FDR died in April 1945, early in his fourth term). These partisan motives of the moment, however, should not be allowed to obscure the enduring arguments for the Twenty-second Amendment, arguments that are consistent with a long and wise tradition in the United States of suspicion of executive power. Indeed, FDR's third and fourth terms were wholly inconsistent with American history and tradition, and the Twenty-second Amendment is properly understood as a restoration of a settled understanding of presidential tenure and, by extension, presidential power.

The framers of the Constitution declined to include term limits for either the president or members of Congress. This was a controversial decision, as it had been the practice of the states to limit the terms of their governors and state legislators. Additionally, although there was no presidential office under the Articles of Confederation, federal legislators were also term limited. Most importantly, colonial Americans' rejection of British authority had been specifically directed at the English monarchy. For many critics, a presidency with unlimited reeligibility opened the door for a long-serving executive not unlike the English king. As Thomas Jefferson put it in a letter to James Madison (commenting on the not-yet-ratified Constitution): "Experience concurs with reason in concluding that the first magistrate will always be re-elected if the constitution permits it."[1] For Jefferson and other critics of unlimited reeligibility, the issue was straightforward: The longer an executive stayed in office, the more likely that power would be abused.

In response to those criticizing the lack of a term limit for the new presidential office, Alexander Hamilton defended the convention's decision in *Federalist #72*, making now-classic arguments in favor of "unlimited reeligibility." These include concerns for experienced and emergency leadership, as well as for incentives to good behavior and electoral checks on bad behavior. Most of these arguments are ably articulated and defended by David A. Crockett in his essay. However, those who are suspicious of executive power and wish to limit presidential terms have an even stronger tradition and more powerful arguments on their side.

George Washington is sometimes cited as founding the "two-term tradition," that is, presidents voluntarily stepping down after two terms in office, but it was actually Jefferson who established the two-term tradition as a necessary part of a healthy democracy.[2] As Jefferson explained in 1807, "[b]elieving that a representative government, responsible at short periods of election, is that which produces the greatest sum of happiness to mankind, I feel it a duty to do no act which shall essentially impair that principle." With those words, President Jefferson announced his intention not to seek a third term and thereby founded the two-term tradition.[3] Jefferson had long been a supporter of term limits, or "rotation" as he called it, and there were three main reasons for this support, reasons that remain salient today.

First and foremost was the traditional concern that long executive tenure resulted in the abuse of power. A president who stayed in office beyond his term would naturally grow not only more powerful but also become arrogant and insulated. Such a president could easily become an elective monarch and abuse the powers of the office as well as the rights of the citizens.

Second, Jefferson believed that term limits would help to refresh the political system by mandating a change of leadership. Even if the retiring president and the new president were from the same political party, the new president would promote different ideas, interests, and perspectives. A president who holds power for a long period of time will invariably focus on preserving his power and protecting his policy commitments and the positions of those he has appointed to office. Where supporters of long tenure see stability, Jefferson saw administrative rigidity and inertia.

Finally, Jefferson worried that without term limits a president might serve well beyond what his physical and mental capacities would allow. Jefferson did not mince words. Without a limit, the "danger is that the indulgence and attachments of the people will keep a man in the chair after he becomes a dotard."[4] Even in Jefferson's day, the office of the presidency was a demanding one, and men did not advance to the office until past middle age. In his mind, two terms were more than enough to sap the strength of the president.

Each of these three arguments shows that although Jefferson was a great fan of "the people" and democracy, he did not trust elections to always produce the best leaders. It is not so much that he blamed the people, but, rather, that he realized officeholders, especially presidents, have tremendous powers at their disposal that can enable them to stave off serious challenges and thereby perpetuate themselves in office.

The historical experience of the United States as well as contemporary experiences in other nations suggest the wisdom of Jefferson's position and the limitations of Hamilton's. Despite Hamilton's dire warnings of former presidents roaming the United States like "discontented ghosts,"[5] early American presidents had few qualms about following the two-term tradition, with James Madison, James Monroe, and Andrew Jackson all stepping down willingly after two terms. In fact, reflecting Americans' wariness of executive power, support for a "one-term tradition" developed in the pre-Civil War era. President James Polk, for example, announced early in his first (and only) term that he would not seek reelection. In 1864, Abraham Lincoln became the first president to run for reelection since Martin Van Buren did so in 1840 (Van Buren was unsuccessful), and even amidst a Civil War, there were some who questioned Lincoln's pursuit of a second term. When President Ulysses S. Grant sought a second term in 1872, the Democratic Party (as well as the breakaway Liberal Republican Party) pledged in its platform that "it is imperatively required that no President shall be a candidate for re-election."[6]

Increasingly, though, presidents and their supporters would not only seek second terms but third ones as well. In both 1876 and 1880, Grant's supporters pushed for a third term; supporters of President Grover Cleveland promoted him unsuccessfully for a third term in 1896; Theodore Roosevelt ran unsuccessfully for a third term in 1912; and Woodrow Wilson, though his party foreswore a *second* term for presidents in its 1912 platform, not only won a second term in 1916 but was seriously discussed for a third term in 1920 (prior to his debilitating stroke).[7] The increasing pursuit of a third term corresponded, not coincidentally, with the growing power of the office, in the late nineteenth and early twentieth centuries. As the powers of the office grew, the office became more attractive and presidents more and more reluctant to leave it. One only has to look at the experiences of other nations in the last several decades to witness the enduring link between tenure and power. Over and over we see powerful executives—Venezuela's Hugo Chavez is archetypal—seeking to change their constitutions to allow them to serve beyond their set terms.

This chronology leads us back to FDR, whose shattering of the two-term tradition brought about passage of the Twenty-second Amendment. Opponents of the Twenty-second Amendment often point to FDR's reelection to a *third* term in 1940 to make the case against a term limit. Here was an experienced incumbent leading the nation through an emergency, in this case World War II. No one else, so the argument goes, was better suited to lead the nation during this crisis. What is more, the people themselves decided to vote for a third term, and isn't that proof enough that FDR's pursuit of a third term was born out of necessity and self-sacrifice rather than opportunism and the pursuit of power?

Regard for the national welfare no doubt influenced FDR's third-term decision in 1940, and FDR's leadership during World War II is generally praised by scholars. However, we also know that those within Roosevelt's inner circle were already considering a third term *before* World War II broke out in Europe in order to consolidate the New Deal reforms passed in the first and second terms.[8] What is more, there were complaints within the party leading up to the 1940 election that Roosevelt was orchestrating his own renomination. As the *New York Times* put it, "'The draft' of President Roosevelt for a third nomination . . . was never able to shake off the quotation marks," since it was initiated by "members of the White House inner circle."[9] FDR was not selflessly heeding the call of the voters to serve a third term so much as he and his advisors were creating public demand for his "indispensable" services.

Moreover, it is worth recalling that FDR's second term was characterized by audacious assertions—one might even say abuses—of executive authority, notably his infamous "Court-packing plan," as well as his attempted "purge" of anti-New Dealers from his own party in the 1938 midterm elections. The Court-packing plan, in particular, displayed Roosevelt's growing power and ambition. The plan would have allowed the president to appoint a new Supreme Court Justice for every member of the Court that was then 70 years or older. This plan would have shifted the balance of the Court to a liberal majority that would be expected to ratify Roosevelt's New Deal policies (the Court had previously struck down a number of these policies). Although the plan to increase the size of the Court did not succeed—and, in fact, it was widely criticized, even by Democrats, as executive overreach—it is not hard to see the growth in presidential ambition that even a *second* term brought in the case of FDR.

None of this is to say that Roosevelt did not also provide the United States with strong leadership during the Great Depression and World War II. The debate over term limits is not a simple one, and there are serious arguments against term limits as well as for them. But the point is that even FDR, widely considered to be a great president and public servant, fell into some of the traps associated with long presidential tenure.

Although the perils of long presidential tenure are evident in FDR's second term and his pursuit of a third, it is his fourth term that most clearly reveals the wisdom of a presidential term limit. Although it was not publicly known at the time, FDR was in very poor health for much of his third term.[10] So significant were his health problems that some scholars have questioned whether Roosevelt was up to the demands of the job during the latter stages of his third term. According to one estimate, Roosevelt was so ill during his last year in office that he was only capable of about four hours of work each day.[11] FDR died less than three months after taking the oath of office for the fourth time. That he and his advisors pursued a fourth term in the face of FDR's debilitating health problems suggests either that they only cared about the maintenance of power or that they had become so insulated during their long tenure in office that they could no longer exercise good judgment. Neither explanation bodes well for unlimited reeligibility. Roosevelt may not have been a "dotard" during his last year or more in office, but as Jefferson rightly put it, "no office . . . less admits the indulgence of age."[12]

That the American people were not informed of FDR's health problems casts into serious doubt the idea that elections can fulfill the power-checking function of a term limit when faced with the desire of political elites to hold on to power at all costs. One of FDR's less-heralded predecessors, Calvin Coolidge, shrewdly diagnosed the dynamics of power that could push presidents and their supporters to perpetuate themselves in office, to the detriment of the country. "It is difficult for men in high office," Coolidge wrote, "to avoid the malady of self-delusion. They are always surrounded by worshippers. They are constantly, and for the most part sincerely, assured of their greatness. They live in an artificial atmosphere of adulation and exaltation which sooner or later impairs their judgment. They are in grave danger of becoming careless and arrogant. The chances of having wise and faithful public service are increased by a change in the Presidential office after a moderate length of time."[13] Coolidge's warning is, if anything, even more true today than it was in Roosevelt's time.

Perhaps most problematic about FDR's fourth term is that vice president Harry S. Truman, added to the ticket in 1944 largely for political reasons, was not taken into the confidence of the administration and upon FDR's death in April 1945 was woefully underprepared to assume the burdens of the office. According to Truman biographer David McCullough, Vice President Truman met personally with President Roosevelt only two times, and "neither time was anything of consequence discussed."[14] That Truman acquitted himself well as president—he is now remembered as a "near great" president who expertly navigated the perilous early years of the Cold War—further undermines a key assumption of term limit opponents, namely that a president or leader is indispensable. FDR's supporters assumed that only their man could successfully lead the country through the war and its aftermath. And, yet, a relatively inexperienced Truman, a "mousy little man from Missouri"[15] who was completely unlike the aristocratic and charismatic FDR, rose to the challenges of the office.

In short, although FDR's presidency is often adduced as a key piece of evidence against the wisdom of the Twenty-second Amendment, his tenure in fact provides a powerful argument for keeping the Twenty-second Amendment that wisely restored the two-term tradition. All three of Jefferson's concerns about long executive tenure—abuse of power, administrative inertia, and presidential fatigue—are illustrated by FDR's time in office. His Court-packing plan and attempted "purge" of members of his own party in Congress, not to mention his ostensible orchestration of his own renomination in 1940, suggest that FDR was not immune to the desire to consolidate power that accompanies long executive tenure. Even before war broke out in Europe in 1939, top officials within the Roosevelt administration were planning for a third term in order to consolidate and extend the New Deal, which illustrates the problem of administrative inertia. And by 1944, administration officials were so determined to hold power and consolidate the New Deal that they nominated a "dying president"[16] for a fourth term.

Since the ratification of the Twenty-second Amendment in 1951, five two-term presidents have been prohibited from seeking a third term: Eisenhower, Reagan, Clinton, George W. Bush, and Obama. In the cases of Eisenhower and especially Reagan, the president's advanced age probably would have discouraged a third-term pursuit. If they had sought and won third terms (which is certainly possible, given their popularity), they may not have become "dotards" in office, but the likelihood that they would have had vigorous and successful third terms seems slim. In Reagan's case especially, it is likely that he was in mental decline toward the end of his second term in office; in fact, he was diagnosed with Alzheimer's just five years after leaving office.[17] A third Reagan term could have been disastrous for the country. The jury is still out on

Obama, but in the case of Bush, his unpopularity during the second term would have precluded the pursuit of a third term. Only Clinton was clearly young enough, ambitious enough, and popular enough to have sought and won a third term. Thus, of the ten presidents who have served since the passage of the Twenty-second Amendment (not counting Obama), only three—Eisenhower, Reagan, and Clinton—had a reasonable chance of winning a third term, and only one, Clinton, was relatively young and healthy at the time of the potential third term. In none of these cases would the third term have come at a time of crisis or emergency.

The worry voiced by opponents of the Twenty-second Amendment that we will be denying ourselves a proven leader in a time of crisis seems a rather remote possibility. Crises rarely follow the rhythms of election cycles. Yet again, Jefferson proved prescient on this point. As he put it, commenting on the need to rigorously adhere to the two-term limit: "no pretext should ever be permitted to dispense with [the principle of rotation] because there never will be a time when real difficulties will not exist, and furnish a plausible pretext for dispensation."[18] It is no stretch at all to conclude that, without the Twenty-second Amendment, most presidents after FDR would have been tempted, by their own ambitions and the opportunism or even honest adulation of their supporters, to prove their own indispensability and, like FDR, serve beyond a second term.

Notably, since the passage of the Twenty-second Amendment (and arguably throughout American history), presidential *second* terms have been almost uniformly unsuccessful, prompting scholars to popularize the concept of "second-term blues."[19] One need only call to mind Nixon's resignation, Reagan's Iran-Contra scandal, Clinton's impeachment, and Bush's poor handling of both Hurricane Katrina and the Iraq War, to consider the power of this phenomenon. Indeed, the tendency of second-term presidents to face scandal and disgrace is offered by some as an argument for limiting presidents to *one* term. While examination of the one-term presidency reform would take us too far afield, it is fair to ask why we should even consider third terms when second terms are already so unsuccessful.

None of this is to say that the two-term limit does not bring some problems of its own. Although the "lame duck" effect is surely exaggerated, presidents do become somewhat diminished in power and influence in their second terms, especially in the last two years. This diminished influence is often caused principally by other factors, such as scandal, but knowledge that a president cannot be reelected does cause Washington actors especially to turn their attention to the next would-be presidents. What is more, although the chance is remote, there may come a day when a term-limited president will be forced to step down in the middle of a crisis. But, as political scientist Thomas Cronin has noted, there is no reason why a term-limited ex-president could not be a key advisor in a new administration.[20] And that one man or woman is the only available leader out of well over 200 million voting age Americans not only strains credulity but is inconsistent with the very premises of American democracy.

At the end of the day, then, the Twenty-second Amendment strikes a balance between power and restraint. Presidents are not restricted to just one term and thus have ample time—the better part of a decade—for significant accomplishments and a lasting legacy. And, yet, from the start they know that their time in office will come to an end, and that they are not indispensable. It is a healthy compromise for executive leadership in our democracy.

NOTES

PRO

1. For an interesting set of essays advocating repeal of the Twenty-second Amendment, see *Restoring the Presidency: Reconsidering the Twenty-Second Amendment*, National Legal Center for the Public Interest (Washington, DC, 1990).
2. Jeffrey K. Tulis, *The Rhetorical Presidency* (Princeton, NJ: Princeton University Press, 1987), 41–45.
3. Alexander Hamilton, James Madison, and John Jay, *The Federalist Papers*, ed. Clinton Rossiter (New York, NY: Mentor, 1999), 418.
4. Ibid., 391–395.
5. Thomas Jefferson, "Letter to the Vermont Legislature," in *The Evolving Presidency*, 2nd ed., ed. Michael Nelson (Washington, DC: Congressional Quarterly Press, 2004), 64.
6. David E. Kyvig, *Explicit and Authentic Acts: Amending the U.S. Constitution, 1776-1995* (Lawrence: University Press of Kansas, 1996), 327–334.
7. For the metaphor of a shadow, see William E. Leuchtenburg, *In the Shadow of FDR: From Harry Truman to Ronald Reagan* (Ithaca, NY: Cornell University Press, 1983). The classic work on presidential regimes is Stephen Skowronek, *The Politics Presidents Make: Leadership from John Adams to George Bush* (Cambridge, MA: Harvard University Press, 1993).
8. Hamilton et al., *The Federalist Papers*, 404.
9. *Congressional Quarterly Weekly Report*, various editions.
10. Paul C. Light, *The President's Agenda: Domestic Policy Choice from Kennedy to Reagan*, rev. ed. (Baltimore, MD: Johns Hopkins University Press, 1991), 36–39.
11. Kenneth R. Mayer, *With the Stroke of a Pen: Executive Orders and Presidential Power* (Princeton, NJ: Princeton University Press, 2001), 96–97.
12. Herbert S. Parmet and Marie B. Hecht, *Never Again: A President Runs for a Third Term* (New York, NY: MacMillian, 1968), 174–177.

13. Michael B. Grossman, Martha Joynt Kumar, and Francis E. Rourke, "Second-Term Presidencies: The Aging of Administrations," in *The Presidency and the Political System*, 6th ed., ed. Michael Nelson (Washington, DC: Congressional Quarterly Press, 2000), 227–231; John C. Fortier and Norman J. Ornstein, "Introduction," in *Second-Term Blues: How George W. Bush has Governed*, eds. John C. Fortier and Norman Ornstein (Washington, DC: Brookings/American Enterprise Institute, 2007), 2–4.

CON

1. *The Portable Thomas Jefferson*, Merrill D. Peterson, ed. (New York, NY: Penguin, 1975), 430.
2. Although he did step down from the presidency after serving two terms, Washington did so for personal more than principled reasons, even intimating in his famous "Farewell Address" that he would have served a third term had the state of the nation been unsettled.
3. "Thomas Jefferson to the Legislature of Vermont, December 10, 1807," in *The Writings of Thomas Jefferson*, ed. Andrew A. Lipscomb and Albert Ellery Bergh, Vol. XVI (Washington, DC: Thomas Jefferson Memorial Association, 1905), 293.
4. "Thomas Jefferson to John Taylor, January 6, 1805," in *The Writings of Thomas Jefferson*, XI, 57.
5. "Federalist #72," in *The Federalist Papers* (New York, NY: Oxford University Press, 2008), 357.
6. Democratic Party Platforms: Gerhard Peters and John T. Woolley, "Democratic Party Platform of 1872," July 9, 1872, *The American Presidency Project*, accessed September, 23, 2015, http://www.presidency.ucsb.edu/ws/?pid=29580.
7. Prior to Wilson's death in February 1924, some supporters were talking about a third-term run in the upcoming election.
8. See "Third Term Move Possible, Ickes Says," *New York Times*, October 20, 1938.
9. Arthur Krock, "'Draft' of Roosevelt is Traced to Inner Circle of the New Deal," *New York Times*, July 18, 1940.
10. See, for instance, Hugh E. Evans, *The Hidden Campaign: FDR's Health and the 1944 Election* (Armonk, NY: M. E. Sharpe, 2002).
11. Robert H. Ferrell, *The Dying President: Franklin D. Roosevelt, 1944-1945* (Columbia: University of Missouri Press, 1998), 4.
12. "Thomas Jefferson to Citizens of Philadelphia, February 3, 1809," in *The Writings of Thomas Jefferson*, XVI, 329.
13. Calvin Coolidge, *Autobiography of Calvin Coolidge* (New York, NY: Cosmopolitan, 1929), 241.
14. David McCullough, *Truman* (New York, NY: Simon & Schuster, 1992), 339.
15. This characterization was made by *Time* magazine, quoted in McCullough, *Truman*, 320.
16. The phrase comes from Ferrell, *The Dying President*.

17. Although there is debate among scholars, pundits, and even Reagan family members as to whether Reagan was in the early stages of Alzheimer's disease in his second term, most would agree that he was losing his sharpness and vitality as the second term wore on, whether due to normal aging or Alzheimer's. Interestingly, new research studying Reagan's presidential speeches suggests that he did develop Alzheimer's disease while in office. See Lawrence K. Altman, "Parsing Ronald Reagan's Words for Early Signs of Alzheimer's," *New York Times*, March 30, 2015.

18. "Thomas Jefferson to Henry Guest, January 4, 1809," in *The Writings of Thomas Jefferson*, XII, 224.

19. See, among others, John Fortier and Norman Ornstein, *Second-Term Blues: How George W. Bush Has Governed*, eds. John C. Fortier and Norman J. Ornstein (Washington, DC: Brookings Institution Press, 2007).

20. Thomas E. Cronin, "Two Cheers for the Twenty-second Amendment," *Christian Science Monitor*, 23 February, 1987.

18

RESOLVED, bring back the bureaucrats

PRO: John DiIulio

CON: Brad DeWees

Let's play an association game—not word association (we say *sun*, you say *hot*) but picture association. What picture comes to mind when we say . . .

President. The White House? Mount Rushmore? The coins and bills in your pocket? The current president of the United States?

Now . . . *Congress.* The Capitol building? C-span? Frock-coated legislators from long ago such as Daniel Webster or Henry Clay? Your own representative or senators?

The Supreme Court. An ornate courtroom? The Court's majestic building in Washington? Distinguished-looking men and women in long black robes?

One more: *bureaucracy.*

Not too many pictures form in your mind when you hear that one, we would guess (although a color might: gray). So let's try words instead.

If you're in any way a typical American, the words you associate with *bureaucracy* aren't positive. What's interesting is the different ways in which prevailing connotations of that word are negative.

Compare these two lists:

First: timid, indecisive, flabby, overpaid, lazy, slow to accept new ideas, reluctant to abandon approaches that don't work, impersonal, red tape.

Second: meddlesome, arrogant, condescending, intrusive, empire builders, social engineers, a self-anointed power elite.

It may be that all of these words ring true. They are certainly all harshly critical. But the words on the first list add up to an image of a bureaucracy that is inert. The words on the second list add up to an image of bureaucracy as hyperactive.

One of the great things about political science is that it takes important but highly abstract components of government and politics and brings them down from the level of impressions to the level of understanding. Bureaucracy, as political scientists who study American national government understand it, is the constellation of large, complex organizations that constitute most of the executive branch. Its purpose is to carry out the nation's laws and spend the money in the federal budget. In Washington, that means organizations such as the Department of State, the Department of Defense, the Department of Education, the Central Intelligence Agency, and the Environmental Protection Agency.

Together these departments and agencies oversee the spending of about $4 trillion each year, a much higher federal budget than existed fifty years ago even if you adjust that figure for inflation. Yet, the number of federal civilian employees has remained roughly the same over the past half century: about 2 million. How has this static work force handled the increasing volume of business? By outsourcing the work to state and local governments, private businesses, and various nonprofit organizations.

John Dilulio calls this new form of big government "Leviathan by proxy" and argues that we would do better to "bring back the bureaucrats"—that is, hire more federal civil servants and have them do more of the work of the government themselves. In contrast, Brad DeWees maintains that if we want "an innovative government, there is no practical alternative to government by proxy" because "the very nature of government bureaucracy is inherently resistant to change."

PRO: John DiIulio

We all know that the federal government has gotten a lot bigger in the past half century. In 2013, Washington spent more than $3.5 trillion. Adjusted for inflation, that was five times what it spent in 1960. This expansion in federal spending was accompanied by an expansion of the federal bureaucracy. Dozens of bureaucratic agencies created after 1960, including the Environmental Protection Agency (1970) and the Department of Homeland Security (2002), dot the federal landscape today. And during the last fifty years, the total number of pages in the Federal Register, which catalogues federal government policies, programs, and regulations, has increased about fourfold (to more than 80,000 pages).

And yet the number of federal civilian workers (excluding postal workers) has barely budged. When George W. Bush became president in 2001, the executive branch employed about 1.8 million civilians, about the same as when John F. Kennedy won the White House. There were in fact more federal bureaucrats (about 2.2 million) when Ronald Reagan won reelection in 1984 than when Barack Obama was elected in 2008 (about 2 million).

How is this possible, when Washington is doing so much more and spending so much more than it was a half century ago?

The answer is that "big government" in America has become a Leviathan by proxy, in which an expanding mass of state and local government workers, for-profit contractors, and nonprofit grant recipients administers a vast portion of federal money and responsibilities.

Members of Congress and blue-ribbon panels calling for cuts in the federal workforce are missing the real problem. We don't need fewer federal workers; we need more of them—a lot more. More direct public administration would result in better, smarter, more accountable government.

Right now, that administration is too diffuse. Look first at the states, where the federal government spends more than $600 billion per year on more than 200 grant programs for state and local governments, a 10-fold increase, in constant dollars, since 1960. And while the post-1960 federal civilian workforce has remained steady, the state and local government workforce has roughly tripled to more than 18 million. Many state workers function as de facto federal bureaucrats. For instance, the largest single item in most state budgets is the federal-state Medicaid program, and Washington covers about half of that program's administrative costs. And more than 90 percent of EPA programs are administered by state and local agencies that together employ many times the EPA's workforce of less than 20,000.

The federal government also spends more than $500 billion a year on contracts with for-profit firms. The Pentagon alone obligates more than $300 billion each year to private contractors, much of it through more than 100,000 single-bid contracts. The contractors do everything from design and deliver major weapons systems to supply on-the-ground security forces. The Defense Department has roughly 800,000 civilian workers—plus the equivalent of about 700,000 full-time contract employees. In 2010, the Department of Homeland Security had more contract employees (about 200,000) than federal bureaucrats (about 188,000). And the Energy Department spends about 90 percent of its annual budget on private contractors, who handle everything from radioactive-waste disposal to energy production.

Even less well understood than the military-industrial complex is the entitlement-nonprofit complex. The nonprofit sector has grown to encompass about 1.6 million organizations registered with the Internal Revenue Service, plus thousands more tax-exempt groups that are not required to register. The registered nonprofits have about $2 trillion in annual revenue. Roughly a third of that money comes from government grants, along with fees from the government for services and goods.

These three players—state and local governments, contractors, nonprofits—are often involved simultaneously in large federal programs. For instance, the American Recovery and Reinvestment Act of 2009 was a roughly $800 billion "stimulus bill" that dedicated about $250 billion to 80,000 federal grants, contracts, or loans to state and local governments, for-profit businesses, and nonprofit groups.

America's Leviathan by proxy consumes as large a share of the nation's gross domestic product (more than a third) as many supposedly more statist European governments do. What is distinctive about big government or "the state" in America is not how much it spends or borrows but how the nation's policies, programs, and regulations are administered. Most European democracies restrict "outsourcing" far more than the United States does. For example, German law dictates that all persons involved in administering national policies must be directly supervised by a government official."

We now have a government that cannot predictably, reliably, and cost-effectively do what our laws dictate that it must—whether cleaning up toxic-waste sites, collecting income taxes, supplying eligible low-income children with meals in the summer, or getting major weapons systems delivered on time and within budget.

In the United States, Medicare and Medicaid account for about a fifth of the federal budget, and each program has more than 50 million beneficiaries, yet each is "run" by a tiny Department of Health and Human Services (HHS) unit, the Centers for Medicare and Medicaid Services, which has fewer than 5,000 federal employees. As Donald Kettl has observed, Washington "does not so much run" Medicare and Medicaid "as leverage them."

When Kettl's own late mother-in-law ended up in a nursing home with multiple medical maladies, Medicare and Medicaid paid all her bills. During the two years before she died, she saw or spoke to doctors, nurses, ambulance drivers, pharmacists, health aids, hospital administrators, bill processing agents, and myriad other persons, but "she never met a single government employee. Not one." Throughout those two years of taxpayer-financed care, Kettle noted, "no one was in charge." Her experience typifies "the paradox of government service payment without government service provision" and its "corollary of government spending without government control of the decisions that shape the costs and the quality" of the care and service supplied.

Leviathan by proxy has had its well-publicized implosions. Just over the past decade, we've witnessed the Federal Emergency Management Agency's failed response in 2005 to Hurricane Katrina, which hit when FEMA had only about 2,100 permanent, full-time employees and had recently lost many senior managers. And the 2013 launch of the Obamacare health insurance exchanges, which involved scores of contractors and was overseen by a federal center with fewer than 5,000 employees. And the recent scandal at Veterans Affairs hospitals, whose "contract officer's representatives" are too few to properly monitor what the small armies of contractors at VA medical centers do.

Beyond such well-publicized meltdowns, the Leviathan by proxy routinely courts administrative debacles on chores as distinct as handling plutonium or regulating the use of pesticides. Worse, with little regard for performance or results, Washington's proxies lobby for federal policies, programs, and regulations that they are paid to administer. The proxies rarely lose, which is a big reason government never stops growing.

For instance, in 2011, during a threatened government shutdown, the bipartisan congressional "supercommittee" made noises about finding ways to trim the federal budget. In response, proxy-government providers within and across every federal government policy domain were on high alert and went more public than usual. Speaking at the National Press Club, the president and CEO of the Aerospace Industry Association noted that the "industry supports 2.9 million jobs across all 50 states" and urged federal lawmakers to "consider whether eliminating hundreds of thousands of jobs over the next decade is at all consistent with the national imperative to create jobs." Echoing that plea, Independent Sector, an umbrella organization that advocates for hundreds of nonprofit leaders, urged its members to remind Congressmen that "our sector is a powerful engine that employs 13 million workers."

Big government masquerading as state or local government, private enterprise, or civil society is still big government. And privatization that involves "acquisition workforce" bureaucrats contracting out work to entrenched interests is not really privatizing. The growth of this form of big government is harder to constrain, and its performance ills are harder to diagnose and fix than they would be in a big government more directly administered by an adequate number of well-trained federal bureaucrats.

Today's federal civil service is not bloated—it is overloaded. We have too few federal bureaucrats monitoring too many grants and contracts and handling too many dollars. Many federal agencies are in crying need of more workers.

Take, for instance, the Social Security Administration (SSA), which administers three main programs: Old Age and Survivors Insurance, Disability Insurance, and Supplemental Security Income. The SSA pays for states' Disability Determination Services (DDS) agencies. The SSA has more than 80,000 state (DDS and other) and federal employees in about 1,700 facilities nationwide (regional offices, field offices, processing centers, hearing offices, Appeals Council, and more). Each day, about 1,800 people visit SSA offices in person, and more than 450,000 call SSA offices.

By 2025, the number of Social Security beneficiaries will exceed 85 million, and the Social Security Administration will disburse nearly $1.8 trillion a year. But the SSA projects that it could lose nearly a third of its workforce by 2020, when some 7,000 headquarters workers and 24,000 field employees become eligible for retirement. Unfortunately, in recent years, because of a congressionally mandated hiring freeze, the SSA has been unable to fill positions left open by employee retirements.

Thus, the SSA's workload is increasing, but its workforce is decreasing. It is clear that "without a sufficient number of skilled employees, backlogs and wait times could significantly increase and improper payments could grow." The short-staffed SSA has already experienced security breakdowns in its computer systems and networks. You need not be a human resources expert or a personnel management guru to guess why "low morale and a feeling of being stretched too thin are hastening retirement among those who are eligible."

SSA is at least popular with both politicians and the public. Not so with the Internal Revenue Service (IRS). In part for that reason, for more than two decades now, Congress and successive presidents have ignored report after report documenting how the IRS's workforce was gradually imploding beneath the weight of nonstop increases in its workload.

Between 1992 and 2001, the IRS lost 16 percent of its fulltime workforce, and major administrative problems erupted. However, calls to bolster the agency's "human capital" were either ignored or lampooned on Capitol Hill. Nothing much changed in the 2000s. In 2011 and 2012, the IRS lost about 10,000 more full-time employees even while the tax code continued to grow in size and complexity.

Short-staffing the IRS must take the prize as the last half century's single most pennywise but pound-foolish federal workforce policy. For several decades now, billions of dollars owed in federal taxes have gone uncollected each year. In 2006, the "tax gap" was $450 billion, three times in constant 2006 dollars what it had been in 1973. This tax gap problem has grown worse as the IRS has become ever more short-staffed both in absolute terms and relative to the size and complexity of its duties.

Donald F. Kettl, the great public administration scholar at the University of Maryland, has been warning about these distortions of America's government for a quarter century. He argues that progressively fewer federal bureaucrats have been progressively more responsible not for managing government programs but for managing proxies who manage programs on the government's behalf.

So how can we both shrink and improve our Leviathan by proxy? It may be that the only practical way is to slowly cut funding for the nonessential proxies and rely more on full-time federal civil servants to directly administer federal policies, programs, and regulations. Paradoxical though it may sound, more federal bureaucrats means less big government, and more direct public administration means better government.

A 2011 report by the National Academy of Public Administration and the Kettering Foundation concluded that programs operated by civil servants receive "significantly higher" scores for management and effectiveness than those run by "grant- and contract-based third parties." Efforts like the one underway at the Department of Transportation to reduce the number of information-technology contractors, for example, are promising. Over time, hiring more federal workers while pruning proxies will not only reduce the size of government but will produce a federal government less beset by grant-seeking and contract-mongering special interests, one that is more faithfully executed by the executive branch, and one that is less bungled by Congress and its dozens of dysfunctional administrative oversight committees and subcommittees.

Of course, there are many steps on this path. We need to reinvent federal grants-in-aid to states, drain the federal for-profit contracting swamps, and wring more public value from grants to nonprofits. But we also need to hire more federal bureaucrats and do a far better job of training, equipping, and—not least—respecting them.

How many more federal bureaucrats are needed? Here's a rough measure: In 1965, the ratio of full-time federal civil servants (1.9 million) to the total U.S. population (193 million) was about 1 to 100. In 2013, with a civilian workforce of 2.1 million and a U.S. population of 316 million, that ratio was about 1 to 150. The Census Bureau estimates that the nation's population by 2035 will be about 370 million.

If the federal workforce grew back to its 1965 ratio, then by 2035 it would need to have 3.7 million employees. If, instead, the federal workforce merely maintained its 2013 ratio, then by 2035 it would have about 2.5 million workers. The midpoint would land the federal personnel roster at about 3 million by 2035, with roughly 1 federal bureaucrat for every 125 citizens.

Crude as it is, that calculation is probably in the ballpark of what's needed: 1 million more full-time federal civilian workers by 2035. Looking at present and potential personnel needs agency by agency, it is hard to imagine doing with fewer federal bureaucrats by then, not unless we intend to have each worker managing still more tasks, more money, and more proxies.

As Table 18.1 makes plain, the number of federal bureaucrats varies among and between cabinet departments and independent agencies. But regardless of their respective workforce totals, some federal departments and agencies need a bigger workforce just to begin to catch up to a workload that has grown bigger over the decades, and others need more or accelerated hires to cope with new duties or larger citizen-client populations that are already mounting or definitely coming. And almost all need more people to more effectively monitor, manage, and measure the performance of their proxies. The expansion in federal hiring would be most efficacious if it were to be front-loaded so that more than half of the increase occurred over the next decade, starting with the Social Security Administration. And help-wanted signs should be hung out now for the assorted units within federal agencies that specialize in contract planning, awarding, and overseeing.

The way to restore limited government is to roll back leveraged government. Of course, even if we hire and train 1 million more federal bureaucrats over the next two decades, Big Brother will still be outsourcing more than it did a half century ago. The Leviathan by proxy is here to stay. But it can be tamed, trimmed, and improved. It is past time for we the people to understand it—and to accept our collective responsibility for it.

Table 18.1

Number of Federal Civilian Employees,* 2010

Defense	772,000
Veterans Affairs	313,000
Homeland Security	191,000
Justice	118,000
Treasury	113,000
Agriculture	98,000
Health and Human Services	84,000
Interior	72,000
Social Security Administration	70,000
Independent Agencies**	68,000**
Transportation	58,000
Commerce	45,000
Environmental Protection Agency	19,000
NASA	19,000
Energy	17,000
Labor	17,000
General Services Administration	13,000
State	12,000
Housing and Urban Development	10,000
Education	5,000
TOTAL	**2.1 million**

Source: Adapted from Curtis W. Copeland, *The Federal Workforce: Characteristics and Trends* (Washington, DC: Congressional Research Service, April 19, 2011), 6, Table 4, reporting data from OPM's FedScope database.

*Rounded to nearest 1,000.

**All excluding SSA, EPA, NASA, and GSA, each of which is listed here separately.

CON: Brad DeWees

On April 23, 2015, Secretary of Defense Ash Carter traveled to Stanford University, just outside Silicon Valley, to deliver a speech that he hoped would eventually change the way the Department of Defense (DOD) operates.[1]

Speaking on behalf of the single biggest bureaucracy in the U.S. Government, his message was simple: Silicon Valley understands how to innovate, and the DOD needs to learn from it. The DOD, like all other components of government bureaucracy, exists in a rapidly changing world. If it does not learn how to adapt itself, the world will leave it behind.

To this end, Secretary Carter announced the formation of a cutting edge office to pioneer the DOD's innovation efforts. It would be called "Defense Innovation Unit X" (DIUx), and its mandate would be to forge closer ties with Silicon Valley and "import" lessons on innovation from the Valley's entrepreneurs. Though he did not know it, Secretary Carter was creating an interesting test case for this debate.

John Dilulio argues that the government should "bring back the bureaucrats" rather than rely on outsiders to execute government—which he calls "Leviathan by proxy," or "Lev-pro." Secretary Carter argued for just this when setting up DIUx. The crucial work of innovation should be done "in-house" by the DOD's professionals, specifically the professionals in DIUx. Bureaucrats would be the men and women to lead the change. (Just to be clear, active duty military are comparable to other federal bureaucrats when not involved in a wartime or combat situation.) To be sure, Secretary Carter does not want the DOD to start its own Googles, Amazons, or Facebooks. But he does want DOD professionals to learn to adapt to their environment in the same rapid manner as the entrepreneurs of Silicon Valley. As a specific example, Secretary Carter cited the need for the DOD to protect civilian infrastructure from cyber-attacks, like the one launched against Sony Pictures prior to the release of *The Interview*.[2] Defending the U.S. civilian infrastructure would entail a massive overhaul of how the DOD is organized, how it hires experts in the field of cyber defense, and how the DOD works with nonmilitary entities whose data are at risk. Secretary Carter admitted that the DOD was not yet capable of this, hence the need for an office that could teach the DOD to learn to adapt from the inside.

After making his case and laying out this vision for a more adaptable DOD, Secretary Carter left Silicon Valley. All that remained to be done was for the bureaucracy to follow through and put his vision into practice. The rest of the story will test whether "Bringing Back the Bureaucrats" is a *feasible* option for improving government, however theoretically sound the advice may appear.

In evaluating Carter's proposal, the first step is to define what "improving government" means. In the twenty-first century, an improved government is more capable of adapting to rapidly changing circumstances. In the case of the Sony cyber-attack, improved government would have been the ability to adapt to "cyber-crime"—a tactic that was difficult to imagine just two decades ago. Rapid change is not just a problem for defense officials or law enforcement. In education, the environment, the world economy, and healthcare, "improvement" and "ability to innovate" should be synonymous.

Given the need for an innovative government, there is no practical alternative to government by proxy short of completely reforming bureaucracy, and such reform is highly unlikely for the time being (though not unprecedented, as discussed below). As the story of DIUx shows, the very nature of government bureaucracy is inherently resistant to rapid change.

After Secretary Carter announced DIUx in April 2015, work turned to staffing the unit. Yet, it was nearly three months before the new unit had a commander. As of this writing in September 2015, the unit still is not fully staffed or resourced. Compared to the entrepreneurial speed of Silicon Valley, where hiring decisions can be made on the spot, this was an abysmal start. Yet, it was predictable. The personnel decisions for the unit had to be staffed through agencies divided among all the branches of the military. Personnel officers—rough equivalents to human resource managers in the private sector—had to make decisions based on predefined career paths, and serving in a new innovation unit did not fit a predefined career path. The result was a unit largely in name only.

As the head of the DOD, why did Secretary Carter not just order the change to happen faster? He could have, were he to devote daily attention to setting up the office. But with military operations ongoing in Afghanistan, Iraq, and other parts of the Middle East, along with Iranian nuclear negotiations and a host of other issues, asking Secretary Carter to devote attention to a single unit was implausible. Instead, he was forced to rely on the bureaucracy beneath him to carry out his orders. Despite the vision from the top, the DOD could only be as innovative as its bureaucratic structure would allow. This structure is characterized by *hierarchy,* a narrow definition of personnel *merit,* and decision-making based on *standard operating procedures.* Each category is explored below.

HIERARCHY

By a hierarchy, I mean that bureaucrats operate in a chain of command. Whether civilian or military, a bureaucrat has several levels of supervisors above him or her. The pay scale of the federal civilian workforce reflects this: There are 15 grades in the federal "General Schedule" for federal civilian employees; within each of those grades there are 10 steps. Above this are still more layers of the Senior Executive Service (SES), which also has its own steps, and above the SES is presidentially appointed political leadership. Though some grades in the scale are infrequently used, the system is conducive to interminable layering from top to bottom.* Most of the functions of a chain of command are benign: A chain helps to organize people into small groups, allows for direct supervision, and implies a sense of order. But one consequence of a chain of command is almost entirely negative: Layers of hierarchy allow for the diffusion of responsibility. As more layers accumulate between the street-level employees who do the work of government and the highest levels of leadership, it becomes more difficult to pinpoint who is responsible for the work that is done (or not done).

In the setup of DIUx, Secretary Carter was too many layers removed from the new unit to directly affect its setup. The personnel officers who would decide how to staff the unit were responsible for thousands of other personnel assignments in addition to DIUx. The result was that unfilled positions within the DOD's unit for innovation waited in line with all the other positions to be filled.

The challenge of staffing DIUx is a miniature version of the bureaucratic problem of coordination, which is simply aligning the efforts of multiple people or agencies. According to bureaucracy scholar Don Kettl, failure to coordinate is one of bureaucracy's "most persistent" shortcomings.[3] Because individuals within a bureaucracy prefer autonomy to supervision in performing their work, and because multiple layers in the hierarchy make it difficult to mandate unity of effort, coordination runs against the grain of bureaucracy.

An example of poor coordination was the federal government's response to Hurricane Katrina in late 2005. In August of that year, Hurricane Katrina made landfall to the east of New Orleans. The storm had recently been downgraded from a category 5, but the hurricane itself was not the primary threat. Flooding overwhelmed the city as rain and wind destroyed the levees protecting New Orleans. Eventually, 80 percent of the city was under water, and local government was nonexistent; government officials could not phone the outside world for two days.[4]

The Federal Emergency Management Agency (FEMA) was in charge of the federal government's response. It was not caught completely off guard by the storm: The Agency's Director, Mike Brown, had said before the storm that he believed Katrina could be "a catastrophe within a catastrophe."[5] Still, FEMA was not able to respond once the storm hit. Though the agency had enough resources to deliver food and water after the flooding, the challenge of coordinating the requisite local, state, and federal agencies proved too difficult to adequately respond in a timely way to the need in New Orleans. FEMA initially had trouble making contact with local officials; it did not coordinate with the DOD to move food supplies from military warehouses into the area; and

---

*The military uses ranks rather than grades, but the layering effect is the same.

though the Department of Transportation offered to help with logistics, FEMA did not give it the opportunity. The result was a tragedy for the people of New Orleans and an embarrassment for the federal government. Over 1,700 people were killed and hundreds of thousands were forced to flee their homes.[6]

Though Hurricane Katrina was an extreme environmental disaster, the story of the federal government's response to Katrina is mundane. FEMA's response is a macroscale of the story of staffing DIUx. Coordination across staff agencies or hierarchical levels is by nature difficult for bureaucracy. Short of direct and sustained involvement by top leadership, agencies tend to work autonomously. Coordination is lumbering at best, impeding the bureaucracy's ability to respond quickly to changing circumstances.

MERIT

While hierarchy and the problem of coordination affect a bureaucracy's short-term response time to a crisis or demand for reform from the top, an arguably more important factor affects bureaucracy's long-term ability to adapt. How qualified and talented are its personnel? What is "merit" in the context of government bureaucracy?

For much of the country's history, federal jobs were distributed based on political favors or personal connections. This was referred to as the "spoils system." Reform eventually led to the "merit system," which means that bureaucrats are hired for their talent and job qualifications rather than their political connections.

The merit system still characterizes how bureaucrats are hired—with a couple of caveats. First, hiring someone based on "merit" is not the same as hiring the best. In 2014, the *Washington Post* reported that millennials were rejecting the federal workforce in favor of employment in the private and non-profit sectors. Turned off by the pay and hiring freezes triggered by government shutdowns and sequestration, the newest generation was turning elsewhere for fulfilling work. As a result, the share of the federal workforce under age 30 dropped to a meager 7 percent, its lowest in over a decade.[7] In contrast, about 25 percent of the overall American workforce is under 30. As the government loses the "war for talent" among workers under 30, how meritorious will its workforce be even a decade from now?

Perhaps more important, though, is how the federal government develops the merit that it initially hires. The decisions of who to retain and develop, and how to do so, shape the caliber of the government workforce as much as the initial decision of whom to hire. On this measure of employee development, the federal government's track record is poor. A 2009 survey found that federal employees thought the government did a consistently worse job of providing opportunities for improvement than did employees in the private sector. Only 30 percent of federal employees at all levels thought that the government did a good job of managing talent, and only 42 percent felt that the federal government did a good job of offering engaging work opportunities. Both numbers were much lower than the same responses given in the private sector.[8] These low scores translate into a difficulty in retaining talented employees. This is nowhere more true than in DOD.

For example, a 2010 report by the Strategic Studies Institute of the Army War College found that "prospects for the Officer Corps' future have been darkened by . . . plummeting company-grade officer [young, 25-30 years-old] retention rates." The reported reasons for the drop in retention did not name deployments to the wars in Iraq and Afghanistan as the main reasons for lower retention rates. Instead, the problem was a "deeply anti-entrepreneurial" personnel management system.[9] In a survey of Army officers still on active duty, economist Tim Kane found that 93 percent "believed that half or more of 'the best officers leave the military early rather than serving a full career.'"[10] Military officers and civilian employee personnel management are driven out by the same critical flaw: Entrepreneurial leadership is not valued. Instead, it is frowned upon by the personnel management system.

Rather than describe bureaucrats as merit based, a better description would be that bureaucrats are *initially* hired for other than political reasons, but the importance of merit quickly diminishes over time and is replaced by a predilection to maintain the status quo. If improvement in government is equivalent to the ability to adapt, maintaining the status quo cannot be a good definition of improvement.

STANDARD OPERATING PROCEDURES (SOPS)

The hiring and promotion practices of government bureaucrats directly affect how they do their work. Bureaucracies are routinized, which is to say that bureaucrats follow standard operating procedures (SOPs) when accomplishing tasks. The government bureaucracies of today came of age when the "task environment"—what workers did on a daily basis—was simple and unchanging. In this environment, operation by SOPs could be efficient.[11] But we no longer live in a world requiring tasks that are simple and unchanging. The medical world is a good example.

The recent bestseller *Being Mortal: Medicine and What Matters in the End*, by Dr. Atul Gawande, discusses how the medical advances of just the past 20 years have upended how our society thinks about end-of-life medical care.

Options for prolonging life, though not necessarily increasing life's quality, have become mainstream in American medicine.[12] Should a son or daughter opt for treatment that will prolong the life of a parent that is suffering? At what cost? This balancing process, fraught with some of the most ethically difficult questions that humanity faces, is the "task environment" of a Medicare actuary. This balancing process is the work of the federal bureaucracy, but the environment is far from simple and reproducible.

The environment in which DIUx will find itself is also changing at a rapid pace. DIUx was set up in part as a response to the threat of cyber-attack, a tactic that did not exist when most current military leaders joined the service. In both cases—end-of-life care and adapting to the threat of cyber-crime—bureaucrats are faced with a rapidly changing world. Many of the challenges they face today did not exist a decade ago; the same will likely be true a decade from now. In this debate over the future of bureaucracy, the measure of success should be whether the government will be capable of rapidly adapting to future changes. An organization's ability to adapt lies in its structure, and government bureaucracy's current structure stifles adaptation. Bringing back the bureaucrats to the same structure will only exacerbate the problem.

INNOVATION AND "TASK ENVIRONMENT"

Bureaucracy's "task environment" must be reformed to describe a process for innovation. In a work recently published in the *Stanford Social Innovation Review*, Clayton Christensen, author of *The Innovator's Dilemma*, concluded that a few tasks in particular make government innovation more likely: a platform for regular experimentation, a means of regular feedback from end users to government employees, and employee ownership of and responsibility for their performance and budget.[13] Using DIUx as an example, this would mean that the commander in charge of the unit would have control over whom to hire and how to spend the unit's money, rather than rely on the personnel and budget agencies of the different military services. The unit would also offer a "platform for experimentation," which in practical terms means a space in which operations could be tested without regard for current SOPs.

Increasing bureaucratic autonomy over hiring practices, budgets, and SOPs sounds easy enough but would entail wholesale reform that is not likely in the near term. Short of such reform, government by proxy is the alternative. Government by proxy can be more adaptable because proxy institutions do not necessarily need to be constrained by the same structure as government bureaucracy. Take the National Reconnaissance Office (NRO), a federal government agency. The NRO is responsible for providing satellite imagery (photos) to other federal government intelligence agencies such as the Central Intelligence Agency (CIA) and parts of the DOD. The NRO has traditionally relied on launching large satellites several years apart. Yet, this process entails an unnecessarily high level of risk. If a satellite is lost during launch or fails to work properly once deployed, the NRO can fall several years behind schedule. The "CubeSat" approach has changed this—"CubeSats" are small satellites that can be launched much more frequently and at lower cost. Private companies such as Alphabet (the recently renamed Google) have capitalized on the CubeSat approach and begun to deliver high-quality imagery of their own.[14] Skybox imaging, a subsidiary of Google, launched a satellite five years after the company was founded, and they are contracted to launch a dozen satellites next year.[15] Even in the extremely complex and expensive field of satellite imagery, a private contractor can adapt faster than the federal government.[16,17] If adaptability is a measure of improved government, the federal government is better off relying on the more nimble nature of government by proxy.

Dilulio and I are in complete agreement on one thing: Bureaucrats want to make a positive difference for their country. Dilulio makes this point clearly in his book *Bring Back the Bureaucrats*, and his well-known article titled "Principled Agents: The Cultural Bases of Behavior in a Federal Government." Where we differ is on what well-intentioned bureaucrats are capable of in today's bureaucracy. The characteristics of bureaucracy, in particular its hierarchical nature, narrow definition of merit, and tendency to operate by SOP, make innovation in government bureaucracy difficult even for the most motivated bureaucrat. Ideally, this would lead us to rethink the nature of government bureaucracy. But until that is possible, "Lev-pro" might be our best bad option in a rapidly changing world.

NOTES

CON

1. Ash Carter, "Drell Lecture: 'Rewiring the Pentagon: Charting a New Path on Innovation and Cybersecurity,'" April 23, 2015, http://www.defense.gov/Speeches/Speech.aspx?SpeechID=1935.
2. "Sony Drops 'The Interview' Following Terrorist Threats," *New York Times*, December 17, 2014, http://www.nytimes.com/2014/12/18/business/sony-the-interview-threats.html.
3. Kettl, Donald F. *System Under Stress: The Challenge to 21st Century Governance*, 3rd Edition, (Thousand Oaks, CA: CQ Press, 2014), 49.
4. Ibid., 72-88.

5. Ibid., 78.

6. "Times Topics: Hurricane Katrina," *The New York Times*, September 25, 2012, http://topics.nytimes.com/top/reference/timestopics/subjects/h/hurricane_katrina/index.html.

7. "Millenials Exit the Federal Workforce as Government Jobs Lose their Allure," *The Washington Post*, December 15, 2014, http://www.washingtonpost.com/politics/millennials-exit-the-federal-workforce-as-government-jobs-lose-their-allure/2014/12/15/ea3d4418-7fd4-11e4-9f38-95a187e4c1f7_story.html.

8. "Improving Worker Performance in the U.S. Government," *McKinsey Quarterly*, Public Sector Practice, November 2009, http://www.mckinsey.com/insights/public_sector/improving_worker_performance_in_the_us_government.

9. Tim Kane, "Why Our Best Officers Are Leaving," *The Atlantic*, January/February 2011, http://www.theatlantic.com/magazine/archive/2011/01/why-our-best-officers-are-leaving/308346.

10. Ibid.

11. James Q. Wilson, *On Bureaucracy: What Government Agencies Do and Why They Do It* (New York, NY: Basic Books, 2000), 339.

12. Atul Gawande, *Being Mortal: Medicine and What Matters in the End* (London, UK: Profile Books, 2014).

13. Nikhil Sahni, Maxwell Wessel, and Clayton Christensen, "Unleashing Breakthrough Innovation in Government," *Stanford Social Innovation Review*, Summer 2013.

14. Skybox Imaging is a subsidiary of Google/Alphabet Inc. that sells imagery taken from small satellites: http://www.skyboximaging.com/. For history of satellite development, see: http://www.skyboximaging.com/company#history.

15. "Vega to Launch Skybox Satellites," *Spacenews.com*, March 17, 2015, http://spacenews.com/vega-to-launch-skybox-satellites.

16. "National Reconnaissance Office Innovation Campaign: The CubeSat Program," http://www.nro.gov/about/innovation/2013-05.pdf

17. The NRO has launched of its own, though its program took over twice as long as Skybox Imaging's to become operational (thirteen years rather than five). To compare timelines, see endnotes 14 and 15 for information on Skybox, and endnote 16 for information on the NRO.

RESOLVED, the terms of Supreme Court justices should be limited to eighteen years

PRO: David Karol

CON: Ward Farnsworth

Among the "repeated injuries and usurpations" by King George III detailed in the Declaration of Independence was the complaint that "he has made Judges dependent on his Will alone, for the tenure of their offices." In doing so, the rebellious colonists believed, the king was violating a fundamental principle of English law and liberty, as laid down in the Act of Settlement of 1701. In previous centuries, judges served at the pleasure of the king, and when the king died the judges' terms ended. One of the achievements of the Glorious Revolution of 1688 was that judges now served during good behavior and could be removed only if they were convicted in regular judicial proceedings.

Many of the state constitutions drafted in the immediate aftermath of the Declaration included a provision that judges would, in the words of Virginia's constitution of 1776, "continue in office during good behavior." At the Constitutional Convention in 1787, there was much debate about who should appoint federal judges. Some thought they should be selected by the legislature, and others preferred that they be appointed by the executive, but everyone agreed that judges should serve "during good behavior." In *Federalist* No. 78, Alexander Hamilton stressed that the "good behavior" provision of Article III, Section 1 ("The Judges, both of supreme and inferior Courts, shall hold their Offices during good Behavior") was among the least objectionable and most important parts of the Constitution. Having judges serve during good behavior, Hamilton argued, was essential to preserve the independence and integrity of "the least dangerous" branch.

Legal scholars disagree, however, about what the framers meant by "good behavior." According to many scholars, the clause means that the only way that judges can be removed is through impeachment, which is authorized by Article II, Section 4: "The President, Vice President, and all other civil Officers of the United States shall be removed from Office on Impeachment for, and Conviction of, Treason, Bribery, or other High Crimes and Misdemeanors." Of the seventeen federal officers who have been impeached by the House of Representatives (seven of whom were convicted by the Senate), ten were federal judges, including, in 1805, Supreme Court Justice Samuel Chase. A few scholars argue, in contrast, that the framers of the Constitution intended that judges could be removed without being impeached so long as due process was followed.

Whatever the framers' original intent, it is clear that today good behavior is widely construed to mean that federal judges may serve for life so long as they do not commit an impeachable offense. The most important question is not what the framers intended but rather whether the framers' handiwork meets the needs of the twenty-first century. David Karol answers this question in the negative. He argues that the framers were wrong to think that life terms—as opposed to fixed terms of a specified length—were essential to judicial independence and strength. Ward Farnsworth rejects that argument. The framers, he says, got it right: Life tenure makes not only for a more robust, independent judiciary but also for a more stable legal system.

PRO: David Karol

I t is time for a constitutional amendment that would establish an eighteen-year nonrenewable term for Supreme Court justices. The Supreme Court today has far more power than the founders ever anticipated, and justices serve far longer than the founders ever could have imagined. In its first seven decades the Court struck down federal laws only twice; today the Court routinely strikes down federal statutes. Not only does the Court have a larger impact on society today, but also individual justices have much longer careers. From 1789 to 1970, the average length of service for a Supreme Court justice was about fifteen years. Since 1970, the average has been well over twenty-five years. Chief Justice William Rehnquist died in office in 2005 after having served more than thirty-three years on the Court. Justice Scalia served more than twenty-nine years before dying in office in 2016.[1]

The Court's growing power and the increasing length of terms are two of the most commonly raised objections against life tenure. In this essay, I discuss four additional reasons why eighteen-year terms are superior to life tenure. First, eighteen-year terms fix the problem of the huge and random disparities in the number of appointments to the Supreme Court that presidents make. Second, they eliminate the possibility of "strategic retirement." Third, they reduce the risk that justices will continue to serve despite diminished capacities. Fourth, they check the tendency of justices to become out of touch with society. In addition, viewed from a comparative perspective, the eighteen-year term is not a radical or unconventional idea; indeed, it is life tenure for high court justices that is the outlier among the world's democracies as well as among state supreme courts in the United States.

HOW THE EIGHTEEN-YEAR TERM WOULD WORK

Under the proposed reform, each current justice would be assigned a term of from two to sixteen years in reverse order of seniority, so that the most senior justice's term would expire first, followed by the next most senior, and so on. At the expiration of these shortened terms each justice would be replaced by a new appointee serving an eighteen-year term. Under this new system, one justice would ordinarily retire every two years, creating two vacancies in each presidential term. If a justice were to leave office before his or her term expired, the next appointee would be appointed to a shortened term. In this way, deaths and midterm retirements would not permanently disrupt the schedule of regular turnover on the Court.

The amendment creating the eighteen-year term could be written to take effect some years after ratification to minimize the immediate political implications of the change.[2] The amendment could also stipulate that retired justices would be ineligible to hold federal or state office, so as to remove any possibility that sitting justices would seek to please elected officials or political parties as they looked toward life after the Court. Given the age of the retiring justices, however, this is unlikely to be a major concern.

REDUCING ARBITRARINESS IN THE APPOINTMENT PROCESS

Ensuring regular turnover among justices is important because under the current life-tenure system, presidents vary greatly in the impact they are able to have on the Supreme Court's composition. President Jimmy Carter did not have the chance to appoint a Supreme Court justice. President George W. Bush was unable to appoint a justice until his second term. President Bill Clinton named two justices in his first term and none in his second. By contrast, President Richard Nixon made four appointments during his first term. Nor is this variation a new phenomenon. William Howard Taft, a one-term president, appointed five justices to the Supreme Court. Abraham Lincoln also appointed five justices in four years.[3]

At issue is not fairness to individual presidents but rather ensuring that the Court does not overrepresent one president or party because of the randomness of mortality and retirement decisions. If one believed that the justices were simply technicians applying straightforward constitutional and statutory provisions to cases, such variation in the numbers of justices presidents appoint would not be problematic, and the very idea of the Court as a representative institution could be rejected. The view of justices as mere legal technicians is a myth, however. The Constitution and statutes are often ambiguous or contradictory, especially in the "hard cases" that reach the Supreme Court. Nor are the justices' political affiliations irrelevant. Studies show that party affiliation is a strong predictor of how justices vote.[4] That makes it highly problematic that some presidents, through mere chance, make a disproportionate number of Supreme Court appointments.

STRATEGIC RETIREMENT

The absence of a mandatory retirement age or fixed-length terms means that the timing of a justice's departure is usually his or her own decision. This is objectionable because it means that public policy rests on the whims of an unelected official whose only democratic legitimacy stems from having been appointed and confirmed in office decades earlier.

The extent to which justices decide to retire based on political considerations remains a matter of some controversy, since this is not a motivation justices typically are willing to discuss publicly. Still, there is evidence that departing justices take political factors into account, a process termed "strategic retirement."[5] Justices cannot choose their successors, but life tenure allows a justice to retire at a time when the president can be expected to appoint a replacement who shares many of the retiring justice's views. In most cases, this means retiring during the administration of a president from the justice's party. In 1987, Justice Lewis Powell, then seventy-nine years old, received a long memo from his friend and former clerk outlining "the political reasons why Justice Powell would want to retire in the twilight of Republican Ronald Reagan's second term as President if he did not want to be forced to leave due to ill-health during a Democratic administration." Two days later, Powell announced his retirement.[6]

Similarly, Justice Byron White, while more conservative than many other Democratic justices, apparently retained some loyalty to the party of President John F. Kennedy, who appointed him. White reportedly told his former clerk, then a Clinton aide handling judicial nominations, that "despite everything he remained a Democrat, and he wanted a Democrat to name his successor."[7] Although strategic retirement typically means leaving the bench so a president from the party that appointed the justice may choose the successor, there are exceptions. A minority of justices find themselves voting more with justices of the other party, whether because their own views have evolved or because the parties' principles have changed.[8] For example, Justice Harry Blackmun, a Nixon appointee but also the author of the Court's decision in *Roe v. Wade*, "began to consider retirement" only after President Bill Clinton was elected in 1992.[9] More recently, the retirements during the Obama administration of Justices David Souter and John Paul Stevens, Republican appointees who mostly took liberal positions, are examples of ideologically based strategic retirement.

Admittedly, some justices who seek to retire strategically may be stymied by failing health and unhelpful election results. Justice Thurgood Marshall was unhappy with the likely choice to replace him in the Carter administration and then tried to wait out Reagan and George H. W. Bush, whom he saw as hostile to his values, but he was forced to retire at eighty-three for health reasons. The first President Bush was still in office, and he appointed Justice Clarence Thomas, whose views were at odds with Marshall's. Most justices, however, have been successful in retiring strategically so as to enable presidents of the same party or ideology to appoint their successors.[10]

LINGERING TOO LONG

Under the life-tenure system, justices may continue to serve long after their abilities are greatly diminished by age. In his last years, Marshall relied heavily on clerks, became befuddled during oral argument, and lost interest in many issues the Court faced.[11] Cancer-stricken Justice Rehnquist missed dozens of oral arguments in the year before his death in 2005.[12] Justice William O. Douglas's diminished capacity disturbed his colleagues so much that they quietly agreed to set aside his vote if they reached a 4–4 tie.[13]

The reasons that justices choose to remain in office when they have lost some of their abilities vary from justice to justice. Some simply cling to office for emotional reasons. Others may hope to retire strategically, while still others may not realize how much their faculties have dimmed. In any case, justices have the leeway to linger without the public being aware of such dereliction of duty. Unlike other top government officials, Supreme Court justices operate largely out of the spotlight and may delegate most of their duties to their clerks, who are typically in their twenties and neither elected nor appointed by anyone who was. In theory, incompetent justices can be impeached and removed from office by Congress, but in all of U.S. history, this has never happened.

OUT-OF-TOUCH JUSTICES

Another problem stemming from the life-tenure system is that justices can become increasingly out of touch with the society they purportedly serve. Again, this would not be a problem if the justices' duties were merely technical in nature, but the role of a justice is a complex one that requires value trade-offs and prudential judgments about the consequences of rulings that are invariably informed by justices' understanding of society and politics. For example, the Court's unanimous ruling in *Clinton v. Jones* (1997), requiring President Clinton to testify in a sexual harassment lawsuit against him while in office, was based on the dubious premise that such testimony would be "highly unlikely to occupy any substantial amount of petitioner's time."[14] This miscalculation led to the impeachment controversy that preoccupied Clinton as well as the Congress in 1998 and early 1999. Another example of justices becoming out of touch with a changing society is offered by Justice Powell. Powell cast the key vote in the 1986 case *Bowers v. Hardwick,* in which the Supreme Court upheld a Georgia law banning sodomy—a decision that was explicitly overturned by the Court seventeen years later in *Lawrence v. Texas.* Powell, then seventy-eight years old, told one of his clerks, who was—unbeknownst to Powell—gay, "I don't believe I've ever met a homosexual."[15]

COMPARING A FIXED TERM WITH A MANDATORY RETIREMENT REQUIREMENT

One alternative reform often suggested is a mandatory retirement age for justices. Such age limits for judges exist in many countries as well as in most American states. A mandatory retirement age might be an improvement on the status quo. An age limit would address some of the problems noted above, including the possibility that justices would continue to serve despite diminished capacity, the risk of strategic retirement, and the extent to which members of the high court become out of touch with society after many years in office.

A fixed term, however, can address all of these problems at least as well as a mandatory retirement age can, and a mandatory retirement age would not ensure that appointments be spread as evenly as possible across presidential terms. Instead of one justice's term expiring every two years, giving chief executives equal opportunities to affect the composition of the Court, the possibility of great variation in presidents' opportunities to appoint justices would remain.

A mandatory retirement age would also increase the incentive for presidents to find younger nominees, so as to maximize the number of years their appointees could serve on the Court. There is nothing wrong with having some young appointees, but a mandatory retirement age would encourage presidents to give this factor excessive weight at the expense of other considerations. In contrast, a fixed term would make nominees' ages less of a factor in presidents' decisions than it is now, since every justice, no matter how old at the time of appointment, would be eligible to serve only eighteen years.

WHY THE FOUNDERS' ARGUMENT FOR LIFE TENURE NO LONGER HOLDS

Admittedly, a rule that has been in place for centuries should not be reformed lightly. Before the Constitution is amended, some consideration of both the founders' views and the practices in other judicial systems at home and abroad is advisable. The provision of the Constitution that justices serve "during good behavior" was agreed upon on at the Constitutional Convention on June 5, 1787.[16] James Madison's *notes* suggest that there was no discussion of this

Table 19.1

Supreme Court Retirement and Reappointment Provisions in Advanced Democracies

Country	Retirement age	Term limit	Reappointment process
Australia	70	None	None
Austria	70	None	None
Belgium	70	None	None
Canada	75	None	None
Costa Rica	None	8 years	Congress
Denmark	68	None	None
Finland	67	None	None
France	None	9 years	None
Germany	68	12 years	None
Iceland	70	None	None
Ireland	70	None	None
Israel	70	None	None
Italy	None	9 years	None
Japan	70	10 years	Election
Luxembourg	68	None	None
Netherlands	70	None	None
New Zealand	70	None	None
Norway	70	None	None
Sweden	67	None	None
Switzerland	68	6 years	Parliament
United Kingdom	70	None	None
United States	**None**	**None**	**None**

Note: In some countries, multiple "high courts" have different jurisdictions. In those cases, this table reports the judicial tenure provision for the court charged with constitutional interpretation.

provision, which must have been uncontroversial among the delegates. Delegates to the Constitutional Convention were more concerned with how justices were to be appointed (should presidents or Congress make appointments?) than they were with how long they would serve. Yet by turning to *The Federalist Papers* we can get a sense of the founders' justification for the "good behavior" clause.

In *Federalist* No. 78, Hamilton argued for the "permanent tenure of judicial offices." Life tenure would, he asserted, protect judicial independence against "legislative encroachments." By contrast, a renewable appointment would reduce judicial independence vis-à-vis the legislative and executive branches. Of course, a nonrenewable eighteen-year term would alleviate this concern about judicial independence. However, Hamilton also argued that there would be few candidates who possessed both the legal knowledge and the requisite integrity to serve on the Court and that a term limit "would naturally discourage such characters from quitting a lucrative line of practice to accept a seat on the bench."[17]

Whatever the force of Hamilton's arguments in his day, they have little relevance in a country one hundred times more populous and containing a vast bar, a well-endowed legal academy, federal and state court systems employing thousands of judges, and a Supreme Court far more powerful and prestigious than it was in the founders' era. It is not plausible that there would be a shortage of qualified aspirants to the high court today simply because justices' terms would be limited.

LIFE TENURE IN COMPARATIVE PERSPECTIVE

If Hamilton's objections to limiting justices' terms are based on dubious and outdated assumptions, the question remains whether term limits are associated with successful governance in our own time. To answer that question, we can look to many examples both abroad and in U.S. state courts.

As Table 19.1 shows, the American system of life tenure is not used by any of the world's other stable democracies.[18] Most common is a retirement age, usually set at around seventy. However, in several countries, high court judges are appointed for fixed terms. Of these, France, Germany, and Italy have nonrenewable terms of nine, twelve, and nine years, respectively. High court judges' terms are renewable by the legislature after six years in Switzerland and after eight years in Costa Rica. In Japan, Supreme Court members face the voters every ten years, but retirement is mandatory at seventy. Justices in Japan are customarily of advanced age when they are appointed, so in practice they serve at most one full term.[19] The list of nations in Table 19.1 demonstrates that life tenure for high court justices is not necessary for the survival of democracy and civil liberties.

Cross-national studies also confirm that there is not a strong relationship between judicial independence and life tenure. In its 2011–2012 report, the World Economic Forum presents the results from a survey that asked executives from around the world, "To what extent is the judiciary in your country independent from influences of members of government, citizens, or firms?"[20] All the countries listed in Table 19.1 ranked relatively high in the survey, which covered 142 countries, many with weak democratic traditions. However, the United States did not do well compared with other stable democracies, finishing in thirty-sixth place, substantially ahead of only Italy (sixtieth) and just ahead of France (thirty-seventh) and Costa Rica (thirty-eighth). All the other nations listed in Table 19.1 ranked well above the United States.

We also have evidence closer to home of judicial systems that function without life tenure for the leading judges. Under the American federal system, every state has its own judiciary, with varying selection and retention mechanisms. Table 19.2 reveals the great variation in state judicial tenure provisions. Thirty states have a mandatory retirement age, most frequently seventy. All but three states also require review of supreme court justices at intervals of six to fourteen years. In most cases, this review is by voters, be it in retention elections or in potentially competitive nonpartisan or partisan elections. In nine states, justices must win reappointment and confirmation from elected officials or nominating commissions. Massachusetts and New Hampshire allow their high court judges to serve without any review once appointed but require retirement at seventy. Only in Rhode Island is the system of life tenure in use. Studies of the quality of state supreme courts based on various metrics, including surveys of lawyers and the extent to which the courts' opinions are cited by other courts, do not find Rhode Island's high court to be among the leading state supreme courts.[21]

In practice, state supreme court justices are rarely rejected or replaced by voters or officials, but these judges are at least modestly accountable and often are also subject to mandatory retirement ages. The great discrepancy between the life terms U.S. Supreme Court justices enjoy and the provisions governing tenure of state supreme court judges reflects the fact that most state constitutions are newer and easier to amend than the U.S. Constitution. As such, they reflect more democratic values that became widespread in American society as far back as the first half of the nineteenth century.

In sum, the system of life tenure under which U.S. Supreme Court justices serve is not in use in *any* other long-standing democratic country. Even in the

Table 19.2

State Supreme Court Retirement and Review Procedures in the Fifty States

State	Retirement age	Term limit (years)	Review process
Alabama	70	6	Partisan election
Alaska	70	10	Retention election
Arizona	70	6	Retention election
Arkansas	None	8	Nonpartisan election
California	None	12	Retention election
Colorado	72	10	Retention election
Connecticut	70	8	Governor and legislature
Delaware	None	12	Governor, nominating commission, and senate
Florida	70	6	Retention election
Georgia	None	6	Nonpartisan election
Hawaii	70	10	Nominating commission
Idaho	None	6	Nonpartisan election
Illinois	None	10	Retention election
Indiana	75	10	Retention election
Iowa	72	8	Retention election
Kansas	None	6	Retention election
Kentucky	None	8	Nonpartisan election
Louisiana	70	10	Partisan election
Maine	None	7	Governor, confirm by senate
Maryland	70	10	Retention election
Massachusetts	70	None	None
Michigan	70	8	Nonpartisan election
Minnesota	70	6	Nonpartisan election
Mississippi	None	8	Nonpartisan election
Missouri	70	12	Retention election

(Continued)

(Continued)

State	Retirement age	Term limit (years)	Review process
Montana	None	8	Retention election
Nebraska	None	6	Retention election
Nevada	None	6	Nonpartisan election
New Hampshire	70	None	None
New Jersey	70	7	Governor, confirm by senate
New Mexico	None	8	Partisan election then retention re-election
New York	70	14	Governor, nominating commission, and senate
North Carolina	72	8	Nonpartisan election then retention for re-election.
North Dakota	None	10	Nonpartisan election
Ohio	70	6	Nonpartisan election
Oklahoma	None	6	Retention election
Oregon	75	6	Nonpartisan election
Pennsylvania	70	10	Retention election
Rhode Island	None	None	None
South Carolina	73	10	Re-election by legislature
South Dakota	70	8	Retention election
Tennessee	None	8	Retention election
Texas	75	6	Partisan election
Utah	75	10	Retention election
Vermont	70	6	Vote of general assembly
Virginia	70	12	Re-election by legislature
Washington	75	6	Nonpartisan election
West Virginia	None	12	Partisan election
Wisconsin	None	10	Nonpartisan election
Wyoming	70	8	Retention election

Source: "Judicial Selection in the States" American Judicature Society, http://www.judicialselection.us.

United States, it is rejected by forty-nine of the fifty states. In forty-seven states, high court judges are reviewed by voters or other officials every fourteen years or more frequently. Viewed in this comparative context, an eighteen-year non-renewable term for U.S. Supreme Court justices is a modest reform that preserves judicial independence while mitigating the ills that come from extended service and life tenure.

CONCLUSION

The time has come to institute fixed terms of office for U.S. Supreme Court justices. The public is ready for the change; a recent New York Times poll found that 60 percent of respondents agreed that "appointing Supreme Court justices for life is a bad thing because it gives them too much power."[22] Fixed terms will end the arbitrariness of the current arrangement in which some presidents are able to reshape the Court while others have no impact on it. They will bring a regular stock of new ideas to a stuffy institution and reduce the likelihood that justices will become out of touch with society. Fixed terms will reduce both the risk of strategic retirements and the possibility that justices will linger in office when they are no longer capable of doing the job. They will also make age less of a factor in presidents' appointment decisions. We can implement fixed terms without significantly reducing the independence that justices must enjoy in order to do their jobs. Evidence from other judicial systems around the world and in the fifty U.S. states suggests that limited terms for justices are compatible with stable democracy and well-functioning court systems.

Fixed terms will not solve all problems or yield all the benefits that some reform advocates suggest. Given the great power that even term-limited justices will have, claims that this reform will reduce the partisan bitterness of confirmation fights, for example, seem questionable. Still, if it is not a panacea, limiting justices' terms is a very worthwhile and overdue reform. Supreme Court justices play a valuable role, but they are human beings and their positions are a public trust, not their private property.

CON: Ward Farnsworth

I defend life tenure for U.S. Supreme Court justices on two main grounds. First, by slowing down the rate of turnover on the Court, life tenure puts a useful brake on political majorities who want to change fundamental legal doctrines by filling the Court with justices who will do their bidding. Fixed terms of eighteen years, by contrast, would guarantee every two-term president the power to remake the Court dramatically—a result that would destabilize the law and place too much trust in the judgment of short-term majorities. Second, term limits would add to the political character of the Court's work; they would turn Supreme Court nominations into an explicit spoil of every presidential election and might well increase the justices' sense of obligation to carry out the views of the presidents who have nominated them. Some of these arguments have a speculative quality, but then so do the arguments in favor of fixed terms, and this counsels in favor of leaving well enough alone. Later I also comment on specific arguments that Professor Karol offers; some of them are plausible, but they nevertheless have limited force.

FASTER AND SLOWER LAW

It is natural to think of life tenure mostly as a feature of the justices' working conditions—a measure meant to improve their performance by insulating them from worries about what they will do after they leave the bench. But the length of their terms also dictates how often openings on the Court arise and thus how quickly electoral majorities can remake the Court and so produce tectonic shifts in the law. From this perspective the optimal length of judicial terms depends on how much we trust judgments made by majorities over shorter time periods. Life tenure reflects a high level of distrust, as it makes the justices' terms as long as possible and so makes the rate of public influence on the Court's work as slow as possible. The distrust of the whims of short-term majorities is salutary.

The gradual rate of turnover on the Supreme Court causes Americans to live under two types of law: fast moving and slow. The faster law is made by members of Congress, state legislators, and other political actors who face elections every few years. The slower law mostly is made by a committee of officials known as Supreme Court justices. Since the justices keep their jobs for a long time, it takes a long time to replace them if the public doesn't like what they do. The Supreme Court is thus conservative—not in the modern sense of being "right-wing," but in the traditional sense of being slow to change. The most fundamental decisions in our legal life are put on a track that requires a sustained expression of public will before they can be reversed.

The Supreme Court's case law on federalism provides a good example. A sea change in that area of law took place in the 1990s; the Court made small but important steps to enhance the rights of the states and limit the powers of the federal government. That shift was not caused by any quick or transitory change in public mood. It was the result of twelve consecutive years of Republican control over the White House (and resulting appointments to the Court), plus the presence of a holdover from the Nixon years (William Rehnquist). The Court's work thus came to reflect, in a slightly delayed fashion, certain national preferences that were durably expressed through the political process. Major shifts in the Court's jurisprudence tend to be of this character, sometimes changing from generation to generation but rarely from year to year.

The value of the Court as a slow lawmaker is that it resists short-term or even medium-term majoritarian judgments so that long-term majorities can prevail. Changing the slower law takes a long time, and this frustrates many people. Fixed shorter terms for the justices would reduce that frustration; it would make it easier, for example, to get *Roe v. Wade* reversed. Maybe that is a good thing, and maybe it isn't, but everyone should have a clear sense of the stakes in this debate. Every generation has its unpopular Supreme Court decisions. The question is whether we should take structural steps to make those decisions easier to undo.

Partisans on both sides would like to see all sorts of decisions by the Supreme Court reversed. On the right there are those who want to limit gun control or to limit the right to privacy, and on the left there are those who want to limit Court-imposed restrictions on affirmative action or gun control. Both left and right are dismayed by the Supreme Court's frustration of their projects, and some in both camps clamor for more public control over the law the Court makes. But most people are more cautious than that, and rightly so—and this is one reason the movement for fixed terms has not picked up steam. Speeding up the rate of change at the Supreme Court would create winners and losers, but it is hard to be sure who they would be, and in the meantime most Americans enjoy a combination of expansive liberties and social stability that makes them understandably risk-averse. They might fairly conclude that any institution capable of bringing so much exasperation to both conservatives and liberals must be doing something right.

Here is a last way to put the point. Having justices serve for eighteen years would guarantee every two-term president at least four appointments to the Court. That would give every two-term president the ability to create a near majority on the Court, which easily could become a majority with the addition of an interim appointment or the presence on the Court of a like-minded justice appointed prior to the beginning of the president's term. This can happen already, but it usually does not. The question is whether we should ensure that it always does. I am skeptical. A two-term president may reflect a single national mood, and there is value in a Court that cannot be remade by one such gust. We should be slow to assume that the country would be better off if the same ideological fads that can elect a two-term president were to regularly produce decisive changes in the Court's membership as well.

THE SUPREME COURT AS A POLITICAL SPOIL

Apart from slowing the pace of fundamental legal change, life tenure also makes the process of appointment to the Court less explicitly political than it would be with fixed terms of eighteen years. First, fixed terms would facilitate the work of interest groups trying to influence the composition of the Court. If justices served terms of eighteen years, one no longer would speak of the *possibility* that the winner of a presidential election might make appointments to the Court. Every winner would be guaranteed two of them. The stakes for the Court in every campaign thus would be higher than they currently are; interest groups would see larger expected returns from pressuring candidates to make and keep promises about how they would use their two nominations if elected. Fixed terms also would make it easier to coordinate pressures further in advance. Everyone would know years ahead of time when the next vacancy will arrive and what seat will be involved. Campaigns to have it filled would begin far in advance, just as a new political campaign begins as soon as the prior one ends. Depriving pressure groups of a clear target, as life tenure does, makes it harder for them to organize their efforts and concentrate their energies.

A second and related drawback of fixed terms is that they might well increase the justices' sense of obligation to carry out the wishes of whoever appointed them. If everyone knows that two seats on the Court are a spoil the president won fair and square, those seats may be regarded as the president's to fill in a stronger sense than we currently see, and the nominees may feel more pressure to carry out the president's agenda. The justices will be Republican appointees or Democratic appointees in a more explicit sense than they now are. Some may therefore view their own roles in a manner a little more political and less lawlike.

Finally, fixed terms resemble the arrangements in the legislative and executive branches of the government and so may cause justices to think of themselves as political officeholders in a more traditional way than they now do. Indeed, some of the proposals for fixed terms are pitched expressly as efforts to make the Court more responsive to the popular will. New justices will be familiar with the rationale of such a plan if it is enacted; they will understand that they are serving fixed, limited terms precisely in order to keep the Court accountable to current political values. The implication is that the justices are supposed to give effect to those values and to popular sentiment when they make their decisions—but this is just how we don't want them thinking about their jobs when it comes time to decide cases. The justices negotiate all the time between their own preferences and the pressure exerted, sometimes weakly, by the legal materials in front of them. We should hesitate before taking any measure that would increase even a little the justices' sense that their charge is political.

THE ALLOCATION OF NOMINATING CHANCES TO PRESIDENTS

Professor Karol rightly points out that fixed terms would spread nominations to the Court evenly among presidents. The argument has some merit but nevertheless is not as strong as it seems. First, there are countervailing influences on the appointment process that help smooth out misallocations of chances to the two parties. Most importantly, the Senate helps compensate for the lumpy way in which nominations are distributed to presidents. The Republican presidents who appointed Justices John Paul Stevens and David Souter wanted to avoid trouble in the Senate and so deliberately chose nominees who carried more ideological risk than the alternatives. The risk paid out badly; both of those justices ended up joining the Court's "liberal" wing. Pressure from the Senate thus helped prevent flukes in the timing of the justices' retirements from causing a comparable shift in the balance of ideologies on the Court. The Senate works as a hedge against the vicissitudes of election cycles and retirements from the Court.

Note that, for this hedge to work, the Senate must reject the idea that it should not second-guess Supreme Court nominations on ideological grounds. Deference of that sort magnifies the effects of the uneven distribution of nominating chances between presidents. Life tenure therefore presupposes a robust political role for the Senate in the Supreme Court appointment process.

Notice, too, that presidential elections are themselves lumpy, winner-take-all events. There is no guarantee that a political minority representing a certain percentage of the population will carry the same percentage of elections. Even a large minority may never win any presidential elections and so may not see its views represented at all on the Court. In addition, the narrow winner of a presidential election gets no fewer nominating chances than a candidate who wins by a landslide. If one wants ideological control over the Court tied in a satisfying way to the ideological composition of the polity, using institutional checks is therefore a sounder strategy than trying to make sure every president gets the same number of appointments. The obvious check would be to shift more power in the nominating process to an institution that reflects a wider range of inputs: again, the Senate. True, the Senate has great shortcomings as a representative institution, but at least both parties always are represented there at the same time and so create possibilities for debate and compromise that are missing if the choice is given to the president alone. Giving two appointments to every president will make only a small contribution to political equity if the Senate has a weak role, whereas if the Senate's role is strong, the distribution of appointments to presidents will become less important.

If a strong role for the Senate is salutary, notice that it is likely to be reduced by giving the justices fixed terms. The two appointments presidents would make during their terms would likely be claimed as their own to spend as they see fit. They earned them. No doubt many in the Senate and elsewhere would resist this way of thinking, but the case for deference to a president's choices undoubtedly would be strengthened relative to where it currently stands because at present the Senate justly can resist a president's nominations on the grounds that the chance to make them was delivered by luck. By weakening this argument, fixed terms would enlarge the president's powers and worsen the distortions created by putting nominations into a single person's hands.

MENTAL DECREPITUDE

Professor Karol makes another argument that has plausibility but again is less forceful than at first appears: Fixed terms would reduce the risk of justices who remain in office when they become mentally decrepit. The first point to appreciate in response is that the problem of decrepitude is less serious than it sounds. According to David Garrow's study, justices have become mentally decrepit eleven times since 1900, and in no case did the problem last more than a year or two.[1] Thus, of the roughly nine hundred man-years of service provided by Supreme Court justices since the start of the twentieth century, perhaps ten or twenty of those years—between 1 and 2 percent of them—were tainted by serious mental deterioration. When it did occur, it was mitigated in two ways. First, its impact was diluted by the presence of the eight other justices; a decrepit justice may serve as a swing vote but otherwise cannot do anything significant unless four colleagues go along with it. Second, the onset of mental infirmity causes the justice's responsibilities to devolve to law clerks, who generally can keep a chamber running without a drop-off in quality remotely commensurate with the justice's drop-off in functionality. This may sound appalling, and of course there are good reasons not to want it to occur, but in fact the devolution can help control—it undoubtedly has helped control—the consequences of decrepitude until the justice leaves the Court. We should pause before trading away the advantages of life tenure to address a problem that sounds bad but has been minor as a practical matter.

STRATEGIC RETIREMENT

An undeniably bothersome feature of life tenure is that the justices—or at least those who retire before death, which includes most of them—decide for themselves when to leave the Court and thus determine who will choose their replacements. As in the case of mental decrepitude, however, it is not clear that the problem of strategic retirement is very serious. The plausible window of retirement for a justice tends to be small enough to make such decisions hard to carry out. Some have speculated that William Douglas, Thurgood Marshall, and William Brennan tried to hold out in the hope of being replaced by a Democrat; if so, all three failed. Meanwhile, other justices seem to enjoy their positions enough to make strategic retirement a low priority. They leave no sooner than they must. The net result during the twentieth century was that a seat on the Court rarely stayed in the hands of the same party more than twice in a row. The most prominent counterexample is the seat now held by Justice Sonia Sotomayor, which from 1914 until 1956 was held by a series of four justices named by Democrats, but three of them (James F. Byrnes, Wiley Blount Rutledge, and Sherman Minton) served brief terms. Democrats likewise filled the seat now occupied by Justice Clarence Thomas three times in a row from 1940 until 1991. If we reach back to the nineteenth century we find a few other such examples, but on the whole it does not appear that monopolization of a seat by a party, whether by strategic retirement or by chance, has yet been a significant practical problem.

CONCLUSION: THE CLAIMS OF THE STATUS QUO

Life tenure for Supreme Court justices has practical consequences. As just shown, however, a recurring problem in debates about life tenure is that most claims about the details of those consequences (and the consequences of any alternatives) are speculative. Terms of eighteen years would cause more frequent turnover than we now see; this may or may not have good or even noticeable effects on the Court's output. Fixed terms might decrease the intensity of the politics that surround the confirmation process or might make it worse. They would even out the chances for presidents to make nominations, a good thing, but they might cause justices to feel more responsibility to the parties who chose them, a bad thing. They would reduce the risks of strategic retirement and mental decrepitude but then so would the simpler solution of age limits—and in any event, it is far from clear that either of those problems is great as a practical matter.

There is much to be said for leaving the Constitution alone unless it is clear that revising it would create net benefits. Our current arrangements, which most would say have served the country tolerably well for around 230 years, are entitled to some respect on that ground alone. The costs of adjusting to a new order and taking the risk that it will be worse than the old are worth incurring only if it is clear that the expected gains are large. Those who wish to end life tenure for Supreme Court justices have a high standard of proof to satisfy, and in my judgment they have thus far come up short.

NOTES

PRO

1. "Members of the Supreme Court of the United States," Supreme Court of the United States website, http://www.supremecourt.gov/about/members_text.aspx.

2. For more discussion of this proposal, see James E. DiTullio and John B. Schochet, "Saving This Honorable Court: A Proposal to Replace Life Tenure on the Supreme Court with Staggered, Nonrenewable Eighteen-Year Terms," *Virginia Law Review* 90 (2004): 1093–1149.

3. See Daniel J. Meador, "Thinking about Age and Supreme Court Tenure," in *Reforming the Court: Term Limits for Supreme Court Justices,* ed. Roger C. Cramton and Paul D. Carrington (Durham, NC: Carolina Academic Press, 2006).

4. See Stuart S. Nagel, "Political Party Affiliation and Judges' Decisions," *American Political Science Review* 55 (1961): 843–50; and C. Neal Tate, "Personal Attribute Models of the Voting Behavior of U.S. Supreme Court Justices: Liberalism in Civil Liberties and Economics Decisions, 1946–1978," *American Political Science Review* 75 (1981): 355–67.

5. See Timothy M. Hagle, "Strategic Retirements: A Political Model of Turnover on the United States Supreme Court," *Political Behavior* 15 (1993): 25–48; and Artemus Ward, *Deciding to Leave: The Politics of Retirement from the United States Supreme Court* (Albany: State University of New York Press, 2003).

6. See DiTullio and Schochet, "Saving This Honorable Court,"1102–3.

7. See Jeffrey Toobin, *The Nine: Inside the Secret World of the Supreme Court* (New York, NY: Anchor Books, 2007), 73.

8. For discussion of the latter phenomenon, see David Karol, *Party Position Change in American Politics: Coalition Management* (New York, NY: Cambridge University Press, 2009).

9. See DiTullio and Schochet, "Saving This Honorable Court,"1104–41.

10. See Juan Williams, *Thurgood Marshall: American Revolutionary* (New York, NY: Times Books, 1998).

11. David J. Garrow, "Mental Decrepitude on the U.S. Supreme Court: The Historical Case for a 28th Amendment," *University of Chicago Law Review* 67 (2000): 1073.

12. Lawrence S. Wrightsman, *Oral Arguments before the Supreme Court: An Empirical Approach* (New York, NY: Oxford University Press, 2008), 8.

13. Garrow, "Mental Decrepitude on the U.S. Supreme Court," 1052–56.

14. *Clinton v. Jones* (95-1853), 520 U.S. 681 (1997), http://www.law.cornell.edu/supct/html/95-1853.ZO.html.

15. Quoted in John Calvin Jeffries, *Justice Lewis F. Powell, Jr.* (New York, NY: Fordham University Press, 2001), 521.

16. "Madison Debates, June 5," Avalon Project, Yale Law School, http://avalon.law.yale.edu/18th_century/debates_605.asp.

17. Alexander Hamilton, *Federalist* No. 78, http://www.constitution.org/fed/federa78.htm.

18. I draw my comparison set of countries from Robert Dahl's list of twenty-one nations aside from the United States that have been stable democracies since 1950. See Robert A. Dahl, *How Democratic Is the American Constitution?* (New Haven, CT: Yale University Press, 2001).

19. On Japan, see Tom Ginsburg, *Judicial Review in New Democracies: Constitutional Courts in Asian Cases* (New York, NY: Cambridge University Press, 2003), 46.

20. Klaus Schwab, ed., *Global Competitiveness Report, 2011–2012* (Geneva: World Economic Forum, 2011). Also see Lars P. Feld and Stefan Voigt, "Economic Growth and Judicial Independence: Cross Country Evidence Using a New Set of Indicators" (CESifo Working Paper No. 906, Center for Economic Studies, Ludwig-Maximilians-Universität Munich, 2003).

21. Stephen J. Choi, G. Mitu Gulati, and Eric A. Posner, "Which States Have the Best (and Worst) High Courts?" (John M. Olin Law & Economics Working Paper No. 405, University of Chicago Law School, 2008).

22. Adam Liptak and Allison Kopicki, "Approval Rating for Justices Hits Just 44% in New Poll," *New York Times*, June 7, 2012, http://www.nytimes.com/2012/06/08/us/politics/44-percent-of-americans-approve-of-supreme-court-in-new-poll.html.

CON

1. See David J. Garrow, "Mental Decrepitude on the U.S. Supreme Court: The Historical Case for a 28th Amendment," *University of Chicago Law Review* 67 (2000): 995–1087.

RESOLVED, Americans should receive four more years of free public education

PRO: Robert Samuels

CON: Neal McCluskey

The United States is commonly portrayed as a welfare state laggard. Compared to Europe, the United States lags behind in vacation time, mandated paid leave, universal health care, and welfare spending. Scholars disagree about how large the gap is and about how best to explain the differences: a fragmented system of checks and balances that advantages the well organized and frustrates change, antistatist values and antitax attitudes, or the absence of a viable socialist party and a weak and divided labor movement. But in one area of domestic spending, the United States has been a leader not a laggard: public education. The United States spends more per student than almost any other nation. Education spending accounts for about 30 percent of all state spending, and in some states (Utah and Vermont, for instance) the number is more like 40 percent.

In *The Audacity of Hope* (2006), then-U.S. senator Barack Obama explained why. "Education has been at the heart of a bargain this nation makes with its citizens: If you work hard and take responsibility, you'll have a chance for a better life."[1] The bargain has long included giving every American, regardless of race, class, or gender, twelve years of free public schooling. That gift is premised on the assumption that without an education, Americans will not be able to live productive lives and be good citizens. The economy and our democracy depend on education.

Americans believe in the importance of education. A 2014 Gallup survey found that 95 percent of Americans said that a high school education was either extremely important or very important to a person's ability to succeed in life. Only 1 percent said it was unimportant. Not quite as many say that a college education is very important, but still nearly 4 in 5 respondents said a college education was extremely or very important. Only 4 percent said it was unimportant.[2]

Americans' notorious distrust of government spending never extends to spending on education. There has never been a public opinion poll that found Americans wanted the government to spend less on education rather than more. In 2011, on the heels of the Republican takeover of the House of Representatives, a Pew survey found that 62 percent of Americans wanted to see an increase in spending on education, and only 11 percent wanted to see a decrease in education spending. No other area of government spending was as popular, not spending on veterans, not health care, not combating crime, not environmental protection, and certainly not military defense.[3] Not surprisingly, candidates of both parties vie with each other to show that they are the best person to bolster public education. Spending on education is viewed not as a government handout but as a crucial part of fostering a culture of self-reliance and equal opportunity.

Americans have always prided themselves on being an education leader, particularly when it comes to higher education. And for good reason. "As recently as the 1980s," observes political scientist Suzanne Mettler, "the nation was the undisputed international leader in the percentage of students graduating from college."[4] Not anymore. Now Americans lag behind many other countries in college graduation rates. A 2014 report by the Organization for Economic Cooperation and Development (OECD) ranked the United States 19th out of 28 countries. Almost thirty percent of American men today have less education than their parents, compared to twenty percent who have more education than their parents. In OECD countries, there is less downward educational mobility (only 19 percent of men in OECD countries have less education than their parents) and more upward education mobility (28 percent of men in OECD countries have higher education levels than their parents).[5]

How can we restore the United States' position as an education leader? In 2015, President Obama proposed a $60 billion initiative (America's College Promise Act) that would make community college free for low-income students through federal matching funds. Two states (Tennessee and Oregon) have already passed laws making community college free for eligible students. In the 2016 presidential campaign, each of the principal Democratic candidates unveiled a plan to deal with the problem of mounting student debt and the corresponding decline in graduation rates. During the primary, Hillary Clinton proposed spending $350 billion over ten years to help students pay tuition without taking out so much in loans. Her opponent Bernie Sanders's proposal was simpler: free college education at public universities financed by a tax on Wall Street.

Sanders's idea is defended in this debate by Robert Samuels, who sees free college education as a way not only to restore America's position as an education leader but to combat the growing problem of income inequality in the United States. For Samuels, free college education is a matter of simple justice. Neal McCluskey, however, cautions us that if something sounds too good to be true it probably is. "Free" public education would in fact be hugely costly and not just to taxpayers. The real solution to what ails our inefficient education system, McCluskey counters, is not to have government play a larger role in subsidizing education but instead to get government out of the business of subsidizing expensive college degrees that often seem to turn out to be worthless.

PRO: Robert Samuels

We should make public higher education free because higher education plays a crucial role in a democracy. Thomas Jefferson argued for a free public university because he knew that a flourishing democracy requires highly educated citizens. "It is safer," Jefferson proclaimed, "to have the whole people respectably enlightened than a few in a high state of science and the many in ignorance."[1] Jefferson believed that public universities were necessary "to develop the reasoning faculties of our youth, enlarge their minds, cultivate their morals, and instill into them the precepts of virtue and order; to enlighten them with mathematical and physical sciences, which advance the arts and administer to the health, the subsistence and comforts of human life; and, generally, to form them to habits of reflection and correct action, rendering them examples of virtue to others and of happiness within themselves."[2] Jefferson did not say that the main goal of higher education was to prepare students for future jobs; rather, he rightly insisted that universities need to cater to the whole person by helping students to develop better reasoning skills, form moral attitudes, and become happier people.

These broad goals of higher education are being undermined by the high cost of tuition and related expenses that drive students to go into debt and force them to focus on pursuing a high-paying job to pay off their student loans. The average student graduates with over $35,000 of debt.[3] Furthermore, universities are now stressing that the major advantage of going to college is that people will earn more, and the unintended effect of this argument is that higher education is seen as a private good purchased by an individual student. This privatizing rhetoric leads states to conclude that they can cut funding for universities and let the responsibility for paying the increased costs fall on the individual student, who is seen as making a down payment on a future job.

The current system has also increased wealth inequality by motivating public universities and colleges to accept students who can pay the full bill or who get large aid packages due to their high SAT scores. One result is that the best public universities are reducing their number of low-income and minority students in order to chase after wealthy American students and foreign students who pay full tuition without financial aid. If we leave the current system unchecked, we will only increase the growing inequality in American society. Recent research has shown that unequal educational attainment goes hand and hand with income inequality, as well as with higher rates of crime and lower health standards.[4] In other words, the more public higher education becomes privatized, the more it becomes unequal—and the more society suffers.

One strong indicator of how unequal higher education has become can be found in the following statistic: In 1970, 55 percent of students from the top income quartile who started college attained bachelor degrees, and in 2013 that percentage increased to 99 percent; meanwhile, students from the lowest quartile who started college in 1970 had a BA attainment rate of 22 percent, which is slightly more than the mere 21 percent who attained a BA in 2013.[5] During this same period, the United States moved from having the highest percentage of college graduates per capita to being number sixteen in the world. We are now behind most European nations and even Russia.[6]

This drop has occurred even though an increasing number of students go to college. The problem is that while many students enroll in college, a declining number finish. Graduation rates have fallen to around 40 percent, and on-time graduation rates are closer to 20 percent. These dismal completion rates are due largely to the expense of college.[7]

Making public higher education free would have several important effects. Because the main reason students drop out of colleges and universities is that they cannot afford the high cost of continuing, it would enable more students to attain degrees. Moreover, many students who do not drop out nonetheless fail to graduate in a timely fashion because they spend so much time working in order to afford the increasing costs of tuition and room and board.[8] If public higher education were free, students could stay in school and graduate on time, and decreasing the average time to graduate would allow more students to get college degrees.

Free public higher education sounds almost too good to be true. Critics of this idea say we can't afford it. They are wrong. How much it would cost to make all public higher education free to all Americans who wanted it? In 2012 to 2013, there were 6.7 million full-time-equivalent undergraduate students enrolled in public universities and 4.2 million enrolled in community colleges. The average cost of tuition, room, and board for undergraduates at public four-year institutions was $17,474; at two-year public colleges, it was $8,928.[9] If we multiply the number of students in public higher education by the average total cost, we discover that the cost of making all public universities free would have been $117 billion in 2012 to2013, with an annual cost of $37 billion for all community colleges—or a total of $154 billion.

While $154 billion seems like a large figure, we need to remember that in 2011 to 2012, the federal government spent $33.6 billion on Pell grants and $104 billion on student loans, while the states spent at least $10 billion on financial aid for universities and colleges and another $76 billion for direct support of higher education.[10] Furthermore, looking at various state and federal tax breaks and deductions for tuition, it might be possible to make all public higher education free by just using current resources in a more effective manner.

It is important to stress that current tuition rates are inflated because schools increase their sticker price in order to subsidize institutional financial aid for low-income students and to provide merit aid for wealthy, high-scoring students. If we eliminated the current aid system and each school instead received a set amount of money for each student from the state and federal governments, we could significantly reduce the cost of making public higher education free in America. Moreover, by eliminating the need for student loans, the government would save billions of dollars by avoiding the current cost of nonpayment of loans, servicing and subsidizing them, and borrowers' defaults.

Rather than directly funding public higher education institutions, state and federal governments have often relied on tax deductions and credits to support individual students. The tax code has been used to fund higher education because it is easier for Congress to pass a tax break than it is to get funding for a particular program. However, this system provides a huge subsidy for upper-middle-class and wealthy families, while lower-income students are forced to take out large loans to pay for their education. According to a 2012 study, "From 1999 to 2009, the government spent $70 billion on tax breaks aimed at subsidizing higher education for families [and] about 13 percent, or $9.4 billion, of that total went to families making more than $100,000 a year. At the same time, only 11 percent went to the neediest families, those making less than $25,000. Families in the middle—those making between $25,000 and $99,999—received the lion's share of the aid, taking in slightly more than three-quarters of the benefits." The report also indicates that much of the direct funding now goes to the wealthiest Americans as well. Whereas "nearly 83 percent of the higher education tax benefits distributed from 1999 to 2001 went to families earning less than $75,000 per year [and] no benefits went to those earning more than $100,000," by 2010 "families making between $100,000 and $180,000 received nearly a quarter of the benefits [and] the share going to middle-income families sharply declined."[11]

The tax system subsidizes affluent students in numerous ways. In 2010, the federal government provided the following tax subsidies, breaks, and credits for higher education: student interest rate exemption ($1.4 billion); exclusion from taxation of employer-provided educational assistance ($1.1 billion); exclusion of interest on student-loan bonds ($0.6 billion); exclusion of scholarship and fellowship income ($3.0 billion); exclusion of earnings of qualified tuition programs—savings account programs ($0.6 billion); the HOPE tax credit ($5.4 billion); the Lifetime Learning tax credit ($5.5 billion); parental personal exemption for students age nineteen or over ($3.4 billion); and state prepaid tuition plans ($1.8 billion).[12] There's also the stimulus package's American

Opportunity Tax Credit ($14.4 billion) and the part of the deductibility of charitable contributions for gifts to educational institutions ($4.9 billion). In total, the federal government lost over $40 billion in tax revenue due to higher education in 2010. And poor students benefitted very little from all this generosity on the part of the federal government.

If we made all public higher education free, not only could we do away with all these tax credits and tax breaks that little benefit those who need it most, but we could also stop the flow of public funds to expensive private and for-profit universities and colleges. Most people do not realize that the use of financial aid and tax subsidies for students has resulted in a system in which much of the governmental support for higher education ends up going to private institutions that cater to the super rich or to low-achieving and predatory for-profit schools. In fact, during a 2012 congressional investigation of for-profit colleges, it was discovered that up to a quarter of all federal Pell grant money is now going to these corporate schools, which charge a high tuition and graduate very few students.[13]

In short, if we took all of the state and federal money that is lost each year due to these tax credits, deductions, and shelters, we could make public higher education free for millions of Americans.

Moreover, free public education would help to drive down the cost of private education as well. One side effect of the current system is that private universities are able to charge higher tuition because they know that the parents of many of the incoming students will pay only a fraction of the full price thanks to merit aid, institutional aid, and tax breaks. Furthermore, once the private universities increase their tuition, they raise the bar for everyone else, making tuition increases at public universities appear more tolerable. And since the top public universities compete with the top private universities for star faculty and administrators, the more the private institutions are able to increase their tuition, the more the public ones have to pay their star faculty.

Making all public higher education free, by moving us away from the current emphasis on tax breaks and tax shelters, would help to contain rising tuition at private universities and end the subsidization of high-cost, low-value for-profit schools. Replacing the current mix of financial aid, institutional aid, tax subsidies, and grants with direct funding for public institutions would give the government a way to control costs at both public and private universities and colleges. The federal government could also require states to maintain their funding for public institutions in return for increased federal support, and once we stabilize funding and make higher education free, there will be no need for so many students and institutions to go into debt.

Higher education should not turn a generation of students into debtors. By making public higher education free, we can increase graduation rates and control costs. However, a key to this change is to see public higher education as a right, in the same way that we now see K-12 education as a universal public value. We can afford to make public college free. All we need is to return to the idea that higher education is a public good and not a private investment.

CON: Neal McCluskey

E ducation is good. We need to be literate to do everything from reading a menu, to understanding a contract, to contemplating *Where the Wild Things Are*. We need to be numerate to calculate a tip or finance a home. And education encompasses more than just basic skills, including everything from art appreciation to learning to cook. But just because education is good does not mean it is wise to make it free.

Food is also good—get too little and you die. But eat too much, or the wrong thing, and you could also die. Similarly, we can consume too much education, or too much junk food labelled "education," and suffer for it. Indeed, there is powerful evidence that the United States is already sick from too much free schooling.

HISTORY

Since education is generally good, you would expect people to seek it out, and this they did in great numbers well before there was broad, free provision of it. Of course, people are being educated all of the time. Children learn much about how the world works by observing their parents, or nature, or just playing with toys. Babies learn the fundamentals of language not from school but listening to and interacting with others and experimenting with sounds. And for much of history, many people learned skills and even reading, writing, and mathematics not in schools, but in daily household work or apprenticeships with skilled artisans.

Prior to 1837—the year common-schooling "father" Horace Mann started as the first education secretary of Massachusetts—there was little government provision of education in the United States, and what existed wasn't free. Yet, by the best-but-limited historical records we have, there is good reason to believe that literacy was very high, at least among the White Americans who, unlike many Blacks, were not legally barred from receiving an education.

Historian Kenneth Lockridge has estimated that in New England between 1650 and 1670 about 60 percent of White males were literate, a proportion that grew to 85 percent by 1762 and about 90 percent by 1795. New England did see government-compelled—but not free—provision of formal education, but literacy rose even as compliance evaporated.[1] Even in the more sparsely populated South, literacy grew. Examining signatures versus the leaving of marks on land deeds, historian Robert Gellman has estimated that free male literacy in Perquimans County, North Carolina—a fairly typical county—rose from 67 percent between 1661 and 1695 to 79 percent between 1748 and 1776.[2] Similarly, in the eighteenth century back country of South Carolina, Robert Meriwether has surmised that roughly 80 percent of White males were literate.[3] Finally, economists Claudia Goldin and Lawrence F. Katz note that "by the mid-nineteenth century, the [school] enrollment rate among children and youth in the United States exceeded that of any other nation in the world."[4]

If education was so widespread before public schooling, why did we eventually see the triumph of "free" public education? In part, precisely because people were already consuming education. As historian Michael B. Katz has explained, "the ease with which public education entered social life stands out as truly remarkable. Most people, by and large, did not need to be coerced to send their children to school."[5] Indeed, small communities were establishing *colleges* at tremendous rates.[6]

Importantly, the primary rationale behind public schooling was not increasing skills and knowledge but fostering unity and democracy. Benjamin Rush, the Surgeon General of the Continental Army and a prominent Pennsylvanian, wrote in proposing public schooling that, "Our schools of learning, by producing one general and uniform system of education, will render the mass of the people more homogeneous and thereby fit them more easily for uniform and peaceable government."[7] Noah Webster wrote that publicly provided education would "implant in the minds of American youth the principles of virtue and of liberty."[8] And Horace Mann said that free schooling is the only institution "capable of diffusing" the "general intelligence . . . indispensible to the continuance of a republican government."[9]

Just as history suggests there was no need for schooling to be free for the large majority of Americans to be educated, it indicates the need for public schooling to foster democratic unity was overstated. In the absence of widespread government provision of education, the American colonies declared national independence; did so with a Declaration that enshrined bedrock American values; defeated the most powerful military force in the world; adopted a Constitution still in effect today; and grew far larger than the original thirteen colonies. Later, we saw immigrant groups assimilate *despite* an often hostile public schooling system.[10]

As time went on, of course, we saw increasing government provision of education, but that does not mean it was necessary. Not only did people consume education before there was major government involvement, advances typically came through the private sector first. Illustrative of this is the growth of secondary schooling, which largely began with private academies. As Goldin and Katz report, "The number of public high schools probably did not equal the number of private academies until the 1880s, and the number of public high school students probably did not exceed those in private academies and preparatory departments of universities and colleges until the 1890s."[11]

Eventually, public schooling won out, so it is impossible to show definitively that people form the late nineteenth century to today would have been educated without widespread government provision. But assuming basic human motivations remained constant, and the value of education remained the same or greater than it was through roughly 1850, it is logical to assume that people would have continued to consume education consistent with their needs.

DOES FREE EDUCATION WORK?

There are two primary phenomena that cause free education to work poorly. The first is that we are not as strongly incentivized to demand efficiency and quality from things we do not pay for as things we do. That is one reason that researcher James Tooley, comparing for-profit and public schools serving the poorest people in the world, has found that the former outperform the latter: Families demand the best possible teaching from schools for which they are paying.[12]

The second major problem is that when government provides something, it sets up an incentive imbalance that gives the people providing the service disproportionate power. It is a matter of concentrated benefits and diffuse costs: Small groups that benefit from something government does focus laser-like on that thing, while the people paying for it have much less at stake in that specific piece of the pie. Public school employees have their livelihoods at stake in education policies, while taxpayers have to worry about everything from defense spending to transportation funding. Even parents do not have the same motivation; they care about their children but also have full-time jobs and only limited ability to get involved in education politics.

This would not be a problem if the interests of students, taxpayers, teachers, and administrators were naturally aligned. But they are not. Like anyone else, teachers and administrators want the best possible compensation and, ideally, no one holding them responsible for their performance. Meanwhile, taxpayers want the most bang for their buck and families want responsive, effective schools.

In free markets, differing incentives are balanced by providers having to earn the business of consumers who can vote with their feet, while consumers cannot demand that people furnish something from which they cannot earn a living. The check on providers, especially, is why Tooley has found that for-profit schools in the world's poorest slums are more effective than the public schools—they have to earn their money.

We see the deleterious effects of undisciplined consumption and imbalanced political incentives in K–12 and higher education. Both have seen huge increases in funding accompanied by little discernable improvement in outcomes, and both feature big lobbying operations by providers. Inflation-adjusted, total cost per-pupil of a public K–12 education rose roughly 190 percent between 1970 and 2012, while 17-year-olds' scores on the Long-Term Trend National Assessment of Educational Progress—a federal, nationally representative test—barely budged.[13] The scores are better for some subgroups of students but are poor overall.[14] The results are little better for high school graduation rates: In the 1969–1970 school year, 79 percent of students who had entered as freshman four years earlier received regular diplomas. That dipped to a low of 71 percent in 1995–1996 and only in 2011–2012—the latest year with available data—broke 80 percent.[15]

The advocacy force to maintain the system, meanwhile, is huge. Numerous associations representing public school employees have headquarters in Washington, DC, and state affiliates are often similarly situated in state capitals. All bring influence, and some bring a lot of money. In the 2014 midterm elections, the two major national teachers' unions spent at least $60 million to influence the outcomes of races.[16] Moreover, funds spent by unions not counted as "political"—for instance, for collective bargaining—are inherently political, since public schooling is a government function.

The situation in higher education is a bit fuzzier than in K–12 schooling because we have no single measure of learning, and the system is much more heterogeneous. Public institutions get direct state and local subsidies but also typically charge tuition and fees, and students have to cover room and board, which may or may not be provided by the school. Private, non-profit institutions typically get no direct government subsidies and have much higher sticker prices but pay little in taxes, while their donors get very favorable tax treatment. For-profit colleges get neither direct subsidies nor tax breaks, but all of these sectors take students who can get federal grants, loans, and work study.

What all these subsidies have a tendency to do is decrease the incentives for prospective students to think hard about whether to go to college, where, what to study, and how hard to work. The results have been poor.

The first impact has been on prices. As illustrated in Figure 20.1, aid per student—the bulk of it federal—has skyrocketed since 1990, though it has trailed off in recent years. Much has come in the form of loans, but grants have also ballooned. Meanwhile, tuition, fee, and room and board costs have also leapt up. This is not a coincidence, with numerous studies supporting what logic suggests: Because they are staffed by self-interested human beings, schools raise their prices, or decrease their own aid, to, essentially, capture aid dollars.[17]

One argument against the conclusion that aid fuels price increases is that states have been cutting their subsidies for public institutions. With the Great Recession, state and local appropriations dropped from $86.1 billion in 2008 to $75.0 billion in 2013. On a per-pupil basis, the decrease was even more dramatic—from $8,554 to $6,960—because, in recessions, at the same time tax revenues are falling people flock to schools to change their skills and credentials.[18]

No doubt such cuts affect prices. But changes in state subsidies do not affect private institutions, which have seen big price increases. More directly, as we see

Figure 20.1

Percentage Change from 1990–1991 Baseline in Aid per FTE Undergraduate and Published Tuition, Fees, Room, and Board for Public 4-Year Colleges

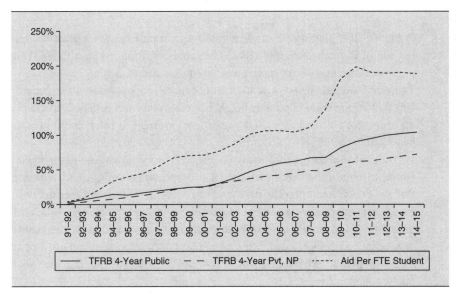

Source: Prepared by author from data in College Board, *Trends in College Pricing 2015*, Table 2, and *Trends in Student Aid 2015*, Table 3.

Note: Aid data are for undergraduates only, and 2014–2015 aid data is estimated.

Figure 20.2

State Appropriations per FTE Student vs. In-State Tuition, Fees, Room, and Board at Public 4-Year Colleges, 1984–1985 to 2014–2015, Inflation Adjusted

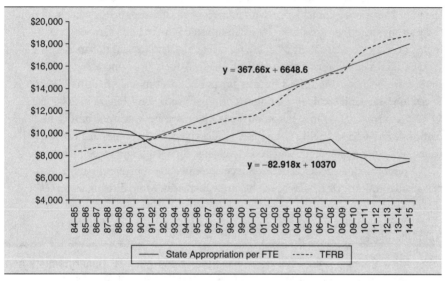

Source: Prepared by author from data in College Board, *Trends in College Pricing 2015*, Fig. 16B and Table 2.

in Figure 20.2, plotting per-student changes in state subsidies against tuition, fee, room, and board charges reveals that public institutions have raised their prices both when state appropriations have fallen and when they have risen.

Even if aid has fueled price increases, it has also likely goosed enrollment. Isn't that a good thing? Probably not. While on average it is beneficial to graduate from college, that does not mean that spurring greater enrollment is beneficial.

The first problem is that many people who enroll in college never finish, failing to obtain the credential crucial to improving earnings and repaying student debts. According to data from the National Student Clearinghouse Research Center, only 74 percent of students entering in 2008 had completed their four-year program at private, nonprofit institutions within six years; only 63 percent had completed at four-year publics; only 38 percent had finished at four-year private, for-profits; and only 39 percent had finished at *two-year* public colleges.[19]

A large part of the problem appears to be that students who are not prepared for college-level work are enrolling, likely encouraged by low-cost options such as community colleges and federal aid. In the 2011–2012 academic year, nearly a third of first-year undergraduate students had to take at least one remedial course, with a high of 40 percent at community colleges.[20] Students who require remedial courses are much less likely to graduate than those who do not.

Huge noncompletion rates are just the beginning of the poor outcomes. Next is the oversupply of degrees. According to the Federal Reserve Bank of New York, roughly a third of Americans holding bachelor's degrees are in jobs not requiring the credential.[21] No wonder: There are 35.6 million Americans ages 25 to 64 with top educational attainment of a bachelor's degree, but only 26 million jobs requiring that credential for entry.[22]

We also suffer from credential inflation: Employers increasingly want job seekers to have degrees, but often not, it seems, because they represent specific skills or knowledge. Degrees often just give basic signals about applicants—do applicants have baseline smarts and the ability to complete things?—that it costs employers little to ask for. This has been borne out in research that has found that often much greater shares of ads for numerous types of jobs call for degrees than the share of current job holders hold them, without evidence that the skills and knowledge needed to do the jobs have significantly changed. In other words, more employers are asking for degrees, but the jobs themselves have not changed.[23]

It also appears that degree holders are less literate than they used to be. According to the National Assessment of Adult Literacy, administered in 1992 and 2003, the "prose" reading proficiency rates for college graduates dropped from 40 percent to 31 percent, and for people with postgraduate studies from 51 percent to 41 percent. For "document" literacy, the drops were from 37 percent to 25 percent and 45 percent to 31 percent.[24]

Further bolstering the credential inflation theory are measures of time students spend studying and socializing. Over the last several decades, the latter has ballooned while the former has shrunk, and researchers Richard Arum and Josipa Roksa have found that students gain little academically while in college.[25] This should come as little surprise, with colleges seemingly providing more pure entertainment, right up to on-campus water-parks.[26] This amenities race is likely driven by the demands of heavily subsidized students: According to one study, other than for academically high achieving students, amenities have a big impact on where students decide to matriculate.[27]

Higher education has become a vicious cycle: More people are getting expensive but often empty degrees, forcing even more people to do the same. To exit the cycle, we must reduce subsidies and thereby encourage people to seek out low-cost ways of obtaining skills and signals that they have them, such as "badges" when they master specific skills.

As with K–12 education, those who benefit from the current system have huge incentives to engage in politics, and there are numerous higher education advocacy organizations in Washington, DC, usually pressing for more money and limited accountability for outcomes. Indeed, in 2014, higher education employed the third most lobbyists of any industry, trailing only pharmaceuticals/health products and electronics manufacturing/equipment.[28] Meanwhile, taxpayers must still deal with every slice of pie and cannot counter the power of the higher education lobby. Students are also an ineffective counterbalance; while they have incentives to change things, their time horizon is relatively short, and their advocacy groups tend to focus more on getting increased aid—or easier debt relief—than phasing aid out. Of course, students also often enjoy the amenities for which their aid enables them to pay.

CONCLUSION

Looking at American education, not only should we not have four more years of free education, we should make education less "free" than it is now. When people pay for something they are incentivized to think hard about what they want and find the most cost-effective way to get it. When someone else pays, those incentives decline. And when government pays, including providing the service directly, it creates a huge disincentive to make efficient choices and gives political advantages to education providers. "Free" education, like non-stop binge eating, ends up being very costly.

NOTES

INTRO

1. Barack Obama, *The Audacity of Hope: Thoughts on Reclaiming the American Dream* (New York. NY: Three Rivers Press, 2006), 159.

2. Jeffrey M. Jones, "In U.S., 70% Favor Federal Funds to Expand Pre-K Education," September 8, 2014, http://www.gallup.com/poll/175646/favor-federal-funds-expand-pre-education.aspx.

3. "Fewer Want Spending to Grow, But Most Cuts Remain Unpopular," February 20, 2011,http://www.people-press.org/2011/02/10/fewer-want-spending-to-grow-but-most-cuts-remain-unpopular.

4. Suzanne Mettler, *Degrees of Inequality: How the Politics of Higher Education Sabotaged the American Dream* (New York, NY: Basic Books, 2014), 21.

5. Liz Weston, "OECD: The US Has Fallen Behind Other Countries in College Completion," *Business Insider*, September 9, 2014, http://www.businessinsider.com/r-us-falls-behind-in-college-competition-oecd-2014-9.

PRO

1. National Park Service, "Thomas Jefferson's Plan for the University of Virginia: Lessons from the Lawn," http://www.nps.gov/nr/twhp/wwwlps/lessons/92uva/92uva.htm.

2. Jefferson, *Report of the Commissioners for the University of Virginia*, quoted at http://www.nps.gov/nr/twhp/wwwlps/lessons/92uva/92facts3.htm.

3. Jillian Berman, "Class of 2015 Has the Most Student Debt in U.S. History," *MarketWatch*, May 9, 2015, http://www.marketwatch.com/story/class-of-2015-has-the-most-student-debt-in-us-history-2015-05-08.

4. See Kate Pickett and Richard Wilkinson, *The Spirit Level* (New York, NY: Bloomsbury Press, 2011).

5. "Indicators of Higher Education Equity in the United States, 45-Year Trend Report," (2015), http://docplayer.net/377884-Indicators-of-higher-education-equity-in-the-united-states-45-year-trend-report-2015.html.

6. Daniel de Vise, "U.S. Falls in Global Ranking of Young Adults Who Finish College," *Washington Post*, September 13, 2011, https://www.washingtonpost.com/local/education/us-falls-in-global-ranking-of-young-adults-who-finish-college/2011/08/22/gIQAAsU3OK_story.html.

7. http://completecollege.org/wp-content/uploads/2014/11/4-Year-Myth.pdf.

8. See Marc Bousquet, *How the University Works: Higher Education and the Low-Wage Nation* (New York University Press, 2008), https://academictrap.files.wordpress.com/2015/03/marc-bousquet-how-the-university-works-higher-education-and-the-lowwage-nation.pdf.

9. National Center for Education Statistics, "Digest of Education Statistics," https://nces.ed.gov/fastfacts/display.asp?id=76.

10. For statistics on Pell grants, see Sandy Baum and Michael McPherson, "Pell Grants vs. Tuition Tax Credits," *The Chronicle of Higher Education* (2011), http://chronicle.com/blogs/innovations/pell-grants-vs-tuition-tax-credits/30663. For state spending on higher education, see Doug Lederman, "State Support Slumps Again," *Inside Higher Ed*, January 23 2012, https://www.insidehighered.com/news/2012/01/23/state-funds-higher-education-fell-76-2011-12; and "State Support for Student Aid 2009–10," *Chronicle of Higher Education*, http://chronicle.com/article/Sortable-Table-State-Support/128153. For federal support for student loans, see Department of Education, "Student Loans Overview," https://www2.ed.gov/about/overview/budget/budget14/justifications/s-loansoverview.pdf; and Kelly D. Edmiston, Lara Brooks, and Steven Shepelwich. "Student Loans: Overview and Issues." *Federal Reserve Bank of Kansas City Research Working Paper* 12-05 (2012), https://www.kansascityfed.org/publicat/reswkpap/pdf/rwp%2012-05.pdf.

11. Stephen Burd, "Moving on up: How Tuition Tax Breaks Increasingly Favor the Upper-Middle Class. Charts You Can Trust," *Education Sector* (2012), http://eric.ed.gov/?id=ED531248.

12. The federal tax breaks for higher education are itemized at Subsidy Scope, "Tax Expenditures in the Education Sector," http://www.pewtrusts.org/~/media/legacy/uploadedfiles/pcs_assets/2012/subsidyscope_education_sector.pdf.

13. For statistics on how many Pell grants for-profits colleges are using, see Andrea Fuller, "For-Profits Hit Hardest by End of Year-Round Pell Grant Program," June 29, 2011, http://chronicle.com/article/For-Profits-Hit-Hardest-by-End/128089.

CON

1. Kenneth A. Lockridge, *Literacy in Colonial New England: An Enquiry into the Social Context of Literacy in the Early Modern West* (New York, NY: W.W. Norton & Company, 1974), 19–20.

2. Robert E. Gallman, "Changes in the Level of Literacy in a New Community of Early America," *The Journal of Economic History* 48, no. 3 (September 1988): 574.

3. Robert L. Meriwether cited in Lawrence A. Cremin, *American Education: The Colonial Experience, 1607-1783* (New York, NY: Harper Torchbooks, 1970), 543.

4. Claudia Goldin and Lawrence F. Katz, *The Race between Education and Technology* (Cambridge, MA: Harvard University Press, 2008), 130.

5. Michael B. Katz, "The Origins of Public Education: A Reassessment," in B. Edward McClellan and William J. Reese, eds., *The Social History of American Education* (Urbana, IL: University of Illinois Press, 1988), 110.

6. Frederick Rudolph, *The American College and University: A History* (Athens, GA: University of Georgia Press, 1990), 44–67.

7. Benjamin Rush, "Thoughts upon the Mode of Education Proper in a Republic," in Frederick Rudolph, ed., *Essays on Education in the Early Republic* (Cambridge, MA: The Belknap Press of Harvard University Press, 1965), 9.

8. Noah Webster, "On the Education of Youth in America," in *Essays on Education in the Early Republic*, 45.

9. Horace Mann, "Report for 1846," in Mary Mann, ed., *Life and Works of Horace Mann* (Boston, MA: Horace B. Fuller, 1868), 531.

10. See, for instance, Milton M. Gordon, *Assimilation in American Life: The Role of Race, Religion, and National Origins* (New York, NY: Oxford University Press, 1964).

11. Goldin and Katz, *The Race between Education and Technology*, 186.

12. James Tooley, *The Beautiful Tree: A Personal Journey into How the World's Poorest People are Educating Themselves* (Washington, DC: Cato Institute, 2010).

13. See chart "Trends in American Public Schooling Since 1970," in Cato Institute, "Educational Freedom: An Introduction," http://www.cato.org/education-wiki/educational-freedom-an-introduction.

14. Scores broken down by subgroup are available at National Center for Education Statistics, The Nation's Report Card, Long-Term Trends, http://www.nationsreportcard.gov/ltt_2012/, accessed November 4, 2015.

15. U.S. Department of Education, National Center for Education Statistics, *Digest of Education Statistics*, Table 219.10, https://nces.ed.gov/programs/digest/d13/tables/dt13_219.10.asp?current=yes, accessed November 4, 2015.

16. Lyndsey Layton, "Teachers Unions Spent $60 million for the Midterms and Still Lost Many Elections," *The Washington Post*, November 4, 2014.

17. For a list of studies finding "capturing" effects, see Neal McCluskey, "The Newly Updated Help-That-Hurts List," SeeThruEdu, http://www.seethruedu.com/the-newly-updated-help-that-hurts-list, January 7, 2016.

18. Calculations based on data from College Board, *Trends in College Pricing 2015*, Figure 16B, http://trends.collegeboard.org/college-pricing/figures-tables/institutional-finances#Institutonal%20Revenues%20and%20Expenditures.

19. National Student Clearinghouse Research Center, "Signature Report 8: Completing College: A National View of Student Attainment Rates–Fall 2008 Cohort," http://nscresearchcenter.org/signaturereport8, accessed November 4, 2015.

20. *Digest of Education Statistics*, Table 311.40, https://nces.ed.gov/programs/digest/d14/tables/dt14_311.40.asp?current=yes, accessed November 4, 2015.

21. Jaison R. Abel, Richard Deitz, and Yaqin Su, "Are Recent College Graduates Finding Good Jobs?" *Current Issues in Economics and Finance 20, no. 1*, Federal Reserve Bank of New York, http://www.newyorkfed.org/research/current_issues/ci20-1.pdf, 2014.

22. Data on bachelor's holders from *Digest of Education Statistics*, Table 104.30, https://nces.ed.gov/programs/digest/d14/tables/dt14_104.30.asp?current=yes, accessed November 4, 2015. Data on jobs for bachelor's holders from U.S. Bureau of Labor Statistics, "Employment 2012 and projected 2022, by typical entry-level education and training assignment," http://www.bls.gov/emp/ep_table_education_summary.htm#1, May 7, 2015.

23. Burning Glass Technologies, "Moving the Goalposts: How Demand for a Bachelor's Degree is Reshaping the Workforce," September 2014.

24. U.S. Department of Education, National Center for Education Statistics, "A First Look at the Literacy of America's Adults in the 21st Century," http://nces.ed.gov/NAAL/PDF/2006470.PDF, 15.

25. Richard Arum and Josipa Roksa, *Academically Adrift: Limited Learning on College Campuses* (Chicago, IL: University of Chicago Press, 2011).

26. For examples see Neal McCluskey, "How Am I Supposed to Learn Anything without a Lazy River and Wet Wall," SeeThruEdu, http://www.seethruedu.com/how-am-i-supposed-to-learn-anything-without-a-lazy-river-and-wet-wall, May 19, 2005.

27. Brian Jacob, Brian McCall, and Kevin M. Stange, "College as Country Club: Do Colleges Cater to Students' Preferences for Consumption Goods?" National Bureau of Economic Research, January 2013.

28. Brody Mullins, Douglas Belkin, and Andrea Fuller, "Colleges Flex Lobbying Muscle," *The Wall Street Journal*, November 8, 2015.

RESOLVED, national security would be strengthened by requiring the government to keep fewer secrets and become more transparent

PRO: Michael Colaresi

CON: Stephen F. Knott

By most accounts, people who were watching television, listening to the radio, or surfing news sites on the web on the morning of September 11, 2001, had the same thought when they learned that a passenger jet had crashed into the north tower of the World Trade Center in New York City: "What a terrible accident." Less than seventeen minutes later, at 9:03 a.m. Eastern Time, people changed their minds when a second plane carrying passengers crashed into the south tower. One crash might be accidental but not two. Nearly everyone realized that what White House chief of staff Andrew Card whispered to President George W. Bush, who was reading to a class of elementary school students in Sarasota, Florida, was true: "America is under attack." As if further confirmation were needed, a third plane soon hit the Pentagon just outside Washington, DC, and a fourth crashed in the Pennsylvania countryside.

On September 12, one day after the attacks, Bush told Attorney General John Ashcroft, "Don't ever let this happen again," signaling that he wanted his administration to focus on preventing future attacks by any means necessary. Two days after that, Congress voted almost unanimously to approve Bush's request to authorize the use of military force "to prevent any future acts of international terrorism against the United States." The Bush administration quickly concluded that the 9/11 attacks, which killed almost 3,000 people, had been inspired by an international terrorist organization called Al Qaeda. In a September 20 address to Congress, Bush vowed to wage a "war on terror." In a later speech, he described the effort as "a different kind of war with a different kind of enemy"—not a country or alliance of countries as in America's previous wars but a nonstate actor whose combatants wore no uniform and lived in no particular place. Combatting this new kind of enemy required, as Vice President Dick Cheney told an interviewer on September 16, that the administration work "the dark side."

During the next decade, through leaks, enterprising reporting, and Congressional oversight, the public discovered some of what the Bush administration had been doing in working the dark side of the war on terror, including the warrantless surveillance of Americans' electronic communications and severe treatment of captured enemies in secret prisons (so-called black sites) operated by the Central Intelligence Agency. Critics of the Bush administration charged that the war on terror had become an assault on freedom. By shrouding the war on terror in secrecy, critics argued, the administration denied citizens and elected members of Congress the information they needed to evaluate these practices.

In 2008, Democratic presidential candidate Barack Obama carried the critics' banner by pledging to end the Bush administration's overreliance on secrecy. Once in the Oval Office, however, Obama preserved many of the Bush administration's policies—and in some cases his administration was even more vigilant in its defense of secrecy, for instance in its aggressive prosecution of whistleblowers who revealed national security secrets.

In his essay, Michael Colaresi raises the banner for greater transparency that he contends Obama needlessly dropped. He argues that secrecy in the United States has reached a "counterproductive and dangerous" level that not only undermines America's democratic values but makes the country less safe by sowing distrust of the American government both domestically and abroad. Stephen F. Knott rejoins that secrecy has always been necessary to preserve American national security, and that the terrorist threat makes it more essential than ever before.

PRO: Michael Colaresi

Secrecy in the United States has reached counterproductive and dangerous levels. The government has been keeping more secrets from the public at an increasing rate, escalating its prosecutions of journalists for pursuing stories of potential abuse and corruption of government, sanctioning unprecedented spying on Congressional overseers, and swelling the justifications for classifying information to include politically embarrassing facts, instead of only those secrets that are necessary to protect national security.

Given this unfortunate excess of secrecy, greater transparency will not only strengthen democracy in America but make us safer in the process. No one would argue for unfettered access to all government information, including the secrets of stealth technology or the known vulnerabilities of airport security screening systems. Yet, in a democracy, transparency must be the rule and secrecy the exception; not the other way around. Without sufficient information on what the government is doing, particularly in the area of national security, the public cannot hold leaders to account or guide policy.

If we choose not to reassert democratic control over secret intelligence agencies, we have to ask ourselves, as others are starting to question, whether American policies are serving to further individual freedom and justice or whether those goals are simply empty rhetoric. To keep details about the imprisonment, torture, and killing of potentially innocent civilians by the Central Intelligence Agency (CIA) in the extraordinary rendition program and drone-strike program secret for many years after specific operations occurred is inconsistent with the democratic ideals of the U.S. Constitution. We innovated new forms of transparency in response to excessive secrecy during the height of the Cold War, thereby staying true to our democratic values. We must do the same today in the fight against extremist groups.

IN SECRECY WE TRUST?

Over the last fifteen years, the balance between public transparency and government secrecy has been flipped on its head. Understandably, after 9/11, the United States strengthened executive counterterrorism powers, rearranged the intelligence agencies, and created the Department of Homeland Security. Unfortunately, the empowering of largely secret bureaucracies to carry out new classified programs has outpaced efforts to innovate methods to ensure that the public and its representatives can accurately observe the long-term costs and benefits of post-9/11 policy decisions.

The United States government reports that it spent at least 15 billion dollars on secrecy in government in 2014 alone. That is 100 times more than the budget for the office tasked with disseminating information on the government, the Government Printing Office. And it is about four times what the government spent annually on the same activities in the years immediately prior to 9/11.[1] Despite the winding down of the Iraq and Afghanistan wars, the government divulged that it made at least 77,552,436 classification decisions in 2014.[2] Moreover, these numbers understate secrecy in the United States since several intelligence agencies, including the CIA, have classified the amount they spent on keeping secrets and the number of classification decisions they made. Experts from within the Department of Defense and National Security Council have stated that they believe up to 90 percent of classified documents could safely be made public.[3]

The government is not only keeping more secrets, it is also threatening those in the press and legislature that attempt to investigate national security programs and events. The Obama administration has subpoenaed phone logs and e-mails from reporters and has formally accused a reporter from Fox News of being "an aider, abettor and/or conspirator" in a leak investigation. *New York Times* reporter James Risen, a two time Pulitzer Prize winner, faced a seven-year legal fight for publishing information on U.S. actions toward Iran.[4]

This clamping down on transparency comes on the heels of the aggressive use of the Espionage Act by the Obama administration to prosecute whistleblowers who leak classified information. The Obama administration has referenced the Espionage Act in seven cases they have brought against potential whistleblowers, including Edward Snowden, who revealed the existence of previously secret surveillance programs that collected information on U.S. citizens and international allies by the National Security Agency. That is three more cases than all other presidents since 1945 combined.[5]

The executive branch's obsession with secrecy means that our enemies sometimes know more about U.S. policies and programs than the American public. For example, at the confirmation hearing for David Petraeus, Obama's nominee to head the CIA, Republican Senator Roy D. Blunt asked the nominee to discuss "the use of drones." While the American public, and enemy nations, know that the CIA is operating drones in conflict areas, Petraeus could not discuss the issue at his confirmation because the CIA's use of drones was still technically classified. Similarly, information that is in the public domain from the Snowden leaks is still considered classified. So while enemies have access to this information online, public discussion and debate on U.S. policies is stifled by worries that the United State government will prosecute or harass academics or members of the public that engage with this information.[6]

One might argue that these prosecutions and tightening the lid on information are valid responses to the leaking of secrets by Edward Snowden and before him Bradley Manning, who released information on Iraq, Afghanistan, and global diplomatic cables to Wikileaks. However, this gets the relationship between secrecy and whistle-blowing backwards. The increasing trend toward secrecy began just after 9/11, before these leaks, as reports by the Information Security Oversight Office make clear.[7] Second, both Manning and Snowden have written extensively about the fact that they were motivated to leak information due to increasing classification and because they believed that the public was not afforded the information to either consent to or hold leaders accountable for national security policy. Excessive secrecy was responsible for these leaks, not transparency.[8]

IS DEMOCRACY OBSOLETE?

Today, the digital and computing revolutions have introduced technologies that allow the government to secretly record and store information on citizens' everyday behaviors and communications without their knowledge, launch assassinations without due process, as well as run a network of secret prisons around the globe outside of the scope of judicial or legislative review. In fact, we now know that the U.S. government was pursuing each of these policies for years, without the knowledge of the public, consent of the legislature, or effective oversight of these actions.

We can see the current imbalance between secrecy and transparency in the frustrations of those who are attempting to grapple with the public costs and benefits of controversial intelligence programs. The then vice chair of the Senate Select Committee on Intelligence Senator John D. Rockefeller IV, saw the growing irrelevance of legislative oversight in 2003 when he wrote to Vice President Dick Cheney that new surveillance "activities . . . raised profound oversight issues." The increased technical complexity of secret data collection programs, in particular, meant that even the committee specifically tasked with understanding the pros and cons of intelligence activities could not serve its function. Senator Rockefeller was not allowed to even discuss the details of the new surveillance programs, as well as other intelligence operations, with his staff or council. He noted that since he was "neither a technician nor an attorney . . . [and] given . . . [his] inability to consult staff or counsel on my own, [he felt] unable to fully evaluate, much less endorse these activities."[9] Public oversight was so poor that we did not even learn about Senator Rockefeller's letter until two years after it was written. Through the leaks by Edward Snowden, we learned that these programs were used controversially to spy on leaders of allies such as German Chancellor Angela Merkel.

Politicians have also been troubled by their inability to evaluate the secret drone-strike program. Until recently, the Fifth Amendment of the U.S. Constitution was supposed to ensure an open and fair trial and due process to those accused by the government of a crime. However, now, the U.S. government has the ability and has been in the practice of launching secret, unmanned drone strikes to kill suspected threats, even American citizens. The speed with which these decisions would need to be made to issue such strikes led then U.S. Attorney General Eric Holder to declare in March 2012 that a secret but careful review by the executive branch, not the judicial branch, could be considered "due process." At issue here is not the justice of the program itself necessarily but the fact that the public has no available information on which to base its consent of the program. An open trial is meant to ensure that the public can judge whether justice or a corruption of justice was the outcome. In contrast, the "due process" for the drone program is secret. Moreover, civilian casualties and mistakes from the drone strikes are also classified. Here again, secrecy is outpacing transparency, depriving the public of information to judge whether the policy is serving its interests.

The upshot of secrecy outpacing transparency has been that the public now knows very little about what our government does on national security policy. Are drone strikes effective at reducing terrorism, or do they inflame conflict and feelings of injustice and cause more insecurity for the United States in the long run? Does U.S. surveillance of leaders of democratic and NATO allies such as Germany increase American security or lead to greater distrust and make coordinating international reactions to threats such as ISIS more difficult? No one can say there is enough public information to answer these basic but crucial questions. This is a significant problem for a democratic polity interested in supporting liberty and freedom at home and abroad. There will always be a diversity of opinions on what are the best policies to pursue given current circumstances. Yet, absent an open and balanced debate about the facts and what has worked and failed in the past, American citizens cannot be participants in their own government.

A MORE SECRET UNION IS A LESS SAFE UNION

Excessive secrecy is not only troubling for our democracy but has practical national security costs. The stakes in this debate could not be higher. As I write this, the largest military in the world is unable to stop sworn enemies from making territorial gains in Iraq, Syria, Afghanistan, Yemen, and Somalia.[10] There have been recent attacks traced to transnational threats in Africa, Europe, and the United States, while Russia has significantly increased its assertiveness in the Middle East and Eastern Europe and China, likewise, in the South China Sea.

These setbacks and emerging challenges have not resulted from inadequate secrecy or insufficient intelligence powers but from the inability of the U.S. government to coordinate and mobilize robust and productive responses among its own citizens, international allies, and individuals around the world. The violent challenge from ISIS was allowed to grow in large part because the United States could not persuade legislative representatives to support more robust intervention in Syria at an earlier stage. After the failures of intelligence in Iraq, skepticism may have been warranted, but the result was an absence of proactive policy by the United States to control the Syrian conflict from which ISIS reemerged with significant territory. Even now, there is not a consensus in the United States on how to meet the ISIS threat.

Skepticism of U.S. policy extends to allies such as the United Kingdom, France, and Germany. The Iraq war still casts a shadow over U.K. public opinion about military cooperation with the United States. A June 2015 poll in the United Kingdom found that 51 percent of respondents thought the war was "wrong," and only 26 percent answered that it was "right."[11] A report compiled by the House of Commons Foreign Affairs Committee "warns that the perception of the UK after the Iraq war as America's 'subservient poodle' has been highly damaging . . . [and concludes] . . . that British prime ministers have to learn to be less deferential to US presidents and be 'willing to say no' to America."[12] This skepticism has constrained what help the United Kingdom was willing to offer in Syria.

More dramatically, while the 2003 Iraq War was criticized deeply in France and Germany, the CIA-led drone strikes and torture programs and NSA surveillance of European leaders has further reduced trust in the United States. Even after the terrorist attacks in Paris on November 13, 2015, the French government turned to the European Union, invoking article 42.7 of the EU treaty for the first time, and not US-led NATO, to coordinate their response. Tensions between Germany and the United States have been running high after it was revealed that the United States had been spying on German Chancellor Angela Merkel. The Chancellor compared U.S. tactics to the infamous dictatorial surveillance by the East German Stasi. The number of Germans who believe the United States government respects freedom dropped from 81 percent in 2013 to 43 percent in 2015.[13]

Perhaps most troubling, potential partners within conflict zones doubt U.S. motives. In Iraq, the American forces were viewed as occupiers by a large section of the populace, sparking a civil war. In the Middle East region, a 2014 Pew poll found that 90 percent of respondents in Jordan and 87 percent in

Egypt disapproved of the U.S. drone strike program specifically. Both of these countries are crucial allies for U.S. policy. The same poll showed deep distrust of the United States throughout Latin America and in Asia where coordination in response to Chinese pressure is vital.[14] In Syria, the United States has thus far not only failed to mobilize its own armed group of local combatants to end the conflict, but what small force they were able to muster in the summer of 2015 was attacked and eviscerated by another rebel group that should have ostensibly been on the same side fighting with the United States against ISIS.[15] Hillary Clinton recently described ISIS, not the United States, as the most effective recruiter in the World. How do we change these perceptions?

America needs to be able to credibly communicate its ideals and goals to mobilize like-minded individuals against the violent world view of ISIS, in particular. Secrecy and antidemocratic policies such as torture play into the enemy's hands because they suggest that liberty and justice are empty sentiments. The common thread linking these past failures is that the U.S. government, despite having the world's largest military and most effective intelligence resources, has been unable to convince people—Americans as well as international allies—to follow its lead. Increasing transparency offers a way for the United States to decrease distrust and to lead by example.

TRUST, BUT VERIFY AGAIN

This is not the first time a disconnect has occurred between intelligence agency powers and democratic transparency. During World War II and the beginning of the Cold War, and particularly with the Manhattan Project and public worries about Soviet domestic spying, intelligence agencies grew in power and funding, while public oversight was nearly nonexistent. In the 1970s, in reaction to Watergate, which included CIA involvement in the cover-up, as well as to press reports that intelligence agencies were running programs that, among other things, authorized assassinations of foreign leaders, Congress improved public oversight of the intelligence agencies. The creation of the world's first specifically designed intelligence oversight committees in the Senate and House of Representatives was made possible because television had raised the profile of congressional hearings. In addition, the ability to copy and disseminate government documents at lower costs helped make possible passage the Freedom of Information Act, which enabled citizens and the media to gain greater access to information about government activities.

Even the former head of the CIA William E. Colby saw the necessity of democratic, public oversight of intelligence policies. He explicitly wrote that the new legislative committees would "strengthen American intelligence" and help to create a new meaning for the CIA as "constitutional intelligence for America."[16] Colby was proven correct. Renewed credibility for the intelligence community led to broad public support for significant investments in national security such as smart weapons, modern carriers, and stealth technology. These investments not only paid off in winning the Cold War but also in the successful first Gulf War in 1991, where direct Iraqi aggression against Kuwait was rolled back by a truly international coalition led by the United States.

Technology, of course, has evolved since the 1970s, but increased transparency is still the best way to build the necessary consensus among United States citizens and allies around the world to confront the many security challenges. Temporary secrecy to protect specific operational details of ongoing missions is necessary, as is the classification of technical details about weapons and vulnerabilities. But, over time, the value of keeping individual secrets declines. We do not have to wait generations for information on previously secret operations to become public. After an operation has finished, agents are no longer in harm's way. Over the years, methods change, technologies advance, and competitors learn the information anyway. We can afford retrospective transparency on specific operations such as renditions, which are supposedly long over, and previous drone strikes, some of which occurred almost a decade ago.

The Russian proverb, trust but verify, echoed by Ronald Reagan during Cold War negotiations, is an apt description of how a classification system should work in democracies. American citizens, as well as allies, must trust the U.S. government with the tools of national security, including the discretion to temporarily classify information. However, the use, and absence of abuse, of these powers must be verified by public oversight.

A PLAN FOR INTELLIGENT OVERSIGHT

There are several commonsense ways that the United States can increase transparency, retrospectively, to enhance national security. The first is to improve the United States Freedom of Information laws. Currently, the U.S. government does not have to release national security information to the public, even if an independent body recommends that citizens would benefit from the release of this information. Other democracies such as Australia subject the review of classified information to a balance test. If the public benefits of transparency are judged to outweigh any harm, then the information should be released. A bill proposing to move in this direction, that also included other important increases in transparency, has received near unanimous support in Congress but has yet to be passed due to obstruction by the party leadership.[17]

Second, the intelligence oversight committees in the House and Senate have increasingly found it difficult to provide substantive oversight of highly technical programs of surveillance and drones. It is difficult, if not impossible, for busy legislators to be experts on Internet protocols at the same time as learning about the international laws governing noncombatant status. Creating a committee of independent experts that can issue public (and private) reports and warnings to the appropriate committees and members of both parties would help to restore high quality intelligence oversight. These type of groups already have been created in Canada and Norway to rebalance what politicians rightfully saw as an excess of government secrecy.

Finally, the administration should step back from prosecuting journalists for investigating national security policies. The government regularly provides classified information to reporters on background to justify their preferred policies. It is not just hypocritical but undemocratic to suggest that the government can legally leak to reporters to sell its preferred policies, but information that might be politically awkward for the executive branch, when revealed, is evidence of treason punishable under the Espionage Act. In a democracy, the public needs to have access to sufficient information on both the pros and the cons of a policy to judge its usefulness. Moreover, without a credible check on executive information, why would anyone believe that the president or CIA director is revealing the whole story. To be credible, just as in the 1970s, the intelligence agencies need public oversight, and a vibrant press is an essential part of achieving that oversight.

SUMMARY

To improve national security, both U.S. citizens and potential partners around the globe must trust that the leader of the world's strongest military is acting to enhance individual liberties and promote just causes and not operating based on narrow, short-term personal or bureaucratic interests. More intelligent oversight and transparency is necessary to renew faith and credibility in U.S. policy after 15 years of accelerating opacity. Those who argue that emerging threats require ever greater levels of classification forget that not everyone blindly trusts or follows the United States' lead. Without transparency, there is ample room for reasonable citizens and leaders to doubt U.S. intentions and judgment. To effectively mobilize American resources, as well as to coordinate with allies, the U.S. government needs public support at home and abroad. Increasing secrecy has bred distrust, particularly among younger generations who have come of age during revelations of U.S. intelligence failures (notably the failure to find "weapons of mass destruction" that were a central part of the

Bush administration's justification for the Iraq war) and secret programs, such as drone killings without due process, torture in the CIA-led Extraordinary Rendition program, and surveillance of U.S. citizens and allied leaders.[18]

The continued classification of mistakes does not instill confidence that better policies will be chosen next time, only facing the truth does. We need stronger and smarter oversight of intelligence in the United States to strengthen national security by reducing distrust in American policies around the world. The 1970s saw leaders and the public resolved to practice what they preached on democracy and transparency. Even intelligence community leaders embraced the reemergence of intelligence oversight as strengthening U.S. security in the face of growing secrecy and skepticism. Those innovations in oversight helped the United States maintain its moral standing and differentiate its worldview from that of the Soviets. A similar resolve to strive toward American ideals and increase public transparency is needed today. With some simple practical steps, we can demonstrate to the world the attractiveness of democracy, liberty, and the rule of law. In the overarching battle of ideas on the world stage, security comes from being right, not being silent.

CON: Stephen F. Knott

Secrecy is as American as apple pie. The governing document of the American political order, the United States Constitution, was drafted under strict rules of secrecy. The windows in Independence Hall were shut and the heavy curtains drawn despite the sweltering heat to keep the press and the public from overhearing the proceedings. One of the first orders of business was the adoption of a measure "that nothing spoken in the house be printed, or otherwise published or communicated" without the consent of the convention.[1] Secrecy prevailed both during the Constitutional Convention and long after, as James Madison's notes were not released until 1840, over fifty years after the close of the convention. During the early years of the new republic, the United States Senate met in secret, mimicking the example set by the Continental Congress, which also operated behind closed doors. The Supreme Court still deliberates behind closed doors while making its decisions. The founding generation understood that secrecy fostered the best kind of decision making; one where all matters, particularly awkward or uncomfortable matters, could be discussed without fear of retribution.

Those, such as Congressman Justin Amash, who argue that "you can't have a free society with secret laws" are not the heirs of those who drafted the document they profess to venerate.[2] The Founding Fathers were averse to transparency (as their secret drafting of the Constitution reveals) and believed that America's defense rested in part on secrecy and on the use of clandestine operations. This approach to defense, by the way, was designed to protect American liberty, which critics of secrecy frequently overlook. Amash, Senator Rand Paul, and defector Edward Snowden claim that "rogue" agencies such as the Central Intelligence Agency and the National Security Agency represent a threat to American liberty. Many who hold these views argue that openness and accountability are the foundation of a legitimate foreign policy, and that secret agencies, and secrecy itself, are antithetical to the American experience.

A few more examples from the founding era will suffice to show that modern advocates of openness and transparency are at odds with the principles and practices of the American founders. George Washington knew how to tell a lie in the public interest and was ruthless in his pursuit of intelligence, urging his agents to "leave no stone unturned" in their pursuit of secrets. The founding fathers engaged in covert mail opening throughout the revolutionary war, for as General Washington noted, this would provide "innumerable advantages" for the American cause. Washington went so far as to provide instructions on successful mail opening techniques: "contrive a means of opening them [letters] without breaking the seals, take copies of the contents, and then let them go on."[3] Mail opening in 1780 was the equivalent of NSA snooping on e-mail in the wake of 9/11.

Influenced by Lockean notions of strong executive power in defense of the nation, the architects of the Constitution sought to ensure that never again would the Commander in Chief's ability to defend the nation's security be impeded by the endless congressional delays and leaks that bedeviled George Washington during the American Revolution. The founders created a republic in which power is delegated to elected representatives who are entrusted with policymaking. They did not create a participatory democracy. In the case of national security and foreign policy, the president is held responsible, as head of state, for the conduct of external, or as John Locke put it, "federative" matters. The "business of intelligence," as John Jay wrote in *Federalist* #64, depends for its success on executive "secrecy" and "dispatch." The founders considered the participation of the House of Representatives in these matters as especially undesirable, as Jay noted in the same essay.[4]

President Washington, in his First Annual Message to Congress in 1790, requested and ultimately won approval for a Secret Service Fund that was exempt from traditional congressional oversight. This fund allowed the president to spend money for services of a sensitive nature without revealing to

Congress how those monies were spent.[5] Washington, Madison, Jefferson, and Alexander Hamilton differed on many of the great issues of their day, but they all shared a belief that the conduct of American foreign policy was the responsibility of the president. Washington and Jefferson (Madison less so) adopted a Hamiltonian conception of executive power as Hamilton outlined in *The Federalist Papers*, one in which an "energetic executive" acted with secrecy and dispatch in the arena of foreign affairs and national security. "Vigor and expedition" can be expected from a single executive, Hamilton argued, and this was especially critical "in the conduct of war" where "the energy of the Executive is the bulwark of the national security."[6]

It was this line of thinking that led Presidents Washington, Jefferson, and Madison to withhold information from the people's representatives when they believed this was in the national interest. As Washington observed when he invoked executive privilege during the debate over the Jay Treaty in 1795, "success must often depend on secrecy."[7] Jefferson echoed Washington's sentiments when he noted that "all nations have found it necessary, that for the advantageous conduct of their affairs" certain secrets should "remain known to their executive functionary only." Jefferson also added on another occasion that the Senate "is not supposed by the Constitution to be acquainted with the concerns of the executive department."[8] If Jefferson saw a limited role for the Senate, he saw even less of a role for the House. The American founders understood that men were not angels, and that the Byzantine world of international relations was an arena of dogged competition marked by treachery and deceit. In recognizing this, they grasped something openness advocates miss: That for liberty to prevail one must see the world as it is and act accordingly.

DAY OF FIRE

The notion that something changed radically in the American political order after 9/11 is simply not true. George W. Bush's conduct as commander in chief was Hamiltonian in nature and compatible with the principles and practices of the founders and with his presidential predecessors. Bush's actions were also in concert with the controversial doctrine of prerogative power. This doctrine is based on the idea that out of necessity, in times of an emergency, the executive may act where the law is silent, or in some cases, in defiance of the law. Abraham Lincoln believed that the Constitution gave the president the power to engage in extraordinary measures in a time of emergency, while Thomas Jefferson believed this power was extraconstitutional, but that the laws of necessity would require its exercise in extraordinary circumstances. At the very least, Thomas Jefferson, Abraham Lincoln, Theodore Roosevelt, Woodrow Wilson, and Franklin Roosevelt would all disagree with a constrained interpretation of the power of the president to deal with national security emergencies. These presidents exercised executive secrecy and dispatch in its rawest form. George W. Bush was in good company.

It is important to remember that September 11, 2001, was the deadliest day in the United States since the Battle of Antietam in September 1862.[9] The toll on 9/11 was higher than that of the attack on Pearl Harbor or on the first day of the American landings on D-Day. Compounding the shock of 9/11, we now know that in October 2001, President Bush was told that Al Qaeda had smuggled a 10 kiloton nuclear weapon into New York City. It was alleged that Al Qaeda had obtained this weapon after the collapse of the Soviet Union. The nuclear emergency search team was dispatched to New York City to search for the weapon, while Vice President Cheney and several hundred federal employees were relocated to a secure underground bunker. No weapon was ever found, but that same month biological detectors in the White House registered the presence of botulinum toxin for which there was no reliable antidote. The president was told that "those of us who were exposed to it could die."[10] Recalling this atmosphere helps us understand why President Bush approved certain extraordinary measures to prevent a second 9/11 or something even worse from happening.

On September 12, 2001, at a National Security Council meeting, President Bush told Attorney General John Ashcroft, "Don't ever let this happen again."[11] It was an order that any responsible president would have given that day. It was from this directive that many of Bush's so-called "abuses" of power flowed. Bush gave this order as the Pentagon and the World Trade Center still smoldered, and the reality set in that the Capitol or the White House came within twenty minutes of being destroyed. Al Qaeda was an organization, as Steven Simon, a senior counterterrorism official during the Clinton years put it, whose destructive dreams knew no bounds. Simon noted that the United States "had other source reporting that indicated he [bin Laden] was thinking in terms of a quote, unquote, 'Hiroshima' for the United States. . . . This was a guy whose idea of violence was stupendous."[12] In light of this, the water boarding of Khalid Sheik Muhammed and two other ranking Al Qaeda members can be defended as a necessary, measured response, as was circumventing the Foreign Intelligence Surveillance Act (FISA; 1978), which was written during the dark ages of technology, prior to the advent of cellphones or the development of the World Wide Web. The decision to circumvent FISA produced an uproar when it was exposed by *The New York Times* in December, 2005.[13] Once again, it was assumed that policies enacted in the 1960s and 1970s were in line with the intentions of the founders, and it was alleged that they would be appalled at such a flagrant abuse of power. Yet, scrutinizing personal communications for intelligence purposes has deep American roots despite what Snowden and assorted critics prefer to believe.

Another highly successful secret program, the Terrorist Finance Tracking Program (TFTP), allowed the government to track the finances of individuals affiliated with Al Qaeda. Two reporters for *The New York Times*, Eric Lichtblau and James Risen, won a Pulitzer Prize in 2006 for their exposé of this program, which effectively killed it. This program had led to the capture of the mastermind of the Bali bombing of October 2002, which killed 202 people, and had identified a man from Brooklyn, New York, who was laundering money for Al Qaeda. Jack Goldsmith observed that the exposure of TFTP "helped terrorists to avoid forms of communication that we were good at monitoring, and instead switch to channels of communication in which we lacked comparative advantage."[14]

All of these programs were briefed to the senior members of the House and Senate Intelligence Committees, which prompted some committee members to urge the Central Intelligence Agency to take more aggressive measures. Later, when the threat subsided, and these programs were exposed, some of these members feigned surprise and condemned the administration and the CIA for their lawlessness.

TRANSPARENCY WILL NOT IMPROVE CITIZEN AWARENESS OR PARTICIPATION

Today's transparency advocates are motivated in part by a belief that technological advances have progressed to a point where the voices of the citizenry should play a more assertive role in the political process. Due to technological advances, it is argued, the American people are better informed and better educated (so it is believed) than they were 220 years ago, and they have a right to more information than they are currently receiving. Democratized decisions lead to better policy, so the argument goes; "crowd sharing" leads to more representative and smarter policy. This is also a far more egalitarian form of decision making than a select few members drawn from the elite of the American foreign policy "establishment," an ill-defined group if there ever was one but one repeatedly cited by critics on both the right and the left.

The notion that increased citizen awareness of and participation in national security decision making will produce better or more just results is not borne out by experience. The founders understood that the public can err, sometimes tragically so. Franklin Roosevelt struggled for years, at times covertly, to nudge his reluctant fellow citizens toward recognizing the threat presented by Adolf Hitler. The American public's support for the war in Vietnam was strong, if not stronger, than support for the war from the nation's elites. In March 2003, a Pew Research

Center poll indicated that 72 percent of the American public supported President George W. Bush's decision to use force in Iraq.[15] Couple these views with the stunning ignorance frequently found regarding the public's understanding of international affairs, and you have a prescription for disaster. For instance, a 2006 Roper poll found that only 37 percent of Americans between the ages of 18 and 24 could find Iraq on a map. This was three years after the United States invaded that country. That same year, 88 percent of these Americans could not locate Afghanistan on a map, five years after that invasion.[16] In 2002, 11 percent of 18- to 24-year-olds could not find their own country on a map.[17]

No increase in transparency will serve to enlighten those whose primary source of information is *The Daily Show* or a Twitter feed emanating from the basement of a tin-foil hat wearing conspiracy monger. Those Americans who know nothing of their own history or government, and even less of the rest of the world, are unlikely to be weaned away from their ignorance or their embrace of conspiracy theories (see for example the 9/11 "truthers" whose material is widely circulated on the Internet or the 7 percent of the American public who believe the Apollo 11 moon landing was fake)[18] by an expansion of the Freedom of Information Act or other steps toward governmental openness.

Confidence in the American government is at near-record lows.[19] It is frequently assumed that more openness, more governmental responsiveness, will reverse this persistent downward trend. Yet, the trend in recent decades has been to greater openness and responsiveness. A strong case can be made that our increasingly democratized, poll-driven politics fails to inspire and, in fact, serves to demoralize the citizenry. Public opinion polls, remarkably enough, have even been dictating who gets to participate in the Republican Party's presidential debates for the 2016 election. "Hyperdemocracy" is the term coined by political scientist Hugh Heclo to describe the phenomenon of the displacement of the Constitution and of deliberative representation with a politics of "participatory openness" that has polarized the electorate and made thoughtful decision making problematic. Compromise and civility are lost in the din of "publicity, exposure, investigation, [and] revelation" in our 24/7 media-saturated environment.[20] Confounding the hopes of openness advocates, the rejection of deliberation and the courting of public opinion has contributed to the mistrust and alienation that characterizes the American political order in the twenty-first century.

SUMMARY

The architect of the Constitution, James Madison, believed that the permanent interests of the community were enhanced through a republican form of government rooted in representation and resistant to the whims of public opinion. While Madison rejected the notion of parroting the will of the public, a more transparent system where the Internet becomes a tool to force elected officials "to think twice," as Congressman Amash has put it, is as far removed from Madison's claim in *Federalist #10* that representation will "refine and enlarge" the public views as one can get. James Madison was opposed to pandering to the public and rejected the type of populist, demagogic appeals that would inevitably emerge from a more transparent and democratized system.

The naïve views of Justin Amash, Rand Paul, and Edward Snowden, the last of whom fled to one of the most secretive regimes on the planet and who exposed far more overseas intelligence operations than he did domestic abuses, were rejected by the American founders. They rightly understood that diplomacy cannot be conducted under the glare of public scrutiny, and that covert operations are an important tool in America's arsenal of defense. They knew that secrecy has its place in protecting sources and methods used by intelligence agencies, in encouraging candid advice to policy makers, and in a larger sense, assisting in the implementation of shrewd and coherent American foreign policy. That the policies of the American government are not always shrewd and coherent does not mean that more openness will produce better results. The more voices involved in national security, the more incoherent American foreign policy will appear to both the American public and to foreign nations.

Open policy openly arrived at will diminish the possibility of strategic breakthroughs, such as President Richard Nixon's opening to China in 1972, which was hatched entirely in secret, or Barack Obama's opening to Cuba in 2014 to 2015.[21] Openly formulated policies are also more subject to the whims of the day, and as Hamilton once candidly noted, *"the people are turbulent and changing; they seldom judge or determine right."*[22] The point of a system of representation, as previously mentioned, was to "refine and enlarge" opinions, to filter the best ideas from the worst. It was to allow for the possibility that "reflection and choice," to borrow from Hamilton in *Federalist #1*, might prevail. That this ideal is not always realized and that the government sometimes fails to achieve its foreign policy objectives or overreaches in terms of the information it classifies is no reason to scrap a system that has helped to keep this nation safe for over two centuries.

Secrecy remains an important tool for American policy makers and one that is essential to America's superpower status. The ultimate tribute to American secrecy comes from our opponents, including the hostile regimes of China and Russia, whose government-sponsored hackers go to remarkable lengths to unearth American secrets, which they seem to find of great value. It is not in our nation's interest to make their task any easier.

NOTES

PRO

1. Information Security Oversight Office Report to the President, FY2014, p. 26, and Budget of United States Government Printing Office, http://www.gpo.gov/fdsys/browse/collectionGPO.action?collectionCode=BUDGET.

2. Annual Information Security Oversight Office report to the President, FY2014, p. 6.

3. "America's Unnecessary Secrets" by Elizabeth Goitein, Brennen Center, November 7, 2011, http://www.brennancenter.org/analysis/america's-unnecessary-secrets.

4. Matt Apuzzo, "Times Reporter Will Not Be Called to Testify in Leak Case," *New York Times*, January 12, 2015, http://www.nytimes.com/2015/01/13/us/times-reporter-james-risen-will-not-be-called-to-testify-in-leak-case-lawyers-say.html?_r=0.

5. See Cora Currier, "Charting Obama's Crackdown on National Security Leaks," *ProPublica*, http://www.propublica.org/special/sealing-loose-lips-charting-obamas-crackdown-on-national-security-leaks; John Greenberg, "CNN's Tapper: Obama Has Used Espionage Act more than all Previous Administrations," *Politifact*, January 10, 2014, http://www.politifact.com/punditfact/statements/2014/jan/10/jake-tapper/cnns-tapper-obama-has-used-espionage-act-more-all.

6. Scott Shane, "A Closed-Mouth Policy Even on Open Secrets," October 4, 2011, http://www.nytimes.com/2011/10/05/us/politics/awlaki-killing-is-awash-in-open-secrets.html?_r=2.

7. See Annual Information Security Oversight Office report to the President, FY2014.

8. See for example, Barton Gellman and Jerry Markon, "Edward Snowden Says Motive behind Leaks Was to Expose 'Surveillance State,'" *Washington Post*, June 9, 2013, https://www.washingtonpost.com/politics/edward-snowden-says-motive-behind-leaks-was-to-expose-surveillance-state/2013/06/09/aa3f0804-d13b-11e2-a73e-826d299ff459_story.html.

9. See Letter from Senator John D. Rockefeller IV to Vice President Richard Cheney, July 17, 2003, available at http://fas.org/irp/news/2005/12/rock121905.pdf. See also the discussion in Greg Miller and Maura Reynolds, "U.S. Spying Plan Lacked Congress' Scrutiny, Leading Democrat Says," *Los Angeles Times*, December 20, 2005, http://articles.latimes.com/2005/dec/20/nation/na-rockefeller20.

10. Ken Dilianian, Zeina Karam and Bassem Mroue, "US Intelligence: ISIS Is no Weaker than a Year Ago," *Associated Press*, http://www.businessinsider.com/us-intelligence-isis-is-no-weaker-than-a-year-ago-2015-7; "US to Abandon Training new Syria Rebel Groups," *BBC*, October 9, 2015, http://www.bbc.com/news/world-middle-east-34486572.

11. "Memories of Iraq: Did We Ever Support the War?" *YouGov*, June 2015, https://
   yougov.co.uk/news/2015/06/03/remembering-iraq.

12. Foreign Affairs Committee, Session 2009-2010, Fourth Special Report, April 9,
   2010, "Global Security: UK-US Relations" available at http://www.publications
   .parliament.uk/pa/cm/cmfaff.htm.

13. Adam Taylor, "Germans Don't Think America Stands for Freedom Anymore,"
   Washington Post, June 25, 2015, https://www.washingtonpost.com/news/
   worldviews/wp/2015/06/25/germans-dont-think-america-stands-for-
   freedom-anymore.

14. "Global Opposition to US Surveillance and Drones, but Limited Harm to
   America's Image," Pew Research Report, July 14. 2014, http://www.pewglobal
   .org/2014/07/14/global-opposition-to-u-s-surveillance-and-drones-but-
   limited-harm-to-americas-image.

15. Anne Barnard and Eric Schmitt, "Rivals of ISIS Attack US-Backed Syrian Rebel
   Group," *New York Times*, July 31, 2015, http://www.nytimes.com/2015/08/01/
   world/middleeast/nusra-front-attacks-us-backed-syrian-rebel-group.html?_r=0.

16. See http://query.nytimes.com/mem/archive/pdf?res=9E02E7D6153DE036A0575
   5C2A9649C946790D6CF.

17. http://www.pbs.org/wgbh/pages/frontline/media/push-to-reform-the-freedom-of-
   information-act-collapses-in-house.

18. See for example, Drew Desilver, "Most Young Americans Say Snowden Has
   Served the Public Interest," January 22, 2014, Pew Research Report, http://www
   .pewresearch.org/fact-tank/2014/01/22/most-young-americans-say-snowden-has-
   served-the-public-interest.

CON

1. John R. Vile, *Founding Documents of America: Documents Decoded* (Santa
   Barbara, CA: ABC-Clio, 2015), p. 179.

2. Quoted in Ashe Schow, "Lindsay Graham, John McCain on the Extreme Fringes
   of American Society, says Justin Amash," *Washington Examiner*, September 20,
   2013.

3. Stephen F. Knott, "If George Washington Were Alive, He'd Be Reading Your
   Email," *Foreign Policy*, January 29, 2014, http://foreignpolicy.com/2014/01/29/
   if-george-washington-were-alive-hed-be-reading-your-email.

4. *Federalist #64, The Federalist*, Jacob Cooke, ed. (Middletown, CT: Wesleyan
   University Press, 1961).

5. See Knott, *Secret and Sanctioned: Covert Operations and the American Presidency*
   (New York, NY: Oxford University Press, 1996), Ch. 3.

6. *Federalist #70.*

7. Mark J. Rozell, *The Dilemma of Secrecy and Democratic Accountability* (Baltimore,
   MD: The Johns Hopkins University Press, 1994), p. 35.

8. See Stephen F. Knott, *Secret and Sanctioned*, p. 82.

9. I am excluding natural disasters such as the Brownsville Hurricane of 1900 or the San Francisco earthquake of 1906.

10. Graham Allison, "Nuclear Deterrence in the Age of Terrorism," *MIT Technology Review*, October 20, 2008, http://www.technologyreview.com/article/411022/ nuclear-deterrence-in-the-age-of-nuclear-terrorism; Peter Baker, *Days of Fire: Bush and Cheney in the White House* (New York, NY: Doubleday, 2013), pp. 168–170.

11. Jack L. Goldsmith, *The Terror Presidency: Law and Judgment Inside the Bush Presidency* (New York, NY: W.W. Norton, 2009), pp. 74–75.

12. Quoted in "9/11 for the Record," *Now with Bill Moyers, pbs.org/now,* September 10, 2004.

13. Stephen F. Knott, *Rush to Judgment: George W. Bush, The War on Terror, and His Critics* (Lawrence: University Press of Kansas, 2012), pp. 117–131.

14. Ibid., pp. 122–124.

15. Stephen F. Knott, "When Everyone Agreed About Iraq," *The Wall Street Journal*, March 15, 2013, http://www.wsj.com/articles/SB100014241278873245320045783 60574070682516.

16. Final Report, National Geographic-Roper Public Affairs 2006 Geographic Literacy Study, http://www.nationalgeographic.com/roper2006/pdf/FINALReport2006 GeogLitsurvey.pdf.

17. "Survey: Young People Lack Geography Skills," *USA Today*, November 20, 2002, http://usatoday30.usatoday.com/news/nation/2002-11-20-geography-quiz_x.htm.

18. Public Policy Polling, "Conspiracy Theory Poll Results," April 2, 2013, http://www. publicpolicypolling.com/main/2013/04/conspiracy-theory-poll-results-.html.

19. Justin McCarthy, "Confidence in U.S. Branches of Government Remains Low," *Gallup*, June 15, 2015, http://www.gallup.com/poll/183605/confidence-branches-government-remains-low.aspx.

20. Hugh Heclo, "Hyperdemocracy," *The Wilson Quarterly*, 23(no. 1, Winter, 1999): pp. 62–71.

21. Carol Morello and Karen DeYoung, "Secret U.S.-Cuba Diplomacy Ended in Landmark Deal on Prisoners, Future Ties," *Washington Post*, December17, 2014, https://www.washingtonpost.com/world/national-security/secret-diplomacy-with-cuba-ended-in-breakthrough-deal/2014/12/17/c51b3ed8-8614-11e4-a702-fa31ff4ae98e_story.html.

22. Noble E. Cunningham, Jr., *Jefferson vs. Hamilton: Confrontations That Shaped a Nation* (Boston, MA/New York, NY: Bedford/St. Martin's Press, 2000), p. 21.